Co-Enrollment in Deaf Education

Perspectives on Deafness

Series Editors
Marc Marschark
Harry Knoors

Innovations in Deaf Studies: The Role of Deaf Scholars
Annelies Kusters, Maartje De Meulder, and Dai O'Brien

Educating Deaf Learners: Creating a Global Evidence Base
Edited by Harry Knoors and Marc Marschark

Evidence-Based Practices in Deaf Education
Edited by Harry Knoors and Marc Marschark

Teaching Deaf Learners: Psychological and Developmental Foundations
Harry Knoors and Marc Marschark

The People of the Eye: Deaf Ethnicity and Ancestry
Harlan Lane, Richard C. Pillard, and Ulf Hedberg

Deaf Cognition: Foundations and Outcomes
Edited by Marc Marschark and Peter C. Hauser

How Deaf Children Learn: What Parents and Teachers Need to Know
Marc Marschark and Peter C. Hauser

Diversity in Deaf Education
Edited by Marc Marschark, Venetta Lampropoulou, and Emmanouil K. Skordilis

Bilingualism and Bilingual Deaf Education
Edited by Marc Marschark, Gladys Tang, and Harry Knoors

Early Literacy Development in Deaf Children
Connie Mayer and Beverly J. Trezek

The World of Deaf Infants: A Longitudinal Study
Kathryn P. Meadow-Orlans, Patricia Elizabeth Spencer, and Lynn Sanford Koester

Approaches to Social Research: The Case of Deaf Studies
Alys Young and Bogusia Temple

Deaf Education Beyond the Western World
Harry Knoors, Maria Brons, and Marc Marschark

Co-Enrollment in Deaf Education
Edited by Marc Marschark, Shirin Antia, and Harry Knoors

Co-Enrollment in Deaf Education

Edited by
Marc Marschark
Shirin Antia
Harry Knoors

OXFORD
UNIVERSITY PRESS

OXFORD
UNIVERSITY PRESS

Oxford University Press is a department of the University of Oxford. It furthers
the University's objective of excellence in research, scholarship, and education
by publishing worldwide. Oxford is a registered trade mark of Oxford University
Press in the UK and certain other countries.

Published in the United States of America by Oxford University Press
198 Madison Avenue, New York, NY 10016, United States of America.

Library of Congress Cataloging-in-Publication Data
Names: Marschark, Marc, editor. | Antia, Shirin D., editor. | Knoors, Harry, editor.
Title: Co-enrollment in deaf education / edited by Marc Marschark, Shirin Antia,
Harry Knoors. Description: New York, NY : Oxford University Press, [2019] |
Series: Perspectives on deafness | Includes bibliographical references.
Identifiers: LCCN 2018039927 | ISBN 9780190912994 (hardcover)
Subjects: LCSH: Deaf children—Education—Cross-cultural studies. |
Inclusive education—Cross-cultural studies.
Classification: LCC HV2430.C57 2019 | DDC 371.91/2—dc23
LC record available at https://lccn.loc.gov/2018039927

9 8 7 6 5 4 3 2 1

Printed by Sheridan Books, Inc., United States of America

Contents

Preface vii

Contributors ix

1. Co-Enrollment and the Education of Deaf and Hard-of-Hearing Learners: Foundations, Implementation, and Challenges 1
   Shirin Antia, Harry Knoors, and Marc Marschark

2. TRIPOD: Answer to the Seeds of Discontent 25
   Carl J. Kirchner

3. Co-Enrollment in Toowong, Australia 41
   Michelle Baker, Cameron Miller, Elizabeth Fletcher, Caroline Gamin, and Breda Carty

4. Learning Together by Deaf and Hearing Students in a Japanese Primary School 69
   Takashi Torigoe

5. Essential Ingredients for Sign Bilingualism and Co-Enrollment Education in the Hong Kong Context 83
   Chris Kun-man Yiu, Gladys Tang, and Chloe Chi-man Ho

6. Co-Enrollment Models of Preschool for Deaf and Hard-of-Hearing Children in Israel 107
   Dalia Ringwald-Frimerman, Sara Ingber, and Tova Most

7. Bilingual, Inclusive, Mixed-Age Schooling in Vienna 133
   Silvia Kramreiter and Verena Krausneker

8. Establishing a Bimodal Bilingual Co-Enrollment Program in Germany: Preconditions, Policy, and Preliminary Data 149
   Johannes Hennies and Kristin Hennies

9. Include to Grow: Prospects for Bilingual and Bicultural Education for Both Deaf and Hearing Students 165
   Lucrezia Di Gregorio, Vincenzina Campana, Maria Lavecchia, and Pasquale Rinaldi

10. The Best of Both Worlds: A Co-Enrollment Program for
    DHH Children in the Netherlands   183
    Annet de Klerk, Daan Hermans, Loes Wauters, Lilian de Laat,
    Francien de Kroon, and Harry Knoors

11. Conditions for Effective Co-Enrollment of Deaf and
    Hearing Students: What May Be Learned from Experiences
    in Belgium   211
    Magaly Ghesquière and Laurence Meurant

12. Four Co-Enrollment Programs in Madrid: Differences and
    Similarities   235
    Mar Pérez, Begoña de la Fuente, Pilar Alonso, and Gerardo Echeita

13. Willie Ross School for the Deaf and Partnership
    Campus: A Dual-Campus Model of Co-Enrollment   257
    Louis Abbate

14. The Growth and Expansion of a Co-Enrollment
    Program: Teacher, Student, Graduate, and Parent
    Perspectives   277
    Kathryn H. Kreimeyer, Cynthia Drye, and Kelly Metz

15. The Tucker Maxon Story: Mainstreaming in Place   301
    Jennifer M. Hoofard, Glen C. Gilbert, Linda Goodwin, and
    Tamala Selke Bradham

16. Visions of Co-Enrollment in Deaf Education   325
    Marc Marschark, Harry Knoors, and Shirin Antia

Index   347

Preface

A FUNNY THING HAPPENED ON THE WAY TO
THE ACROPOLIS

In 2015, the 22nd International Conference on the Education of the Deaf met in Athens, Greece. One group planning to present at the conference included several individuals who had created and implemented a new approach to educating deaf and hard-of-hearing (DHH) children: a bilingual (signed and spoken/written language) program embedded in a local mainstream school, a co-enrollment program. At least they thought it was a new approach. It was not until the teacher/parent/ linguist team arrived in Athens, not far from the Acropolis, that they realized that they were not alone, that there were others who had developed similar programs in several different countries. This story, told by a team from Namur, Belgium (see Ghesquière & Meurant, this volume), led to efforts to identify co-enrollment programs around the world and, ultimately, to this volume. The chapters that follow all were written by people involved, in one way or another, with co-enrollment programming for DHH (and hearing) learners. As they describe, such programs vary widely, and the ones included here may not be considered by everyone to be co-enrollment programs in the "classic" sense that is just now being defined. Nevertheless, all of the programs represented here, in theory, share some central features of co-enrollment, even if practical issues associated with their location, educational culture, and the DHH learners they serve make for significant differences.

Asking individuals busy with the day-to-day functioning of academic programs to write book chapters describing how those programs came about, how they function, and where they are going was asking a lot. All of the contributors stepped up, however, in the hope that sharing information about the potential benefits of co-enrollment would contribute to making education more accessible and more successful for DHH learners in the future. To them and their colleagues who have made such programs a reality, we extend our sincere thanks.

Marc Marschark
Shirin Antia
Harry Knoors
November, 2018

Contributors

Louis Abbate
Willie Ross School for the Deaf
(Emeritus)
Longmeadow, MA, USA

Pilar Alonso
Regional Department of
Education
Madrid, Spain

Shirin Antia
College of Education
University of Arizona
Tucson, AZ, USA

Michelle Baker
Toowong State School
Toowong, Australia

Tamala Selke Bradham
Vanderbilt University Medical
Center
Nashville, TN, USA

Vincenzina Campana
Tommaso Silvestri Institute-ISISS
Margotto, Italy

Breda Carty
Renwick Centre
Royal Institute for Deaf and Blind
Children
Parramatta, Australia

Francien de Kroon
OBS de Bolster
Sint-Michielsgestel, the
Netherlands

Begoña de la Fuente
Regional Department of
Education
Madrid, Spain

Lilian de Laat
Royal Dutch Kentalis
Sint-Michielsgestel,
the Netherlands

Lucrezia Di Gregorio
Tommaso Silvestri Institute-ISISS
Margotto, Italy

Cynthia Drye
Miles Exploratory
Learning Center
Tucson, AZ, USA

Gerardo Echeita
Universidad Autónoma
de Madrid
Madrid, Spain

Elizabeth Fletcher
Toowong State School
Toowong, Australia

Caroline Gamin
Toowong State School
Toowong, Australia

Magaly Ghesquière
Centre Scolaire Sainte-Marie
Namur, Belgium

Glen C. Gilbert
Tucker Maxon School
Portland, OR, USA

Linda Goodwin
Tucker Maxon School
Portland, OR, USA

Johannes Hennies
Heidelberg University of
    Education
Heidelberg, Germany

Kristin Hennies
Herbert Feuchte Foundation
    Association
Heide, Germany

Daan Hermans
Royal Dutch Kentalis
Sint-Michielsgestel,
    the Netherlands
and
Behavioural Science Institute
Radboud University Nijmegen
Nijmegen, the Netherlands

Chloe Chi-man Ho
Centre for Sign Linguistics and
    Deaf Studies
Chinese University of
    Hong Kong
Shatin, Hong Kong

Jennifer M. Hoofard
Tucker Maxon School
Portland, OR, USA

Sara Ingber
School of Education
Tel Aviv University, Israel

Carl J. Kirchner
Sherwood Forest, CA, USA

Annet de Klerk
Royal Dutch Kentalis
Sint-Michielsgestel, the
    Netherlands

Harry Knoors
Royal Dutch Kentalis
Sint-Michielsgestel, the
    Netherlands
and
Department of Special Education
Behavioural Science Institute
Radboud University Nijmegen
Nijmegen, the Netherlands

Silvia Kramreiter
University College of Teacher
    Education Vienna
Vienna, Austria

Verena Krausneker
University of Vienna
Vienna, Austria

Kathryn H. Kreimeyer
University of Arizona
Tucson, AZ, USA

Maria Lavecchia
Tommaso Silvestri Institute-ISISS
Margotto, Italy

Marc Marschark
Center for Education Research
    Partnerships
National Technical Institute for
    the Deaf
Rochester, NY, USA
and
School of Psychology
University of Aberdeen
Aberdeen, Scotland

Kelly Metz
University of Southern
    Mississippi
Hattiesburg, MS, USA

Laurence Meurant
F.R.S-FNRS
University of Namur
Namur, Belgium

Cameron Miller
Toowong State School
Toowong, Australia

Tova Most
School of Education and
Department of Communication
  Disorders
Tel-Aviv University
Tel-Aviv, Israel

Mar Pérez
Regional Department of
  Education
Madrid, Spain

Pasquale Rinaldi
Italian National Research Council
Institute of Cognitive Sciences
  and Technologies
Rome, Italy

Dalia Ringwald-Frimerman
School of Education
Tel Aviv University, Israel
and
Ministry of Education
Department of Special Education
Jerusalem, Israel

Gladys Tang
Centre for Sign Linguistics and
  Deaf Studies
Chinese University of Hong Kong
Shatin, Hong Kong

Takashi Torigoe
Department of Special Needs
  Education
Hyogo University of Teacher
  Education
Hyogo, Japan

Loes Wauters
Royal Dutch Kentalis
Sint-Michielsgestel, the
  Netherlands

Chris Kun-man Yiu
Centre for Sign Linguistics and
  Deaf Studies
Department of Linguistics and
  Modern Languages
Chinese University of Hong Kong
Shatin, Hong Kong

1

Co-Enrollment and the Education of Deaf and Hard-of-Hearing Learners: Foundations, Implementation, and Challenges

Shirin Antia, Harry Knoors, and Marc Marschark

Co-enrollment is a word that, broadly defined, refers to educating groups of deaf and hard-of-hearing (DHH) students with their same-age hearing peers in the same educational environment. Co-enrollment and mainstreaming can be distinguished by making the assumption—at least for the present purposes—that mainstream programs most often place a single DHH student in a general education classroom, with or without educational or communicative support, whereas co-enrollment programs purposefully enroll several DHH students within a single classroom.

Mainstreaming and co-enrollment also typically differ in their philosophical and pedagogical underpinnings. Co-enrollment is based on the assumption that DHH and hearing students should be equal participants with equal status in the classroom—that is, fully included in all aspects of the socioeducational setting (Stinson & Antia, 1999). From a placement perspective, inclusion à la co-enrollment requires that DHH students are physically together in the classroom. From a philosophical perspective, classroom instruction is managed so that all students can benefit to the maximum extent possible. Co-enrollment thus is an educational arrangement that theoretically and pragmatically should allow for the best possible academic and social integration of DHH and hearing students. Co-enrollment could be considered a form of mainstreaming, one point along the continuum of educational placements (see Abbate, this volume). But it is also possible to think of co-enrollment as a different model of placement, one that embraces full inclusion and membership of all participants (teachers as well as learners) at several different levels (see, for example, Yiu, Tang, & Ho, this volume).

Co-enrollment as an educational model is in line with the globally accepted policy described in the 2006 United Nations Convention of the Rights of People with Disabilities (UNCRPD). Similar to earlier policy documents such as the Salamanca Statement (UNESCO, 1994) and the United Nations Standard Rules (UN, 1994), the UNCRPD promotes inclusive education, but unlike earlier policies it avoids the actual label "inclusive education." Instead UNCRPD states: "Ensuring that the education of persons, and in particular children, who are blind, deaf or deafblind, is delivered in the most appropriate languages and modes and means of communication for the individual, and in environments which maximize academic and social development." The Convention calls for universal design of environments and services, making sure that these "may be usable by all people, to the greatest extent possible, without the need for adaptation or specialized design. 'Universal design' shall not exclude assistive devices for particular groups of persons with disabilities where this is needed." As will be seen throughout the chapters in this volume, one of the purposes of co-enrollment programs is the enhancement of social and academic development of DHH students in a classroom that is universally accessible.

As originally envisioned by Kirchner (1994), the intent of co-enrollment classrooms was not to modify curricula or to develop new teaching strategies. Instead, the intent was to allow DHH students to be members of rather than visitors to the general education classroom (see Kirchner, this volume). In other words, in co-enrollment classrooms, DHH students are not present provisionally or on sufferance, just as their hearing peers are not present provisionally or on sufferance. Each student has a right to be in the classroom, and with that right, each student has the responsibility for being part of the classroom community. Being part of the classroom community necessarily involves being physically present in the classroom, but it also means following classroom rules, participating equally with peers in classroom instruction, and being able to communicate with peers and teachers. In fact, Kirchner (1994) advocated creating universally designed educational environments specifically so that they would be accessible to both hearing and DHH students in order to enable learning on an equal basis in the same classroom. And he did so decades ahead of the UNCPRD!

Despite our highest ideals, having DHH students be members of a classroom in which most of the students are hearing and the teacher has no knowledge of, or experience with, the communicative or other needs of DHH students is a pragmatic challenge. Co-enrollment thus usually also involves co-teaching by the regular classroom teacher and a "teacher of the deaf" ("ToD" in North America), someone specifically trained in teaching DHH students or, in some cases, a special education teacher. Co-teaching shares many of the same philosophical underpinnings as co-enrollment. Both teachers, sometimes with additional support staff, partner in providing classroom instruction in a classroom that typically includes students with and without special needs. The purpose of co-teaching is to ensure that students who have special educational needs have access to specialized instruction, while also having access to the general education curriculum (Friend, Cook, Hurley-Chamberlain, & Shamberger, 2010). The assumption underlying the co-teaching model is that the general educator or classroom teacher will have the content expertise while the teacher of the deaf or special educator will have the expertise in specific instructional strategies required by students.

Neither co-enrollment nor co-teaching is strictly defined and, as the following chapters make clear, in practice they may take many different forms. Most contributors to this volume would agree that co-enrollment classrooms include both DHH and hearing students, and that the ratio of DHH to hearing students is sufficient for the former to form a visible and substantial group within the classroom. Co-enrollment classrooms are likely to be co-taught by professionals whose differing expertise combine synergistically to provide the best possible classroom experience for both DHH and hearing students. Co-enrollment and co-teaching thus ideally should go hand in hand, but co-enrollment can occur without co-teaching, and co-teaching can occur without co-enrollment. As is evident in this volume, the manner in which co-enrollment is conducted thus can vary considerably, although the philosophy of equal access and full membership remains paramount.

Co-enrollment is not yet a widespread model in any one country, but the fact that there are co-enrollment programs in the United States, several European countries, Hong Kong, Japan, and Australia speaks to the growing belief that these programs can provide at least a partial answer to some of the pragmatic and philosophical challenges faced in educating deaf students in mainstream educational settings and also assist in "raising the bar" for academic achievement for deaf students. Our hope is that the chapters in this book will provide educators a window into how different co-enrollment programs are established, how they are administered and managed, and how they are maintained. The successes and challenges of these programs should inspire us to both emulate good ideas and to avoid some previously encountered difficulties.

WHY HAVE CO-ENROLLMENT PROGRAMS?

Historically, DHH students in the United States and other countries attended special schools for deaf children (Hermans, de Klerk, Wauters, & Knoors, 2014; Perez Martin, Valmaseda Balanzategui, & Morgan, 2014). These schools were often far from home, and students were unable to be with their families except during weekends or vacations. Special schools often served the role of enculturating students into the Deaf community, but they also could segregate and isolate DHH children as well as their teachers. In the United States, legislation spurred the movement of DHH students from traditional residential schools for the deaf (now termed center schools) to public school (mainstream) classrooms. As a result of legislation beginning with the Rehabilitation Act of 1973 and the Education for All Handicapped Children Act in 1975 (U.S. Department of Education, 2017), every child with a disability has had a right to a free and appropriate education (FAPE) in the least restrictive educational environment (LRE). The FAPE and LRE requirements opened the doors for parents to send their DHH children to schools within their local school districts and have greater input into their children's educational programming. Similar legislation has been passed in other countries (e.g., Australia, Netherlands, New Zealand, and Spain). As a result of such legislation, many DHH students now attend mainstream schools. For example, 87% of DHH students in the United States and 83% of all Australian children attend mainstream schools (National Center for Education Statistics, 2016; Punch & Hyde, 2010). Unfortunately, legislation regarding access to quality education for students with special needs, including those who are DHH, is still sorely lacking in many parts of the world (see Knoors, Brons, & Marschark, in press).

One advantage of DHH students' attending mainstream schools is that they can have access to the regular academic curriculum at a pace and in the same manner it is taught to typically hearing students. In practice, of course, instruction within the curriculum would have to be communicatively accessible for the DHH students, communication being the most common barrier they face in mainstream education settings. Such curricular access can result in higher achievement than is typically reported for DHH students (Antia, Jones, Reed, & Kreimeyer, 2009). At the same time, however, students with more severe hearing loss, those with language or cognitive delays, and those with communication needs that are not easily met in classrooms with hearing peers may continue to lag in achievement.

Because DHH students are few and far between, most local schools will enroll only one or two students each year (Mitchell & Karchmer, 2006). School personnel thus may not have the time or the motivation to develop expertise in including these students academically and socially into the classroom. Further, when DHH students have limited access to ongoing communication in the mainstream classroom, they may participate in social activities with their hearing peers (Antia, Jones, Luckner, Kreimeyer, & Reed, 2011) but may not have the opportunity to develop close friendships with them. At the same time, being the only DHH student, or perhaps one of a handful of DHH students, in a mainstream school means that access to DHH peers also is limited, and they may not have the opportunity to become part of a larger community of DHH students. DHH students in co-enrollment programs, unlike their DHH peers in more typical mainstream settings, have opportunities to interact with same-age DHH and hearing peers and can develop friendships based on common interests rather than on hearing status or communication ability. Several studies have demonstrated that co-enrollment also increases the likelihood of DHH students being accepted by hearing peers and decreases the chances of loneliness and isolation (Hermans, de Klerk, et al., 2014; Wolters, Knoors, Cillessen, & Verhoeven, 2011; Yiu & Tang, 2014).

Because DHH students in the mainstream are scattered so widely across school districts, they typically are served by itinerant teachers of the deaf who travel from school to school and provide either *pull-out* or *push-in* services to the students on their caseloads. When providing pull-out services, itinerant teachers see each student in a one-on-one situation and supplement or complement classroom instruction. When providing push-in services, itinerant teachers might co-teach with the classroom teachers or work individually with the DHH student while physically within the classroom. While itinerant services are beneficial, there is little information available on how itinerant teachers make decisions about the services that they provide or the effectiveness of such services (Antia & Rivera, 2016). DHH students also may receive services from other professionals (e.g., from audiologists or speech-language pathologists), but these professionals, including the general education teachers, often do not have sufficient time for joint planning or coordinating services. The result is that services can sometimes be fragmented and duplicative rather than complementary (Kirchner, 1994). Also, because there may only be one or two DHH students in the school, it is easy for administrators and teachers to overlook the needs and accommodations for these students. DHH students may encounter noisy classrooms (Nelson & Soli, 2000), teachers who are unwilling to support communication by cooperating with sign language interpreters or using of FM systems (Reed, Antia, & Kreimeyer, 2008), and the lack of qualified interpreters (Schick, Williams, & Bolster, 1999; Schick, Williams, & Kupermintz, 2006).

Co-enrollment can solve some of the problems encountered by DHH students in school systems that predominantly serve hearing individuals. Because they are full members of the co-enrollment classroom, communication by and with DHH students becomes an integral part of the classroom culture, and various activities and practices evolve to ensure that all students have communication, academic, and social access. In addition, because general education teachers in co-enrollment classrooms are likely to work intensely and over a continuous period of time with DHH students, they implicitly or explicitly

will develop expertise in teaching DHH students. Most general education teachers are unlikely to develop such expertise because they
work with DHH students sporadically, on an incidental basis. As several of the following chapters demonstrate, general education teachers'
gaining of expertise with regard to the academic strengths and needs of
DHH students is one of the foundational components of co-enrollment
programs.

DOCUMENTED BENEFITS TO DHH STUDENTS IN CO-ENROLLMENT PROGRAMS

There are several reasons why co-enrollment programs exist. One of
the stated purposes for placing DHH students in mainstream schools
is to promote social and academic integration, but researchers have
expressed doubts about whether mainstreaming actually results in such
integration. Proponents argue that co-enrollment programs are more
likely to result in both academic and social integration and, furthermore, can improve academic achievement of DHH students. Several
of the chapters in this volume provide information in this regard from
their own programs, but let us provide some background.

Social Integration and Benefits

Stinson and Antia (1999) defined social integration as the ability to interact with, make friends with, and be accepted by a community of
peers. Various observers and authors predicted that the movement of
DHH students from schools for the deaf to mainstream schools would
result in a generation of lonely and isolated students who could neither
communicate with their hearing peers nor have access to other DHH
peers (Bunch, 1994; Ramsey, 1997). Early research with DHH students
in mainstream settings seemed to bear out this prediction. Researchers
reported that DHH students interacted infrequently with hearing
peers (Antia, 1982) and had trouble gaining access or maintaining
conversations with hearing peers (McKirdy & Blank, 1982). DHH
students, while not rejected by their hearing peers, were also not fully
accepted or chosen as friends (Antia & Kreimeyer, 1996; Nunes &
Pretzlik, 2001).

More recent studies have yielded mixed results. In a longitudinal
study of DHH students who spent a majority of their day in general
education classrooms, Antia et al. (2011) found that classroom teachers
rated a majority of them as having average social skills. DHH students'
self-ratings also showed similar results. Thus, these students did not
appear to have difficulty interacting with peers or learning school social
mores. Whether these positive social findings imply that DHH students
always are accepted by and are popular among hearing classroom
peers is not clear. In a large study of social acceptance and popularity

of DHH students in the Netherlands, Wolters et al. (2011) reported that DHH adolescents attending mainstream schools scored significantly below their hearing peers in popularity but not in social acceptance. Even while the DHH students scored lower than their hearing peers on conversational and pragmatic language skills, they scored comparably, overall, to hearing peers on measures of prosocial, antisocial, and withdrawn behavior. It thus appears that many DHH students in mainstream schools have social skills, are socially accepted, and participate in social activities with peers. Such social comfort and participation may depend to a considerable extent on individual DHH children's ability to interact using spoken language (Archbold & Wheeler, 2010; Jambor & Elliott, 2005).

Are social outcomes any better in co-enrollment classrooms? In one of the earliest studies of outcomes from co-enrollment programming, Kreimeyer, Crooke, Drye, Egbert, and Klein (2000) reported that, at the beginning of the school year, when students initially joined the co-enrollment program, interaction between DHH and hearing peers was minimal, both in the classroom and in the lunchroom. Over the course of the school year positive peer interaction increased for all the observed students. In a more recent study of the same co-enrollment program, McCain and Antia (2005) reported that DHH and hearing students in an upper elementary, co-enrollment classroom had similar scores (within the normal range) on student-reported and teacher-reported social behaviors. Perez Martin et al. (2014) similarly reported that 17 of 18 DHH students in a co-enrollment program in Madrid scored within the normal range for social competence, affective expression, and adjustment on a teacher- and caregiver-reported rating scale. The results of these studies, taken collectively, suggest that DHH students in co-enrollment programs are socially well adjusted.

Beyond relationships among individual students, one of the reasons for co-enrollment is to create an integrated social community of DHH and hearing students (see Kirchner, this volume). The studies by McCain and Antia (2005), and Perez Martin et al. (2014) used information from rating scales completed by teachers, parents, or students. While important, data from rating scales do not provide information on the presence of close friendships or feelings of identification with the community (Deaf or hearing), nor do they identify why individual students might feel isolated. To obtain a more in-depth picture of social integration for mainstreamed students, Reed et al. (2008) conducted a series of interviews with the parents and teachers of 25 DHH students ranging from elementary to high school. Many of these mainstreamed students had fulfilling social lives, but several had experienced difficulties, particularly if they attended rural schools. Some of these students were not able to access extracurricular after-school activities, an important factor in promoting social interaction and integration, because of the lack of sign language interpreters and adequate transportation. Because of their geographical isolation from other DHH students, few had DHH peers as friends. Thus, although mainstreaming does not of necessity lead to isolation, the potential for isolation exists, especially in less densely populated communities. In co-enrollment programs, the presence of numerous DHH students and a deaf-friendly hearing community can mitigate these problems but, clearly, the establishment of such programs depends on having a sufficient number of DHH students available. Thus, several co-enrollment programs described in this volume have created multi-age/multi-grade classrooms (see Baker et al., this volume; Kreimeyer, Drye, & Metz, this volume; Krausneker & Kramreiter, this volume).

Whether in multi-grade or single-grade classrooms, the membership assumption of co-enrollment programs should lead to social acceptance and friendships across hearing-status groups. The results of studies of friendship and acceptance of DHH students and hearing peers are am-biguous. Bowen (2008) examined social acceptance between DHH and hearing students in co-enrolled third/fourth-grade classrooms. She re-ported that the DHH and hearing students in the co-enrollment class-room had similar numbers of positive and negative peer nominations. However, the co-enrolled DHH students received mostly negative nominations from hearing students in the same school, although not from their co-enrolled classmates. Thus, co-enrollment seemed to con-tribute to positive acceptance, but only from those hearing classmates who had extensive contact with the DHH students.

Unfortunately, Bowen's (2008) study included very few children. Additional positive evidence of social acceptance across hearing status groups in co-enrollment programs comes from the co-enrollment pro-gram in Hong Kong (described by Yiu, Tang, & Ho, this volume). Yiu and Tang (2014) asked DHH and hearing students to rate how much they liked to study or to play with their DHH and hearing peers. Both DHH and hearing peers received high ratings (4.5 on a 5-point scale) from peers. About 30% of DHH students gave "like to play" ratings to hearing peers, and a similar percentage of hearing students gave "like to play" ratings to DHH peers. Interestingly, 60% of DHH students gave "like to play" ratings to DHH peers, and most of the DHH students re-ported having both DHH and hearing friends. Hermans, de Klerk, et al. (2014) reported social acceptance findings from a group of 16 DHH and 96 hearing students in a co-enrollment program in the Netherlands. They found that DHH students received significantly fewer positive nominations and significantly more negative nominations than their hearing peers, and also that all students showed preferences for peers of similar hearing status and gender.

Although social outcome reports from co-enrollment programs are generally positive as regards acceptance across hearing-status groups, we clearly need more in-depth information about friendships and feelings of identification with the school and larger community. The results from the Hong Kong and Dutch programs point to the possibility that self-segregation by hearing status might occur in co-enrollment programs. This may be either negative or positive, depending on the goals and desired outcomes of the programs.

Academic Integration and Benefits

Stinson and Antia (1999) suggested that academic integration can be examined through academic performance or achievement of the DHH students and also their participation in the academic life of the classroom, including participation and communication with peers and teachers during academic activities. Historically, the achievement of DHH students has been considerably below their hearing peers (Qi & Mitchell, 2012), but several studies have found that DHH students appear to benefit from access to the general education curriculum (Antia et al., 2009; Kluwin, 1993). DHH students who attend general education classrooms, however, also are more likely than other DHH students to have parents who speak the predominant language of the school community and may have higher socioeconomic status compared to those in schools for the deaf. The students themselves tend to have a lesser degree of hearing loss and prefer to use spoken language (Kluwin, 1994; Kluwin & Gonter Gaustad, 1992; Stinson & Kluwin, 2003). Therefore, they may not represent the population of DHH school students who have severe and profound hearing loss and who prefer signed communication. These DHH students are likely to need more support than the few hours a week typically provided by an itinerant teacher. Nevertheless, national data from the United States, involving a randomly selected sample of approximately 500 DHH high school students, indicated that having attended only mainstream schools was one of the best predictors of academic achievement across the curriculum (Marschark, Shaver, Nagle, & Newman, 2015). Meanwhile, it also remains unclear whether students enrolled in most co-enrollment programs are representative of their age and geographical DHH cohorts.

What we do know is that for students to learn and therefore achieve, they need to be actively engaged in classroom academic activities (Hermans, Wauters, de Klerk, & Knoors, 2014; Reyes, Brackett, Rivers, White, & Salovey, 2012). For DHH students, academic engagement requires that they have full access to classroom communication and content. This might mean creating a physical classroom environment that allows visual access or engaging in teaching practices that allow students to devote sequential rather than simultaneous visual attention to classroom content. It also may mean that DHH students should be able to engage in academic activities with peers with whom they can communicate directly and easily. At this point in time, however, academic benefits to students in co-enrollment programs are less well documented than social benefits. We have some information on teachers' expectations of DHH students in co-enrollment classrooms, data on student participation and engagement within these classrooms, and some data on academic achievement as represented by standardized test scores. Chapters that follow in this volume add to this evidence base.

Academic expectations of teachers in general education classrooms have been shown to influence (hearing) students' achievement (Rubie-Davies, Peterson, Sibley, & Rosenthal, 2015). However, too often teachers hold low expectations of the ability of DHH students to understand content, justifiably or not. Either way, low expectations can result in teachers of DHH students providing them with immediate help anytime they encounter the slightest difficulty (Gaustad, 1999), thus leading to a lack of self-determination and an attitude of dependence on others.

Anecdotes of observations conducted in co-enrollment classrooms present a different picture. Antia recalls that while observing at a co-enrollment program in California, she saw that one of the DHH students in an upper elementary grade did not complete homework as required. Antia fully expected the classroom teacher to assume that the homework was too difficult for a deaf student and to arrange for tutoring help from the teacher of DHH. Instead, to her surprise, the classroom teacher calmly informed the student that he had been in class the previous day when the content was covered, that he was therefore expected to know the content and to request help before the homework was due, and that he would be required to complete the homework independently during recess. On another occasion Antia observed that three DHH students (in a co-enrolled group of about 15 students) were not paying particular attention to the teacher during a science lecture. She remembers thinking that the behavior of these DHH students was similar to behavior she had observed in other classrooms where individual DHH students were mainstreamed. Antia immediately assumed that the reason for the inattention of the DHH students was their inability to follow the classroom instruction (which she also assumed was too difficult for them). After the teacher lecture, the students in the co-enrollment classroom were divided into smaller groups, comprising both DHH and hearing students, to complete an activity pertaining to the science topic. The DHH students, far from being passive or clueless as she expected, were active participants in the small group activity. They initiated providing information to the group, obtained information from the sources available to them, asked questions of the other students, and were not shy about contradicting the other members of their group when necessary. The teacher informed Antia that these

DHH students had mastered the content of her lecture the previous day and did not need the preview she had provided.

The issue of teacher expectations is highlighted in illustrative excerpts from teacher interviews. Teachers of DHH students in self-contained classrooms typically have little day-to-day knowledge of the pace and content of instruction in general education, while in co-enrollment classrooms both teachers and students encounter the general education curriculum as part of their daily teaching and learning. A teacher of DHH students in a self-contained classroom mentioned that she generally aimed her lessons at the students with the lowest level of language proficiency and cognitive skill (Hermans, de Klerk, et al., 2014). In contrast, a teacher of DHH in a co-enrollment classroom stated that she did not let the children "get away with anything" and believed that all students needed to take care of their responsibilities because doing so was a basic skill of adult life (Jimenez-Sanchez & Antia, 1999).

Qualitative studies of teacher, parent, and student perceptions of co-enrollment programs reveal that the DHH students are perceived as having good access to curriculum and instruction. Teachers of two co-enrollment classrooms reported that co-enrolled DHH students were expected to master content information appropriate to their grade level, were held to the same standard as other students, and learned appropriate study skills and behaviors (Luckner, 1999). Parents of these students and school administrators who were interviewed believed that the DHH students benefited by becoming independent learners who were accountable for their own learning, rather than being dependent on teachers and tutors. Hermans, de Klerk, et al. (2014) reported findings from a questionnaire given to hearing and DHH students in a Dutch co-enrollment program. They found that the DHH students felt greater academic pressure and also reported less teacher support than their hearing peers. However, there was no difference between DHH and hearing students in their perception of the structure of lessons, the effectiveness of teacher explanations, and the classroom climate, indicating that all students were able to access instruction in the co-enrollment classroom.

Unfortunately, participation and engagement in classroom academic activities in general education classrooms can be difficult for DHH students. Students who use a sign language interpreter to gain access to classroom communication can encounter difficulties due to the lack of qualified interpreters (Sapere, LaRock, Convertino, Gallimore, & Lessard, 2005; Schick et al., 2006), the rapid pace of classroom discussions, and the necessity of giving simultaneous visual attention to the interpreter, the teacher, and the classroom materials (Stinson & Liu, 1999). Students who depend primarily on spoken language also may have difficulty participating and, ultimately, learn less in the classroom because of their inability to follow spoken communication in poor acoustic conditions (Crandell & Smaldino, 2000; De Raeve, 2015).

Difficulties in participation are easily overlooked in classrooms where only a single DHH student is enrolled. However, in co-enrollment classrooms with a substantial number of DHH students and a teacher of DHH as a co-teacher, participation inequalities are more likely to be noticed and successfully addressed. As will become evident in the following chapters, many co-enrollment classrooms are also bilingual, with sign language and spoken language used for instruction and for interaction. When sign language interpreters are needed in such programs, their role is likely to be understood and valued, although interpreters new to co-enrollment sometimes find their roles very different from their expectations (e.g., Kreimeyer et al., this volume). Also, because of the prevalence of sign use in the classroom, general education teachers and hearing students may frequently be able to communicate directly with the DHH students, unmediated by an interpreter. Classroom teachers who work with DHH students daily are more likely to be aware of how the pace of classroom talk and the physical and acoustical parameters of the classroom influence participation. Thus, one would expect that DHH students in co-enrollment classrooms would participate and be as academically engaged as their hearing peers.

Equal participation by DHH and hearing students in the co-enrollment classroom would provide evidence of academic benefits. Two studies from a single co-enrollment program in the United States indicate that the inequalities in academic participation and engagement between DHH and hearing students are not completely erased by co-enrollment. To obtain information on student perceptions of participation, McCain and Antia (2005) asked hearing and DHH students in the co-enrollment classroom to complete the Classroom Participation Questionnaire (Stinson et al., 2001), which provides information on how well students feel they understand the classroom teacher and their classmates, and their positive and negative affect toward the classroom. The authors found that on all four scales (Understanding Teacher, Understanding Students, Positive Affect, and Negative Affect), DHH students without disabilities scored consistently lower than hearing students, although the differences were not statistically significant. DHH students with disabilities scored significantly lower on all four scales than the hearing students.

Metz (2013) observed the academic engagement (defined as student attention, participation, and on-task behavior) of nine DHH and nine matched hearing students in two early elementary co-enrollment classrooms. She found no differences between DHH and hearing students in overall academic engagement. However, DHH students were more likely to be passively engaged (i.e., paying attention) and less likely to be actively engaged (i.e., participating in activities such as reading, writing, or answering questions) than their hearing peers. Neither group of students engaged in off-task behaviors. In general, the DHH and hearing students showed similar patterns of engagement during academic activities such as reading, listening to a lecture, or engaging in independent seat work. However, hearing students were more likely than DHH students to be engaged during activities that involved student discussion. For hearing students, academic engagement was highest in small group activities, while for the DHH students, academic engagement was highest during one-to-one instruction. Taken together, these two studies (both from the same co-enrollment program but conducted several years apart) indicate that DHH and hearing students in co-enrollment classrooms may differ in the degree of their active and passive engagement depending on the nature of classroom activities. Further research is needed on academic engagement in these different situations as well as the extent to which differing levels of academic engagement might influence academic achievement.

The ultimate question, of course, is whether co-enrolled DHH students who have good access to the regular education curriculum and where instruction is adapted to their communication needs achieve at a higher level than DHH peers in other academic settings, and whether any of these factors have greater influence than others. Data on academic achievement in co-enrollment programs are relatively scant and, like academic engagement, provide a mixed picture. Kreimeyer et al. (2000) reported that reading vocabulary scores for the DHH students in the co-enrollment program were not significantly different than the national grade-level norms. Reading comprehension scores of the DHH co-enrolled students were lower than the national norms but higher than the DHH norms. McCain and Antia (2005) similarly reported that on teacher ratings of academic competence the DHH students scored within the low-average range when compared to national norms. On standardized assessments of reading, mathematics, and language they scored below the national grade-level norms but above the national norms for DHH students.

Hermans, de Klerk, et al. (2014) reported a large gap in achievement of DHH and hearing students in a co-enrollment program in the Netherlands. Most of the hearing students at the school scored within the 81st to100th percentile in reading, spelling, and mathematics, while DHH students scored within the 1st to 40th percentile. Importantly, the few reports of achievement among DHH learners in co-enrollment programs come primarily from the programs described by Kreimeyer et al. (this volume) and de Klerk et al. (this volume). Because the studies were conducted in different countries with children who vary in several ways (e.g., degree of hearing loss, family involvement, years in co-enrollment programming) in addition to program differences, their results are not strictly comparable (Antia & Metz, 2014). Several later chapters in this volume provide additional evidence with regard to the achievement of DHH and hearing students in co-enrollment program settings, but further study is clearly needed.

Co-Enrollment and Language Proficiency

If DHH students are co-enrolled with hearing peers, does this influence DDH students' proficiency in spoken language? Or in sign language? And if so, positively or negatively? These questions have not been studied comprehensively yet, but a few research studies into co-enrollment of DHH students offer at least a glimpse into these matters.

Perez Martin et al. (2014) reported scores on tests and scales measuring spoken and sign language proficiency in DHH children in bilingual co-enrollment programs in Madrid. Using the Spanish CDI for expressive vocabulary and the PPVT for receptive vocabulary, scores were generally above the hearing age (the number of months after cochlear implantation or provision of hearing aids) of the 12 DHH children tested, but lower than might be expected given their chronological age. Grammatical proficiency in spoken Spanish in a group of 11 somewhat older children showed scores in the lower ranges of hearing peers, but variability was high. In receptive and expressive Spanish Sign Language, progress over time was very positive, revealing a typical pattern of comprehension preceding production. Again, however, variability was high.

Tang, Lam, and Yiu (2014) described the spoken language proficiency in Hong Kong Cantonese, the comprehension of grammatical structures in written Chinese, and production and grammaticality judgments of Hong Kong Sign Language in 20 DHH children co-enrolled in the Hong Kong sign bilingual program. Eight of these children had fewer than five years' exposure to these languages. Results showed significant positive relationships in proficiency among all three languages. No adverse effects were found from the acquisition of Hong Kong Sign Language for the development of spoken Cantonese and written Chinese. No comparisons were made with language acquisition of DHH children in other educational programs, so it is not possible to attribute the results directly to the co-enrollment program itself.

Hermans, de Klerk, et al. (2014) studied proficiency in spoken Dutch and Sign Language of the Netherlands in 12 DHH students in a co-enrollment program. Upon entry in the program, the students had less severe delays in spoken Dutch compared to peers in bilingual special schools for the deaf, although variability was high. In fact, spoken language proficiency was one of the criteria used to select these students for the co-enrollment program. The results with respect to spoken Dutch vocabulary showed a surprisingly positive growth over the years. Nevertheless, receptive vocabulary scores of DHH students still showed lags compared to their hearing peers. With respect to Sign Language of the Netherlands, the already high proficiency of co-enrolled DHH students upon entry in the program remained above average over the years, compared to the sign language proficiency of students in bilingual deaf education. This seems in line with the positive effects on sign language proficiency that Bowen (2008) found in her study of a U.S. co-enrollment program.

In summary, results of the few studies of language proficiency of DHH students in co-enrollment programs show some progress in spoken and sign language over the years, and this may be valued positively. However, whether this progress is more or less than that of DHH students in other programs is hard to establish. To what extent program elements lead to progress in language proficiency is impossible to determine. What seems similar to language proficiency scores of DHH students in other educational program is the high variability.

THE INTERSECTION OF CO-ENROLLMENT AND BILINGUAL PROGRAMS

Although co-enrollment programs are not necessarily bilingual, to achieve the ideal of equal access to curriculum many programs use both sign and spoken language as the languages of the classroom. Ideally, for DHH and hearing students to participate fully in all aspects of the academic and social life of the classrooms, all teachers and students should share an effective means of communication, and that may mean having the ability to use both the spoken and the sign languages of the community. In practice, it is unlikely that everyone in the classroom will be fluent in both languages, a challenge described in several of the later chapters. Even so, both previous reports (Bowen, 2008; Kreimeyer et al., 2000) and chapters in this volume indicate that DHH students in co-enrollment classrooms are motivated to use spoken language because of the presence of hearing peers, while hearing students seem motivated and willing to learn sign language because of the presence of their DHH peers. McCain and Antia (2005), for example, found that the DHH students reported that they most often preferred to use spoken language when interacting with hearing peers, while 44% of the hearing students reported that they used speech and sign with DHH peers; 67% reported that they preferred to use speech and sign with hearing peers as well.

In bilingual co-enrollment programs, targeted efforts are made to ensure that hearing students learn sign language. These programs typically offer sign classes and expect all students to sign during some school periods. Informal observations (Antia & Metz, 2014; Luckner, 1999) indicate that visitors are not always able to distinguish DHH and hearing students on the basis of the communication mode they use in the classroom (see also Kirchner, this volume). Hearing students have been observed interpreting for visiting adults who do not sign, interacting with their DHH classmates in sign during collaborative activities, and signing during school assemblies (see Yiu et al., this volume).

These efforts at promoting the use of sign seem to have had positive results. Kreimeyer et al. (2000) reported that by the end of the first year in the co-enrollment classroom, most of the hearing students were able to use sign language to some extent during presentations. Teachers reported that hearing students conversed with the DHH students in voice-off sign about 50% of the time. Bowen (2008) went further and evaluated the sign language abilities of hearing students. She found that co-enrolled hearing students received higher ratings on their sign ability from deaf adults than students in the traditional (non–co-enrollment) classroom.

General education teachers in co-enrollment programs also learn to sign, some with sufficient fluency to conduct classes in sign themselves (Kreimeyer et al., 2000). Bilingual co-enrollment programs, therefore, appear to offer a positive alternative for those DHH students in general education classrooms who use sign and otherwise would likely receive all of their instruction mediated through an interpreter. Within the co-enrollment program, the presence of DHH and hearing peers—as well as adults—with whom students can communicate directly makes social and academic integration possible. Once again, however, there is no necessity that co-enrollment programs be bilingual or even bimodal. Even if the original co-enrollment model assumed a bimodal–bilingual approach (Kirchner, 1994, this volume), other co-enrollment program classrooms can be monolingual but still enhance learning by creating a classroom climate in which DHH students can communicate, participate, and learn.

BARRIERS AND CHALLENGES TO CO-ENROLLMENT

Although co-enrollment programs are being developed worldwide, they continue to be relatively rare compared to self-contained or traditional mainstreamed programs. Given the potential for social and academic integration, one has to wonder why co-enrollment programs are not more prevalent. The challenges to initiating and maintaining co-enrollment programs are detailed in several chapters in this book. Some challenges, however, have already been documented based on interviews with teachers and administrators in U.S. co-enrollment programs (Antia & Metz, 2014).

One administrative challenge is that co-enrollment classrooms require a substantial number of DHH students. While it may be possible to enroll sufficient numbers of DHH students in urban and suburban schools, schools in more rural areas may have difficulty attracting and transporting a sufficient number of DHH students to a single school program (Baker et al., this volume). Another administrative challenge is convincing principals, school supervisors, teachers, and parents that co-enrollment will not be detrimental to the school curricular program or to the hearing students (Kreimeyer et al., this volume; Yiu et al., this volume). Finally, if the co-enrollment program is also co-taught, the presence of two teachers in a classroom may be seen as a financial liability even if it is possible to find appropriately qualified individuals, something that is not always possible (Hoofard, Gilbert, Goodwin, & Bradham, this volume; Perez et al., this volume).

Co-teaching is often a challenge for teachers, who may have to change their beliefs, attitudes, and behaviors. Teachers are sometimes unwilling to share control of the classroom and recognize the co-teacher as an equal partner in the classroom. Perceptions of teachers' roles may also need to change. Special education teachers (including teachers of DHH students) are often perceived as specialists who deal primarily with difficult-to-teach students, while the general education teacher primarily delivers curriculum. The temptation in co-enrollment classrooms is for the teacher of DHH to work mainly with the DHH students and the general education teacher to work with the hearing students, thus de facto segregating rather than integrating the classroom. To avoid such segregation, which essentially negates the purpose of co-enrollment, teachers may have to rethink their expectations and attitudes toward all students. They may have to unlearn assumptions that DHH learners are academically incompetent, requiring a lot of one-to-one assistance. They may also have to reconsider their automatic supposition that all learning difficulties encountered by DHH students are due to hearing loss rather than inattention, mischief, or other reasons common to all students. Teachers need to learn how to focus on the similarities among DHH and hearing learners and also to understand how adapting instruction for different learners benefits all learners. Ultimately, for teachers to work together, they must have sufficient time and incentive to do so. Partnering with another teacher requires planning time over and above that normally available during the school day, a theme returned to many times in the chapters to follow.

Communication challenges are also present in co-enrollment programs, almost by definition. Although the ideal is for all adults and children in those programs to communicate with all other adults and children, the reality is that learning a second language (whether signed or spoken) requires persistence, motivation, and support. Not all hearing staff (and perhaps some deaf staff) will be able to become fluent in sign language, given that not all adults are successful second-language learners. Even for those highly motivated individuals who ultimately will be successful, gaining sign language fluency will take different amounts of time, effort, and resources that the individuals and their programs may or may not be able to accommodate. Similarly, many deaf staff will not be fluent in spoken language, and others will prefer not to use it for a variety of reasons. While the social benefits of the dual-language environment seem to be consistent and positive the academic benefits to the DHH and hearing learners are more difficult to pin down (Hennies & Hennies, this volume; Marschark, Knoors, & Tang, 2014).

Finally, expense might be a barrier, especially if co-enrollment classes are co-taught by both a general education teacher and a teacher of DHH. Itinerant teachers who work with DHH students in main-stream classes can have 10 to 20 students or more on their caseloads. In contrast, the teacher of DHH in a co-enrollment program might work with as few as six DHH children. However, it is important to keep in mind that self-contained classrooms of DHH children in center schools or mainstream schools are often quite small and might have a similar student–teacher ratio. Additional expense also might be incurred if students need to be transported to a centrally located school instead of to local schools. Again, these costs may not be any more than those incurred for students who attend a center school. Expense in terms of teacher time for teamwork and professional development might be the greatest barrier.

BACK FULL CIRCLE: WHAT DO WE NEED TO KNOW ABOUT CO-ENROLLMENT PROGRAMS?

As yet, our information about co-enrollment programs and their outcomes is limited. Is co-enrollment better seen as one option along a continuum of options for DHH students or somewhere in between self-contained programs and mainstream programs? Does it have the potential of being the ideal integrated environment, "the best of both worlds"? If co-enrollment is considered only one option among many, we have to ask whether co-enrollment classrooms are good for some DHH students and not for others. If so, which students benefit—or ben-efit the most—from co-enrollment? And if only some DHH students benefit, should these students be chosen based on some academic or social criteria? If DHH students have to earn the right to be in a co-enrollment program, then co-enrollment cannot be considered a truly integrated environment with DHH students welcomed as members who have a right to be in the classroom. Is co-enrollment another term for group inclusion (as termed in Ringwald-Frimerman, Ingber, & Most, this volume) or reverse mainstreaming? We also need to answer some more basic questions about the kind of variability within and among co-enrollment programs. Are there specific criteria that co-enrollment programs should meet? What do these programs have in common and how much do they vary? How do, or how should, characteristics of the programs that are seen as essential vary with the cultural, legal, and sociological context of the program site? Unless we can define these programs using even a limited number of parameters, it is unlikely that we can study them with any degree of rigor or compare results from different co-enrollment programs. The chapters in this book will start the conversations; we hope that these eventually lead to some answers.

In terms of the benefits of co-enrollment, while we have some information on the social benefits to DHH students, we have relatively little information as to whether these positive social outcomes are greater than or equal to social outcomes of students who are mainstreamed or who attend self-contained classrooms in center schools or mainstream schools. It is also worth noting that social outcomes reported in most studies thus far are primarily for elementary-age students. We do not know yet whether these positive social outcomes are maintained as DHH and hearing students move into higher grades. Some of the programs described in this book that provide co-enrollment from preschool through high school may provide us with answers to these concerns.

The field also needs information on the academic outcomes of DHH students in co-enrollment programs. In theory, the opportunity to access the general education curriculum and to be challenged by high expectations from teachers should result in better academic achievement as long as students are equipped cognitively, linguistically, and emotionally to deal with the curricula and the expectations. However, the data available in this regard are scarce and variable. The little information we have on academic achievement seems to indicate that co-enrolled DHH students outperform DHH peers in other settings, but the extent to which they should be expected to match achievement of hearing peers is a much larger question beyond the scope of the present volume. In any case, there are a host of variables that can affect these outcomes. Among these are the length of time students have spent in the co-enrollment program, the actual (rather than the perceived) access to the curriculum, and, of course, the variables that affect achievement of all students, such as socioeconomic status, time spent in instruction, the quality of such instruction, and the extent to which student language and cognitive abilities match academic demands. Although academic engagement is a necessary component for academic achievement, we know almost nothing about such engagement in co-enrolled, self-contained, or mainstreamed classrooms. We know even less about the quality of the instruction provided to DHH students in the different kinds of classrooms.

The issue of communication access and ease is central to the education of DHH students and is one of the drivers of co-enrollment programs. Most of the co-enrollment programs described in the literature (prior to the publication of this volume) are bilingual, using both the signed and spoken language of the communities in which they are situated. The purpose behind bilingual co-enrollment programs can be quite varied. In some cases the primary purpose is to ensure that DHH students are able to learn using sign language instead of being confined to learning through spoken language alone, as they might be in other educational environments. In other cases the purpose is to ensure that the DHH students have direct access to instruction and in addition have the ability to learn from and interact with hearing peers and teachers.

We have some data to show that hearing students in co-enrollment classrooms learn to sign and can interact with their DHH peers using sign language. What we do not know is whether they sign well enough to engage in academic activities with DHH peers unsupported by sign language interpreters. We have little information about how sign language is acquired by these hearing peers. Some programs provide sign language classes to all students, but we do not know any details on the depth or intensity of sign language instruction needed to create a sign bilingual classroom for both DHH and hearing students. Others use the "hope and pray" method, assuming that the opportunity to be in an environment where signing is accepted will result in sign acquisition.

We know from program descriptions in this volume as well as interviews conducted by researchers that the teachers involved often view co-enrollment programs in a positive light. Positive perceptions are also reported by administrators and parents and by students themselves. We also know that for programs for DHH students to be successful, collaboration among teachers and other service providers (speech therapists, audiologists, sign language interpreters) is crucial. In co-enrollment programs, successful collaboration is possible and welcomed; it may be one of the critical contributions of such programs to the education of DHH students. Co-teaching is a common component of co-enrollment. It can take many different forms, but all require collaboration and sharing of responsibility among teachers. Collaboration can also lead to the inclusion of teachers of DHH children, deaf professionals, and the Deaf community into the larger school community, something seen as essential by most of the co-enrollment programs described in this volume. While such collaboration is certainly possible within self-contained or traditional mainstream programs, the structure of co-enrollment programs makes the need for such collaboration obvious and therefore probably more likely.

LOOKING AHEAD

This volume is intended not to provide definitive evidence of the effectiveness of co-enrollment programs but to offer a collection of pedagogical and didactic descriptions of programs that see themselves as consistent with co-enrollment ideals. We undertook this effort out of concern that the field lacks practical, pedagogical, and organizational information about what works and what does not work for co-enrollment programming in different settings. Some co-enrollment programs are not even aware that others exist! This volume therefore is aimed at sharing with a broad audience what we have learned about teaching DHH learners in co-enrollment programs. Chapters focus on how co-enrollment programs work and "variations on the co-enrollment theme."

This collection is not intended as a research volume. Contributors were asked to provide information about the organization of their programs, the manner in which the programs seek to support access for all learners, how teachers and other stakeholders collaborate, and how student progress is monitored. The book thus focuses on the efforts that these programs have made to create and sustain co-enrollment programs and the ways in which they are evaluating the benefits (and challenges) of those programs.

The existence of co-enrollment programs in countries around the globe is a development to be celebrated. Eventually, to sustain these programs, we will need to not only describe them but also to engage in a continuing program of inquiry, including reports of student academic and social outcomes over time. It is our hope that by raising awareness of co-enrollment programs, describing the wide variety of such programs, and providing initial information about their promise, the community of educators, researchers, and consumers of deaf education will sustain and expand the programs and provide evidence of their effectiveness.

REFERENCES

Antia, S. D. (1982). Social interaction of partially mainstreamed hearing-impaired children. *American Annals of the Deaf, 127*, 18–25.

Antia, S. D., Jones, P., Luckner, J., Kreimeyer, K. H., & Reed, S. (2011). Social outcomes of students who are deaf and hard of hearing in general education classrooms. *Exceptional Children, 77*, 487–502.

Antia, S. D., Jones, P., Reed, S., & Kreimeyer, K. H. (2009). Academic status and progress of deaf and hard-of-hearing students in general education classrooms. *Journal of Deaf Studies and Deaf Education, 14*, 293–311.

Antia, S. D., & Kreimeyer, K. H. (1996). Social interaction and acceptance of DHH children and their peers. *Volta Review, 98*, 157–180.

Antia, S. D., & Metz, K. (2014). Co-enrollment in the United States: A critical analysis of benefits and challenges. In M. Marschark, G. Tang, & H. Knoors (Eds.), *Bilingualism and bilingual deaf education* (pp. 424–443). New York: Oxford University Press.

Antia, S. D., & Rivera, M. C. (2016). Instruction and service time decisions: Itinerant services to deaf and hard-of-hearing students. *Journal of Deaf Studies and Deaf Education, 21*, 293–302.

Archbold, S., & Wheeler, S. (2010). Cochlear implants: Family and young people's perspectives. In M. Marschark & P. Spencer (Eds.), *The Oxford handbook of deaf studies, language, and education* (Vol. 2, pp. 226–240). New York: Oxford University Press.

Bowen, S. (2008). Coenrollment for students who are deaf or hard of hearing: Friendship patterns and social interactions. *American Annals of the Deaf, 153,* 285–293.

Bunch, G. (1994). An interpretation of full inclusion. *American Annals of the Deaf, 139,* 150–152.

Crandell, C., & Smaldino, J. (2000). Classroom acoustics for children with normal hearing and with hearing impairment. *Language, Speech and Hearing Services in the Schools, 31,* 362–370.

De Raeve, L. (2015). Classroom adaptations for effective learning by deaf students. In H. Knoors & M. Marschark (Eds.), *Educating deaf learners: Creating a global evidence base* (pp. 573–593). New York: Oxford University Press.

Friend, M., Cook, L., Hurley-Chamberlain, D., & Shamberger, C. (2010). Co-teaching: An illustration of the complexity of collaboration in special education. *Journal of Educational and Psychological Consultation, 20,* 9–27.

Gaustad, M. G. (1999). Including the kids across the hall: Collaborative instruction of hearing, deaf, and hard of hearing students. *Journal of Deaf Studies and Deaf Education, 4,* 176–190.

Hermans, D., de Klerk, A., Wauters, L., & Knoors, H. (2014). The Twinschool: A co-enrollment program in the Netherlands. In M. Marschark, G. Tang, & H. Knoors (Eds.), *Bilingualism and bilingual deaf education* (pp. 396–423). New York: Oxford University Press.

Hermans, D., Wauters, L., de Klerk, A., & Knoors, H. (2014). Quality of instruction in bilingual schools for deaf children: Through the children's eyes and the camera's lens. In M. Marschark, G. Tang, & H. Knoors (Eds.), *Bilingualism and bilingual deaf education* (pp. 272–291). New York: Oxford University Press.

Jambor, E., & Elliott, M. (2005). Self-esteem and coping strategies among deaf students. *Journal of Deaf Studies and Deaf Education, 10,* 63–81.

Jimenez-Sanchez, C., & Antia, S. D. (1999). Team teaching in an integrated classroom: Perceptions of deaf and hearing teachers. *Journal of Deaf Studies and Deaf Education, 4,* 215–224.

Kirchner, C. J. (1994). Co-enrollment as an inclusion model. *American Annals of the Deaf, 139,* 163–164.

Kluwin, T. N. (1993). Cumulative effects of mainstreaming on the achievement of deaf adolescents. *Exceptional Children, 60,* 73–81.

Kluwin, T. N. (1994). The interaction of race, gender and social class effects in the education of deaf students. *American Annals of the Deaf, 139,* 465–471.

Kluwin, T. N., & Gonter Gaustad, M. (1992). How family factors influence school achievement. In T. Kluwin, D. F. Moores, & M. Gonter Gaustad (Eds.), *Toward effective public school programs for deaf students* (pp. 66–82). New York: Teachers College Press.

Knoors, H., Brons, M., & Marschark, M., Eds. (in press). *Deaf education beyond the Western world.* New York: Oxford University Press.

Kreimeyer, K. H., Crooke, P., Drye, C., Egbert, V., & Klein, B. (2000). Academic and social benefits of a coenrollment model of inclusive education for deaf and hard-of-hearing children. *Journal of Deaf Studies and Deaf Education, 5,* 174–185.

Luckner, J. (1999). An examination of two coteaching classrooms. *American Annals of the Deaf, 144,* 24–34.

Marschark, M., Knoors, H., & Tang, G. (2014). Perspectives on bilingualism and bilingual deaf education. In M. Marschark, G. Tang, & H. Knoors (Eds.), *Bilingualism and bilingual deaf education* (pp. 445–476). New York: Oxford University Press.

Marschark, M., Shaver, D. M., Nagle, K., & Newman, L. (2015). Predicting the academic achievement of deaf and hard-of-hearing students from individual, household, communication, and educational factors. *Exceptional Children, 8,* 350–369.

McCain, K., & Antia, S. D. (2005). Academic and social status of hearing, deaf, and hard-of-hearing students participating in a co-enrolled classroom. *Communication Disorders Quarterly, 27,* 20–32.

McKirdy, L. S., & Blank, M. (1982). Dialogue in deaf and hearing preschoolers. *Journal of Speech and Hearing Research, 25,* 487–499.

Metz, K. (2013). *Academic engagement of deaf and hard-of-hearing students in a co-enrollment program.* Ph.D. thesis, University of Arizona, Tucson.

Mitchell, R. E., & Karchmer, M. A. (2006). Demographics of deaf education: More students in more places. *American Annals of the Deaf, 151,* 95–104.

National Center for Education Statistics. (2016). Digest of Education Statistics 2015 (NCES 2016-014). Retrieved from https://nces.ed.gov/fastfacts/display.asp?id=59

Nelson, P., & Soli, S. (2000). Acoustical barriers to learning: Children at risk in every classroom. *Language, Speech and Hearing Services in the Schools, 31,* 356–361.

Nunes, T., & Pretzlik, U. (2001). Deaf children's social relationships in mainstream schools. *Deafness and Education International, 3,* 123–136.

Perez Martin, M., Valmaseda Balanzategui, M., & Morgan, G. (2014). Sign bilingual and co-enrollment education for children with cochlear implants in Madrid, Spain. In M. Marschark, G. Tang, & H. Knoors (Eds.), *Bilingualism and bilingual deaf education* (pp. 368–395). New York: Oxford University Press.

Punch, R., & Hyde, M. (2010). Children with cochlear implants in Australia: Educational settings, supports, and outcomes. *Journal of Deaf Studies and Deaf Education, 15,* 405–421.

Qi, S., & Mitchell, R. E. (2012). Large-scale academic achievement testing of deaf and hard-of-hearing students: Past, present, and future. *Journal of Deaf Studies and Deaf Education, 17*(1), 1–18.

Ramsey, C. (1997). *Deaf children in public schools: Placement, context and consequences.* Washington, DC: Gallaudet University Press.

Reed, S., Antia, S. D., & Kreimeyer, K. H. (2008). Academic status of deaf and hard-of-hearing students in public schools: Student, home, and service facilitators and detractors. *Journal of Deaf Studies and Deaf Education, 13,* 485–502.

Reyes, M. R., Brackett, M. A., Rivers, S. E., White, M., & Salovey, P. (2012). Classroom emotional climate, student engagement, and academic achievement. *Journal of Educational Psychology, 104,* 700–712.

Rubie-Davies, C. M., Peterson, E. R., Sibley, C. G., & Rosenthal, R. (2015). A teacher expectation intervention: Modelling the practices of high expectation teachers. *Contemporary Educational Psychology, 40*, 72–85.

Sapere, P., LaRock, D., Convertino, C., Gallimore, L., & Lessard, P. (2005). Interpreting and interpreter education—Adventures in Wonderland? In M. Marschark, R. Peterson, & E. Winston (Eds.), *Sign language interpreting and interpreter education: Directions for research and practice* (pp. 283–298). New York: Oxford University Press.

Schick, B., Williams, K., & Bolster, L. (1999). Skill levels of educational interpreters working in public schools. *Journal of Deaf Studies and Deaf Education, 4*, 144–155.

Schick, B., Williams, K., & Kupermintz, H. (2006). Look who's being left behind: Educational interpreters and access to education for deaf and hard-of-hearing students. *Journal of Deaf Studies and Deaf Education, 11*, 3–20.

Stinson, M. S., & Antia, S. D. (1999). Considerations in educating deaf and hard-of-hearing students in inclusive settings. *Journal of Deaf Studies and Deaf Education, 4*, 163–175.

Stinson, M. S., & Kluwin, T. N. (2003). Educational consequences of alternative school placements. In M. Marschark (Ed.), *Oxford handbook of deaf studies, language and education* (pp. 52–64). New York: Oxford University Press.

Stinson, M. S., & Liu, Y. (1999). Participation of deaf and hard-of-hearing students in classes with hearing students. *Journal of Deaf Studies and Deaf Education, 4*, 191–202.

Stinson, M. S., Long, G., Reed, S., Kreimeyer, K. H., Sabers, D., & Antia, S. D. (2001). *Communication Participation Questionnaire*. University of Arizona, Tucson.

Tang, G., Lam, S., & Yiu, K. C. (2014). Language development of deaf children in a sign bilingual and co-enrollment environment. In M. Marschark, G. Tang, & H. Knoors (Eds.), *Bilingualism and bilingual deaf education* (pp. 313–341). New York: Oxford University Press.

UNESCO. (1994). *The Salamanca statement and framework for action on special needs education.* Retrieved December 21, 2017, from www.unesco.org/education/pdf/SALAMA_E.PDF

United Nations. (1994). *Standard rules on the equalization of opportunities for persons with disabilities.* Retrieved February 9, 2018, from https://www.un.org/development/desa/disabilities/standard-rules-on-the-equalization-of-opportunities-for-persons-with-disabilities.html

U.S. Department of Education. (2017). Individuals with Disabilities Education Act. Retrieved from https://sites.ed.gov/idea/?src=policy-page

Wolters, N., Knoors, H., Cillessen, A. H. N., & Verhoeven, L. (2011). Predicting acceptance and popularity in early adolescence as a function of hearing status, gender, and educational setting. *Research in Developmental Disabilities, 32*, 2553–2565.

Yiu, C., & Tang, G. (2014). Social integration of deaf and hard-of-hearing students in a sign bilingual and co-enrollment environment. In M. Marschark, G. Tang, & H. Knoors (Eds.), *Bilingualism and bilingual deaf education* (pp. 342–367). New York: Oxford University Press.

2

TRIPOD: Answer to the Seeds of Discontent

Carl J. Kirchner

THE 1970 REQUEST FOR PROPOSAL

The success story of TRIPOD (Toward Rehabilitation Involvement by Parents of the Deaf) began in 1970 when the federal government issued a Request for Proposal (RFP) to address the need for rehabilitation services to serve deaf and hard-of-hearing (DHH) students because basic rehabilitation services had been shown to be inadequate. After reviewing the RFP, Dr. Ray L. Jones, director of the National Center on Deafness, California State University—Northridge, felt that it should not be limited to the rehabilitation service issue but should incorporate two other basic components to be effective—parenting and education. These additional components were based on the premise that rehabilitation services cannot stand alone without the involvement of parents and educators. As assistant professor in the Special Education Department, I was asked to develop and expand this vision. This required input from parents, educators, rehabilitation personnel, and Deaf community leaders. Input sessions with selected individuals from around the nation were held, and the information received was carefully crafted to fit the basic RFP requirements. TRIPOD was the title given to identify the grant awarded to the National Center on Deafness (Culton, 1971). The framework comprised three components: rehabilitation services, parenting, and education; thus, the TRIPOD approach.

The format involved an initial conference and eight three-day regional conferences around the country that allowed participants from each of the designated groups to participate without traveling great distances. One family was chosen from each state. Families were deaf, hard-of-hearing, or hearing with DHH children using various communication modes. Renowned individuals at the national level who were involved in current deaf issues—David Denton, James Hanson, Kathryn Meadow, and Hilde Schlesinger—were selected to be the presenters at the conferences. After the initial conference (April 1971), regional conferences began and continued into 1972. By the last conference and the ending of the grant, parents who had been selected from each state to attend the regional meetings, along with a new cadre of parents, requested continuance of TRIPOD. These regional conferences addressed their need for support, for education, and for their involvement in the education of their children.

The educational philosophy that developed from the TRIPOD conferences resulted in the following eight educational recommendations:

- Be more open to innovation.
- Listen to parents.
- Implement the Total Communication philosophy at all levels.
- Provide more realistic counseling for parents and be more truthful.
- Recruit and further prepare interpreters for integrated classes.
- Raise schools for the deaf to higher standards approximating the academic standards of public schools.
- Treat and educate students as individuals.
- Make provisions for special groups (e.g. DHH students with multiple handicaps [DHH-MH]).

Over the next eight years (1972 to 1980), the recommendations were shelved, implemented in part, or modified by some school or county programs. However, no local school districts, county programs, or state schools for the deaf attempted to implement the entire package. These recommendations were often acknowledged but without follow-through.

THE START OF THE TRIPOD PRESCHOOL PROGRAM

In the fall of 1980, parents of a male infant diagnosed with a hearing loss contacted me for initial information regarding the issues of deafness, educational implications, and communication strategies. My response was, "Attend my class, which is an introduction to deafness, and then we can have a follow-up discussion." The parents complied. This initial meeting was followed by subsequent meetings and discussions. In July 1982, a meeting concluded with the comment, "We would like to establish a preschool program for deaf children." They asked if I was willing to be the cofounder and educational director. The parents assured fiscal support. After further discussion, the question was asked, "What will this program be called?" Without hesitation, I responded, "TRIPOD." This decision was based on the following premises:

- The TRIPOD name was already nationally known.
- Parents wanted the continuation of the TRIPOD conference concept.

- The new educational program would incorporate the 1970 TRIPOD recommendations.

The fiscal foundation would be derived from the movie industry, where the parents had connections and there were opportunities for sophisticated fundraising events. TRIPOD was incorporated as a nonprofit organization in 1982.

Current practices were the rationale for establishing an effective inclusive learning environment to serve the DHH school-aged population. Self-contained classes, with a wide range of age and skill levels, provided limited or no peer language models for individual growth. Teachers were left to develop the students' language skills, placing DHH students in educational "straitjackets." Adherence to one specific curriculum program designed for DHH students using a single communication mode provided little opportunity for student self-discovery and also limited access to a stimulating learning environment. Reading skills of DHH students usually plateaued at the fourth-grade level, resulting in limited comprehension and writing skills and fostering intellectual stagnation. As a result of inadequate language, the communication skills and intellectual capabilities of DHH students were deemed to be below normal. This observation surfaced in the early 1960s with the publication of "The Psychology of Deafness" by Helmer Myklebust (Myklebust, 1964).

Responding to the parents' previous request, the TRIPOD Grapevine was established in 1983 as a national, unbiased, one-stop resource/information call center. A parent was hired as the director. Its purpose was to provide information resources for parents and others having questions about communication issues, Individualized Education Programs, and advocacy.

With five students (ages 2.5 to 6), TRIPOD opened in February 1984 as a unique, tuition-free private preschool for DHH children regardless of any additional disabilities. Inclusion of hearing siblings was a key component (foreign to the educational practices at the time). The TRIPOD school was based on Montessori principles. Maria Montessori, the Italian medical doctor and pedagogue, established a school for so-called defective children (children with special educational needs) in 1898. She developed materials and methods allowing these children to perform far beyond their perceived capacity. With all the key components in place, the cofounders formulated TRIPOD's mission statement: "To help families raise and educate their deaf and hard-of-hearing children in a supportive environment."

Realizing that the future of deaf education was foreshadowed by the 1975 Education for All Handicapped Children Act (PL 94-142; federal legislation requiring all states to provide services to all students with disabilities, 0–22 years of age) and that there was also no inherent value in recreating the status quo in deaf education, the cofounders set out to establish a unique, avant-garde early childhood program. In other words, it was not the continual modifications of the subject matter and practices, or adoption of new trends but a change in the educational environment/setting needed to convey learning experiences for the students. This also required the teachers to change their attitudes and traditional approaches. Preparing the students for the twenty-first century required severing the ties to theories that had no proven success. Selfish motives such as what makes educators or programs look good, or maintaining programs for financial success at the expense of quality education, did not results in adequate student success.

KEY COMPONENTS OF THE TRIPOD PROGRAM

For the TRIPOD program to be successful, key program components were identified. The first was a Montessori-based philosophy and curriculum. The introduction of the Montessori curriculum provided a child-centered approach to meeting the early developmental needs of DHH students. The program started with a Montessori-trained teacher with a DHH credential who also served as the program supervisor. An additional teacher was needed, so a DHH-credentialed teacher was chosen to take the one-year Montessori training, with the training funded by TRIPOD. Early childhood DHH programs in existence around the nation were teacher-centered, based on the assumption that the children needed constant teacher direction for cognitive and language development. Maria Montessori stated, "The importance of my method does not lie in the organization itself, but in the effects which it produces on the child. It is the child who proves the value of this method by his spontaneous manifestations, which set to reveal the laws of man's inner development" (1914/1964, p. 114). Therefore, it can be said that the teacher's task is not to talk, but to arrange motives for cultural activity in a special environment made for the child, namely the Children's House.

The second component was the Total Communication philosophy, which served as the foundation for language development. This philosophy promotes the application of a full spectrum of language modes: child-devised gestures, formal sign language, speech, speechreading, fingerspelling, reading, and writing (Denton, 1972). The students could send and receive information in a relaxed communication environment. The development of speech and auditory skills and the use of technological devices were included as part of the program. DHH students need to be exposed to all communication functions and modes as they move into adult years. They need to be able to comfortably code-switch using these multiple communication modes so they can interact with various styles of expressive and receptive language use. The many modes and strategies that are part of the Total Communication philosophy and are part of visual learning activities for DHH students also benefit general education populations.

Sign Language classes were held either at home or at school. Entire families were involved so that parents and siblings could develop their communication skills based on the sign language continuum. Hearing preschool-aged siblings or relatives served as a building block both at home and in the pre-K program. Their participation provided the opportunity to develop family relationships through education, communication, and shared experiences. This proved that every individual (parents, siblings, other relatives, and even friends) should be involved in all aspects of the program and provided the foundation for family bonding and early access to English-language development.

EXPANSION OF TRIPOD: THE ELEMENTARY COMPONENT

The kindergarten year was the original end of the TRIPOD program. The administrator and educational director, as well as teachers and parents, asked the board of directors to take the next step and extend the preschool/kindergarten program by adding an elementary school component. This request, and the subsequent expansion of the program, was made in response to the observed language development of the TRIPOD students, which was identified as being more substantial than that of DHH students of the same age educated in self-contained classes in surrounding school districts.

A small private school was chosen for expansion of the program. The site administrators and teachers were willing to embrace the TRIPOD philosophy and accommodate a team-teaching situation. The elementary program continued based on the TRIPOD philosophy. Students were to be enrolled in a general education class, which was a requirement for student success. The Montessori curriculum was no longer possible at the elementary level, but the experiences it provided allowed the DHH students to make a positive social and educational transition into a much larger class in a school environment with hearing students. The DHH children had no difficulty making this transition based on their preschool and kindergarten experience.

A credentialed teacher of DHH students team-taught with the general education teacher. In this environment, both the general education teacher and the DHH teacher worked with all the children. A formal class to develop sign skills for both the general education teacher and hearing student classmates was instituted. This, in addition to the daily involvement by all, created an inclusive educational environment. The regular school curriculum and teacher activities were not modified for the DHH students, although the content of the lesson or activities could be expanded for language or concept clarification. This benefited both the DHH students and the hearing students. All aspects of the Total Communication philosophy remained in place. Private school tuition was required for the DHH students. The team teacher's salary and the student tuition were subsidized by TRIPOD. The students worked at grade level and ranked academically in the middle third of the class.

TRANSFER TO THE BURBANK UNIFIED SCHOOL DISTRICT

August 1989 brought a substantial change to the educational component of TRIPOD: the program moved from the private sector to the public school arena. The superintendent of the Burbank Unified School District (BUSD), Dr. Arthur Pierce, an educator with vision, was very interested and willing to work with the TRIPOD administration and board of directors in advancing the TRIPOD program and philosophy. TRIPOD was offered space on a preschool campus and an elementary school campus. The offer was welcome due to the increased tuition charged by the private school and the implications of PL 94-142 guaranteeing parents a free education program for their child. The move to the public school district paved the way for a permanent home and the opportunity to develop a program spanning parent–infant through high school.

With the additional space, TRIPOD was able to keep the Montessori curriculum and establish the parent–infant component (ages 0 to 3). With the original philosophical base intact, the elementary years required practical and innovative building blocks; thus, additional philosophical stepping-stones were added.

To adhere to the 1972 parent recommendations and the philosophy establishing the TRIPOD program, the "contractual" arrangements (in reality a handshake) requested and approved between TRIPOD and BUSD began with the recognition of the TRIPOD program and staff as an integral part of the district. The TRIPOD administrator and educational director would have the freedom to interact with BUSD personnel at all levels, as though they were district employees, in meeting the needs of the DHH students.

The elementary students would be located at a school site where the principal and staff were open to the TRIPOD philosophy and where students would be completely mainstreamed in team-taught classrooms. If a student had a designation as DHH-MH, pull-out tutoring would be provided. (The MH designation refers to a student with more than one diagnosed disability in addition to deafness, such as cerebral palsy or a physical, emotional, or learning disability.) However, at the time no additional funding was allocated for a DHH-MH student. When the principal of the elementary school was contacted about DHH students being assigned to her program, she stated that she knew nothing about deafness, but "children are children and I can learn" (Joan Baca, first principal, personal communication). Initially, parents of hearing students thought that including DHH students would lower academic standards, but within two years, those parents and others were requesting placement for their children in classes with DHH students. This was a result of several factors: two teachers in the classroom; more attention and interaction between students and teachers; parents and students who appreciated learning with differently-abled students and the opportunity to learn a second or third language (American Sign Language [ASL]).

It was also during the first year in Burbank that the co-enrollment designation emerged. The term was coined by Dr. Barry Griffing, Assistant Director of Special Education, State of California, and myself. The sign configuration was borrowed from Japanese Sign Language meaning "equal study" and now has become part of the American sign system (Fig. 2.1).

The elementary, middle, and high school sites were chosen for their proximity to each other and for the ease of continued program development and services. This also provided the opportunity for hearing students to interact with DHH students and to move from class to class

Equal   Study

Figure 2.1. Japanese Sign Language sign meaning "equal study," now an ASL sign for "co-enrollment."

with them based on their communication skills. This continuity would be kept even if they lived in another school catchment area.

The TRIPOD board of directors would underwrite the fiscal costs for its administrators, the teachers involved in the DHH team-teaching situation, and specialty services (audiology and speech and language personnel) needed by DHH students. Out-of-district DHH students and siblings would be accepted into BUSD provided a release was authorized by their home school district. Parents residing outside the area of the Special Education Local Plan Agency (SELPA) in California were responsible for transporting their child. A number of students traveled on their own over 60 miles one way on the public rail system.

Once the DHH students entered the high school program, ASL classes were initiated for all students and credited as a foreign language. Interpreters were hired at the middle and high school levels to support students in classes that were not team-taught. The teachers holding a California Education Specialist: Deaf and Hard of Hearing credential included deaf, hard-of-hearing, and hearing personnel. Throughout the years of program development from 1989 to 1994, when the high school program began, the following educational principles constantly intersected:

- Montessori philosophy: developed independence, cognitive processing skills, and orderly response to the environment
- Co-enrollment: provided for equal education instruction, with DHH students using the same curriculum and taking the same tests
- Modeling: played a powerful role in language skills development and observation, teaching DHH students how to participate in classroom activities as well as appropriate behavior
- Responsibility: taught DHH students how to accept the results of their positive or negative behavior, how to complete school work and assigned tasks, and how to seek assistance when needed
- Communication: built self-confidence, provided freedom to be oneself, and opened doors to the world
- Parenting: provided additional learning experiences for parents through communication and support

These principles are the foundation to fulfilling one's potential.

The decision to share the educational successes beyond BUSD came from the encouragement of professional educators at all levels (both those in favor or skeptical of mainstreaming). This included parents, administrators, and deaf community members. But most of all, the belief of general educators and special staff involved in implementing the program at all levels showed that the TRIPOD philosophy and educational structure can make a difference in the lives of students with hearing loss and in the lives of their hearing peers.

In 2000, BUSD decided to limit enrollment to students who lived within the SELPA. This decision caused parents who wanted their child to have a TRIPOD education to move into the communities that the SELPA comprised: Burbank, Glendale, La Canada, and Pasadena. However, students who were in districts outside the SELPA could no longer be accepted. This created an enrollment decline. The TRIPOD program became known as the TRIPOD/BUSD/Foothill SELPA program (Betton & Merritt, 2009), and in 2001 it was officially designated Burbank/SELPA DHH, but the TRIPOD program philosophy did not change.

SEEDS OF DISCONTENT

The passage of PL 94-142 in 1975 brought upheaval and change to the educational scene for DHH students. The 1980s and the following thirty-plus years continued to bring confusion regarding appropriate educational programs, especially regarding placement in the least restrictive environment, which was defined as mainstreaming. School districts and county offices were unprepared to adequately or appropriately serve the needs of students with hearing losses. Placement in a regular classroom with an interpreter who had no supervision or teacher guidance provided a very poor quality of mainstreaming. Many traditional ideas were discussed in educational circles. These included the opinion that educational materials specifically created for DHH students must be adhered to and instruction must be teacher-directed. DHH students cannot be taught the same material designed for their hearing peers. Adding to this was the belief that ASL should be the primary communication mode for instruction. Seeds of discontent were being sown. TRIPOD sought to address these concerns, providing both a philosophy and structure to transform DHH education.

THE BENEFITS OF TRIPOD

Over the thirty-three years of the TRIPOD co-enrollment program, student and teacher success can be evaluated by what has happened as the result of participation. Teachers involved in the team-teaching situation as well as teachers who used interpreters in co-enrolled classes have witnessed better academic results and requested that the teaming concept continue even in classes where no DHH students are assigned (see also Kirchner, 1994).

Table 2.1 gives the number of individuals who formally graduated or received certificates of high school completion. Students who left

Table 2.1. DHH Graduation Statistics, 2015–2017

Year	% Graduated with Standard HS Diploma	Graduated with Standard HS Diploma		Certificate of Completion	Certificate of Attendance	Total
2016–17	100	3				3
2015–16	50	1			1	2

1998–2014

Year	% Graduated with Standard or Differential Standards Diploma	Graduated with Standard HS Diploma	Graduated with Differential Standards Diploma	Graduated with CAHSEE Exemption Diploma	Certificate of Attendance	Total
2014–15	86	6		1		7
2013–14	100		2			2
2012–13	100	4				4
2011–12	67	2		1		3
2010–11	100	4	3			7
2009–10	86	4	2		1	7
2008–09	75	3		1		4
2007–08	77	7	2			9
2006–07	88	6	1		1	8
2005–06	100	3				3
2004–05	100	1	1			2
2003–04	78	7			2	9
2002–03	75	3			1	4
2001–02	80	4			1	5
2000–01	100	4				4
1999–2000	100	6	1			7
1998–99	100	3				3
1997–98	100	5				5

Data from BHS registrar's office. As of this publication, forty students who have left the TRIPOD program (for varied reasons) have been tracked. Thirty-two are high school graduates, eight are nongraduates, and a number are lost to follow-up.

sometime during their high school program are not recorded on the chart, although there is a footnote on some.

The percentage of students receiving standard high school diplomas is far greater than those receiving certificates of completion. According to Garberoglio, Cawthon, and Sales (2017), "In 2015, 83% of deaf adults in the United States had successfully completed high school compared to 89% of hearing adults. . . . Only 18% of deaf adults in the US had completed a bachelor's degree or more compared to 33% of hearing adults" (p. 4).

The 83% statistic refers to the number of DHH students who have matriculated the four years but does not identify those students who have earned a standard high school diploma (Cawthon, personal communication). In contrast, 80% of TRIPOD's students over the past twenty years have received the standard California high school diploma.

Since 2000, when the SELPA limited enrollment, there have been fewer DHH students in the program. In Table 2.1, DHH students matriculating four years at Burbank High School (BHS) are listed by the certificate achieved in the twenty years since the first graduates from BHS. The State of California, Department of Education, has changed the requirements and titles recognizing general student success except for the standard high school diploma. The certificate of attendance and the California High School Exit Exam (CAHSEE) exemption diploma have been eliminated. Currently, California DHH students fall into one of three categories: those receiving a standard Diploma, a certificate of completion, or a certificate of attendance. Prior to 2015, there were four diploma designations, the first three (rather than the first two) designating course requirement proficiency.

A majority of the students completing the high school program have gone on to postsecondary programs with a significant number completing a four-year college program. Career choices for TRIPOD DHH students have covered the gamut: teaching, college professorship, classroom paraprofessional, business ownership, fashion design, accounting, structural engineering, business administration, Teacher Corps (in foreign countries), graphic design, security, automotive, beautician, jewelry making, and construction. One student was asked to speak at his high school commencement.

Over the years, ASL classes increased in number and levels, as well as in the number of students enrolled. Hearing students who were part of this program and studied ASL as a foreign language now use these skills as sign language instructors in public and private high schools, in postsecondary programs, in the legal profession, as educational paraprofessionals, as community service workers, and as teachers of DHH students. Many also serve as interpreters.

The results indicate that DHH students with a strong inclusive educational foundation can have successful careers, and that those who interact with them have a positive impact.

In reviewing the program operations, some changes had to be made to meet the California state regulations and constraints. These changes might include a modification to the team-teaching structure or a replacement of the team-teaching structure with a classroom teacher who held dual state credentials—one for teaching students in general education and the other for teaching DHH students. Teachers hired for this program had to demonstrate the ability to use and understand ASL and to effectively incorporate all parts of the Total Communication continuum. Educational interpreters were needed to cover middle and high school classes when only general education teachers were available. However, contracting with interpreting agencies to provide interpreters can be problematic because interpreters assigned this way are often not trained in educational interpreting. Also, the cost of agency interpreters can be up to three times more than those hired by a school district.

TRIPOD is sometimes referred to as a clinical study with positive results. The foremost positive result was observing the faster rate of language development in DHH students, which was attributed to the influence of their hearing peers. In addition, the following benefits can be noted:

- Co-enrollment provided greater opportunity for academic success. This implied a change from the traditional learning environment, curriculum content, and class placement for DHH students.
- At the end of the school year, DHH student achievements were recorded from test results. Their scores were distributed across all levels and not clustered at the bottom.
- Student self-confidence emerged early in the program.
- Communication skills were expanded, which fostered code-switching. Colloquial language and slang became part of the students' vocabulary.
- Students joined with their hearing peers on the playground at the preschool and elementary levels and participated in various sports teams and in artistic programs in middle and high school.
- The previous fourth-grade reading plateau was shattered.
- DHH students with additional disabilities were mainly educated in inclusive class settings with the use of appropriate learning strategies and support.
- Diplomas rather than certificates of completion became the norm, according to the BHS registrar's office.
- The TRIPOD program and philosophy continued when new teachers entered the program even though there was little or no supervision. The teaching staff has been the key to their inculcation.
- General education teachers, not holding a DHH credential, have proven that with the propèr support, DHH students assigned to their classes can succeed.

These benefits are reflected in the following testimonials. A few examples are presented by way of illustration, the first two from former students:

> The Tripod Program had a positive impact on my life. It created a special connection between me and my hearing family. This program required hearing parents of a deaf child to have a deaf person come to their home once a week. The deaf person taught my parents and me how to sign and develop a bond. Another positive impact on my life was how my teachers invested in me and believed that I would be successful once I finished school. They gave me hope, made me feel secure and allowed me to be free. Today, I'm a successful business owner and will obtain a Master of Business Administration degree in two months. I think the TRIPOD program should be the model for all mainstreaming programs to study and copy. (Male student, Class of 2008)

> My personal experience of growing up in the TRIPOD program with hearing classmates has given me, as a college professor, a unique perspective of the world. The collaboration I learned at TRIPOD I continue with my students. It has enabled me to understand different visual languages and perspectives while conveying the same message. I'm able to connect easily with both hearing and deaf students as well as colleagues. I genuinely believe I wouldn't have this teaching ability if it weren't for the amazing and superior teachers at TRIPOD. They nurtured my strengths and helped me reach my full potential so that I could relate to my students, and I credit them for shaping me into the teacher I am today. (Female student, Class of 2000)

The next two testimonials are from former professionals at TRIPOD.

> In 1994 Burbank High School (Burbank, California) accepted a new program of DHH inclusion called TRIPOD. A cadre of teachers (one from each discipline) was tapped to work with the TRIPOD DHH administrators, teachers and interpreters in co-enrolled classes. None of us had prior experience teaching DHH students but all of us used a combination of methodologies and scaffolding to deliver our curriculum. We were adventurous and, most of all, positive about the challenge.
>
> In the early years, several of the students would (I think) use their deafness as an excuse for poor or incomplete work. Once given the tools, the students responded with better and better work. Co-enrollment was a huge component. This made group work accessible, along with peer editing and even explanation. As an educator, I learned so many things about instructional delivery that helped all of my students. I soon realized that deafness is no hindrance

to student achievement. All of this is just good teaching and I am so grateful to TRIPOD for allowing me to become a better teacher. (English teacher, Burbank High School)

I used to love the puzzled looks I got from visitors when I escorted them around to visit our TRIPOD classrooms. "Which ones are the deaf students?" they would ask, because the only way the deaf students stood out was by their hearing aids. The teachers and the students were signing and speaking, and all around the rooms were working partnerships and collaborative groups with deaf students as full participants. Amazed visitors accustomed to the more typical programs for deaf and hard-of-hearing students saw our students learning, socializing and behaving like any other children. The classrooms were carefully designed, managed and taught but on any given day in one of our TRIPOD classrooms, what seemed to be happening was pure magic. It was my pleasure and my honor to be part of such an innovative and successful program—a true high point in my long career in education! (Second principal [hearing] of the elementary school program at Washington Elementary, previously working as the middle school teacher at TRIPOD who coordinated and taught the co-enrollment program)

Over the years, some negative comments have also surfaced. The attitude was held by many educators that DHH students cannot successfully achieve in the inclusive academic setting, let alone be accepted socially by general education teachers and hearing students. Yet this thirty-three-year program has dispelled that belief. The TRIPOD model does not succeed without planning ahead. With a supervisor holding only a general education credential or a general special education credential (not for DHH students), the program will have limited or no success. Students being placed in an inclusive setting can take up to a year to become effective and self-sufficient learners. If administrators at the district or school site are unwilling to be involved or do not provide a sustained commitment, the program is doomed. Some administrators, teachers, and parents want to abandon the program shortly after it is put into place due to a perceived lack of quick results, but inclusion takes time. Traditionally DHH community members see no value for students being placed in inclusive settings due to cultural beliefs. Some administrative personnel believe that the implementation of a TRIPOD program (or a modification thereof) is more expensive than a self-contained program with limited mainstreaming or a state residential school placement, even though it has been shown to be less expensive.

The lesson to be learned for the future success of DHH students in an inclusive setting is very simple. The traditional learning environment must be changed. If not, DHH students will continue to be locked within themselves because they will lack many of the fundamental skills necessary to experience the world in which they live. To break these shackles, the current status quo must be changed to challenge students to develop their potential.

From an administrative point of view, placement of interpreters in the inclusive setting has become a quick, easy, and fiscally effective way to fulfill federal and state legislation requirements. However, without proper training for classroom assignments, with no supervision by an appropriate administrator, or with only reliance on interpreter certification scores, the DHH students they serve are hindered in their learning capabilities. There must be a total commitment by all individuals involved to establish and maintain a successful comprehensive inclusive program. Since the beginning, the program showed steady growth while maintaining its original concept and philosophy, but each step forward required planning and patience to realize implementation.

Based on TRIPOD's innovative approach, one can watch for basic elements of the design to appear in future educational programs:

- Social aspects of Deaf Culture will expand to include the hearing community and vice versa.
- More and more general education classroom teachers in regular pre-K–12 programs will have signing skills to accommodate the inclusion of DHH students.
- Technological advances will provide better access for DHH students to be effectively placed in the general education classrooms.
- Inconsistent agency placement of interpreters in the inclusive classroom will be reduced. Districts will establish permanent educational interpreter positions.
- Career doors previously unattainable will be opened to DHH students.
- The self-esteem of DHH students will rise.
- Self-contained classrooms/day programs will be phased out.
- More DHH role models will emerge in all fields.
- The perennial myths (e.g., need for small class size, aide assistance, repetition rut, communication straitjackets, and reading deficits; Kirchner, 2007) in deaf education will be eradicated.
- Programs for DHH students currently in existence or being developed internationally will incorporate all or parts of the TRIPOD program.

Members of the TRIPOD staff coined a slogan to indicate the flexibility of the program's implementation. They showed commitment and pride in their work and in their student-centered philosophy. With the expression, "Whatever Works," for thirty-three years, TRIPOD has demonstrated that, indeed, planning, flexibility, and commitment lead to success.

REFERENCES

Betton, M., & Merritt, W. (2009). *25-year reunion: TRIPOD/BUSD/Foothill SELPA, 1984–2009.* Burbank, CA.

Culton, P. (1971). *Operation TRIPOD.* Washington, DC: Health, Education and Welfare, Social and Rehabilitation Service, Rehabilitation Services Administration, Division of Training. Grant No. 44-P-4508/9-10.

Denton, D. (1972). A rationale for Total Communication. In T. J. O'Rourke (Ed.), *Psycholinguistics and Total Communication: The state of the art* (pp. 53–61). Washington, DC: Gallaudet University Press.

Garberoglio, C. L., Cawthon, S., & Sales, A. (2017). *Deaf people and educational attainment in the United States: 2017.* Washington, DC: U.S. Department of Education, Office of Special Education Programs, National Deaf Center on Postsecondary Outcomes.

Kirchner, C. J. (1994). Co-enrollment as an inclusion model. *American Annals of the Deaf, 139*(2), 163–164.

Kirchner, C. J. (2007). *Every deaf child a star.* Keynote Presentation, CAL-ED/ IMPACT Conference, April 20, 2007, Burbank, CA.

Montessori, M. (1914). *Dr. Montessori's handbook* (1964 reprint). Cambridge, MA: Robert Bentley, Inc.

Myklebust, H. (1964). *The psychology of deafness.* New York: Grune & Stratton.

3

Co-Enrollment in Toowong, Australia

Michelle Baker, Cameron Miller, Elizabeth Fletcher,
Caroline Gamin, and Breda Carty

*Dedicated to the memory of Gemma Bailey, former student Toowong State
School.*

Toowong State School is a small metropolitan primary school in
Queensland's capital city of Brisbane. The Toowong bilingual bicultural
co-enrollment program began with a single Year 1 class in 2001 and was
phased in over six years until it was offered at all year levels across
the school. Since 2001, the program has celebrated many successes,
conquered challenges, and weathered its critics and has seen several
cohorts of students progress through secondary school into tertiary
education and the work sector. The journey has been one of incredible learning for deaf and hearing children, the families of these children, staff in the school, and the Queensland education system. With
the changing landscape of deaf education, the impact of early detec-
tion and technology (including cochlear implants), and the introduction and implementation of a new national curriculum, this evolving
inner-city school continues to meet the unique needs of its students and
remain true to its founding principles, which include the provision of
equitable access to the curriculum through Australian Sign Language
(Auslan) and English, innovative pedagogy, and support for every
child to achieve his or her potential in the mainstream classroom.

HISTORY OF THE TOOWONG STATE SCHOOL BILINGUAL
BICULTURAL CO-ENROLLMENT PROGRAM

The impetus for the program came from the Queensland Deaf community and a parent community advocating for Auslan to be used with
their deaf children in an environment that provided access to the mainstream. Until this time, most severely and profoundly deaf children
were taught in segregated unit settings attached to mainstream schools
by teachers of the deaf using Australasian Signed English, an artificial

41

sign system. Advocates for a new kind of program examined models of educating deaf children using sign language around the world, and co-enrollment was chosen as the model of operation to deliver a sign bilingual program that would best meet the needs of Brisbane's deaf students. Numerous state schools in metropolitan Brisbane were considered as homes for the program, and Toowong was chosen.

Toowong was chosen because the school was small. The school has a population of approximately 270 students, with a limited capacity to grow much more. It was felt that in a small school a minority culture and language would have the potential to thrive rather than be lost in the majority. Toowong also draws from a broad demographic. Students come from a variety of backgrounds, including families who have English as their second language, families from a range of socioeconomic backgrounds, and families whose parents work at the nearby University of Queensland. Toowong's enrollment catchment plan means it has geographical boundaries, and priority is given to those who live nearby. The school has an addendum to this plan that allows for deaf children, their siblings, and children of deaf adults (CODAs) living outside the catchment boundaries to apply for enrollment at the school.

The number of deaf and hard-of-hearing (DHH) students in the school now sits at about 10% of the population consistently, with CODAs currently making up 5% of the population and siblings of deaf children making up 17% (see Kirchner, this volume). This means that approximately one-third of the school population has a strong connection to deaf people and the Deaf community. As a small school, the use of a mixed-age philosophy and way of working was already well established when the program was implemented. The mixed-age philosophy provides for lots of "places" for all children developing at different rates but equally importantly allows for a greater ratio of deaf children to hearing children than if classes were by single year level.

Another reason that Toowong was chosen was that it had no previous history with educating deaf children. However, the school administration was "pro languages" and valued difference. From the outset, communication from the principal was about the value a cultural group such as the Deaf community could bring to the school rather than any notion of "helping" a disadvantaged or disabled group.

The commencement of education for deaf children in Queensland coincided with a very "oral period" in deaf education after the 1880 Milan conference. This means that Queensland has a relatively oral history of educating deaf children compared to other Australian states whose education of deaf children was founded by deaf teachers. Queensland did have a school for deaf children that ran for the better part of a century, which provided a sense of community and did use sign in instruction for some of its tenure. But as with many such institutions internationally, some deaf adults report experiences of abuse. This, coupled with the vast size of the Queensland state and the reluctance of parents to send their children so far from home to a boarding school, saw the closure of the school for the deaf in the mid-1980s in favor of small special education units attached to schools across a number of city and regional centers. By the year 2000, these units were staffed with experienced teachers of the deaf, most of whom were signed English users with limited experience with a natural sign language. A transition to the use of Auslan in instruction for deaf children statewide and training for these staff was to begin later in the decade. When the Toowong program was established, however, it was decided that choosing a new site for the bilingual program, rather than trying to change teaching philosophies in established "unit" sites, would likely be an easier route.

The Department of Education and Training (DET) employed a project officer for two years prior to the commencement of the program whose work included conducting a literature review around educating deaf children using sign language, examining sign bilingual models internationally, working with key stakeholders to make a decision about an appropriate school and model of operation, and coordinating training for the staff at the site in the lead-up to the commencement of the program.

In 2001, a group of five profoundly deaf children (three from deaf families) enrolled in Year 1 at Toowong. They formed part of a class of 24 children with two teachers—one a classroom teacher from the school learning Auslan and the other a deaf teacher of the deaf (fluent in both Auslan and English). The class also employed a CODA as their Language Assistant (now referred to as a Teacher Aide: Auslan Language Model [TA:ALM]). The project officer continued providing support to the school for the next two years before moving to teach in the program. This support included the coordination of a reference group with representation from all key stakeholders to oversee the implementation of the program in its early years; development, with this group, of a set of guiding principles for the program (still used by the school; Table 3.1); and coordination of training for staff and families in learning Auslan, learning about Deaf culture and community, and coaching the class teachers around co-teaching, bilingual bimodal pedagogy, and ways of working.

As the first cohort progressed through the school, so too did the year levels at which a bilingual option was provided. While there was significant pressure to provide a bilingual, co-enrolled option across the entire school from the outset, it was felt that to maintain the integrity of the program and to ensure highly skilled staff at each level, year-by-year implementation needed to be adhered to. By 2006, the school offered bilingual, co-enrolled mixed-age classes across the entire school.[1]

Table 3.1. Guiding Principles for Toowong State School's Bilingual Bicultural Co-Enrollment Program

1. A child's need for early exposure to an accessible first language is of the utmost importance. For some deaf children, visual communication is the most accessible communication system and Auslan is a first language option.

2. Auslan and English are equally valued within the program. Fluency in both Auslan and English is a desired outcome of the program. Students will have the opportunity to learn in Auslan and in English.

3. Individual communication needs are valued and catered for in the program. Communication modes available in both Deaf and hearing cultures are available to students in the program (e.g., signing, speaking, listening, reading, writing).

4. Contributions from all stakeholders (including parents and the Deaf community) are valued and considered important in the functioning of the program.

5. Deaf and hearing cultures are equally valued within the program. Deaf and hearing role models are an integral part of the program, assisting in the development of children's healthy identity and helping them establish their place in both Deaf and hearing cultures.

6. The role of parents as caregivers and as important language models for their child is critical for the success of the program.

7. The inclusion of Deaf and hearing staff who have or are aiming toward fluency in Auslan and English is critical for the success of the program.

KEY ADMINISTRATIVE COMPONENTS IN RUNNING THE PROGRAM

The school leadership team has consistently valued the program and understood which elements within the school must be considered for the program to continue to be successful. Stable leadership under a principal who advocates for the program at a strategic level in the DET has been a major component of Toowong's success. The leadership team includes the principal, the Head of Special Education Services (HOSES), the Head of Curriculum (HOC), and the Support Teacher for Literacy and Numeracy (STLaN). Both the HOSES and the HOC are trained teachers of the deaf (ToDs) and make key contributions to strategic school direction. The STLaN has also worked within the program as a teacher and thus makes highly informed decisions that include DHH students. Access to language and a bilingual approach to teaching literacy are at the forefront of all decisions made by the leadership team rather than tacked on as an afterthought. This is a major point of difference to other schools offering programs for deaf students, which sometimes don't even have a ToD on staff let alone a school leader with experience educating deaf children.

Program Organization

The organization of the program is complex. The school leadership team reviews the program on a regular basis throughout the year, in particular analyzing future staff arrangements and considering the suitability of hearing students for bilingual classes. In a typical year, there are 11 classes in total across the school, with 4 of those classes being a bilingual bicultural co-enrolled mixed-age class. In 2017, bilingual bicultural classes were Prep, 1/2, 3/4, and 5/6.

Classes encompass children of multiple ages for several reasons. The small size of the school means that often there are around 1.5 classes needed for one year level; pooling students who are DHH from two year levels rather than one results in a larger group of DHH peers in a class. There also are a limited number of staff available with skills to work in the program, and the amount of funding available to the school to use for staffing is not adequate to providing a co-teaching option at every year level unless the classes comprise children of multiple ages.

Students and Families

Class size at Toowong is as per any DET school, ranging from 24 students in the lower years to 28 in the upper years. Class makeup is a mix of hearing and DHH children from hearing and deaf families. Students enrolled are from a variety of backgrounds. Because of the large proportion of students from non-English-speaking backgrounds (45%), a significant part of the school population is already "sold" on a bilingual philosophy and knows the benefits of additional languages. The demand for a place in a bilingual class is high and there is often a waiting list.

There is the usual mix of students with special needs across the entire cohort. The deaf children have a range of abilities and needs: some are working at year level; others have language delay; others have disabilities or learning difficulties; some have spoken language as their first language and others have Auslan as their first language.

When the program was phased in, the school attracted deaf children who had Auslan as their first language. Over time, the demographic of students has evolved to include students who are hard of hearing and students who are cochlear implant users. These students choose to use Auslan as their second language, and their parents value the connection the school has with the Deaf community and the support this provides their child in terms of social-emotional development.

The deaf students at Toowong fall broadly into three literacy categories. One group comprises students who are achieving at year level (or above) in English. These students arrive at school with a primary, face-to-face language intact and ready to begin their reading and writing journey. A second category includes those students working below year level but with some Auslan fluency, connecting to English and making progress with English literacy. These students often arrive at school with Auslan developing but exhibiting a delay, are sometimes those for whom an implant has not been successful in terms of production of spoken language, and are sometimes from English as an additional language/dialect (EALD) homes. A third category consists of those working significantly below year level who are still building a first primary, expressive language, with significant delays in both Auslan and English literacy. These students often arrive at school with very little language at all, are sometimes refugee students, or are students who are deaf with additional needs.

The bilingual bicultural co-enrollment program caters successfully to a very diverse group of DHH and hearing students and to more DHH students than any other model of operation. While many children are working at year level, it is important to point out that there are many children at Toowong (both deaf and hearing) who are working on Individual Curriculum Plans (ICPs) at a different year level to the class in which they are enrolled. These students receive high-quality differentiated instruction and their progress is measured and reported on accordingly. This is the protocol followed by all DET schools.

It is also important to mention that a small number of students have found that the co-enrollment model does not suit them. In the case of hearing children, some children with autism, in particular those who find visual stimulation overwhelming, tend to do better in a nonbilingual class. The leadership team carefully considers membership of the bilingual classes, as it takes equally seriously its commitment to quality education for hearing children in bilingual classes.

For a few DHH students, the program has been less successful, but they almost always have had high needs not directly related to their hearing loss. Sometimes they have a significant intellectual impairment or high medical needs. (Approximately a third of the DHH students attending Toowong do have additional needs and are successfully provided for in the program.) Students least suited to the model tend to require extensive time "outside" the mainstream classroom in order to receive their highly individualized program or to attend to their medical needs. Co-teaching is most successful when both teachers are responsible for the learning of *all* students in the classroom environment (see Kreimeyer, Drye, & Metz, this volume). When the teacher of the deaf removes students for chunks of learning across the day, this ultimately leads to a group of children enrolled only notionally in a mainstream class and results in compromising the basic principles of co-enrollment. Unfortunately, funding models do not allow for both a co-enrolled and segregated model to be made available at the same site (see Abbate, this volume).

Staff

Over the duration of the program's existence, the staff composition has changed as we have learned more about the needs of the classroom as a whole and have been required to adjust to changes in government funding. Over time, the leadership team has come to the realization that, when employing staff, equal weight needs to be given to a teacher's ability to differentiate the curriculum, work in a team, and be committed to developing fluency in Auslan and knowledge of bilingual pedagogy. That is, being a great signer does not mean you will be a teacher well matched to the program. The school supports teachers in developing all the skills required in this complex teaching role and acknowledges that few people come complete with the entire skillset required. To this end, Toowong has a strong commitment to professional development of staff, and a strong coaching model exists in the school: more experienced staff mentor others, and input from outside experts is sought and provided.

When selecting teachers for the program the following aspects are considered:

- Is the teacher an experienced, highly effective classroom teacher?
- Is the teacher a qualified ToD? if not, can he or she be paired with one?
- Can the teacher differentiate for individual children?
- Can the teacher work in a partnership, possessing open communication skills?
- Is the teacher a fluent Auslan user? If not, will he or she make the commitment to learning Auslan and does he or she have the capacity to do so?
- Does the teacher have an awareness of the Deaf community and an understanding of Deaf culture or an eagerness to be immersed?
- Does the teacher have the ability to work as a member of a team and plan for multiple support-staff members?
- Is the teacher able to make links between the curriculum and Deaf culture to ensure that it is valued within the classroom?
- Does the teacher have high expectations for students and believe that they can achieve, rather than operating from a deficit perspective?

Beyond these considerations, an ideal candidate may be deaf, thus often providing a role model to students and staff and possessing a more authentic understanding of the complexities of learning English as a second language. Toowong has had two long-term ToDs who are deaf and who provide on-the-job training and coaching to other staff members, modeling bilingual bicultural pedagogy.

Once teachers are employed, there is a focus on training to enhance their linguistic understanding of Auslan and their cultural understanding through regular discussions with more experienced staff, TA:ALMs, the HOSES and HOC, as well as Deaf community members who have been employed. Staff are encouraged to attend Deaf community events and value authentic experiences. Staff also access departmental training to enhance their Auslan skills and sign bilingual pedagogy when it is available.

As well as teachers, the program is funded to include TA:ALMs. These staff are Deaf community members who work as support staff within the program and fulfill a variety of roles, such as providing deaf role models for students; providing a language model for students, staff, and families; working with one student or a small group of students to achieve curriculum goals; and assisting teachers, interpreters, and students to improve their Auslan skills, through interaction and regular feedback, both spontaneous and planned. They also relay interpret when the language is not at an accessible level to the student due to language delays and so forth.

Teachers' aides employed as educational interpreters (TA:EIs) also are part of the bilingual team. Though direct instruction from the teacher is always prioritized in the school, sometimes interpreters are required. These include specialist lessons such as physical education. Some educational interpreters employed in the school are qualified by the National Accreditation Authority for Translators and Interpreters; others are not. Regardless, all are fluent users of Auslan and English. The educational interpreters employed in the school also have general teacher aide responsibilities and, as fluent signers, are also used for direct support to students alongside their deaf TA:ALM counterparts. Historically, many TA:EIs in the school have been CODAs.

The school has a strong ethical commitment to providing equitable access in Auslan for all deaf students, staff, and parents, and professional interpreters (from outside the school) are employed, for example, for professional development, general staff meetings, Parent and Citizen school community meetings, and meetings with school psychologists.

A Bilingual Bicultural Team meeting is held on a regular basis across term time and conducted in Auslan. During this time, data sharing and case conferencing may occur, assessments are analyzed and shared, challenges are discussed, and new pedagogy and training are delivered. This regular meeting has become an important component in team building in the program and is in addition to year level meetings and whole-of-staff meetings.

HOW TEACHERS WORK TOGETHER

Co-teaching sits at the foundation of the co-enrollment philosophy and the teaching partnership. Co-teaching requires both teachers to be responsible for *all* children, to share planning, teaching, and assessing of all students. Teachers new to this way of working always report that it is initially challenging. It requires an entirely different way of planning and delivery and a level of communicating and preparation greater than teaching solo (see De Klerk et al., this volume).

The teaching relationship can break down when one teacher holds more information, and this tends to lead to disempowerment of the other. Only an ongoing commitment to effective communication can avoid this, and that takes time. Staff working in nonbilingual classes can develop the misconception that having two teachers in the room halves the workload, when the opposite actually applies. At Toowong, it is common for administrators to schedule an additional day per term offline for planning for co-teaching teams in acknowledgment of the extra time required. Teachers generally report that after a considerable investment of time establishing ways of working, including sharing teaching philosophy and planning for lessons and methods of behavior management, then the amount of time they devote to planning does decrease somewhat. All teachers who work in successful team-teaching partnerships report that the investment is worthwhile and the teaching experience is the most valuable in their career:

> I think co-teaching has made me a better teacher of deaf and hearing students. I see good matching of the teaching team as imperative and when this occurs it's a really positive teaching arrangement for staff and students. I enjoy having an authentic sounding board when trying to figure out how best to organise teaching/learning experiences for students of all abilities and I like brainstorming ideas with a person who really understands the context and the issues. It's intensely valuable to have conversations with another person who is equally invested in what you are trying to achieve. Together we can achieve far more than if we were working as silos. (Classroom teacher, bilingual classroom, 2017)

Teachers report that the most successful lessons occur when they are well planned and all adults in the classroom are clear about their role in terms of delivery. When planning, teachers talk about (and record) the content they need to convey, how they will deliver it with consideration for the L1 and L2 Auslan users (along with individual needs of all students), and the roles of the additional support staff during the lesson. Staff members new to signing and co-teaching attend more to their delivery than in regular classrooms. Teaching teams experiment with ways of recording planning and making it available so that at any time support staff can see what is expected of them and what will be covered across a term, week, or lesson. With such a complex program, communication and explicit planning is pivotal to meeting all the children's needs.

Delivery of lessons takes many forms and depends on the objective of the lesson. The presence of two teachers and a TA:ALM in the classroom means that there is a good deal of flexibility in terms of delivery. Two teachers might be at the front of the class (with perhaps one demonstrating Auslan and the other English/contact sign or role-playing examples), or one teacher might do the bulk of the teaching, with the other moving around and supporting students with needs different to the mode of delivery. Alternatively, the class can be broken into groups for direct instruction (this could be by year level, by L1 or L2, by ability) or there can be rotations, with teachers/support staff all taking a group.

PROVIDING ACCESS FOR ALL STUDENTS

Using the toolkits of individual students is the key to providing access and good teaching to every student at Toowong, and identifying the primary/face to face language of each student is important in providing access and ensuring the appropriate pedagogy for every student is used to achieve English literacy. With a mix of students who have Auslan as a first language (L1) and Auslan as a second language (L2) in every class, all members of the team are expected to use sign in the bilingual classroom. Sometimes this will be sign only; sometimes it will be sign accompanied by voice. No deaf person is expected to use his or her voice if it is not his or her preference/way of learning. However, if students are able and need voice in order to learn, teachers plan carefully so key learning times always provide both an English and Auslan version of the learning. At times, some students might use only English, for example during instruction around phonics when cued articulation may be used, when speech training is occurring, or when students choose to present information in spoken English for an oral presentation or during a read-aloud session. In these instances, access for L1 users is provided by a staff member as required. Equally, there will be times when it is appropriate to use Auslan only. All language preferences and types are catered to in the classroom.

The primary classroom is a "repetitive environment." Teachers are very good at providing multiple opportunities to see and hear the same learnings—this is no different in a bilingual bicultural co-enrollment classroom. Children have multiple opportunities to learn in both languages and in spoken/auditory, signed, and written forms. At Toowong, adults become very adept at using a Natural Sign System (NSS) to communicate a message, rephrasing the message in Auslan or in spoken English and then chaining it to written text. However, interpreting is rarely used to achieve access to learning at Toowong. Aside from specialist lessons (such as physical education), mediated instruction (teaching via an educational interpreter) is not the preferred method of instruction at the school. This is a pivotal point of difference between a co-enrolled program and a mainstream program using an educational interpreter (or programs with mixed models). Toowong places a high value on direct teaching. That is, every child has the right to learn directly from a teacher. Mediated instruction changes the dynamic in the classroom, disempowering the deaf children and staff.

In the case of mediated instruction, class teachers can feel they lose ownership of the teaching, leading to interpreters being required to teach/take responsibility for the deaf student's learning, and students can feel disempowered due to issues like time lag, leading to learned helplessness. Students also can feel alienated from the class as they cannot access contributions from peers or communicate with them. Students thus can develop lower self-esteem, which impacts on mental health.

Understanding this fundamental difference between mediated instruction and direct teaching models has been critical for DET human resources personnel. The program requires a different funding model that does not rely solely on the allocation of TA funds based on the need for TA:EIs. Rather, funding needs to be prioritized toward employing teachers for the program who can sign or have demonstrated an aptitude for learning sign, who can develop bilingual bicultural and co-enrollment pedagogical skills, and who are committed to working in a team-teaching relationship, as this delivers a superior program for students:

> The social/emotional benefits for DHH students attending Toowong are profound. Students have a range of both Deaf peers and hearing peers who can communicate with them. There is very little reliance on adult interpreters in student interactions. Deaf students present on assembly, audition for band, are voted into positions as sports captains and school captains. Most importantly, that is seen as "the norm"; it is expected. While I believe all educational settings strive to enable Deaf students to achieve their potential in a supportive setting, the co-enrollment model appears to provide the best environment in which these aspirations can be realised. (ToD, bilingual classroom, 2017)

KEY PEDAGOGIES USED TO SUPPORT THE STUDENT COHORT AND KEY CURRICULUM DIRECTIONS

Languages of Instruction and Modeling Bilingualism

Teachers work hard to ensure the deaf and hearing dynamic in the classroom sends a clear message about valuing both deaf and hearing languages and cultures and that deaf people bring something valued and unique to the classroom. Some teaching teams are a deaf and hearing teacher, and this makes modeling bilingualism easier. But in classrooms where both teachers are hearing, careful planning is required to ensure authentic situations in which deaf TA:ALMs have leadership roles in the classroom, leading to promotion of deaf identity and a promotion of both languages as languages of instruction and equally valued.

Auslan as a Subject

Auslan is offered as a language subject in the school under the Languages Other than English (LOTE) curriculum. While the National Curriculum has only just released its official Auslan curriculum, Toowong has offered Auslan classes to every class in the school since the program's inception. This means that hearing students can move easily between bilingual and nonbilingual classes from year to year and that the school sees itself as a bilingual community. Auslan LOTE has been taught by a number of deaf adults since the program commenced. All deaf teachers have demonstrated skills and experience in teaching Auslan; if they do not have teacher registration, a teacher oversees the programming and delivery.

Auslan as L1 or L2

The foundation of any bilingual program is the need for a strong first language in order to learn a second language, and this is also true in a bilingual bimodal program like the one at Toowong. Fundamental to the delivery of lessons using appropriate pedagogy is the need to identify the primary/face-to-face language of every student. While some children do arrive at school bilingual (with equal ability in both languages), in the Toowong experience, this is rare. In the case of deaf children, it is important to establish in the early years of formal schooling whether Auslan will be their L1 or L2. That is, is their primary/face-to-face language Auslan or is it spoken language, be that English or another language spoken at home? Sometimes this depends on whether the student is from a deaf household, but more often, nowadays, this comes down to success and age of cochlear implantation, and whether the child is deaf with additional needs, or perhaps a refugee arriving with no language.

The reason for identifying primary language is that the pedagogy required for deaf children to be English literate, if Auslan is their L1, is different from that required for those who come with Auslan as their L2. And while it is true that Toowong's demographic has seen a shift to include more Auslan L2 users since it commenced, there is still a significant proportion of deaf students whose L1 is Auslan. Currently, 40% of deaf students at Toowong have Auslan as their L1.

Auslan L2 Deaf Learners

In essence, DHH students with Auslan as their L2 and English (or another spoken language) as their L1 learn to read and write in English in a similar way to their hearing peers. With good access to audition and speech training and the optimal listening environment, these children can "talk their way into text" as hearing children do. That is, they learn to speak words, identify sounds in those words and connect them to letters, develop phonological awareness, and build a strong, primary/spoken language that will map directly to English on the page.

Certainly, many pedagogical considerations are still made for this group at Toowong that are not available elsewhere. For example, Toowong chooses cued articulation (Passey, 1993)—please note this is not cued speech—as a component of the phonics program delivered to students. This program provides visual cues that support the production of speech sounds and uses cues that demonstrate how sounds are made. It's a useful tool that assists all students to talk about the differences between letter names, letter sounds, and how they are produced. This benefits students from EALD backgrounds, can be used as successfully in conjunction with phonics programs for hearing students, and is accessible to deaf students.

Students with usable audition and whose parents are committed to developing speech as part of their English development have access to speech services at Toowong. Complete speech and language assessments are conducted with students. While language development is the responsibility of the class teachers, speech therapists focus on speech and audition with links to literacy and provide programs to be integrated into the students' daily program.

Auslan L2 students also benefit from being enrolled in a school community that understands the learning needs of DHH children and accommodates them well, with more access to teachers of the deaf than they would receive from an itinerant service, classrooms that accommodate visual learners, auditory and speech training programs, and optimal listening environments with use of sound-field/FM systems. These students benefit from being enrolled in a program that promotes bilingualism and gives them another language and all the benefits that brings (Cummins, 1991; see Marschark, Tang, & Knoors, 2014), but above all, they have like peers with whom to identify and have access to a community of successful DHH adults like themselves. Parents value this model because it enhances their child's social and emotional well-being.

Auslan L1 Deaf Learners

The fundamental difference in pedagogy for Auslan L1 and L2 learners is in the approach to teaching English literacy. This is due to the difference in the modes between the first language of students. Some people have likened the deaf, L1 Auslan user to the EALD hearing student, and to some extent this is true. Certainly, *some* of the pedagogical tools used in this domain are transferrable to the bilingual bicultural signing context. However, the critical difference is *the use of audition and speech to get to the print version of the same spoken language* versus *the use of signed mode of one language to get to the written version of a different language*. The sign bilingual pedagogy used with this L1 Auslan group to achieve English literacy is very different from that used with the L2 group. "Signing your way into text" is very different from using speech to "talk your way in."

Of course, this has been understood as a challenge for some time. Certainly the need for a way to represent English on the hands has been mooted by many, including Mayer and Wells (1996) in their Double Discontinuity hypothesis, which questioned the level of transfer possible between a signed and spoken language. However, Johnston (2002), a sign language linguist rather than an educator, outlined just how effectively deaf people do represent the majority spoken language on their hands. It would seem the issue has been that educators have not (until recently) understood enough about the linguistics of sign language and the significance of how deaf adults alter their way of signing to reflect English, and the benefits of this as a way to access English literacy. The linguistic term given to the way the spoken language of the majority contacts with the sign language of the minority is *contact sign, signing in English*, or an *NSS* (Fischer, 1998). Johnston (2002) maintained that deaf people choose to sign in this English-like way while still maintaining visual-spatial grammatical elements of sign language, depending on who they are communicating with and the communication purpose. For example, the deaf person delivering a presentation with an English-heavy PowerPoint to a largely hearing audience might present in Auslan but use a NSS to demonstrate specific English vocabulary or read "aloud" components of the slides. This movement between Auslan and signing in English has been referred to as moving back and forth along the contact sign continuum (Baker & Stark, 2015; Johnston & Schembri, 2007).

Baker and Stark (2015) argue that learning to exploit the continuum as a pedagogical tool forms an important component in a teacher's repertoire in teaching English to the signing deaf child. At Toowong, this is a key underpinning of bilingual bicultural pedagogy, the main tool used to connect Auslan and English and the L1 Auslan child's way of "signing their way into English."

Using the Contact Sign Continuum—Reading

The Language Experience Approach (LEA) and the use of Schick's (2017) Fingerspelling Our Way To Reading Program are pivotal pedagogy used in the early primary years at Toowong and involve the contact sign continuum. As described, in this L1 group there are often children arriving at school without a complete language intact, with delayed sign language development or perhaps no language at all, so building face-to-face/primary language is important before introducing English literacy.

The first step in learning to read and write is to have enough expressive language to be able to retell an experience, and the LEA provides this opportunity. The LEA has been around for a very long time and in its most basic form is the kindergarten child who paints a picture and tells the teacher what it is about, and then the teacher writes that as the caption. The difference for the Auslan user is that modern technology has enabled us to have the final product, a Language Experience Reader (LER), include sign language in the form of an inserted signed version of the experience and/or the English text. In recent times at Toowong, students produce these using an app such as Book-Creator (Red Jumper Limited, 2017) on their iPads. Book-Creator is a multimedia app that allows images, video, audio, and text to be included in an e-book that is copied easily to other devices and can be printed in hard form if desired.

The LEA produces a digital LER that provides an opportunity for the student to read again and again and, in doing so, consolidate new Auslan signs and English vocabulary. Students can take these e-books home, which has the added benefit of parents at home learning new signs as well as providing scaffolded read-at-home tasks. Initially, the students tend to rely on the contact sign in the video to assist in the reading task, but later they will disregard the video and read the text alone. Teachers collate new vocabulary acquired through the process and provide opportunities for multiple exposures (including personalized spelling lists) and monitor the commitment of this vocabulary to long-term memory over time.

As students acquire more Auslan language, the LEA as a reading approach is complemented by the PM series of readers (Smith, Nelley, & Croft, 2010). When students with Auslan as their L1 at Toowong are introduced to these readers, they read them initially with a TA:ALM at school before taking them home for the night. This allows for focus on ensuring the Auslan language around the experience and some teaching of English vocabulary before the task of reading the book at home. Sometimes students will also have Auslan versions of these to take home on the iPad. The idea that the child has the understanding in his or her first language of the story and any new concepts is a foundation of Toowong's bilingual bicultural program and is reflected in teachers' planning of new teaching material. Once the students understand the Auslan version of the story, they can then focus cognitive attention to the English words on the page—that is, the task of reading.

Toowong has also recently implemented the *Fingerspelling Our Way to Reading Program (Schick, 2017)*. This evidence based program from Colorado provides an alternative path via fingerspelling into the phonology of English for those students who do not necessarily have complete auditory access to spoken language. The program has demonstrated incredible success, particularly for Toowong's L1 Auslan students who had previously shown mixed progress in English phonology and English vocabulary development. This program coupled with the LEA are two key components of sign bilingual pedagogy that are imperative for the progress of the L1 child in a mainstream classroom and vastly different to any pedagogical approach used with hearing and HOH students/those with Auslan as their L2.

Using the Contact Sign Continuum—Writing

The challenges associated with deaf children learning to write have been well recorded in the literature, yet little change has been evidenced in the last 80 years (Mayer, 2010). Mayer (2010) summarized common error patterns and divergent structures used by deaf students in their writing. Most of these studies have used traditional grammar approaches to analyzing students' samples and compared data to norms for hearing children. Ironically, little research has actually focused on what makes a difference pedagogically for those signing deaf children who do achieve high levels of English written literacy (Baker & Stark, 2015).

"Deaf children are not simply hearing children who cannot hear" (Marschark & Knoors, 2012). This quote is never truer than when applied to the teaching of writing to Auslan L1 users. We have always taught deaf children to write by drilling what hearing struggling writers need. But if your primary language of expression does not have the same phonological and grammatical rules as the target written language (i.e., the primary mode and the grammatical rules of sign language differ from the primary mode and grammatical rules of English), then how we scaffold to reach the written English target becomes really important and vastly different to what hearing children need.

So, rather than the deficit lens through which deaf children's writing is often viewed, the staff at Toowong has been determined to establish just what children are doing when they write and what resources they are drawing on. Using a functional grammar approach has been a key part of this in terms of analysis and programming. In addition, Dostal and Wolbers (2014) showed that a combination of signing in English, metalinguistic discussion, and direct comparisons/contrasts and inter-activity between the two languages produces improved outcomes in both languages for students. Toowong staff use this method of building metalinguistic understandings between the two languages to enhance students' writing along with functional grammar templates to scaffold children to build the connection between Auslan and the written mode of English.

Writing tasks begin with students "telling" in their first language to a fluent user what they are going to write about. This is often filmed for review/use later, particularly if the L1 of the student is Auslan. Depending on student language goals, sometimes an English word wall will be built with the student to ensure connections have been built between Auslan vocabulary and English vocabulary and to allow cognitive focus on the grammatical structure in writing time. Students sometimes use a story/genre planner and map out their ideas, either pictorially or in English words. Then students begin the task of writing their story.

For some students, support with writing each idea into a sentence using a functional grammar scaffold is necessary initially. For others, using the scaffold independently occurs easily, and for others it is not required at all. After completion, students can self-edit their work according to previous grammar teaching and/or then have a session with an adult fluent in Auslan and English.

Expansion of English vocabulary is a major goal for many students, and building connections between Auslan and English vocabulary might include any or all of several approaches. For example, children can watch the signed sample of the story to unpack additional information not included in the written version, such as unpacking rich depicting verbs, adverbs included in nonmanual features and adjectives included in nonmanual features, or depicting nouns. Teachers can build connections between Auslan and English at word and sentence level using an NSS, perhaps using chaining, mouthing, and fingerspelling to signs or signs to written words/phrases. Students can enrich their story by extending English vocabulary options for signed noun groups (e.g., the girl, Annie, the shy girl, the child, her sister) or English synonyms for a modified sign (e.g., run: sprint, jog, lope, race, dash). In addition to building and connecting vocabulary in both languages, such sessions also allow for a mini-lesson about grammatical rules at a sentence or text level (e.g., ensuring every sentence has a verb, position of adjectives in noun groups, tense and verb agreement, tracing pronoun referents across a text).

This approach to teaching writing is very different from traditional approaches to remediating deaf children's writing. At Toowong great value is placed on the product students deliver when they bring into contact their knowledge of sign language and their knowledge of English—even though their initial product does not always look English-like to the naïve eye. Rather than a deficit view of the written sample and the perspective that it is lacking in some way, a lens that looks at what deaf children are doing as a result of language contact means our interventions and scaffolds will be quite different. Being able to use this lens demands that teachers are fluent users of Auslan and English, are good users of contact sign, and have a good understanding of the linguistics of both languages so that they can scaffold students and build on their strengths in their L1 to connect to the L2.

MONITORING STUDENT PROGRESS

All students at Toowong receive a program that meets the requirements of Australia's national curriculum and its eight subject areas. To complement this curriculum, Queensland has a "Curriculum to Classroom" series of resources that provide teachers with exemplars of units of work and assessment. Students who are not working at year level in some or all subject areas have an ICP that provides a learning program at their level of working and includes appropriate individualized assessment and reporting. In all classes at Toowong there are children on ICPs, both deaf and hearing students. When students require a component in their program that is outside the national curriculum but specific to their individual needs (e.g., auditory or speech training), this is recorded in a support plan. All of this information is recorded centrally in DET using an online tool known as OneSchool.

Monitoring Auslan Development

The Auslan Assessment Tool (adapted by Schembri, Hodge, & Rogers, 2014, and based on the BSL Production and Receptive Tests by Herman, Holmes, & Woll, 1999, and Herman, Grove, Holmes, Morgan, Sutherland, & Woll, 2004) provides teachers with important information about the development and progress of students' Auslan skills in the program. The receptive test measures a child's ability to understand grammatical components of Auslan. The expressive test requires students to watch a short play involving a girl, a boy, and a spider and requires the student to retell the story while also measuring their capacity to use specific grammatical components of Auslan such as depicting signs, modification of signs to include manner, and the use of role shift to show characterization. As well as demonstrating whether students have age-appropriate Auslan vocabulary and grammar, this assessment allows teachers to show areas of strength and weakness in the students' narrative development (Morgan, 2006), an important precursor to being ready to read and write (Baker & Stark, 2015).

Toowong staff collate data from this tool annually along with sign language developmental schedules/checklists (de Beuzeville, 2015) to show how hearing and hard-of-hearing children are progressing in their acquisition of Auslan as their L2. Critically, for deaf children for whom Auslan is an L1, data from these two assessments provide vital information that informs teachers and, consequently, programming about their Auslan and English literacy development. One component of this information consists of areas in which a focus is needed to improve the student's primary language. For example, some children produce only a string of nouns when asked to tell their story, indicating the need for a language program that will immerse them in the use of Auslan verbs and in particular depicting verbs to build their face-to-face language. Results of the assessment also indicate how ready the student is for English literacy. For example, some children with impoverished expressive language cannot tell a story. This is a precursor to being ready to read and write and means an Auslan immersion program, rather than an English literacy program, is required initially. The progress students are making in Auslan language development relates to, for example, the level of expressive language in the primary, face-to-face language is required for students to make connections to English. Students, such as refugees, who arrive at school without this need time to develop expressive language to connect to English. These assessments allow teachers to show progress in primary language development using sign language developmental schedules, even if there are not yet measurable gains being made in English literacy. Finally, the assessments identify areas that might benefit from attention and ultimately result in the enhancement of English. For example, students whose English writing shows difficulties with referent tracking may exhibit the same challenges in their sign language samples, and attention in the Auslan space can assist with English writing.

Monitoring English Development (Reading and Writing)

Monitoring Reading

Toowong staff track the reading levels of all students using various reading assessments, including the PM Benchmark Reading Assessment (Smith et al., 2010). Once they can read at a level 25 or above, students begin to be assessed using the PROBE reading assessment (Parkin & Parkin, 2011). Deaf students with Auslan as their L2 fit neatly into this system of reading levels. However, deaf children with Auslan as their L1 are not as clear-cut, and results are often not a true reflection of progress in their reading. This is because the reading program is designed for students who speak English to map their speech onto print. The distance between the two phonological systems is great, so this group often uses an additional set of strategies when they read. For this reason, reading data for this group are analyzed further and a form of miscue is conducted that identifies further information about the reading strategies used by the student (Easterbrooks & Huston, 2008).

Records from the Language Experience Approach (outlined previously) and the Fingerspelling Our Way to Reading Program (also outlined previously) particularly in the early years, complete the data picture for these students. It should be noted that reading with deaf students includes reading with and to the students, guided reading sessions modeling all strategies, silent reading, and read-aloud time. Read-aloud time (using contact sign) has not received a lot of attention in the literature but has proved a vital part of moving L1 students' reading forward because it gives valuable insight into all the reading strategies the student has at his or her disposal. This has been a major focus for Toowong, and there is significant investment in developing teachers' skills in this area as well as a set of protocols developed by the school for staff to use.

Monitoring Writing

Like all DET schools, a whole-of-school professional development focus is identified annually as part of operational planning. In 2017, the Toowong focus was in the area of teaching writing effectively by focusing on different elements, such as sentence structure and vocabulary. Elements that have always been fundamental to the bilingual bicultural classes are being reviewed with the general staff, such as improving students' vocabulary through semantic webs, word walls, and ladders of intensity. Teachers focus on specific individual goals for students, based on the literacy continuum, which are reviewed in small guided writing groups.

A functional grammar assessment of spontaneous writing samples occurs for deaf children biannually. Baker and Stark (2015) used the work of Halliday (1994) and Deriwianka (2011) to look at the spontaneous written language samples of deaf children through a functional grammar lens rather than one that focused on traditional, linear form only, and this has informed practice at Toowong. Further, work by Menendez (2010) demonstrated that deaf students appear to be "pooling their resources" when they write, and there is some research to show that deaf writers do embed L1 sign language features in their written work (Wolbers, Bowers, Dostal, & Graham, 2014). Certainly, a number of the documented "error" trends in deaf children's writing (Mayer, 2010) can be accounted for by the language contact occurring as children "pool the resources" (Menendez, 2010) they have in both languages when they come to the task of writing (Baker & Stark, 2015).

Conducting functional grammar analysis provides valuable points of comparison in terms of strength of retell in the primary language compared to what a student may be able to produce in a written English sample. Any spontaneous written sample analyzed using functional grammar will demonstrate what students can do with participants (noun groups), processes (verb groups), and circumstances (adverbial information) and allow broad comparisons to be made between narrative in the primary mode and narrative in the written form. This type of analysis provides teachers with vital specific information about what's missing in the written English sample but also for the Auslan

L1 students, in particular, what they need to write in more English-like word order and how their first language can be used to support this growth.

CHALLENGES FACED BY THE PROGRAM

Feeder Programs

Toowong is a primary school enrolling students from Prep (5 years old) to Year 6 (11 years old). A major concern for the school community is that there is no direct mainstream kindergarten program or high school that operates in the same co-enrolled manner as Toowong does. While there is a specialist intervention early childhood center for DHH children under DET that provides a bilingual option for children, it does not provide a full kindergarten program, with the expectation that parents will supplement with a kindergarten program in their local area. Such kindergartens are not set up to provide a bilingual co-enrolled option for children, with the result being that many DHH students arrive at school less "school-ready" than hearing peers. This has been a recent focus of the school, and to this end the school is now working closely with a local kindergarten so that a TA:ALM is employed at the site and all children are encouraged to sign and be bilingual. However, this is a space in which a lot of work is still required. Most DHH children who attend Toowong do not necessarily attend this kindergarten, so this needs to be marketed to parents so that it is a viable option for all future Toowong students. Such an offering would see a reduction in the number of students who arrive at Toowong without an intact L1 and are not school-ready.

Another challenge is that all potential DET feeder high schools are large, in comparison to Toowong's roughly 270 students. This means that although a critical mass of deaf students may be in the high school, proportionate to the hearing students they are few in number and the culture and language of the deaf students will be vulnerable. Deaf students are often widely dispersed across classrooms and often away from deaf and hearing signing peers. In addition, there are few ToDs in these settings, with the assumption often that the deaf student can work using an interpreter in a mediated instruction model. This dilutes the deaf student's connection with the classroom teacher; in addition, such a model demands a strong mastery of both sign language and English, which many students do not have by year 7 (Russell, 2015). Combined with less contact with like peers, this can lead to an isolating experience in stark contrast to their experience at Toowong. Ultimately, this places these students at higher risk of mental health issues. Research suggests that mental health issues in the hearing community are at all-time highs of 25%, and in the Deaf community they are estimated at around 40%

(Montiero, 2014). Anecdotally, this has also been the observation by authors in the adolescent DHH population of students in DET. With the model at Toowong building resilience and mitigating risk factors for poor mental health, it seems a shame this cannot be sustained into high school:

> The biggest difference in high school is teachers can't sign. When I became immersed in high school life I no longer had the direct contact with teachers and peers that could sign and I had to rely on interpreters to access info. So, if they are not skilled enough or they don't understand me or the content then I miss out. It is also an issue that they cannot always represent me appropriately so it impacts on my marks and the class and teacher's opinion of me. In Toowong the teachers could communicate with me directly and understand me so they never underestimated me. Sometimes high school is isolating. I have a bilingual family so my confidence and self-esteem is okay but I think for other deaf students it is really hard. (Former Toowong deaf student)

Supporting Parents to Sign

To support students' academic and emotional well-being, it is vital that parents and caregivers can effectively communicate with their children through a strong L1. DHH students' level of Auslan once enrolled at Toowong often improves at a dramatic rate that does not parallel that of their parents. While some parents avail themselves of the opportunities provided by the school to learn to sign, sadly a proportion of parents do not engage. Thus, another challenge for the school community is to encourage and facilitate all parents and caregivers to develop their Auslan skills to a level that is equal to or superior to that of their children. New ideas to engage with families are always being explored.

Models of Inclusion

There is a trend in education for all students to be educated at their local school and a belief that this is the only model of inclusion that should be considered. This may be appropriate for the majority of children with a high-incidence disability; however, research into education of deaf children, the use of mediated versus direct instruction, and the need for a peer group for healthy social and emotional development strongly suggests that clustering deaf children together for learning is critical (e.g., Hermans, De Klerk, Wauters, & Knoors, 2014; Tang, Lam, & Yiu, 2014; Yiu & Tang, 2014). Unfortunately, with the best intentions by educational organizations to be "inclusive," models of operation, funding models, and information shared with parents often take the "majority-disability" perspective, meaning that an increasing number of parents of deaf children are ill informed and choose a local school without a like-peer group and mediated instruction over direct instruction for their child.

There is little understanding by decision makers that the challenge of educating deaf students is as much a case of sociolinguistic programming (as has been acknowledged in programs for indigenous Australians) as it is about disability. It is imperative that the benefits of bilingual bicultural co-enrollment programs like the one at Toowong are held up as a robust and viable form of inclusion for educating deaf students so that parents receive the information they need to make an informed decision about their child's schooling and so that departmental protocols (e.g., funding and staffing) are flexible enough to accommodate the needs of such programs. Establishing research programs at Toowong and similar schools to enable robust data collection is imperative and overdue:

> Systemic issues (low incidence population in a vast state, enrollment policies, training and availability of specialist staff, adequate resourcing, etc.) continue to be major factors in providing the best educational outcomes for DHH students. It saddens me greatly, especially when parents need to make the monumental decision to relocate their family, that there are no other facilities like Toowong anywhere else in the state. The lives of the families able to access this co-enrollment program appear considerably brighter and enriched. (ToD, bilingual class, 2017)

Staffing the Program

As the program has expanded to four classes, the school has faced significant challenges in employing ToDs and primary teachers who possess both a strong ability to teach the primary school curriculum and a fluency in Auslan, or a capacity to become fluent. Reasons for this include that the school is bound by the department staffing arrangements, which means staff can be transferred at any time and staff without any Auslan skills can be transferred into the school. In addition, a decreasing number of ToDs in the workforce, due to the declining number of courses available to train ToDs nationwide and the perceived lack of need from educational institutions for low-incidence specialists due to the generalized role of special educators and a focus on "local school" inclusion models and the use of mediated instruction, means it is difficult to find teachers with the level of signing skills and pedagogical knowledge required to work in the program.

As a result, responsibility lies with Toowong to find many of its own staff, while still having to work within the confines of DET staffing protocols. Every year, the school is forced to begin again with training for numerous new staff. Putting energy here always takes away from energy that could be invested in developing innovative productive pedagogies for the bilingual classrooms.

BENEFITS OF THE PROGRAM TO ALL INVOLVED

Entire cohorts of students from the program have now moved through the school system with great success. DHH and hearing students have experienced success in employment, with many having completed tertiary studies. A significant number of hearing students from the program have undertaken interpreter studies or are working in some way connected to the Deaf community. A large number of past students return to visit their primary school that so strongly shaped them as young people, and increasing numbers of past students are returning to work as TA:ALMs or TA:EIs. Toowong's bilingual bicultural co-enrollment program delivers a wide range of benefits providing rich social, academic, and identity-shaping experiences for the entire school community, and students remain connected through their secondary years and into adulthood. Although formal research projects have been difficult to establish, collected testimonials from the past and present school community have helped to portray the diverse benefits of the program:

> My involvement in the bilingual program has been a defining part of my life. As a child, it helped to instill pride and confidence: pride in my place in a bilingual/bicultural community, and a confidence to embrace diversity. As an adult I have nothing but praise for the program in defining not only my education but qualities that I consider to be my best. (Former student)

> The fact that it is a bilingual bicultural school not a special needs or a Deaf school is what makes Toowong very unique and extremely important. Deaf children deserve to be in a school where they, their language, cultural and community are celebrated and cherished. Having hearing students part of this school means they will grow up with respect for Deaf people and Auslan—this is what it means to ensure Deaf people are part of society. (Drisana Levitzke-Gray, Young Australian of the Year 2015)

> It is exciting to see the relationships develop between deaf and hearing students. In other schools, the Deaf students would be limited to playing with only those children that can sign (usually a very small proportion of the school), but at Toowong almost all children can sign so they have so much more choice! (Deaf parent)

> From my observations, Toowong's co-enrollment programme has enabled a community of like-minded people to come together with

a view to embrace a minority group, generally labelled with a "dis-ability." The community, through the school, advocates for a culture that is strong, unique and inherently "able." Hearing students see Deaf students with a respected language, self-worth and self-value and this is reflected in their positive interactions. Hearing and deaf and hard-of-hearing peers recognise that each have something posi-tive to contribute and treat each other with respect and transparency. Facilitating a common language improves the ability of the students to connect and share events, deepening their common experience. (Classroom teacher, bilingual class, 2017)

CONCLUSION

Several aspects of the Toowong bilingual bicultural program have made it successful. Most centrally, it is a small school whose dem-ographic is pro-bilingualism and values difference, and it has an administrative team who understand well the needs of deaf chil-dren and the curriculum and who have the needs of deaf children as learners at the forefront of their minds. The school is committed to direct co-teaching, not mediated instruction, and DHH adults are included as equal partners in the educational team. That means the school understands that specialist teachers with Auslan skills, good teaching practice, and strong understanding of sign bilingual pedagogy are vital to achieve equitable programming for DHH students. It helps that the school is in a capital city that has a large enough population to draw a critical mass of DHH students to the school. As a result, enough resources are attracted from DET to run co-enrolled classes and enough staff are available to work in the program. The critical mass of students allows for a large enough community of users and also for efficiency of resources based on economies of scale.

Toowong is visited regularly by families and educational per-sonnel nationally and internationally. Many go away with a plan to implement something similar. Unfortunately, they often stumble because outside a capital city, the critical mass and all that comes with it is simply not achievable. In a world where technology is opening doors never before thought possible, some remote students are being connected to cluster sites by videoconferencing (such as is currently being trialed at Toowong with Skype for one remote stu-dent). However, for a deaf child, Toowong has found nothing that can match daily, quality, face-to-face direct teaching and interaction with deaf peers and adults—and this is what this small inner-city school delivers in spades.

NOTE

1. As with all new things, many teething problems were encountered during the earliest years of the program. It is appropriate at this point to acknowledge with gratitude the work of Cameron Miller (first deaf teacher and current teacher in the program), Anthea Denholm (first principal in the program), Abigail Sawyer (early class teacher in the program), Sally Strobridge (deaf community leader, TA:ALM, teacher, parent with CODAs in the program, and staunch advocate for the program), Glen Lawrence (Director, Deaf/Hearing Impairment Services), Carl Kirchner (Founder of TRIPOD, USA), Michelle Baker (Project Officer), and the entire parent and staff community of Toowong, past and present.

REFERENCES

Baker, M., & Stark, M. (2015). Building connections between the signed and written language of signing deaf children workshop. Melbourne, Victorian Deaf Education Institute. Retrieved from http://www.deafeducation.vic.edu.au/Pages/home.aspx

Cummins, J. (1991). Interdependence of first and second language proficiency in bilingual children. In E. Bialystok (Ed.), *Language processing in bilingual children*. Cambridge, UK: Cambridge University Press.

de Beuzeville, L. (2015). *Auslan Developmental Expectations & Goals Matrix*. Unpublished manuscript, RIDBC Renwick Centre, University of Newcastle.

Deriwianka, B. (2011). *A new grammar companion for teachers*. Riverwood, Australia: Primary English Teaching Association.

Dostal, H. M., & Wolbers, K. A. (2014). Developing language and writing skills of deaf and hard-of-hearing students: A simultaneous approach. *Literacy Research and Instruction, 53*, 245–268.

Easterbrooks, S. R., & Huston, S. G. (2008). The signed reading fluency of students who are deaf/hard of hearing. *Journal of Deaf Studies and Deaf Education, 13*(1), 37.

Fischer, S. D. (1998). Critical periods for language acquisition. In A. Weisel (Ed.), *Issues unresolved: New perspectives on language and deaf education* (pp. 9–26). Washington, DC: Gallaudet University Press.

Halliday, M. A. (1994). *Functional grammar*. London: Edward Arnold.

Herman, R., Grove, N. Holmes, S., Morgan, G., Sutherland, H., & Woll, B. (2004). *Assessing British Sign Language development: Production test (narrative skills)*. London: City University.

Herman, R., Holmes, S., & Woll, B. (1999). Assessing British Sign Language development: Receptive skills test. Gloucestershire: Forest Books.

Hermans, D., De Klerk, A., Wauters, L., & Knoors, H. (2014). The Twinschool: A co-enrollment program in the Netherlands. In M. Marschark, G. Tang, & H. Knoors (Eds.), *Bilingualism and bilingual deaf education* (pp. 396–423). New York: Oxford University Press.

Johnston, T. (2002). The representation of English using Auslan: Implications for deaf bilingualism and English literacy. *Australian Journal of Education of the Deaf, 8*, 23–37.

Johnston, T., & Schembri, A. (2007) *Australian Sign Language: An introduction to sign language linguistics.* New York: Cambridge University Press.

Marschark, M., & Knoors, H. (2012). Educating deaf children: Language, cognition and learning. *Deafness and Education International, 13*(3), 136–160.

Marschark, M., Tang, G., & Knoors, H. (2014). *Bilingualism and bilingual deaf education.* New York: Oxford University Press.

Mayer, C. (2010). The demands of writing and the deaf writer. In M. Marschark & P. Spencer (Eds.), *The Oxford handbook of deaf studies, language, and education* (Vol. 2, pp. 144–155). New York: Oxford University Press.

Mayer, C., & Wells, G. (1996). Can the Linguistic Interdependence Theory support a bilingual-bicultural model of literacy education for deaf students? *Journal of Deaf Studies and Deaf Education, 1,* 93–107.

Menéndez, B. (2010). Cross-modal bilingualism: Language contact as evidence of linguistic transfer in sign bilingual education. *International Journal of Bilingual Education and Bilingualism, 13*(2), 201–223.

Monteiro, B. (2014). *Healthy Deaf Minds Workshop.* Melbourne, Victoria.

Morgan, G. (2006). The development of narrative skills in British Sign Language. In B. Schick, M. Marschark, & P. Spencer (Eds.), *Advances in the sign language development of deaf children* (pp. 314–343). Oxford: Oxford University Press.

Parkin, C., & Parkin, C. (2011). *PROBE-Reading Comprehension Assessment.* Upper Hutt, New Zealand: Triune Initiatives.

Passey, J. (1993). *Cued articulation.* London: STASS Publications.

Red Jumper Limited. (2017). Book-Creator (5.1.2). [iPad application software]. Retrieved from https://www.appstore.com

Russel, D. (2015). Research on mediated education. Deaf education and choices: Interpreted education and direct instruction. Retrieved from http://youtube.com/watch?v=QM7olkiqGFo#action=share

Schembri, A., Hodge, G., & Rogers, I. (2014). *Assessing Auslan (Australian Sign Language) development.* Melbourne: Victorian Deaf Education Institute.

Schick, B. (2017). *Fingerspelling Our Way To Reading.* Colorado: Center on Literacy and Deafness.

Smith, A., Nelley, E., & Croft, D. (2010). *PM benchmark reading assessment resources.* Melbourne: Cengage Learning Australia Limited.

Tang, G., Lam, S., & Yiu, K.-M. (2014). Language development of severe to profoundly deaf children studying in a sign bilingual and co-enrollment environment. In M. Marschark, G. Tang, & H. Knoors (Eds.), *Bilingualism and bilingual deaf education* (pp. 313–341). New York: Oxford University Press.

Wolbers, K. A., Bowers, L. M., Dostal, H. M., & Graham, S. C. (2014). Deaf writers' application of American Sign Language knowledge to English. *International Journal of Bilingual Education and Bilingualism, 17*(4), 410–428.

Yiu, K.-M., & Tang, G. (2014). Social integration of deaf and hard-of-hearing children in a sign bilingual and co-enrollment environment. In M. Marschark, G. Tang, & H. Knoors (Eds.), *Bilingualism and bilingual deaf education* (pp. 342–367). New York: Oxford University Press.

4

Learning Together by Deaf and Hearing Students in a Japanese Primary School

Takashi Torigoe

BACKGROUND

The history of Japanese education for deaf and hard-of-hearing (DHH) children is similar to that of the United States and Europe. When deaf education began in the late 19th century, sign language was accepted and used in schools for the deaf. However, around the beginning of the 20th century, most schools for the deaf became oral. For a long time, the oral (and subsequently the aural-oral) method has been predominant in the education of DHH children in Japan. Even when the Total Communication (TC) approach was spreading in the United States and Europe in the 1960s and 1970s, Japanese teachers at schools for the deaf were reluctant to use signing with DHH pupils in the classrooms, although one school for the deaf did attempt to develop and use manually coded Japanese.

A significant change occurred in the 1990s when, while American and European educators were enthusiastically discussing a bilingual approach to educating DHH pupils, several schools for the deaf had just started to implement signing in their kindergarten classrooms, and subsequently in the primary school–level programs.[1] Although the teachers reported on the positive effects of this approach, such as producing active conversation and interaction among DHH children in the classrooms (Nakamori, 1999; Tanaka, 2000), signing was still incorporated within the framework of the TC approach (Torigoe, 2004). Also during the 1990s, pediatric cochlear implantation was spreading substantially, and most of the children with cochlear implants (CIs) enrolled in regular schools rather than in schools for the deaf. In this inclusive context, the aural-oral method has remained the dominant approach, and sign language is not used for communication and instruction in the regular schools, despite the need for its use by DHH pupils.

Table 4.1 shows the recent numbers of DHH pupils enrolled in regular schools and those in special schools. Roughly speaking, half of the DHH pupils are enrolled in regular primary schools and slightly less than half are enrolled in regular junior high schools.

Three types of inclusive learning situations for DHH pupils can be found in the present Japanese educational system. The first type is fully inclusive. DHH pupils learn in regular classrooms all day, with no official special educational support. We have no information concerning the number of those pupils, as described in Table 4.1. The second type is partially inclusive, using resource rooms for DHH pupils. In this learning situation, DHH pupils learn mainly in the regular classrooms with hearing pupils with no special support. Typically for two hours a week, they go to the resource rooms for DHH at the same school or at the central school of the region. In the resource room, they receive special support from teachers of DHH, depending on their educational needs. The last type is also partially inclusive: DHH students enroll officially in a special class for DHH pupils and occasionally go to a regular class to learn with hearing pupils. This type can be further subdivided into two types. One type is a special class that is attached to the DHH pupil's home school. Because of the low incidence of congenital or early acquired hearing loss, the typical situation is one DHH pupil per school. The second type is a special class attached to the central school for DHH education in the region. In big cities, it is often possible to group together several DHH pupils in a school. Thus DHH pupils have the option of enrolling in the central school for DHH education rather than their home school, which typically results in the group learning situation for DHH pupils at central schools. In both subtypes, DHH pupils usually learn Japanese and mathematics (and English in junior high school) in the special class, where one-to-one or small group instruction is possible. For other subjects, such as social science, science, arts, physical education, and so forth, they attend the regular classrooms and learn with hearing pupils. Thus the central schools for DHH education have the possibility of teaching hearing students and

Table 4.1. Number of DHH Pupils in Special Schools and Regular Schools

	Primary School Level	Junior High School Level	Total
Special school of DHH	3,093	1,882	4,975
Special class of DHH	1,029	410	1,439
Resource room for DHH	1,796	385	2,181

*We do not know the number of DHH pupils enrolled in regular schools without any official special educational support.

The Japanese Ministry of Education, 2014.

DHH (as a group) together in the same classrooms—that is, to practice co-enrollment, as described later.

The academic, social, and psychological challenges of inclusive education for DHH pupils have been reported in Japan (Mino & Torigoe, 2007; Torigoe, 2008), as well as in the United States (Antia et al., 2010; Cerney, 2007; Oliva & Lytle, 2014; Stinson & Antia, 1999). In addition, there are two principal challenges for DHH children in inclusive education in Japan. The first concerns the regular classroom situation, in which DHH pupils learn with hearing pupils. Formally, there is no support in the regular classroom for DHH pupils such as note-taking and/or sign language interpretation, with classes typically consisting of 40 students and just one general education teacher. The second challenge concerns the recruitment system for Japanese teachers. The teachers are employed by the local government, not by the school, and usually they are ordered to change schools periodically by the local board of education, typically every three to five years. Therefore, even if a teacher learns a lot concerning instruction and support for DHH pupils, he or she must move after several years to another school, where there may be no DHH pupils. At the same time, a teacher who has no experience of teaching DHH pupils may come to that school, where he or she becomes responsible for teaching DHH pupils. These situations in Japan further complicate DHH pupils' learning in the regular classroom.

HOW WE STARTED

The present chapter will report the process and some results of a project implementing the sign language, the natural language of the Deaf community, into a regular primary school (the regional central school for DHH education) with special classes for DHH pupils. This school is situated in an urban area in southwest Japan. The school has a total of approximately 180 students, including around 10 to 15 DHH pupils. The school is small in comparison to other urban schools in Japan.

The DHH pupils enrolled in this school had mild to profound levels of hearing loss, and they all used hearing aids or CIs. All the DHH pupils had hearing parents who spoke Japanese as their first language. Most of the DHH pupils used only speech in their daily lives, while some of them knew some signs and sometimes used signing with speech when they talked to each other or to the teachers of special classes.

For the past 10 years, the teachers of the special classes for DHH pupils have used both speech and signing (simultaneous communication) in the classrooms. One teacher noticed that 10 years ago she used speech only in the DHH classroom, but she felt it was difficult for the pupils to understand the lesson contents. Thus, she learned some signs by herself and began to use them gradually. She also reported that signing was needed for the DHH pupils themselves because it seemed like it was difficult for them to communicate, not only with hearing pupils but also (and even more so) with other DHH pupils. Ten years ago in Japan, the use of sign language or just signing in the regular school was very uncommon, although small changes in special schools of the deaf were beginning to occur, as described earlier. When the teacher began to use signing in the DHH classroom, some but not all of the DHH pupils also began using it. The teachers of DHH students also observed that because the school was a small one (with each grade having just one class and hearing and DHH pupils staying in the same regular classroom), some hearing pupils naturally began to learn some signs from the DHH pupils and began to use signing informally in the classroom, on the playground, and in other places at school. Some hearing pupils also began to support DHH classmates spontaneously by gesturing, using simple signs, or fingerspelling. The teachers of DHH students felt that this was a good step toward the full participation of the DHH pupils in regular classes, but further steps were needed because signing was used only sporadically in the classrooms and the learning by hearing and DHH pupils was still less collaborative than wished for. Japanese Sign Language (JSL) instruction or sign language interpretation in regular classrooms still had not been considered in those days. In addition, no Deaf adults were involved in the school's activities.

The author of this chapter became involved in the school's activities as a researcher on the education of DHH pupils. The possibility of sign language use in the classrooms was discussed with the teachers of DHH students and the school's administrators; as a result a small, three-year project to implement the use of sign language at the school was set up. This project consisted of three parts: (1) the instruction of sign language to the DHH pupils by a deaf sign language teacher, (2) the introduction of sign language interpretation into regular classrooms, and (3) the instruction of sign language to hearing teachers and pupils. The first part aimed to improve the level of DHH pupils' sign language ability and to give them an opportunity to interact with deaf adults. The second aimed to give a bilingual environment to DHH pupils, and the third aimed to enhance collaborative learning by DHH and hearing pupils while being co-enrolled.

Torigoe (2014) discussed types of co-enrollment programs for DHH pupils in various places and distinguished two types: interpretation prominent and co-teaching prominent. The present practice would be classified as an example of the first one. Despite the limitations of meditated instruction by interpreters rather than direct instruction in JSL, this option was chosen in the present project because the teacher was employed by the local government and not by the school (as described earlier). Thus, it was more difficult to create and implement a co-teaching approach, while employing a sign language interpreter in the regular classrooms was easier.

THE PROCESS OF INTERVENTIONS

First, a deaf sign language teacher visited the special classes periodically (usually two days per month) and taught JSL to the DHH pupils. How the DHH pupils learned JSL through interaction with the deaf teacher has been reported in other publications (Torigoe, 2012, 2015). Although at first the DHH pupils struggled to negotiate the "speaking culture" of their daily lives with the "silent culture" introduced by the deaf teacher, we found that they learned a substantial amount of JSL as a second language and soon became used to communicating in JSL with the deaf teacher and among themselves. However, we also found that despite becoming sign language users, the DHH pupils would not use signing in their regular classrooms, instead choosing to continue speaking to hearing classmates and general education teachers.

In the second year of this project, the sign language instruction to hearing pupils and general education teachers started. A deaf university student volunteer visited the regular classrooms to teach some signs to the hearing pupils. In addition, we asked the deaf volunteer to stay in regular classrooms with the DHH pupils for a couple of hours after teaching signs to the hearing pupils and to participate in the subjects, learning with the pupils. This situation facilitated the use of signing by the DHH pupils in their regular classes, not only with the deaf volunteer but also with their hearing classmates.

In the same year, sign language interpretation began to be implemented in the regular classrooms. However, because of constraints in funding, sign language interpreters were employed only once a week and were assigned mainly in the social and natural sciences lessons to the fourth- and sixth-grade classrooms, where two DHH pupils seemed to have a greater need for sign language interpretation than the other DHH pupils. The interpreter usually stood in front of the classroom, next to the general education teacher, and interpreted for the DHH pupils. During small group and individual learning activities, the interpreter stayed near the DHH pupils and interpreted for them when needed.

Though the data were not collected systematically and quantitatively concerning, for example, how the interpretation improved DHH pupils' learning and attainment, because the time of sign language interpretation was limited, we obtained comments every day from the teachers and DHH pupils concerning its positive effects, such as the fact that DHH pupils easily participated in the activities and learning through interpretation. One DHH pupil indicated that without interpretation, she could manage to follow the teacher's instruction through

FM systems, but that with interpretation she noticed for the first time how her classmates talked to the teacher and with each other during the lessons, which would be indispensable for her collaborative learning with hearing classmates.

Next, the results and challenges of sign language interpretation are described from the standpoint of learning together by DHH and hearing pupils. When they finished each hour-long interpretation, the interpreters reflected on and summarized their activities by reviewing their completed tasks, what they felt went well, and the challenges they faced. Seventy-three hours of these records were collected and supplemental classroom observations were also conducted. Through qualitative analysis of the challenges of the interpreters' tasks, they could be classified into three categories: (1) challenges related to the DHH pupils, (2) challenges related to the interpreters, and (3) challenges related to the classroom situation.

CHALLENGES OF SIGN LANGUAGE INTERPRETATION

Challenges Related to the DHH Pupils

The challenges related to the DHH pupils can be divided into two categories: their limited sign language proficiency and their limited experience with interpreters. The former challenge concerns the fact that, although the information was interpreted, the DHH pupils sometimes could not understand the signs. Although they were learning sign language and using it in their daily lives, the signs for technical terms or vocabulary used in academic subjects were often unfamiliar to them.

The latter challenge concerns the fact that the DHH pupils had almost no experience with sign language interpretation. Thus, while the information was interpreted, DHH pupils could not use it for their learning. For example, it was observed that often before the interpretation was finished, the DHH pupils shifted their attention from the interpreter to other things (e.g., the visual materials such as the textbooks) and subsequently failed to receive the entire message through the interpreter. In addition, as they did not have interpretation for most of the school day (just one day in a week, as described earlier), they would often try to get the information directly from the teacher's speech. So even when there was an interpreter, the DHH pupils would still first attempt to understand the target content through the teacher. However, they would then give up halfway and shift their attention to the interpreter. This might cause the information they received to be fragmented and inconsistent.

The DHH pupils thus needed more experience with interpretation and had to learn how to use it correctly so they could obtain the information fully and consistently to improve their learning. The interpreters also reported that when they interpreted, the DHH pupils sometimes did not watch them. In these situations, the interpreters would only start signing after the DHH pupils gave them their full attention. However, the interpreters noted that this delayed the information transfer, which meant that just a summary (rather than the full message) would be delivered.

Challenges Related to the Interpreters

In Japan, sign language interpretation in schools is still uncommon, and the interpreters had little experience in classroom interpretation, especially in primary schools. In addition, they had almost no experience in interpreting a teacher's speech to children, nor were they used to children's signing. The content of lessons (e.g., natural sciences) was also unfamiliar to the interpreters, and many technical terms had no corresponding signs. In these situations, the interpreters would sometimes ask for a sign from the DHH pupils or just show written words (writing in the air) or fingerspelling to them. These processes required more time, which resulted in delays in the interpretation of the teacher's speech. The interpreters were able to overcome this challenge through sufficient preparation and their accumulating experience. Collaboration between the teachers and interpreters was thus critical for good interpretation practice; however, the interpreters were employed on an hourly basis, and it was not easy for them to find time for collaboration before and/or after the job.

Challenges Related to the Classroom Situation

Challenges related to the classroom situation can be subdivided into three types: whole class instruction, small group activities, and individual learning.

Whole class instruction occurs when the teacher talks unidirectionally or asks questions to all pupils at once; pupils raise their hands and answer, and then the teacher comments further. This flow of information, namely a "single information flow," was easily interpreted; the DHH pupils were able to follow instruction and fully participated in the classroom activities. However, challenges occurred when several pupils talked simultaneously and among themselves. When some pupils murmured to themselves, or when private talking while thinking occurred, the teacher overheard private conversations and provided the responses/comments to the entire class. In these situations of "multiple flows of information," the interpreters experienced challenges, as it was difficult to interpret the murmurs, private conversations, and simultaneous talking for the DHH pupils. As they could hear all talking and conversations, hearing pupils can discard any irrelevant information, but DHH students are reliant on interpretations. The interpreter must therefore choose which murmurs should be interpreted and control the information flow to facilitate the DHH pupils' understanding.

The teachers usually used various visual materials (e.g., books, videos, real objects, and projected pictures) to help the pupils easily understand the lesson contents. When the teachers talked to the pupils while pointing to these visual materials, interpretation became difficult. This is because sign language is also visual, and DHH pupils cannot watch both the teacher and the interpreter simultaneously. Sometimes, some hearing pupils also talked in these situations; this is confusing to the DHH pupils as they cannot identify who talked to whom about what through interpretations. Another situation was observed in which the teacher or pupils read aloud parts of the textbook while the remaining pupils underlined the text being read. Simultaneous activities, such as listening to a voice (or watching it being interpreted) and completing individual work (e.g., underlining the text), is difficult for DHH pupils. The interpreter reported that she solved this problem using a strategy in which she stopped interpreting when the DHH pupil's attention was distracted and restarted when she regained his or her attention. However, sometimes this did not work because there were two or more DHH pupils in the classroom, and their attention patterns was not same.

The interpreter usually stood next to the teacher. However, the teacher sometimes walked around the classroom while she talked to the pupils. In this situation, the interpreter did not move and remained at the front of the classroom. The DHH pupils needed to decide whom to follow, the teacher or the interpreter. Some of the DHH pupils had substantial residual hearing and could partly understand what the teacher said through their hearing aids or CI. However, this did not always work, and they would rely on the interpreters when, for example, the classroom's sound environment was not ideal. In such situations, the DHH pupils first followed the teacher; if they could not understand teacher's speech fully, then they redirected their attention to the interpreter, or they switched back and forth between the teacher and the interpreter. In these situations, it was difficult for the interpreter to know from where to begin interpreting for the student again. Moreover, the DHH pupils might again receive fragmented or inconsistent interpretations.

In the lessons, the teacher wore an FM microphone and her voice was easily transmitted to the DHH students' hearing aids or CI. However, the pupils' voices were difficult to understand without microphones. When the teacher asked the pupils sequentially to read aloud parts of the textbook, the DHH pupils could not hear the other students' voices and it became difficult for them to follow who was reading which part of the textbook. It was also observed sometimes that a hearing pupil sitting next to a DHH pupil would provide support by pointing at the part of the textbook being read.

As for the textbook usage, in one of the natural sciences classes, the teacher encouraged the pupils to quickly identify as many images of insects in the textbook as possible. In reality, there were many pictures of insects in the textbook. While they scanned the textbook, the pupils shouted, "I found one!" one by one and said what kind of insect was found on which page. In this situation, interpretation did not work because the DHH pupils were also concentrating on scanning their own textbook and could not watch the interpreter. While hearing pupils could listen to what the other pupils said when scanning the textbook, the DHH pupils missed the information completely or received fragments at most.

Small group activities are now very common in Japanese classrooms because they are thought to support active and collaborative learning. However, these activities represent challenges for DHH pupils' learning because the classroom's sound environment deteriorates with multiple student conversations occurring simultaneously. In addition, simultaneous talking among group members can occur, which makes it difficult for DHH pupils to identify who said what and to participate fully in the group discussions and interactions. Small group work is also challenging for interpreters as DHH students may not all be in the same group, and the classroom was too small for the interpreter to freely move between groups. The interpreter would thus only enter the small groups when the DHH pupils requested interpretation; otherwise, the interpreter left the pupils to support each other.

We observed that some hearing pupils used signing or fingerspelling while talking or would talk very slowly to the DHH pupils. A "culture" or atmosphere to support DHH pupils spontaneously developed in the classes. In addition, the interpreters reported that if they went into the groups to interpret too often, the hearing pupils would rely too much on the interpreters to communicate with the DHH pupils, disrupting the group atmosphere. However, this support did not necessarily guarantee the DHH pupils' full participation in their group activities. The information conveyed to the DHH pupil was often fragmented and only in the final stage (rather than being an ongoing process).

One episode was observed in a natural science lesson in which the teacher used a group activity in which the pupils observed how their flowers were growing and discussed these developments in groups while drawing. In group discussions, the DHH pupil was left alone, and only the conclusion was conveyed to her. Finally, she copied the drawing of the flowers to her notes, seemingly without understanding what was being discussed in her group. However, the teacher might believe that the DHH pupil participated fully in the group activity because she finished drawing the flower.

Not only do we need to clarify when and how the interpreters should intervene in the group learning situations, but also the DHH pupils need to accumulate more experience of asking for information or clarifications from hearing pupils.

Individual learning was often implemented in which pupils could individually confirm what they learned and/or extend their learning by tackling more advanced questions at their own pace. The teacher moved around the classroom and supported the pupils individually when needed. When the teacher supported the DHH pupils, the interpreter would sometimes interpret, but other times, the teacher spoke to them slowly and visually without interpreters. In these situations, the challenges the DHH pupils faced concerned overhearing. When the teacher walked around and gave advice to hearing pupils individually, other hearing pupils could overhear and receive some of the information. They could use it in their ongoing work or disregard it because of its irrelevance to what they were doing. However, the DHH pupils missed this information due to the lack of interpretation. The interpreter always tried to give information to the DHH pupils regarding what happened in the classroom, although this sometimes interrupted the students' ongoing work. Therefore, the interpreter always analyzed and judged which information should be interpreted to the DHH pupils based on its relevance. This, however, did not work when there were several DHH pupils in the classroom and when the interpreter did not fully understand each DHH pupil's learning situation. Therefore, collaboration between the teacher and interpreter is necessary to overcome this challenge.

In individual learning situations, interpreters sometimes extended their roles, for example taking on the role of tutor. Occasionally, some DHH pupils asked the interpreter for more detailed instructions when the teacher's instructions were unclear to them. According to the interpreter's role, interpreters should intervene between teachers and DHH pupils to support the learners when more information is required. However, this was not always possible, and the interpreter often provided the DHH pupils with the needed additional information. In this situation, it was observed that a closed space of the DHH pupils and the interpreter would be created in the classroom that would exclude the hearing members of the classroom. In this regard as well, collaboration between teachers and interpreters is needed to overcome this challenge.

Another episode was observed where the DHH children talked with each other or to the interpreter easily as they used sign language. These signed (individual and/or local) conversations were usually not interpreted into speech and were not shared with the hearing class members. The hearing children and teacher could not "overhear" these signed conversations. To combine these two worlds, interpretation would also play an indispensable role. We therefore need to continue clarifying what, when, and how to interpret in inclusive classrooms.

DISCUSSION AND FURTHER PRACTICES

This chapter has reported on the processes and results of a three-year project that implemented a sign language program at a regular Japanese primary school where several DHH pupils were enrolled. I focused on sign language interpretation in regular classrooms.

Various challenges in the implementation of this project were illustrated. The DHH pupils loved learning sign language at school. During the sign language lessons, they learned to use JSL from a deaf teacher and to communicate the way deaf people do, for example without voice. However, the DHH children were reluctant to use JSL in their regular classes. DHH children in this school wore a digital hearing aid or CI and some might have acquired spoken Japanese as their first language, although they still had a need for sign language use, depending on the situation. They were thus learning sign language as a second language. The deaf adult's presence in the regular classrooms was found to facilitate the DHH pupils' use of sign language.

In the present study, two issues were addressed concerning the inclusive learning of DHH pupils in regular classrooms. One issue concerns the multiple flows of information in the classrooms and the other concerns the issue of overhearing/incidental learning by the children.

When learning is constructed socially and/or dynamically (e.g., creative discussion in a small group), children become active and engaged; they talk spontaneously and sometimes simultaneously. In this situation, multiple information flows occur, as compared with the single flow of information in structured, teacher-centered teaching. When many hearing children spoke simultaneously to the hearing teacher and the teacher responded to some of them, the DHH pupils sometimes could not follow these conversations even when the interpreter was interpreting for them. In addition, interpreted speech can be time-delayed and DHH pupils may lose opportunities to make timely contributions to class talk. Thus, when multiple, spontaneous information flows occur in the classrooms, sharing the conversation among the DHH and hearing children was difficult even when an interpreter was present.

In small group learning and/or individual learning situations, teachers moved around the classroom and talked directly to a group or a single pupil. These local conversations (i.e., not involving the whole class) were not usually interpreted for the DHH children if not directed to them. In these situations, however, hearing children could overhear the conversations, and they might learn something from them. Children generally learn a substantial amount simply by overhearing others' conversations. Overhearing thus provides opportunities for incidental learning, but DHH pupils often missed out on these opportunities. In addition, the language input for DHH children is less than that of hearing children. However, if all local conversations were interpreted to DHH pupils instantaneously, this would likely be disruptive to DHH pupils' ongoing learning or activities. Thus, interpreters instead sometimes would summarize what happened in the hearing/spoken world afterwards, if the DHH pupils seemed to have missed any essential information.

Although research on educational interpretation in inclusive learning situations for DHH pupils has been conducted (Cerney, 2007; Ramsey, 1997), the typical situation was one deaf child per classroom or school. Thus, we need to know more about sign language interpretation where several DHH pupils learn in the same classroom. In addition, sign language interpretation is still not common in Japanese educational situations. We need to know more about using sign language interpretation in inclusive classrooms in Japan from the perspective of learning together by deaf and hearing pupils (Torigoe, 2014).

At present, this project has been extended and is now in the eighth year but is facing another challenge. The school was merged with several other small local schools to become a large school of 700 pupils; however, the number of DHH pupils remains virtually the same. Each grade now has three classes, and every two years the classes are shuffled, with two-thirds of their hearing classmates changed to other classes. As a result, many of the hearing pupils and teachers have no personal contact with the DHH pupils in the daily life of the school. We are now thinking of extending the program from being classroom-based to school-based, in which all hearing pupils and teachers in the school would get together with the DHH pupils to learn more about and experience signed language and Deaf culture.

ACKNOWLEDGMENTS

This research was financially supported by the Japan Society for the Promotion of Science from 2010 to 2012 (No. 22531066). I would like to express my gratitude to the DHH and hearing pupils, their parents, the teachers, and the school administrators for giving me the invaluable opportunity to conduct this research.

NOTE

1. Generally speaking, in the Japanese schools of the deaf, upper-level programs (i.e., high school) tended to be more tolerant of sign language use than lower-level programs (i.e., kindergarten and primary school), which tended to strictly eliminate it from the classroom.

REFERENCES

Antia, S. D., Kreimeyer, K. H., & Reed, S. (2010). Supporting students in general education classroom. In M. Marschark & P. E. Spencer (Eds.), *Oxford handbook of deaf studies, language, and education* (Vol. 2, pp. 72–92). New York: Oxford University Press.

Cerney, J. (2007). *Deaf education in America.* Washington, DC: Gallaudet University Press.

Mino, T., & Torigoe, T. (2007). A survey on the support to deaf and hard-of-hearing children in an inclusive environment: A narrative analysis. *Deaf Education, 49*(2), 47–66. [In Japanese]

Nakamori, R. (1999). Creative drama workshop "Wanpaku-dan" with children. *Bulletin of the Nara Prefectural School for the Deaf, 21,* 16–21. [In Japanese]

Oliva, G. A., & Lytle, L. R. (2014). *Turning the tide.* Washington, DC: Gallaudet University Press.

Ramsey, C. (1997). *Deaf children in public schools.* Washington, DC: Gallaudet University Press.

Stinson, M. S., & Antia, A. D. (1999). Considerations in educating deaf and hard-of-hearing students in inclusive settings. *Journal of Deaf Studies and Deaf Education, 4*(3), 163–175.

Tanaka, A. (2000). A report on the teaching Japanese using the sign language. *Bulletin of the Adachi Metropolitan School for the Deaf, 25,* 64–72. [In Japanese]

Torigoe, T. (2004). Deaf education and bilingualism: Signed and spoken languages. *Studies in Language Sciences, 3,* 55–65.

Torigoe, T. (2008). Communication and psychological support of deaf and hard-of-hearing children. In K. Murase & Y. Kawasaki (Eds.), *Clinical psychology for deaf and hard-of-hearing people* (Vol. 2, pp. 75–95). Tokyo: Nihon-Hyoron-Sha. [In Japanese]

Torigoe, T. (2012). How hard-of-hearing children learn a sign language. A sociocultural analysis. Poster presented at the 5th Conference of International Society for Gesture Studies, Lund.

Torigoe, T. (2014). What are the "co-enrollment" practices? A comparison, Paper presented at Symposium on Sign Bilingualism and Deaf Education, Chinese University of Hong Kong.

Torigoe, T. (2015). Sign language learning by inclusive deaf and hard-of-hearing pupils: A longitudinal analysis, Poster presented at the 17th European Conference on Developmental Psychology, Braga.

5

Essential Ingredients for Sign Bilingualism and Co-Enrollment Education in the Hong Kong Context

Chris Kun-man Yiu, Gladys Tang, and Chloe Chi-man Ho

Deaf education in Hong Kong used to be predominantly oral in both deaf schools and mainstream school settings. The white paper "Integrating the Disabled into the Community: A United Effort" (Hong Kong Government, 1977) and the later promotion of the Whole School Approach to Integrated Education for all local schools in 1997 (Hong Kong Education Bureau, 2010) have led to a reduction in the number of deaf schools from four to one, the second to the last just closed down its deaf unit in the summer of 2018. It was in this setting that the Centre for Sign Linguistics and Deaf Studies of the Chinese University of Hong Kong saw the need to establish the Sign Bilingualism and Co-Enrollment (SLCO) program in August 2006. The new approach, which invited partnership with some mainstream schools in Hong Kong, aimed to provide an option to the predominantly oral education for deaf and hard-of-hearing (DHH) children. It was established at a time when parents, educators, and professionals were skeptical about the effectiveness of sign language in supporting DHH children's development; therefore, for sign language to be adopted in an inclusive setting was beyond the public's imagination.

The SLCO program has two overarching principles of organization originating from the fields of sign linguistics and deaf education:

1. In its original conceptualization, sign bilingualism promotes a form of deaf education in which DHH students can access sign language as a first language. Spoken language, especially in its written mode, is acquired as a second language in order to support DHH students' language and literacy development as well as education. Sign bilingualism also highlights the cultural values of sign languages of the Deaf community (Swanwick, 2016). The SLCO program adopts a modified version of sign

bilingualism in light of research findings of bimodal bilingualism (see the section on Pillar 3).
2. Co-enrollment, according to Kirchner (2004), refers to a model of inclusive education that stresses the existence of a critical mass of DHH students to study together with a group of hearing peers. The deaf–hearing ratio may vary from 1:1 to 1:3 or 1:4. The class is co-taught by a teacher for the deaf, deaf or hearing, and a general education teacher.

In the following sections, we will introduce the background of deaf education in Hong Kong, including the city's linguistic landscape and the government's efforts to promote bilingual/multilingual education. Next, we will describe the context in which the SLCO program was established in 2006 and how the system was developed from preschool to secondary education (up to secondary six [grade 12] at the time of writing) within a regular school system. The novelty of such an education model has encouraged researchers and teachers to adopt a reflection-in-action approach in program implementation, which means continuously observing and modifying the pedagogical practices in the SLCO classrooms each year, as new and sometimes unforeseen circumstances challenge the SLCO approach. Based on the 12 years of classroom observation and experiences gained in program implementation, the team has identified four key ingredients that form the foundation of the SLCO program. Finally, we will discuss the challenges the SLCO approach faced during this establishment process.

HONG KONG'S LINGUISTIC LANDSCAPE

There are currently three official languages in Hong Kong. Cantonese is the language of communication used in formal and informal settings by a majority of the society. Written Chinese, a Chinese subject taught in school, is read with Cantonese pronunciation, although the grammar follows that of Mandarin Chinese. The third official language, English, is another core language subject at school.

In the Deaf community, Hong Kong Sign Language (HKSL) is the natural language variety used by local deaf people. Due to a long history of predominantly oral deaf education, only about 3,900 deaf people use HKSL within a population of 155,000 DHH people (Census and Statistic Department, 2014). Some DHH or hearing children are born to deaf families who use HKSL, some learn sign language mainly from their schoolmates when they enter the school for the deaf, and many of them acquire HKSL during adolescence or adulthood. Over the years, the promotion of HKSL in society has led many deaf parents to become more receptive to using it to interact with their children, either deaf or hearing.

DEAF EDUCATION IN HONG KONG

According to the Hong Kong Education Bureau (2013), there are about 700 DHH students who use different types of hearing aids or cochlear implants in Hong Kong. The number of DHH students with relatively mild hearing loss is unclear. In Hong Kong, deaf education became prevalently oral when the government unit responsible for education closed down all learning centers that used sign language to educate DHH children in 1970s (Sze, Lo, Lo, & Chu, 2013). Currently, there are about 70 to 80 DHH students studying in the two special schools for the deaf (Hong Kong Special School Council and Committee on Home School Cooperation, 2017); one of the schools is about to be phased out completely. The remaining 90% of DHH students are attending regular primary and secondary schools, using primarily spoken language without any exposure to HKSL. The global trend of inclusive education supported by advancement in assistive hearing technology and rehabilitation services has drawn parents away from the schools for the deaf and Hong Kong is no exception.

The United Nations Convention on the Rights of Persons with Disabilities (UNCRPD) (United Nations, 2006) clearly ascertains the linguistic status of sign language for adoption as a medium of communication to enable deaf people to access information without barriers. In January 2017, there was an attempt to legalize HKSL as one of the official languages of Hong Kong; however, it did not meet with success due to prevailing misconceptions or lack of understanding of sign language for the deaf. As far as education is concerned, the government's attitudes toward sign language in educating DHH students remain ambivalent. Although the government was requested by the Deaf community and some parents and educators to adopt HKSL alongside spoken language to support DHH children in mainstreamed preschool and school-age settings (Hong Kong Legislative Council, 2014) the Hong Kong Education Bureau (2014, p. 1) stated that they "would . . . refer students with severe or profound hearing loss or those who cannot construct knowledge because of inadequate speech abilities, that is, those students who may need to use sign language in communication and learning, to special schools for children with hearing impairment to receive intensive support services." In other words, the ideology of no sign language in mainstream education for the deaf continues to prevail.

DEVELOPMENT OF THE SLCO PROGRAM

The SLCO program aims to complement the existing oral-dominant education policy toward supporting DHH students in mainstream education. It embraces linguistic diversity and specific education needs of

DHH students through devising school practices to cultivate a learning environment that enhances bimodal bilingual development of DHH and hearing students at an early age. During the past 12 years, the SLCO program has been partnering with a few regular schools to build the system from scratch. Throughout the process we have gained lots of invaluable experience and practice wisdom on how a SLCO program can be set up in a regular school. The program envisions establishing a "through-train," from baby signing to preschool and school-age education before entering higher education, within the mainstream settings. When the program commenced in 2006, parents were reluctant to allow their DHH children to learn HKSL, worrying that acquiring this language would only impede spoken language development and eventually integration into the hearing-majority society.

During this initial stage of program development, the organizer came across orally trained children who had severe or profound hearing loss without any communication abilities even at the age of 5 or above. Obviously, initial deprivation of early language input, no matter whether signed or spoken, had led to language delay (Mayberry, 2007) and cognitive deficiencies (Courtin, 2000; Figueras, Edwards, & Langdon, 2008; Hall, Eigst, Bortfeld, & Lillo-Martin, 2017).

Initially, the SLCO program admitted DHH children into Kindergarten 3, the last year of a three-year preschool education system. The first cohort consisted of 6 DHH and 14 hearing students. Over the past 12 years, the program has been continuously expanding up and down with DHH and hearing students distributed over 14 grade levels, including K1 to K3 at the kindergarten level, P1 to P6 at the primary level, and S1 to S5 at the secondary level. In two years, the first cohort of SLCO students, DHH and hearing, will be taking a public examination and graduating from secondary education.

Here we will identify the four major pillars in the construction of the SLCO program (see also, DeKlerk et al., this volume).

THE FOUR PILLARS

The four pillars are (1) a whole-school approach toward promoting deaf and hearing collaboration; (2) involvement by deaf individuals in school practices, especially deaf–hearing co-teaching practices in the SLCO classroom; (3) an enriched linguistic context to support bimodal bilingual development of DHH and hearing students; and (4) DHH and hearing students' active participation in school and social activities. The four ingredients, each one serving its own independent purposes, partner with the others to steer the program's overall development to realize our goals (see the section "Development of the SLCO Program"). The SLCO program seeks to appreciate the linguistic and cultural context of the Deaf community in Hong Kong and to work within the government's general policy of inclusive education. We will describe how these four pillars have been constructed at the partner schools over the past 12 years. It is anticipated that this chapter can serve as a practical reference for educators and researchers interested in examining the crucial aspects of the SLCO program in the Hong Kong context.

Pillar 1: Whole-School Approach Toward Promoting Collaboration Between Deaf and Hearing Educators

Collaboration Between Deaf and Hearing Educators

Collaboration between special educators (i.e. 'teachers for the deaf' in our case) and general educators is considered an effective way to promote inclusion of DHH children (Luckner, Rude, & Sileo, 1989) and children with disabilities in general (Thomson, 2013). It is a problem-solving process, aiming to bring mutual benefits through concerted efforts between at least two parties. According to Friend and Cook (1990), collaboration is "a style for interaction between at least two co-equal parties voluntarily engaged in shared decision-making as they work toward a common goal" (p. 72). There are different levels of collaboration, such as collaboration or team efforts between administrators, professionals, teachers, and also students, bringing positive impacts on students' academic, social skills, and self-esteem (Jiménez-Sánchez & Antia, 1999). Friend and Cook (1990) regarded collaboration as a predictor for success in school reform.

In addition to collaboration between special and general educators, successful establishment of the SLCO program requires close partnership between a team of teachers for the deaf. These educators include teachers or teacher aides who are deaf as well as bilingual hearing teachers who are knowledgeable about HKSL and deaf education and a team of general teachers well versed in operating a regular school system, especially with the implementation of a mainstream curriculum and integrated education policy of the territory. Therefore, at school, there is close collaboration between the two teams of teachers, including daily teaching and learning, organizing and running extracurricular activities, and consolidating school policies and education philosophy within the constraints of the system. That the two teams of teachers identify themselves as collaborators in the "school venture" has led to expectations that there should be regular meetings to discuss strategies to steer class practices and school developments. Acceptance of the whole-school approach among teachers means their willingness to contribute their efforts to build the SLCO classroom and the school community. Another example of important teamwork to build the SLCO classroom is to establish effective collaboration between teachers for the deaf and general teachers (more descriptions in the next section).

They are scheduled to meet regularly to prepare for lessons and to discuss how different teaching activities should be distributed between them. In fact, collaboration is found at all levels, including principals and supervisors, front-line teachers, parents, and support staff like office clerks, computer operators, and workers at the school kiosks.

A unique characteristic of the SLCO program is that it incorporates into the school environment a multidisciplinary team. In addition to the teachers mentioned above, there are speech therapists, and researchers trained in sign linguistics and deaf education. The researchers are responsible for observing the SLCO classes and collecting data, reviewing the development of the program, and projecting new directions. They facilitate reflective teaching among the general teachers and the teachers for the deaf in order to confirm or disconfirm the effectiveness of school/class practices within the general SLCO philosophy so that collective decisions may be made to sustain or to modify existing practices (Friend & Cook, 1990).

Shared Goals and Resources

The SLCO program emphasizes the importance of having a common goal among the general teachers and teachers for the deaf. If asked what the common goal is, a simple answer from the principals of the partner schools would be "to develop the SLCO approach as a form of inclusive education in school." During an interview in 2014, a former principal who helped to develop the SLCO primary school system recalled what motivated the school to take on this SLCO venture in 2007:

> The program gives our school an opportunity to actualize the philosophy and values of a Catholic school. The SLCO approach triggers us to identify, at a professional level, ways to support students with special educational needs. They are minorities in the school community; but they are in need of support in education and society. If we believe in what we are doing is correct, we can have a greater opportunity to succeed.

Are there any other objectives that both the teachers for the deaf and the general teachers envision to achieve besides program establishment? A burning question from the school stakeholders is whether incorporating a deaf education program in an inclusive setting benefits the school's overall development, especially the education of hearing students. A former vice principal and coordinator of the primary school program made this statement during an interview in 2007:

> There are four "wins" in the establishment of this program at school. Both DHH children and hearing children win as they learn a lot from each other, not only academically and linguistically but also empathy and care for others. For our teachers, they develop better

strategies in classroom teaching, especially knowledge and skills in supporting children with different special needs. Finally, the school wins because the school develops an inclusive culture that is so embracing and accepting.

It is the prospect of pursuing a win–win situation together that allows the two teams of teachers to collaborate on a daily basis to determine what is efficient for both groups of students and for overall school development. Table 5.1 summarizes the different SLCO practices that led to perceivable changes within the system at the SLCO kindergarten and primary and secondary schools resulting in whole-school development at different levels.

The sense of having a common goal permeates the school system, driving the teachers to interact closely with each other and to inform the school administration of new initiatives or modified strategies as soon as possible. Teachers and parents expressed concerns about how the SLCO approach would impact the general development of the schools and students, both with or without hearing loss (see Kreimeyer, Drye, & Metz, this volume). The former principal stated:

> Staff members are crucial in actualizing the program. We need to have the right person to do the right thing. At the very beginning, teachers who were devoted to supporting DHH children and who were ready for challenges were invited to be the vanguard. As time went by, some of them performed better and gained a sense of ownership of the program. What I did was to support them in all aspects. Gradually, more and more stakeholders, including other staff members and parents of hearing students, showed acceptance to the program. Then, the atmosphere and culture of the school became more and more inclusive; and the students became more and more receptive to differences.

As Friend and Cook (1990) stated, to gain trust and respect for each other, a common vision and shared operational objectives between the two teams of educators are necessary. In addition, collaborative efforts were made to include different professionals (speech therapists, audiologists, psychologists and social workers) to support whole-person development of the students. When the vision and operational objectives are transparently expressed, teachers and professionals will engage in different levels of knowledge and experience sharing, an activity essential for inculcating a new school culture. Such sharing also transmits to all stakeholders the school mission in regards to the establishment of the SLCO program.

The two teams also worked together toward making cultural changes in the community when opportunities arose in order to educate the public about the importance of inclusive deaf education through the

Table 5.1. SLCO Practices That Contribute to Whole-School Developments

Domains	SLCO Practices	Whole-school Developments
School culture	Establishing an inclusive culture to support DHH students in school, with enhanced Deaf awareness and respect for sign language	A cultural change in school that accepts diversity and respect for individual differences
School management and administration	Developing a school-based support system for DHH students, including policies for curriculum and examination accommodations as well as adaptations	A school-based student support system in place for not only DHH learners but also students with different types of special educational needs
Learning and teaching	Exploring deaf–hearing co-teaching practices	More attention and support given to students in class and better use of different pedagogical strategies in class
	Training stakeholders in deaf education and inclusive education practices	Enhancing competence of teachers and their practical strategies in handling students with diverse needs
	Training in sign language skills and how they may be applied to classroom teaching	Teachers' use of sign language, gestures, and nonverbal communication in class, in addition to spoken languages
Resource development	Developing visual materials to enhance learning for DHH students, such as PowerPoint slides and worksheets for individual subjects	Attracting the attention of all students and enhancing their learning interests and participation in class
	Developing sign bilingual reading programs	Promoting early literacy among students
	Developing learning packages to support the academic development of DHH students (e.g., packages for word problems in mathematics)	Sharing of learning resources with teachers of non-SLCO classes and those responsible for supporting students with other special needs
Support for special needs children	Training teachers and school staff in deafness and related knowledge	Enhancing teachers' professional knowledge of deafness and language development of children with special needs
Student development	Organizing sign language classes for hearing students and coaching student volunteers to work with DHH students	Acquiring signed language skills, consideration and empathy for people in need

Table 5.1. Continued

Domains	SLCO Practices	Whole-school Developments
Parental involvement	Organizing parents or parent/child sign language classes	Enhancement of parent–child relationships
	Coaching parents to serve as volunteers in DHH students' reading programs and other activities	Parental involvement leading to an appreciation for accepting all special needs children

SLCO approach. These opportunities included school visits and public seminars and participation in teaching awards for special needs children such as the Chief Executive's Award for Teaching Excellence (http://www.ate.gov.hk/english/index.html).

The SLCO program emphasizes capacity building of the SLCO schools. Resource materials that support learning and teaching of different subjects such as Chinese, English, mathematics, and general studies are developed through concerted efforts of the deaf education and general education teams. The materials developed are primarily designed to enhance DHH students' sign language skills, Chinese and English literacy, arithmetic skills, and world knowledge. They are all stored in the school intranet, which is accessible also by teachers of non-SLCO classes. All other teachers may use them in daily teaching to enrich their teaching pedagogies in general or to provide remedial support to students with other special needs, though adaptations may be required.

Training and Seminars to Motivate Changes

Motivated by the need for change, seminars and workshops on HKSL, communication strategies to use with DHH children, sign bilingual education, and deaf–hearing co-teaching practices were organized for different stakeholders. Such in-house training is important to raise school staff's deaf awareness and communication skills and to facilitate administrative practices and decision-making on curriculum matters and discussion on school policies. Some training workshops target support staff such as computer technicians, clerical staff, and workers because they also have direct contact with DHH students and may be assigned to deal with daily routines. In addition to providing professional knowledge and skills, the workshops also include practical tips such as how to establish rapport with DHH students, how to collect and distribute the FM systems to the students, how to take care of DHH children when they visit the toilet, or how to send school notices to deaf parents.

In sum, the development of the SLCO program, unprecedented at least in Hong Kong and Asia, involves a continuous problem-solving process that requires constant reflection, review, and modifications. For each reflection-in-action cycle, by means of shared participation, shared accountability, and shared resources (Friend & Cook, 1990), the two teams identify problems, generate solutions, predict possible consequences, and monitor implementations for any changes and new developments (Luckner, Rude, & Sileo, 1989). In the following sections, we will discuss how deaf teachers' potential strengths are being used in the SLCO program.

Pillar 2: Deaf Individuals' Involvement in School and Co-Teaching Practices

Impact of Deaf Individuals' Involvement

When the co-enrollment program started under the TRIPOD Project (Kirchner, 1994), it emphasized direct communication among the participants to offset the need for sign interpretation. It was achieved through co-teaching between a regular teacher and a teacher for the deaf who may be deaf, hard-of-hearing, or hearing. The SLCO program is characterized by an active involvement of deaf adults as deaf teachers or deaf teacher aides depending on their academic qualifications, whose social and linguistic roles serve as the framework of deaf–hearing co-teaching in the SLCO classroom. Currently, over 60% of the lessons are co-taught by a deaf teacher or deaf teacher aide and a hearing teacher. Due to the history of oral education for the deaf in Hong Kong, many deaf signing adults had failed to receive education in a wide range of subjects. To cope with such a constraint, the fundamental principle for staffing allocation is "the younger the students in the SLCO classes, the greater the significance attached to deaf–hearing collaboration in the co-teaching practices." This principle ensures that there is sustained and enriched bilingual input in the SLCO environment as L1s (see next section), especially during the early years of DHH children. The involvement of deaf adults is a crucial pillar in the SLCO environment, partly for their rich linguistic resources to support the bimodal bilingual development of DHH students (as well as hearing teachers and students) and partly for their ability to instill deaf identity into the DHH and hearing students (Tang, Lam, & Yiu, 2014; Tang & Yiu, 2016). A senior kindergarten teacher noted the significance of deaf individuals' involvement:

> I witness a dramatic impact of employing a deaf adult on the whole school in the development of signing skills of my teachers. When the deaf adult becomes our colleague, we have lots of opportunities for interacting directly with each other in HKSL, sharing our work and concerns.

In fact, almost all hearing teachers for the deaf and the school's general teachers are adult second-language learners of HKSL, bringing with them characteristics of cross-linguistic influence from Cantonese. With these constraints, the deaf teachers are highly valued as their daily interactions with the hearing teachers offer constant practice in HKSL and continual improvement in proficiency.

As about 95% of DHH children are born to hearing parents, it is natural for most DHH children to identify themselves initially as members of the mainstream hearing community. Having a preference for speech over signing, DHH people with an enculturated hearing identity may not feel comfortable perceiving themselves as members of the Deaf community (Bat-Chava, 2000). Thus, many of them may end up with a marginalized identity, holding a confused or negative attitude toward deafness (McKee, 2008). A study on social acceptance of Black children by Jackson, Barth, Powell, and Lochman (2006) has provided solid evidence that the involvement of Black teachers significantly supports social integration of Black children in a regular school. Similarly, the presence of a deaf role model in the daily teaching process supports DHH students in developing a deaf identity and social integration, especially during late childhood and adolescence.

To investigate how students perceived the involvement of deaf teachers in the SLCO program, a survey was conducted with 23 DHH and 64 hearing students from Primary 4 to Secondary 1. The DHH students clearly showed a preference for deaf teachers for academic, social, or emotional support. They affirmed the role of deaf teachers as their guides, especially when encountering personal difficulties (Ho, Yiu, & Pun, 2014).

The coexistence of both a minority and a majority language as the medium of instruction in oral bilingual education facilitates intercultural understanding and thus social integration of students (Meier, 2010). Creating a naturalistic bilingual environment in the SLCO program, students, both DHH and hearing, can assimilate both hearing and Deaf cultures (Bowen, 2008; Kirchner, 1994, 2004). After studying in the SLCO program for nine years, from Kindergarten 3 to Secondary 2, a deaf student of deaf parents remarked:

> I like interacting with both deaf and hearing classmates, for the SLCO program gives deaf students opportunities to get in touch with the hearing culture, we don't want to miss the chance. . . . Regarding my identity, I don't feel strange being deaf. I feel equal like hearing people. Deaf people are able to do what hearing people can. We are the same.

In fact, the daily interactions between the deaf and hearing teachers in class vividly demonstrate how deaf and hearing people can work together, appreciate each other's characteristics, and communicate well in the real world if the communication barriers are removed (Ho, Yiu, & Pun, 2014). This phenomenon was also observed in a co-enrolled classroom with a deaf teacher reported by Jiménez-Sánchez and Antia (1999). Involvement of deaf individuals as teachers helps the hearing students not only to learn a new language but also to achieve a better understanding and a positive attitude toward deafness and deaf people.

Professional Training of Deaf Adults

As suggested in Article 24 of the UNCRPD, "States Parties shall take appropriate measures to employ teachers, including teachers with disabilities, who are qualified in sign language and/or Braille" (United Nations, 2006, p. 17). Almost no deaf adults in Hong Kong had a license to teach when the SLCO program was started in 2006. To enhance their professional recognition, there is a continuous movement to organize training programs to improve their Chinese and English literacy and to enhance their academic knowledge of sign linguistics as well as sign bilingualism in deaf education. For instance, a university-level Diploma in Deaf Education was developed in 2011 to provide deaf and hearing teachers foundational training in deaf education. Over the past three years, two deaf teaching aides have completed a three-year bachelor in education (special needs) program and one completed a postgraduate diploma in education (major in special education). All became registered teachers. Currently, another deaf teaching aide has been admitted into a similar education training program. It is the SLCO program's long-term goal to encourage more deaf people to become professional teachers for the deaf to support deaf education in the future, although Hong Kong's existing education system does not favor deaf people's tertiary education, as there is no guarantee for sign interpretation in class. Indeed, many of the SLCO students have a vision to study education so they can become deaf teachers like their predecessors, who have made tremendous efforts to bring up the next generation of DHH children.

Deaf and Hearing Co-Teaching Practices

Co-teaching in an inclusive education context refers to "the partnering of a general education teacher and a special education teacher or another specialist for the purpose of jointly delivering instruction to a diverse group of students, including those with disabilities or other special needs, in a general education setting and in a way that flexibility and deliberately meets their learning needs" (Friend, Cook, Hurley-Chamberlain, & Shamberger, 2010, p. 11).

In the SLCO program, co-teaching between a deaf teacher and a general education teacher is a preferred practice for the purpose of creating teams of deaf and hearing teachers to support each other in teaching and in daily school practices. They work together to lead the whole class and to initiate change of the school teaching and student-support culture. The spirit for them to "team up" with each other forms the cornerstone of the entire pedagogical and school processes.

But it is not easy to develop effective co-teaching between a deaf teacher and a hearing teacher. Obviously, the signing proficiency of the hearing teachers is an important factor, without which it is almost impossible to achieve mutual understanding and appreciation for bi-modal bilingualism/multilingualism in the SLCO classroom (Jiménez-Sánchez & Antia, 1999). As expressed by a hearing teacher of the primary SLCO program:

> Co-planning for lessons is very important. We talk about what contents we want to cover and in what ways they are imparted to students, using what teaching procedures and strategies. . . . I remember initially I relied a lot on myself in lesson planning; but gradually when the deaf teacher have developed confidence [in teaching], the role of deaf teachers became more prominent. . . . there should be more suggestions about how information should be presented to students, how to teach the topic or how to improve our teaching. . . . Because my sign language is not so proficient, it would be better to have two teachers . . . [the] deaf teacher knows what difficulties DHH students face in learning and is able to suggest what we can do to ensure students' understanding in class.

When the deaf and hearing teachers learn how to appreciate differences and to see each other's linguistic skills as strengths instead of weaknesses, mutual understanding between them gradually develops. In the SLCO program, periods for lesson planning represent times for the deaf and hearing teachers to intensively interact with each other. Such interaction creates opportunities to understand each other's expectations from a hearing or a deaf perspective. While the deaf teacher learns from the hearing partner the concept of adhering to a framework of curriculum development in regular schools and the corresponding teaching strategies, the hearing teacher learns from the deaf teacher how curriculum content may be conveyed through a visual-gestural modality. In essence, it is a mind-broadening experience for both parties. It is a joint venture in the development of day-to-day strategies and practice wisdom for the effective delivery of curriculum content to the students. It is also a time for the hearing teachers to receive contextually HKSL linguistic input so they can practice signing.

For most of the lessons, the teachers use a projector to display major class content on the screen. Such visual strategies provide the deaf teachers and all students the main points they need to follow. Whenever there is speech information that is not accessible to the DHH students or the deaf teachers, the hearing teachers will sign as far as possible, writing the key words on the blackboard for their reference.

When deaf teachers become an integral part of the school community, fully involved in the team teaching practices, "the most viable
benefit was the access of all children to all communication in the classroom . . . where differences were not degraded but viewed as valuable and respected" (Jiménez-Sánchez & Antia, 1999, p. 223). Future
development may require systematic recording and analysis of classroom interactions to uncover classroom pedagogies that are effective
in creating a stimulating and linguistically rich environment for both
DHH and hearing students.

Pillar 3: An Enriched Linguistic Context to Support Bimodal Bilingual Development

The SLCO program aims to remove DHH students' barriers to communication and education as far as possible. From the teachers' perspective, deaf involvement and deaf–hearing co-teaching are some of the
essential features to support bimodal bilingual development of DHH
and hearing participants in class, leading to the creation of a school
community that embraces HKSL alongside spoken languages. In a
questionnaire, principals, teachers, and other school staff, as well as
hearing students and their parents, agreed that deaf teachers are inevi-
tably the major source of sign language input.

In fact, in a bilingual education setting, incorporating a significant
number of students who use a minority language is highly valued
in inculcating social acceptance (Jackson, Barth, Powell, & Lochman,
2006) and in supporting minority language development (Baker &
Wright, 2017). To enhance bimodal bilingual development, it is also
crucial to consider how to boost the "frequency of bilingual input" in
order to advance ultimate attainment in the acquisition process (De
Houwer, 2009). All students, DHH and hearing, need individuals who
sign to them in context to enrich and sustain their HKSL development.
The deaf teachers come in handy.

Therefore, the co-enrollment practice may be interpreted from the
perspective of "two-way immersion" (Lindholm-Leary, 2001). This is
a strategy to engage both the minority DHH and the majority hearing
students in an environment that promotes "dual-language" input and
interactions to trigger bimodal bilingual acquisition at a young age as
far as possible and to facilitate education at a subsequent stage. Over
time, the accumulative critical mass of DHH students and deaf teachers
at school naturally form a small "Deaf community." Through different
interactions with their hearing peers during study and play, they start
to appreciate differences about the hearing-majority school community.
Instead of having just one or two DHH students at school, as in the current practice of integrated education in Hong Kong, the presence of a
critical mass of DHH students as well as deaf teachers naturally raises
awareness of deafness and the linguistic needs of a bimodal bilingual

classroom. The senior teacher of the kindergarten explains why integrating a critical mass of DHH students in a SLCO class is preferred:

> If there is only one deaf student in class, I may forget about him/her when I am busy teaching the whole class. When I need to do some follow-up work with the student, I will do it more on an individual basis like in a withdrawal situation, not in class . . . If I realize that there is a small group [of deaf students], like five, six or seven of them, I would consider a lot more what I could do in class.

Having a critical mass of DHH students, with about 5 or 6 DHH students studying with 14 to 26 hearing students in a ratio of 1:3 to 1:4, also signifies the need for the hearing students or teachers to communicate using HKSL. The use of HKSL in class gradually becomes a symbol for group identity of the SLCO classes; this identity was initially acquired by the DHH students led by the deaf teachers but was gradually extended to the hearing teachers and the hearing students, who value their group membership as being "bimodal bilingual." Further research is necessary to examine how hearing students in the SLCO classroom develop their HKSL knowledge and how they use this linguistic resource to interact with their DHH peers and deaf teachers in school and in accessing curriculum contents in class.

Enriched Linguistic Resources of a Bimodal Bilingual Environment

In the SLCO program, besides natural bimodal bilingual interactions, structured HKSL lessons are arranged for hearing teachers, parents, and students. All students from both SLCO and non-SLCO classes receive HKSL training, one 35-minute session a week. The schools also arrange whole-school activities to provide HKSL exposure to all students (Table 5.2).

The observation that many hearing students favor the learning of HKSL also makes the DHH students quite popular at school. Interestingly, the DHH students also learn how to accommodate their hearing peers' specific linguistic needs by modifying their signing to facilitate comprehension. Indeed, from their interviews, some of the DHH students commented that sometimes they would resort to using signs that follow the Cantonese grammar when interacting with their hearing teachers and peers, although they do not prefer this variety (Tang, Yiu, & Lam, 2015). All in all, the enhancement of the sign language abilities of hearing students facilitates the development of social relationships between the DHH and hearing students as peers and partners in education.

As for the DHH students, while developing spoken language literacy as a sign bilingual strategy is crucial, the SLCO program arranges speech therapy services to bolster their speech development. From our observation, the urge to communicate with their hearing peers/

Table 5.2. Some Major Whole-School Deaf Awareness and Sign Language Activities

Activities	Brief Descriptions
Sign Language Recess	The first recess every day, where every student, no matter DHH or hearing, is supposed to sign in class. A deaf teacher stays in class to encourage signed communication among students.
Sign Language Day	Similar to the organization of English Day, on Sign Language Day everyone in the school will sign to each other. Sometimes there are also sign language booths organized for students to learn more about HKSL.
Sign Bilingual Assemblies	Every day there are sign bilingual assemblies during the second recess. Junior sign interpreters stand on the stage and help interpret for DHH students and deaf teachers. During the assemblies, there are activities that all students sign together, such as sign language songs and weekly signed Bible verses.
Deaf Festival	In response to the call by the World Federation of the Deaf for organizing an International Week of the Deaf on the last full week of September every year, there are special activities organized in schools for about two weeks such as sign language game booths, a quiz on Deaf culture, and sign language competitions.

friends at school also motivates them to practice speech in Cantonese, especially when they perceive that some of them are not proficient in HKSL. Additionally, when a positive social relationship is established between the DHH and hearing students, it guarantees frequent direct interactions and naturalistic input to bolster the DHH students' oral language development.

Pillar 4: DHH and Hearing Students' Active Participation in School and Social Activities

Insufficient oral language skills of DHH students is always a tremendous obstacle in establishing social relations with their hearing peers in mainstream settings. Nunes, Pretzlik, and Olsson (2001) found that DHH students may not always be rejected but are more likely than hearing peers to be neglected and isolated. Major obstacles to forming friendships are often attributed to the communication barriers they have in oral language. Physically integrating DHH students in a regular school may still end up with "segregation" (Stinson & Kluwin, 2003). In the absence of effective communication, DHH students cannot participate in daily classroom learning or extracurricular activities, access the mainstream curriculum, or develop peer relations with hearing students.

In the SLCO program, DHH students are expected to fully participate in in-class or extracurricular activities. This provides many opportunities for them to interact directly with their hearing peers, either in HKSL or spoken languages. Because HKSL is promoted broadly among the hearing participants at schools through various school activities, many hearing students can develop HKSL skills to support social interactions with the DHH students, thereby encouraging the DHH students to get involved more frequently in school activities (Bowen, 2008).

Currently, the schools' policy is that all school activities are open to DHH students, which may include sports, dance and speech recitation, drama and concert performance, and overseas exchange or competitions. To support their participation, a hearing bilingual teacher or a sign language interpreter accompanies them to these activities. If a sign language interpreter is not available, some hearing students usually come forward to provide sign language support for their DHH peers (see Kreimeyer et al., this volume). By learning HKSL at school, these hearing students are aware of their DHH classmates' special needs to access information in different environments. They demonstrate their consideration and empathy for others as well as gain confidence in putting a language they learn to good use.

Seeing that some hearing students make outstanding progress in signing abilities, the SLCO program decided to set up a Junior Sign Language Interpreter (JSLI) training program as an extracurricular activity at school a few years ago. The JSLI is an enrichment program offering talented students additional opportunities to learn HKSL and to support their DHH peers' participation in school. Currently, around 40 students from Primary 2 to Secondary 4, with or without hearing loss, join the weekly training program that is taught by one deaf and one hearing teacher. Handpicked by the deaf teachers for the training programs, these junior interpreters are assigned to interpret into HKSL during assemblies or school-based activities. Parents and teachers are often amazed by their proficient signing skills and their confidence in sign interpretation.

In sum, benefits are observed by encouraging active collaborative participation of DHH and hearing students in both curricular and extracurricular activities. A deaf teacher had the following comments after teaching in the program for seven years:

[I]n the SLCO program, both deaf and hearing students follow the same curriculum. Deaf teachers sign in class and so deaf students can learn from them. Deaf students start interacting with their hearing classmates from an early age. When they grow up and come across other hearing people in their workplace, they can interact with them at ease. . . . For hearing students, the program does them good, too.

Together with their deaf classmates, they develop mutual support with each other, and learn about what are mutual acceptance and respect. In addition, they learn sign language as their second language.

PRELIMINARY EVIDENCE FOR THE PROGRAM

Evidence so far supports the positive development of DHH students in the program. Areas include their signed and spoken/written language development (Lee, Lau, Lam, Lam, Tang, & Yiu, 2014; Sze & Tang, 2016; Tang, Lam, & Yiu, 2014; Tang, Yiu, & Lam, 2015), social integration (Yiu & Tang, 2014), classroom participation (Yiu, 2015; Wong, 2017), and academic attainment (Tang & Yiu, 2016; Yiu, 2017).

The language development of children in a sign bilingual education context is always a concern of parents and educators. To address their misconception that acquiring HKSL would impede the spoken language development in DHH learners, Tang, Lam, and Yiu (2014) examined the development of Cantonese, written Chinese based on Mandarin grammar, and HKSL of a group of SLCO DHH children and found positive growth and interaction among the languages. Not only did the DHH students demonstrate positive growth in the three languages under study, they also developed a sufficient level of metalinguistic awareness to differentiate HKSL and signed Cantonese in the linguistic input embedded in the SLCO classroom (Tang, Yiu, & Lam, 2015). In the SLCO program, both DHH and hearing children are observed to use either signed or spoken language flexibly, depending on the language preference and speech abilities of the interlocutors (Tang, Yiu, & Lam, 2015). In fact, some other studies have already shown that development of one language does not necessarily hinder the development of another; on the contrary it brings additional linguistic resources to the children, whether in a unimodal bilingual context (Baker & Wright, 2017) or a bimodal bilingual context (Lee, et al., 2014; Sze & Tang, 2016). In a three-year longitudinal study to compare the Cantonese development of orally trained DHH children in a mainstream setting and bimodal bilingual DHH children in the SLCO setting, Lee et al. (2014) observed a significantly faster growth rate with DHH students in the SLCO setting than the orally trained DHH children in the mainstream setting, even though there was no significant difference in their initial Cantonese scores.

Inclusive education for DHH children has become the global trend in recent decades. Due to their difficulty in communication, one of the crucial questions is whether they are integrated well in the regular classroom socially and academically (Stinson & Antia, 1999). Yiu and Tang (2014) showed that DHH and hearing students in the SLCO program display social acceptance toward each other. In particular, the hearing students' positive attitudes toward their DHH peers are associated with the number of years of SLCO education that these DHH and hearing peers have undertaken. The positive social relationship between DHH and hearing students helped create an inclusive environment that facilitates their engagement in class. In fact, preliminary analysis by Yiu (2015) on DHH students' classroom participation showed that the SLCO DHH students could achieve a level of participation similar to their hearing peers, despite their restricted hearing and speech perception abilities.

What is the academic performance of the DHH students in the SLCO program? A preliminary analysis of the academic performance of the first four cohorts of 24 SLCO DHH students in 2017 revealed that the average pass percentages from grade 1 to 6 in three major subjects (Chinese, English, and Mathematics) ranged from 82% to 89% (Yiu, 2017). When the same 24 SLCO DHH students were assessed at grade 6 by the Learning Achievement Measurement Kit (LAMK), a standardized assessment based on territory-wide normative samples at primary grade levels developed by the Hong Kong Education Bureau in 2006, the SLCO DHH children had reached a median grade level of grade 6 in English and Mathematics, but in Chinese reading and writing they showed a one-year gap (a median grade level of grade 5; Yiu, 2017). Relative to the academic attainment of high school graduates in the United States in 2003, with median grade levels of grade 4 in reading, grade 6 in mathematical problem solving, and grade 7.5 in mathematical procedures (Qi & Mitchell, 2012), the academic performance of SLCO DHH students is generally satisfactory. Though initial results in language development as well as social and academic outcomes have provided encouraging feedback to the SLCO program, further research is required to document the pedagogical experiences to elucidate how the SLCO program benefits DHH students when they have the opportunity to receive mainstream education with HKSL support.

DISCUSSION

While mainstreaming emphasizes DHH children unilaterally "adapting" themselves to a regular school environment, co-enrollment may be seen as involving a bidirectional inclusive process in which both the deaf and the hearing participants attempt to embrace each other's differences and to benefit from each other's perceived strengths. Such a process is facilitated by the participants' readiness to learn additional languages in order to remove barriers to communication, leading to the development of positive social relations and mutual understanding.

The SLCO program also demonstrates the benefits of learning sign language by DHH children as early as possible by supporting not only their language development but also their development of social interaction skills in the regular school community. Sign language is no longer seen as a language for remediation only. Instead, in the SLCO school community, both DHH and hearing children are observed to use either sign or spoken language flexibly. Both DHH and hearing children are free to explore both HKSL and other spoken languages when communicating with each other, and language choice depends not only on the perceived hearing status but also the proficiency of especially HKSL and Cantonese of the persons communicating with them. Within the two dimensions, we observe the DHH students' and deaf teachers' readiness to moderate the signing variety to satisfy the pedagogical and communicative needs of the hearing participants, who are acquiring HKSL as a second language. In other words, it gives HKSL a new meaning in the school community. It is no longer taken to be a "minority language" adopted to reduce the negative impact of delayed language input, nor is it a language to be restricted to the Deaf community in society. It is simply an acquirable natural language by humans to satisfy the needs for communication, and through which a community of bimodal bilinguals comprising DHH and hearing members is formed within a larger hearing school community. Future research is needed to uncover what cultural values such a community embraces and to what extent such values overlap with those of the Deaf community of the society at large. What we have learned from the school is that the Deaf teachers are performing a very important role of introducing these SLCO students to the Deaf community in society through encouraging them to actively participate in their functions.

Setting up an innovative program from scratch within a predominantly hearing education system has its challenges. One difficulty the program faces is the lack of deaf individuals who are competent or confident enough to teach content subjects like chemistry, information technology, applied mathematics, and geography at the senior level, due to the previously inadequate academic training. Under those circumstances, the program needs to adjust its strategy by partnering a hearing teacher who can sign fluently with a general teacher at the senior levels to ensure that the curriculum content can be imparted to the DHH and hearing students effectively. Recently, the program has recruited a few oral deaf adults who were determined to learn HKSL and engage themselves in sign linguistics training in a higher degree. They are potential teachers for the deaf in the future and may bring in new dimensions in the development of the SLCO program.

CONCLUSION

We have summarized the four major ingredients that serve as the philosophical foundation and drive the development of the SLCO program in Hong Kong. Together they create a school environment that is free from barriers to information accessibility and is inclusive to DHH students while fulfilling the expectations of integrated education as stipulated by the government.

Co-enrollment programming is still maturing in terms of an educational reform in the world. With the concerted efforts from educators in different countries, there is evidence of preliminary success in its impact on the different aspects of child development for both DHH and hearing students (Marschark, Tang, & Knoor, 2014; see the various chapters in this book). Further development requires "thinking out of the box" or a paradigm shift, and more importantly, collaborative research to inform educators and policymakers what we can achieve further by adopting sign bilingualism and co-enrollment in deaf education programs.

ACKNOWLEDGMENTS

The authors acknowledge the generous donations of the Hong Kong Jockey Club Charities Trust, the Lee Hysan Foundation, and the Fu Tak Iam Foundation to support the establishment of Sign Bilingualism and Co-enrollment (SLCO) Education in Hong Kong. Thanks are due also to the deaf and hearing colleagues of the Centre for Sign Linguistics and Deaf Studies who participated in the teaching and research developments of the SLCO program.

REFERENCES

Baker, C., & Wright, W. (2017). *Foundations of bilingual education and bilingualism* (6th ed.). Bristol, UK: Multilingual Matters.

Bat-Chava, Y. (2000). Diversity of deaf identities. *American Annals of the Deaf, 145*, 420–428.

Bowen, S. K. (2008). Co-enrollment for students who are deaf or hard of hearing: Friendship patterns and social interactions. *American Annals of the Deaf, 153*(3), 285–293.

Courtin, C. (2000). The impact of sign language on the cognitive development of deaf children: The case of theories of mind. *Journal of Deaf Studies and Deaf Education, 5*(3), 266–276.

De Houwer, A. (2009). *Bilingual first language acquisition* (MM textbooks). Bristol, UK: Multilingual Matters.

Figueras, B., Edwards, L., & Langdon, D. (2008). Executive function and language in deaf children. *Journal of Deaf Studies and Deaf Education, 13*, 362–377.

Friend, M., & Cook, L. (1990). Collaboration as a predictor for success in school reform. *Journal of Educational and Psychological Consultation, 1*(1), 69–86.

Friend, M., Cook, L., Hurley-Chamberlain, D., & Shamberger, C. (2010). Co-teaching: An illustration of the complexity of collaboration in special education. *Journal of Educational and Psychological Consultation, 20* (1), 9–27.

Hall, M. L., Eigsti, I-M., Bortfeld, H., & Lillo-Martin, D. (2017). Auditory deprivation does not impair executive function, but language deprivation
might: Evidence from a parent-report measure in deaf native signing children. *Journal of Deaf Studies and Deaf Education, 22,* 9–21.

Ho, C. M., Yiu, K. M., & Pun, Y. S. (2014, June 20). *Deaf teachers' involvement
in the SLCO Programme: Views from students.* Paper presented at the 2014
Symposium on Sign Bilingualism and Deaf Education, Hong Kong.

Hong Kong Census and Statistics Department. (2014). *Social data collected via
the general household survey. Special topics report no. 62: Persons with disabilities
and chronic diseases.* Retrieved from http://www.statistics.gov.hk/pub/
B11301622014XXXXB0100.pdf

Hong Kong Education Bureau. (2006). *Learning Achievement Measurement Kit
(LAMK).*

Hong Kong Education Bureau. (2010, May). *Operation guide on the whole school
approach to integrated education* (2nd ed). Retrieved from http://www.edb.
gov.hk/attachment/en/edu-system/special/support/wsa/ie%20guide_
en.pdf

Hong Kong Education Bureau. (2013, September). *Response to views and concerns
raised at the meetings on 18 June and 8 July 2013.* LC Paper No. CB(4)1007/12-
13(01). Retrieved from http://www.legco.gov.hk/yr12-13/english/panels/
ed/ed_ie/papers/ed_ie0618cb4-1007-1-e.pdf

Hong Kong Education Bureau. (2014, July). *Legislative Council Panel of Education,
Subcommittee on Integrated Education Meeting on May 2014.* LC Paper No. CB(4)
935/13-14(02). Retrieved from http://www.legco.gov.hk/yr13-14/english/
panels/ed/ed_ie/papers/ed_ie0528cb4-935-2-e.pdf

Hong Kong Government. (1977). *White paper: Integrating disabled into the community: A united effort.*

Hong Kong Legislative Council. (2014, September). *Panel on Education,
Subcommittee on Integrated Education: Report.* LC Paper No. CB(4)1087/13-
14(01). Retrieved from http://www.legco.gov.hk/yr13-14/english/panels/
ed/ed_ie/reports/ed_iecb4-1087-1-e.pdf

Hong Kong Special School Council & Committee on Home School Cooperation. (2017). *Special school profiles.* Retrieved from https://www.chsc.
hk/spsp/brief.php

Jackson, M. F., Barth, J. M., Powell, N., & Lochman, J. E. (2006). Classroom contextual effects of race on children's peer nominations. *Child Development,
77*(5), 1325–1337.

Jiménez-Sánchez, C., & Antia, S. (1999). Team-teaching in an integrated classroom: Perceptions of deaf and hearing teachers. *Journal of Deaf Studies and
Deaf Education, 4*(3), 215–224.

Kirchner, C. J. (1994). Co-enrollment as an inclusion model. *American Annals of
the Deaf, 139*(2), 163–164.

Kirchner, C. J. (2004). Co-enrollment: an effective answer to the mainstream de-
bacle. In D. Power & G. Leigh (Eds.), *Educating deaf students: Global perspectives*
(p. 161–174). Washington, DC: Gallaudet University Press.

Lee, K., Lau, T., Lam, E., Lam, J., Tang, G., & Yiu, K. M. (2014, June 20). *The oral
language development of deaf children in a sign bilingualism and co-enrollment program.* Paper presented at the 2014 Symposium on Sign Bilingualism and Deaf
Education, Hong Kong.

Lindholm-Leary, K. (2001). *Dual language education (bilingual education & bilingualism)*. Clevedon, UK: Multilingual Matters Limited.

Luckner, J., Rude, H., & Sileo, T. (1989). Collaborative consultation: A method for improving educational services for mainstreamed students who are hearing impaired. *American Annals of the Deaf, 134*(5), 301–304.

Marschark, M., Tang, G., & Knoors, H. (2014) *Bilingualism and bilingual deaf education*. New York: Oxford University Press.

Mayberry, R. I. (2007). When timing is everything: Age of first-language acquisition effects on second-language learning. *Applied Psycholinguistics, 28*(3), 537–549.

Mckee, R. L. (2008). The construction of deaf children as marginal bilinguals in the mainstream. *International Journal of Bilingual Education and Bilingualism, 11*(5), 519–540.

Meier, G. (2010). Two-way immersion education in Germany: Bridging the linguistic gap. *International Journal of Bilingual Education and Bilingualism, 13*(4), 419–437.

Nunes, T., Pretzlik, U., & Olsson, J. (2001). Deaf children's social relationships in mainstream schools. *Deafness & Education International, 3*(3), 123–136.

Qi, S., & Mitchell, R. (2012). Large-scale academic achievement testing of deaf and hard-of-hearing students: Past, present, and future. *Journal of Deaf Studies and Deaf Education, 17*(1), 1–18.

Stinson, M., & Antia, S. (1999). Considerations in educating deaf and hard-of-hearing students in inclusive settings. *Journal of Deaf Studies and Deaf Education, 4*(3), 163–175.

Stinson, M. S., & Kluwin, T. N. (2003). Educational consequences of alternative school placements. In M. Marschark & M. E. Spencer (Eds.), *Oxford handbook of deaf studies, language, and education* (pp. 52–64). New York: Oxford University Press.

Swanwick, R. (2016). Deaf children's bimodal bilingualism and education. *Language Teaching, 49*(1), 1–34.

Sze, F., Lo, C., Lo, L., & Chu, K. (2013). Historical development of Hong Kong Sign Language. *Sign Language Studies, 13*(2), 155–185.

Sze, F., & Tang, G. (2016). Metalinguistic awareness in the bimodal-bilingual acquisition of locative sentences in Chinese and Hong Kong Sign Language by deaf/hard of hearing children. *Journal of Applied Psycholinguistics, 16*(2), 101–132.

Tang, G., Lam, S., & Yiu, K. M. (2014). Language development of deaf children in a sign bilingual and co-enrollment environment. In M. Marschark, G. Tang, & H. Knoors (Eds.), *Bilingualism and bilingual deaf education* (pp. 313–341). New York: Oxford University Press.

Tang, G., & Yiu, K. M. (2016). Developing sign bilingualism in a co-enrollment school environment: A Hong Kong case study. In M. Marschark & P. E. Spencer (Eds.), *The Oxford handbook of deaf studies in language* (pp. 197–217). New York: Oxford University Press.

Tang, G., Yiu, K. M., & Lam, S. (2015). Awareness of HKSL and manually coded Chinese by deaf students learning in a sign bilingual and co-enrollment setting: A Hong Kong case study. In H. Knoors & M. Marschark (Eds.), *Educating deaf learners: Creating a global evidence base* (pp. 117–148). New York: Oxford University Press.

Thomson, C. (2013). Collaborative consultation to promote inclusion: Voices from the classroom. *International Journal of Inclusive Education, 17*(8), 882–894.

United Nations. (2006). *Convention on the Rights of Persons with Disabilities.* Retrieved from http://www.un.org/disabilities/convention/conventionfull. shtml

Wong, F. (2017). *The interactional patterns of hearing, Deaf/hard of hearing (D/HH) students participating in Hong Kong sign bilingual and co-enrollment classroom.* Unpublished doctoral dissertation, University of Hong Kong.

Yiu, K. M. (2015, July). *Classroom participation of deaf and hard of hearing students in a sign bilingualism and co-enrollment (SLCO) education setting.* Paper presented at the 22nd International Congress on the Education of the Deaf: Educating Diverse Learners: Many Ways, One Goal. Athens, Greece: Deaf Studies Unit, University of Patras. Retrieved from https://dl.dropboxusercontent.com/u/6204930/Proceedings_ICED_2015_FINAL.pdf

Yiu, K. M. (2017, July 24). *Academic performance of deaf and hard-of-hearing (DHH) students in the Sign Bilingualism and Co-enrollment in Deaf Education (SLCO) Programme.* Paper presented at SSC/Adept Conference, Scotland.

Yiu, K. M., & Tang, G. (2014). Social integration of deaf and hard-of-hearing students in a sign bilingual and co-enrollment environment. In M. Marschark, G. Yang, & H. Knoors (Eds.), *Bilingualism and bilingual deaf education* (pp. 342–367). New York: Oxford University Press.

6

Co-Enrollment Models of Preschool for Deaf and Hard-of-Hearing Children in Israel

Dalia Ringwald-Frimerman, Sara Ingber, and Tova Most

HISTORY OF CO-ENROLLMENT KINDERGARTENS IN ISRAEL

The first kindergarten co-enrollment classes for deaf and hard-of-hearing (DHH) children in Israel were established during the 1960s. Before then, only self-contained preschool classes were available (Plaut, 2007). The number of co-enrollment classes gradually increased over the next 20 years. This trend in the Israeli educational system reflects a worldwide shift that acknowledges the rights of children with special needs to be educated in the "least restrictive educational environment" that best complies with their educational needs (Al-Yagon, Aram, & Margalit, 2016). In response to these changes in the societal perceptions and attitudes toward individuals with disabilities, the Israeli Special Education Law was passed in 1988, followed by the Act of Inclusion in 2002 and the amendment in 2018 (The national legislation database of the State of Israel, 2018; Israeli Ministry of Education and Culture, 2002). This law mandates an orientation to the least restrictive educational option that best secures the child's educational needs. This policy is taken into consideration in the workings of the "eligibility committees" that decide the extant of child's eligibility for special education services, based on functional behavioral assessments as well as the disability characteristics.

Another important change during this same period was the growing recognition of parents' right to be full partners in their child's educational and habilitation program. In Israel, parents now have the legal right to be present during the deliberations of the eligibility committee and to state their preference for the type of educational framework they want for their child, as well as to be fully informed, participate in planning, and approve their child's individual intervention program (Al-Yagon et al., 2016; Most, Weisel, & Ezrachi, 2009). In most cases, after a discussion with the eligibility committee members, the parents' choice is accepted.

The general trend toward inclusive education[1] in Israel has been driven in part by advances in technology of advanced sensory devices such as digital hearing aids and cochlear implants, the implementation of newborn hearing screening in 2010, and the development of language intervention and other educational programs adjusted to Hebrew and the Israeli culture (Dromi, Fux, Ringwald-Frimerman, & Tzohar, 2003; Dromi & Ringwald-Frimerman, 1999), and the creation of academic programs in DHH education (Most et al., 2009; Most & Ringwald-Frimerman, 2014). As a result, more DHH preschoolers exhibit better spoken language skills than ever before, and more young DHH children are now enrolled in mainstream education. Also, since the majority of the parents of the children have typical hearing, as compared to parents with hearing loss, they prefer to have their child attend an individual inclusion kindergarten in their neighborhood rather than co-enrollment settings that often are further away (Most et al., 2009). For example, Plaut (2007, p. 437) reported that from 2001 to 2005 the percentage of DHH kindergarteners who attended individual inclusion classes in Israel rose from 19.81% to 54.68%, whereas the percentage of children in co-enrollment settings decreased. No self-contained preschool classes were reported during this period.

Currently, three basic types of educational frameworks are available to preschool DHH children in Israel: individual inclusion, co-enrollment classes, and self-contained classes. Current data published on the official website of the Ministry of Education, Special Education Department, Supervision of Education for DHH Students show that about 80% of all DHH children in the Israeli educational system are enrolled in individual inclusion, about 15% in co-enrollment, and only 5% in self-contained educational settings (retrieved September 1, 2017, from https://sites.google.com/a/lakash.tzafonet.org.il/main/demograf).

A number of challenges involved in the successful co-enrollment of DHH preschoolers have been discussed in the literature. These challenges were taken into consideration in constructing the infrastructure of the educational co-enrollment system in Israel. The key issues are reviewed in this chapter, including accessibility to auditory habilitation, teaching communication and language in typical (hearing) preschool environments, the use of various communication methods, ways to support the development of social skills, self-identity, and proactive participation in daily kindergarten life, as well as attitudes of family members toward different educational frameworks along the inclusion continuum. The challenges of working in a multidisciplinary team in inclusion settings with DHH preschoolers are also explored. Then, we describe how the Israeli preschool co-enrollment system for DHH children has been structured to respond to these challenges.

CHALLENGES TO CO-ENROLLMENT OF PRESCHOOL DHH CHILDREN

The period of early childhood is crucial for the habilitation and education of DHH children. Brain plasticity makes intervention programs dealing with these children's auditory habilitation, language development, and the establishment of cognitive and social skills crucial at this vulnerable period of life (Marschark, Lang, & Albertini, 2002). For these reasons, issues related to physical, academic, and social educational environment should be considered when designing and implementing early intervention (EI) programs for inclusion settings where DHH preschoolers learn in regular kindergarten environments.

Auditory Accessibility of DHH Children in Preschool Settings

In early childhood, most DHH children lag behind hearing children in their spoken language development (Marschark & Spencer, 2011), which in turn limits their communicative resources to participate in the complex spontaneous conversations engaged in by their hearing peers (e.g., Blum-Kulka & Hamo, 2010; Hamo & Blum-Kulka, 2007; Kristoffersen & Simonsen, 2014; Spencer & Marschark, 2010). Co-enrollment preschool educational environments are characterized by and encourage parallel interactions among groups of children that take place in an unstructured, spontaneous way (e.g., Kristoffersen & Simonsen, 2014; see Kirchner, this volume). It has been argued that most learning in preschool children occurs through incidental learning in the course of these free play activities (DeHart, Sroufe, & Cooper, 2004). However, many DHH preschoolers experience enormous difficulties acquiring spoken language skills in regular kindergarten environments because of the noisy background and crosstalk that usually characterizes informal activities.

This issue needs to be addressed in the educational management of learning spaces of DHH preschoolers by ensuring prerequisites such as optimal fitting of hearing devices (cochlear implants [CIs], hearing aids, FM systems), monitoring of the acoustic environment, and creating an accessible physical environment that provides adequate conditions for listening as well as visual perception of speech or spatial/visual communication (e.g., sign-supported speech or sign language) (Antia & Levine, 2001; Moeller, Carr, Seaver, Stredler-Brown, & Holzinger, 2013; Uhler, Thomson, Cyr, Gabbard, & Yoshinaga-Itano, 2014).

The Critical Age Hypothesis and the Choice of Communication Method

According to the critical age hypothesis,[2] the human brain is able to acquire a linguistic system spontaneously on a maturational-driven basis during a limited period in early childhood (Kuhl, 2004; Newport,

2006). The overwhelming acknowledgment of the consequences of congenital hearing loss on spoken language acquisition has prompted a
debate in the field of deaf education related to the choice of communication method in early childhood. Proponents of the aural-oral method,
which exposes the DHH child to spoken language alone, argue that
at the critical language-acquisition period the educational endeavor
should be focused on intensive teaching of auditory and spoken language skills without any exposure to signs. This reasoning is based on
studies showing that exposure to signs may limit the efficiency of the
auditory cortex to process speech stimuli or develop spoken language
(Nishimura et al., 1999). These findings have been supported by more
recent studies involving CI users that show that early implantation
reduces the gap between spoken language achievements of "orally" educated DHH children and their hearing age-mates (e.g., Connor, Craig,
Raudenbush, Heavner, & Zwolan, 2006; Waltzman & Roland, 2005).

On the other hand, advocates of the bilingual-bicultural method,
which favors exposing the child to the linguistic systems of both sign
language and spoken language (see Marschark, Tang, & Knoors, 2014),
are concerned that DHH children enrolled in oral-only programming
and who fail to reach a satisfactory level in spoken language during
the critical age period may experience linguistic deprivation. These
children risk not having sufficient knowledge of any language before
they enter school, which is likely to impede their linguistic, cognitive,
and social-emotional development (Fischer, 1998; Humphries et al.,
2012). Studies have shown that early exposure to sign language is crucial, since later exposure (ages 5 to 10) results in limited mastery of
its grammar (Mayberry, 2007; Mayberry & Lock, 2003). According to
proponents of this approach, sign language allows the DHH child to
acquire full-blown language spontaneously during the critical period,
stimulating the language centers of the brain and avoiding delays in
language acquisition (Mayberry, 2007). Proponents of this approach
argue that the acquisition of sign language does not affect auditory habilitation and that spoken language development can take place in parallel (Humphries et al., 2012).

Another common communication approach in DHH education is
known as Total Communication (TC). This philosophy advocates the use
of aural, manual, and oral modes of communication to ensure fluent and
effective communication with DHH children. TC is often implemented
in the form of *simultaneous communication*, which uses spoken language accompanied by signs, most of which are borrowed from the
sign language lexicon, although some have been invented to represent the spoken language grammar visually (Fischer, 1998; Marschark
et al., 2002; Moores, 2001). Advocates of the TC approach claim that
when a toddler experiences a significant lag in acquiring spoken language, exposure to supportive signs may enable the establishment of

meaningful communication with the proximal environment. In addition, supportive signs can pave the way to sign language acquisition or can serve as a supportive method until DHH children master spoken language and can communicate effectively through it (e.g., Knoors & Marschark, 2012; Kovach, 2015). Since the majority of DHH children are born to hearing parents (e.g., Mitchell & Karchmer, 2004) who do not master a formal sign language, simultaneous communication may be easier for them. Thus, it could be argued that simultaneous communication can serve as a primary method of communication as well as a bridge to good proficiency in sign language.

Even today, there is no consensus among researchers and educators as to which communication method is best, and no single method will be best for all deaf children. Further, there is a greater realization that no one method can fit all the needs of DHH children or suit all families' sociocultural background (e.g., deaf families who use sign language as the home language and hearing families that use a spoken language, perhaps one different than is used in school) (Marschark et al., 2014).

The use of sign language and/or simultaneous communication in co-enrollment frameworks is very common, unlike in individual inclusion settings (see Hennies & Hennies, this volume). In co-enrollment settings, DHH children have the opportunity to interact by signing with peers (either DHH peers or hearing peers who have learned some signs). By contrast, in individual inclusion settings, even when a sign language interpreter is available, free-ranging peer interactions through signs are usually impossible, since the hearing peers do not know any signs (e.g., Most et al., 2009).

Supporting Communication Skills in the Educational Setting

One of the main goals of intervention programs for young DHH children is to establish effective communication processes with significant adults (e.g., Spencer, 2003). A key variable in ensuring communication and high-quality interactions in the educational setting is the ratio of number of adults to children in the class (Post, Hohmann, & Epstein, 2011; Theilheimer, 2006). For DHH children this adult/children ratio is particularly important, because a DHH child may miss much of the spontaneous environmental discourse and needs to experience more intensive qualitative-direct interactions with adults.

Studies have shown that even when the adult/children ratio is satisfactory, teachers of mainstream preschool children need guidance in how to interact and mediate language and communication to young children in general (National Academies of Sciences, Engineering, and Medicine, 2016) and to DHH children in particular (e.g., Kristoffersen & Simonsen, 2014). More intensive guidance can take place in co-enrollment settings than in individual inclusion settings when multidisciplinary teams work closely together (e.g., Martin, Balanzategui, & Morgan, 2014).

Peer Relations Between DHH and Hearing Children in Inclusion Settings

The early education setting is a key arena for children outside the familiar boundaries of the family. During this period children experience a range of social relations, some mediated by adults and others spontaneous. They initiate social communication, experience negotiations with peers, and develop socio-pragmatic skills such as how to interact in disagreements, conflicts, and communication failures (Hamo & Blum-Kulka, 2007). Rich social experiences are as important for DHH children as for hearing children. Thus, the type of the inclusion setting has important ramifications in terms of the nature and scope of the child's social interactions with hearing and DHH peers. Co-enrollment settings can provide children in both groups with various opportunities to interact and practice social and communication skills.

However, there are a number of hurdles to overcome. Studies have shown that DHH children in co-enrollment preschool classes tend to play more among themselves and less with hearing peers (Antia & Levine, 2001; Antia, Stinson, & Gausted, 2002; Kluwin, Stinson, & Colarossi, 2002; Most, Ingber, & Heled-Ariam, 2012; Nunes, Pretzlik, & Olsson, 2001). Other studies have reported that in a co-enrollment setting, many DHH preschoolers were less well accepted by hearing children compared to other hearing peers in the same kindergarten, especially when they had poor speech intelligibility (Most et al., 2012; Nunes et al., 2001).

A review of studies on the social relations of young DHH children points to several variables that can affect the success of social integration in co-enrollment settings. Among these is the length of time in the presence of hearing children (Kluwin, et al., 2002; Kreimeyer, Crooke, Drye, Egbert, & Klein, 2000) and the level of speech intelligibility of the DHH child. DHH children with poor speech intelligibility may not be understood by their hearing peers, and this may lead to rejection and with time to lower self-image, fewer social interactions with hearing peers, and loneliness (Bat-Chava & Deignan, 2001; Most et al., 2012).

These findings thus suggest that in comparison to individual inclusion settings, the co-enrollment setting may protect DHH children from being isolated, in that they have the opportunity to interact with other DHH peers, not necessarily through spoken language. Guidance and active involvement of the educational staff will encourage familiarity between the DHH child and hearing children and help DHH children to benefit from the social environment in mainstream educational settings (Kluwin et al., 2002; Kreimeyer et al., 2000).

Adjusting the Curriculum to DHH Children's Needs

Another key goal of the co-enrollment of DHH preschoolers is to enable these children to acquire knowledge and skills to benefit from the general kindergarten curriculum (Kirchner, 1994). The decision to incorporate a DHH child into a partial co-enrollment, full enrollment, or individual inclusion setting should be based not only on the child's language skills but also on the child's ability to be an active learner in the regular kindergarten curriculum (see Abbate, this volume).

Preschool learning primarily involves experiential activities that take place in activities designed by the educational team or in incidental learning situations. Free play, where acquiring knowledge is spontaneous and incidental, is a very important learning context in preschool (DeHart et al., 2004). DHH children may, however, miss out on a considerable amount of the incidental information that is not addressed to them directly. They may miss much in informal situations characterized by multiple-member conversations. In the absence of proper adult mediation, DHH children may experience fragmented information and have difficulties understanding the significance of situations; they may not grasp sequences of events, planning, and reasoning. In addition, the reduction and disruption of the ongoing linguistic input may lead to impaired construction of world knowledge (e.g., Spencer & Marschark, 2010).

The educational team in the co-enrollment kindergarten needs to expose DHH children to multiple teaching strategies so they can participate successfully in the daily routines of the preschool class. These strategies include focusing on the discussion topics, interpreting communicational intent, expansion of utterances, explanations, demonstrations, and description of the activities and circumstances. It also requires introducing the child to the key concepts and keywords that will be taught (Luckner & Cooke, 2010). The most suitable organization of the kindergarten environment should also be considered. If the space in the educational setting is designed properly, it provides children with physical, symbolic, and contextual cues, such as the "shop," the "clinic," and so on (e.g., Inan, 2009).

Parental Involvement in the Decision on the Educational Setting

Parents of DHH children face numerous decisions during the early childhood period, such as the selection of hearing devices (hearing aids and/or CI), choice of communication method, and educational setting (Luterman, 2003; Steinberg, Bain, Li, Montoya, & Ruperto, 2002). All of these decisions are made by the parents when still in the initial phases of adapting to the information that their child is DHH, when they are very vulnerable (Ingber, 2004). The vulnerability and stability of the family is affected by a variety of factors related to the child, the parents, and the family structure (Ingber, Al-Yagon, & Dromi, 2013). EI programs need to establish partnership relations with the parents, should provide assistance to families to facilitate parents' decision making when adapting to the changing needs of their child, and should help parents cope with their own emotional distress (Guralnick, 2017; O'Leary, 2001).

Most hearing parents want to integrate their child into hearing society and thus choose individual inclusion, with the hope that the child will acquire spoken language and will be exposed to the norms of hearing society (Kaiser & Hancock, 2003; Lane, 2005; Lang, 2003). However, other hearing parents prefer to expose their child to signs as well, either by teaching them via bilingual bicultural programming or using simultaneous communication. These parents believe that this choice will help the child communicate fluently from early infancy and feel accepted by DHH peers as a full partner. Deaf parents who interact by sign language tend to choose an educational setting that will expose their DHH child to sign language (Lane, 2005; Mitchell & Karchmer, 2004) and preserve their cultural identity.

To make a decision that fits the child's abilities and needs as well as the aspirations of the parents and family values, parents need the guidance of professionals. Through mutual dialogue, professionals can inform parents about the various implications of educational settings (Beni-Noked, Ingber, & Ringwald-Frimerman, 2014; Eleweke & Rodda, 2000).

Multidisciplinary Teamwork in Early Childhood Settings

The multidisciplinary teamwork approach is broadly recognized in EI programs for young children with special needs and their families (Guralnick, 2017; McGonigel, Woodruff, & Roszmann-Millican, 1994). An intervention designed for DHH children requires the collaboration of experts from different disciplines such as teachers of DHH children (TODHHs), speech-language therapists, otolaryngologists, audiologists, occupational therapists, social workers, and psychologists. This team further expands when DHH children are integrated in preschool settings and also includes members of the regular education staff. To collaborate and work together as a team, differences in attitudes, beliefs, and expectations must be bridged (Guralnick, 2017; Reiter & Schalock, 2008; Sandberg & Ottosson, 2010; Smith & Erevelles, 2004; Westwood, 2009).

The co-enrollment of DHH children in regular educational settings where professionals from different disciplines are involved may elicit disagreements on issues such as the specific responsibilities of each professional member, and the perception of the partnership process. A formal definition of the expectations and the fostering of constructive dialogue between the team members can help improve the multidisciplinary teamwork (Antia et al., 2002; Lieber, Wolery, Horn, Tschantz, Beckman, & Hanson, 2002; Sandberg & Ottosson, 2010). Special attention should be paid to collaboration between the TODHHs and the regular teacher, since the two are simultaneously in charge of the DHH child's education. This type of coordination and cooperation can lead to success (Antia, 1999; Antia et al., 2002; Avramidis & Norwich, 2002).

THE CO-ENROLLMENT PRESCHOOL EDUCATIONAL SYSTEM IN ISRAEL

In general, the co-enrollment preschool settings of DHH children in Israel adhere to the principles of the ecological system theory and address the challenges facing deaf education in EI co-enrollment settings. The philosophy starts from the premise that child development is influenced by different levels of the environmental system, from direct interactions with individuals such as family members, caretakers, and educators up to a more distant macro system that relates to national and cultural institutions, such as laws and authorities (Bronfenbrenner, 2001; Guralnick, 2017). For children with special needs, the interrelationships among components within and between systems at different levels are particularly important (Guralnick, 2001, 2017).

In Israel's national special education system, the DHH co-enrollment preschool settings serve children aged 3 to 7 (Fig. 6.1).Israeli special education laws stipulate that DHH children in co-enrollment classes are eligible for support services that include an acoustic-visual physically accessible learning environment, speech and language therapy

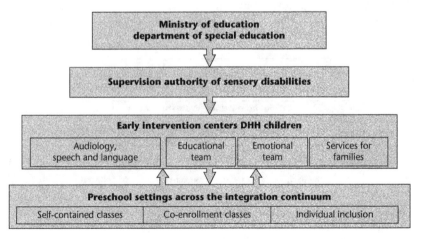

Figure 6.1. The national system of DHH preschool education for 3- to 7-year-olds in Israel.

(two to three hours weekly), adapted instruction by expert TODHHs, accommodations in the regular academic curriculum as well as exclusive educational programs, therapy from health and psychoemotional professionals (e.g., occupational therapy, art therapy), in addition to support services and instructional services for their families. Sign language interpreting services are not provided in preschools because the communication methods used at that age in educational settings in Israel are the oral method and the TC method in the form of simultaneous communication alone. However, sign language interpreting services are provided in school-age co-enrollment and self-contained settings where Israeli sign language is used.

The preschool co-enrollment educational settings operate under the auspices of seven regional multidisciplinary EI centers that supply comprehensive supportive services for DHH children and families. The multidisciplinary teams at each EI center include audiologists, speech and language therapists, emotional therapists, expert TODHHs, and pedagogical instructors.

Representative expert professionals from these local teams take part in leading national instruction teams under the Special Education Department at the Ministry of Education (Fig. 6.2). The national instruction teams are responsible for providing guidance and support to the local multidisciplinary staff at the EI centers and at co-enrollment and individual inclusion kindergartens around the country. These teams develop in-service courses and educational tools for all those involved in working with DHH children in inclusion settings (regular education staffs, deaf education staff, speech-language therapists, families of DHH children), develop educational programs adjusted to the needs of DHH children, and assimilate new programs and educational tools in the field. The guidance and implementation processes are enacted through close collaboration with the local educational staff of the DHH

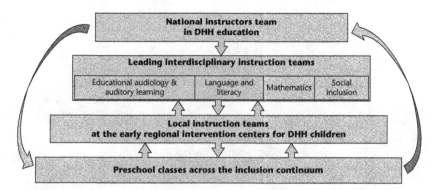

Figure 6.2. The hierarchical structure of national instruction teams in DHH education.

EI regional centers. This structural organization enables (a) an effective information flow from the national leading instruction teams to the regional staff at the EI centers and vice versa, (b) ongoing professional development of the multidisciplinary staff of the EI centers, (c) immediate exposure at the regional EI centers to new educational tools, and (d) the ability to pool resources among the EI centers by sharing accumulating experience, ideas, and local educational initiatives. The advantage of this hierarchical structure of the national instruction teams lies in their ability to implement dynamic changes in the support needs of the professional staff at educational settings around the country.

Characteristics of the DHH Populations in Co-Enrollment Settings

The decision regarding the placement of DHH preschoolers in an educational setting in Israel involves the evaluation of the child's functioning by a professional multidisciplinary team and the assessment of family expectations. Special attention is given to auditory skills, communication, speech and oral language development, social-emotional competence, and academic capabilities. The multidisciplinary team discusses and recommends the educational setting that best accommodates the child's needs with the parents. Family values and available support services are taken into consideration. Frequently, DHH children who are referred to co-enrollment settings present delays in their spoken language development, rely more on visual learning (either pictorial or simultaneous communication), may have additional developmental difficulties, and may manifest difficulties in socioemotional adjustment. Hence, these children need more intensive intervention and professional scaffolding during the school day and in most academic content areas and developmental domains. However, throughout the preschool years children may move from one kind of educational setting to another according to their progress in language, academic, and social functioning. The child's progress is monitored by a yearly interdisciplinary assessment process. The characteristics of the DHH population at co-enrollment preschool settings reflect the process described earlier of the general trend in special education in Israel from separated classes to co-enrollment, and then from co-enrollment to individual inclusion.

Implementation of Three Models of Preschool Co-Enrollment Classes

In Israel, there are a wide variety of co-enrollment preschool classes that differ in terms of the extent of shared activities of DHH children with hearing children as well as in the degree of partnership among the multidisciplinary team members. In all co-enrollment models the kindergarten class has about 25 hearing children and 6 to 10 DHH children. An acoustic-visual accessible environment is available in all kindergarten spaces. The multidisciplinary team comprises the regular kindergarten teacher and an educational assistant and the deaf education staff, which includes an expert TODHH, a special education assistant, a speech-language therapist, an occupational therapist, and an emotional therapist (e.g., art therapist). In addition, there is a supportive staff composed of a social worker, psychologist, and educational counselor who provide regular professional services to the kindergarten (staff, children, and parents).

The DHH children receive a number of individual therapy sessions during the week according to their needs. These individual therapies include speech-language therapy, occupational therapy, or art therapy. Children also attend the EI regional center for hearing assessment, auditory monitoring, and evaluation of hearing devices. The parents receive guidance and support from the professional staff and if needed they have sessions with the social worker or psychologist.

Three examples of different co-enrollment models are described next and their key advantages and disadvantages are discussed. Aspects common to all three models are described, including the communication methods used in the co-enrollment settings, curriculum accommodations and mediation, ways of monitoring children's progress, and ways of encouraging an atmosphere of partnership in the functioning of the multidisciplinary team. Differences in the co-enrollment models are indicated whenever they exist.

Side-by-Side Classes

In this form of co-enrollment there are separate classes for the group of DHH children and the group of hearing children. Shared activities usually take place in the inclusive class space—that is, in the hearing class. In many co-enrollment classes, the separate spaces are connected by a small corridor so children can move from one class's space to another, either freely or when directed to by the teacher. The playground area is usually common. Most of the formal learning activities, such as the morning and noon meetings, and certain language and literacy instruction activities are held in the separate DHH class, but at free play time, on the playground, and during rhythmic lessons and celebrations, the children from the DHH group join the inclusive class.[3] At free play time hearing children may choose to play in the DHH class and vice versa.

The extent of participation in shared activities can vary from one educational setting to another. In most side-by-side classes, the individual teaching program for each DHH child is planned, implemented, and monitored by the deaf education staff. Reports and meetings with parents are conducted by the deaf education staff. Shared activities are jointly coordinated by the teacher for the hearing children together with the TODHHs.

This partial co-enrollment model is designed for DHH children who would have severe social and academic difficulties in an individual inclusion or even in a full-time co-enrollment kindergarten because they need more intensive intervention during the sensitive period of early childhood to acquire basic hearing, language, literacy, and social skills. The disadvantages of this model are (1) the reduced exposure to interactions with hearing children because the partnership between the two groups is limited and (2) the risk of feeling like "visitors" in the inclusion (hearing) class (Antia, et al., 2002).

Partial Co-Enrollment with Heterogeneous Age Group

In this model, the DHH group consists of younger and older kindergarteners between the ages of 3 and 7. Their special education class is located within a complex that serves a cluster of three classes of hearing children. The DHH children start the school day separately in their own class, where they receive adapted teaching and preparation for the shared activities with the regular class. Later on, the group splits according to chronological age when they join the regular classes (ages 3 and 4 and ages 5 and 6). In the regular classes, they are accompanied by the assistant of DHH. These assistants mediate the DHH children's academic activities and social activities but also encourage the children to deal with everyday issues independently. During inclusion time, the TODHHs give individual supportive lessons for the DHH children and also invite small groups comprising a DHH child and hearing peers to take part in a shared activity to encourage social relationships. The small groups may also serve hearing children who need some support in developing social relationships. Shared activities in co-enrollment are coordinated by the TODHHs and the regular teachers. Individual teaching programs for each DHH child are planned separately by the deaf education staff but incorporate the viewpoint of the regular teacher. Reports and meetings with parents are held separately with the deaf education staff and the regular staff; however, the teams may prepare together before meetings with parents.

The main advantage of this model is that it affords intensive support to the DHH children, and it also encourages the development of social relations with hearing peers. The disadvantage is that the staff of DHH needs to coordinate educational activities with the two different teams working with the younger and older regular classes. In addition, only two or three DHH children attend the hearing peer group class together. The hearing class includes about 25 to 30 hearing children. This ratio of DHH children to hearing children is less than that recommended in the published literature on co-enrollment principles in DHH education (e.g., Antia & Metz, 2014).

Full-Time Co-Enrollment

In full-time co-enrollment kindergarten classes, in addition to the large shared activity space, there is a smaller resource room used exclusively for teaching language/literacy reinforcement and pre-preparation classes for the regular kindergarten formal conventions. Additional rooms for speech/language and other therapies are also available. In this model, the DHH group spends almost the whole day in co-enrollment settings with hearing children. Individual adapted teaching is given to the DHH children in a small resource room. Separate DHH group activities with the TODHHs precede the morning co-enrollment integration, so that the DHH children are able to participate in all academic and social events with the hearing children. If needed, the TODHHs mediate the academic and social events by using speech supported by a sign communication method. In this model, the transdisciplinary team approach is fully implemented; thus, TODHHs and general education teachers design almost all the educational activities together, and they support each other during the day. In the co-teaching model, the regular teacher takes responsibility together with the TODHHs for the DHH children's academic and social progress. During the school day, the TODHHs mediate the kindergarten activities for the DHH children, using simultaneous communication or spoken language as needed. This teacher also provides children with enrichment and language lessons that are taught in the resource room. In a kindergarten setting, once a week the DHH group is taught separately in a special class at the EI center where they receive audiological services, individual therapies, and enrichment activities. Once every three weeks, the hearing children and their staff join the DHH children to spend the school day together at the EI center. The rationale for this idea is to let the DHH children feel truly "at home" and have the opportunity to serve as "hosts" (see Antia & Metz, 2014, and Antia et al., 2002, for a critical discussion of the "visitor" idea in group inclusion settings). In the full co-enrollment model, the individual teaching program for each DHH child is first planned separately by the deaf education staff and then discussed with the regular teacher. Some meetings and reports with parents are held by the deaf education staff separately and others together with the regular staff.

The main advantages of this model include full involvement in regular kindergarten activities along with intensive support provided by the deaf education staff. Furthermore, the high level of partnership between the regular teacher and the TODHH contributes to the intervention efficiency and coherency (Guralnick, 2005, 2017). In addition, as DHH children may experience a sense of isolation in individual inclusion settings, the opportunity to develop social relationships both with hearing and DHH peers leads to greater emotional well-being (e.g., Antia & Metz, 2014). The disadvantage of this model is mainly for those DHH children who experience serious difficulties when trying to function socially, linguistically, and academically in these challenging educational environments.

Communication Methods in Co-Enrollment Settings

The DHH groups in co-enrollment settings in Israel are heterogeneous with respect to children's needs and parents' preferences of communication methods. Therefore, an effort is made to accommodate the communication methods used by the deaf education staff to each child's needs. In most co-enrollment settings, simultaneous communication is used in the exclusive group activities and in interactions with most of the DHH children during the school day. In addition, a new storytelling program in Israeli sign language for these classes was recently written and is now being piloted.

In a few co-enrollment classes, the DHH group only uses spoken communication, usually because the children have better spoken language skills. When needed, the deaf education staff mediates the regular teacher's talk in shared formal learning events by using speech supported by signs. In full co-enrollment settings, the regular teacher may try to use some signs in communication with a DHH child. Activities such as teaching songs accompanied by signs to all children may encourage the hearing children to use some signs when interacting with DHH peers. However, these occurrences are sporadic. Regular teachers can enroll in in-service sign language courses, but because this is not mandatory, not all teachers do so.

Curriculum Accommodations and Mediation

The national preschool academic curriculum is implemented in all preschool co-enrollment settings. However, special adaptations are made to meet the needs of DHH preschoolers. In full-time co-enrollment classes, the TODHHs follow the mainstream curriculum more closely since the DHH children spend most of their time with the hearing children. Components of the special intervention programs are integrated by TODHHs when they work in small group activities and in individual supportive lessons. As mentioned earlier, in side-by-side and other partial co-enrollment classes the TODHHs implement the special programs more intensively, since DHH children receive much of their formal teaching separately in their own class. Although Kirchner (1994) has argued for the advantage of full and intensive exposure to mainstream curriculum, many DHH children in the co-enrollment settings in Israel need special accommodations of the mainstream curriculum, as well as the supplement of special programs in order to progress in their academic, linguistic, and social skills in a meaningful learning environment. Special education programs that are developed for DHH children cover active auditory learning, language and literacy, storytelling for signing DHH children (the program demonstrates mediating strategies in storytelling using Israeli Sign Language and/or speech accompanied by signs), teaching mathematical concepts to DHH preschoolers, and promoting social skills for DHH preschoolers in co-enrollment and individual inclusion settings.

Monitoring Progress: Assessment Tools and Reporting Procedures

To monitor progress in the domains of auditory learning, language, literacy, and social skills, the professional team uses a variety of formal and informal evaluation tools. Language and auditory skills are assessed by formal set of standardized tools that were developed in Hebrew or have been adapted to Hebrew. Example of auditory function evaluating tools are the Hebrew Early Speech Perception (HESP) (Kishon-Rabin et al., 1994) and the Imitation Speech Pattern Contrasts (IMSPAC) (Boothroyd, 1995). Language tests to evaluate the child's language level in comparison to hearing norms are also in use, for example the Guralnick Hebrew Preschool Language Screening Test (Guralnick, 1995) and the Preschool Language Scale adapted to Hebrew (Zimmerman, Steiner, & Pond, 2002). Some other tools include a parental questionnaire that evaluates early lexical knowledge (Maital, Dromi, Sagi, & Bornstein, 2000) and was adapted for Israeli DHH children. The speech-language clinician is responsible for the auditory and language evaluation process; however, the TODHHs and the child's parents are also involved in the evaluation process. For example, spontaneous language samples are collected and analyzed from time to time during the individual lessons both by the speech-language clinician and the TODHHs. Monitoring of academic and literacy progress is under the responsibility of the TODHHs. A formal tool is available to examine phonological awareness (Tubul, Lapidot, & Whole, 1995). The child's academic progress is usually assessed by informal evaluation tools based on unstructured observations during the individual lessons and the group activities in the kindergarten.

To evaluate communicative and social functioning in co-enrollment settings, an observation tool is used. This tool examines the child's pragmatic and social behaviors in various contexts in the inclusion setting (e.g., free play, meals, playground, didactic games). Both the regular teacher and the TODHHs complete this observational protocol together. The protocol includes pragmatic categories such as communicative initiations with peers, topic sustain, asking for clarifications, and responding to peers' references and also includes social categories such as the extent of cooperation with peers and coping behaviors during conflict situations. The observation also notes differences in the child's social functioning in quiet versus noisy activity contexts, as well as functioning in multiple-member peer versus dyadic interactions.

Based on the entire evaluation process of the child's functioning in the auditory, linguistic, social, and academic domains, the multidisciplinary team devises an Individualized Education Program (IEP) for each DHH child in the co-enrollment setting. The TODHHs is responsible for managing the IEPs. This is done in close collaboration with the regular teacher. The IEP is presented to parents and the intervention goals are discussed together. Parents are invited to contribute their own viewpoint and goals to the IEP. Parents are then requested to approve the IEP.

Encouraging Role Release Approach and Atmosphere of Partnership

To instill an atmosphere of real partnership between the regular educational staff and the TODHHs, both teams need to acknowledge each other's professional expertise, respect each other, and feel they are enriched professionally by working in multidisciplinary team. Whereas the regular teacher is an expert in pedagogical strategies used with hearing preschoolers and in the regular curriculum, the TODHHs are specialists in the educational needs of DHH children and the adaptations required for their successful co-enrollment. To encourage this multidisciplinary partnership, guidelines have been developed by the national leading instruction teams (see Fig. 6.2). Three key concepts have been derived from ecological theory and the developmental system approach (e.g., Bronfenbrenner, 2001; Guralnick, 2005, 2017): (a) a range of perspectives of the educational agents in the microsystem should be represented: parents, DHH individuals, regular teachers, and DHH expert teachers, (b) guidelines for regular preschool teachers and staff should relate specifically to the unique characteristics of kindergartens as a social and learning environment, and (c) the regular staff should be aware that the educational needs of preschool DHH children unfold in a dynamic, long-ongoing process that call for the implementation of a variety of methodologies. Crucially, in most schools of education in academic institutions in Israel (located in universities and colleges), only one general course is offered that deals with the inclusion of children with special needs in mainstream educational frameworks. Hence, mainstream teachers have limited information about the educational needs of DHH children. This is taken into consideration when developing instructional tools for the regular education staff. Regular teachers receive instruction in the beginning and throughout the academic year.

The tools and guidelines include three components:

1. **An Internet website for the regular preschool teachers.** The website explains and demonstrates how every regular kindergarten environment, by nature, is a challenge for DHH children (even in acoustic-visual accessible classes) and how teachers can use adapted communicative and teaching strategies to help DHH preschoolers to integrate. This website includes video interviews with parents of DHH children as well as with experienced regular teachers who incorporate DHH children in their classes. Some of the important ideas raised in these videos are that (a) integrating DHH children in regular classes contributes to the kindergarten community by promoting the value of acceptance of differences in society, (b) using teaching strategies adapted to DHH children can help other children in the class as well, and (c) working within a multidisciplinary team can be an enriching experience for all participating professionals. Regular teachers who access the website are also invited to participate in the website's forum to share their experiences or ask questions.

2. **Information kit.** The kit includes a CD with explanations and demonstrations of basic issues in DHH habilitation and education processes (e.g., what is a hearing loss, types of hearing loss, hearing loss impact on child development, communicative principles with DHH children, communication methods in DHH education). This CD also includes video interviews with young DHH adults who describe their personal academic and social experiences as students in a regular school. The kit also includes a booklet with authentic examples illustrating adapted teaching strategies and ways to encourage social integration.

3. **In-service courses for the regular teachers.** A virtual course is made available to the regular teachers that provides information about the specific difficulties of DHH children in inclusion educational settings and explains how to implement teaching strategies for DHH students. Face- to-face courses in Israeli Sign Language and simultaneous communication are also offered to the regular teachers by the districts' DHH EI centers. Additionally, once a year, the preschool regular staff attends a seminar day at the EI center. At this seminar, regular kindergarten teachers receive information, guidance, and support on various issues regarding the development of DHH children. A key feature of the seminar day is the opportunity for regular teachers who integrate DHH children in their classes to meet each other and discuss common issues. The DHH educational team also has the opportunity to talk with the regular teachers.

SUMMARY

Early childhood is a sensitive and critical period in the development of every child, let alone a child with hearing loss. During this period, major changes in all developmental areas occur: sensory and motor development, emotional, social development, linguistic and cognitive progress (Bronfenbrenner, 2001; Guralnick, 2017). Hence, the period of early childhood constitutes enormous challenges for the educational and habilitation systems that are involved in or responsible for providing services to DHH children and their families (Moeller et al., 2013; Yoshinaga-Itano, 2014). Educational placement of young DHH children is complex and requires a comprehensive examination covering the child's characteristics (e.g., level of hearing loss, auditory functioning in various acoustic and communicative environments, use of communication method, level of speech intelligibility, spoken and signing skills), the family's aspirations and expectations, the type of educational system, and the ability of the special education and regular education systems to work in collaboration and provide the necessary conditions for the optimal development of the DHH child.

The population of DHH children is very heterogeneous (Marschark, Knoors, & Tang, 2014). In order to meet the needs of each of the children and their families, a range of educational settings is required. In Israel, the continuum of educational frameworks includes a separate special kindergarten for DHH children, a co-enrollment educational setting of different types, and an individual inclusion setting (see Abbate, this volume). Having different paths to integration makes it possible to adjust the level of integration needed for each child's optimal development, so that parental expectations are met and the best EI program to maximize the child's potential and well-being is implemented.

ACKNOWLEDGMENTS

The authors thank Dr. Beni-Noked for her invaluable contribution to this chapter and all the professionals in the co-enrollment and early intervention centers for their assistance in collecting the information.

NOTES

1. Throughout this chapter the term *inclusion* refers in general to any educational setting in which DHH children learn together with hearing children, *co-enrollment* refers to any extent of DHH group integration in mainstream classes, and *individual inclusion* refers to DHH children who are enrolled in a regular class with hearing children and no other DHH peers.
2. Extensive analyses of arguments for and against each of the three main methods of communication in DHH education can be found, for example,

in Marschark (2007) and Moores (2001). In this section, we only relate to the critical age hypothesis arguments.

3. The side-by-side model is reminiscent of the cluster model of group inclusion described by Antia and Metz (2014) and Guralnick (2001).

REFERENCES

Al-Yagon, M., Aram, D., & Margalit, M. (2016). Early childhood inclusion in Israel. *Infants and Young Children, 29*(3), 205–213.

Antia, S. D. (1999). The roles of special educators and classroom teachers in an inclusive school. *Journal of Deaf Studies and Deaf Education, 4*(3), 203–214.

Antia, S. D., & Levine, L. M. (2001). Educating deaf and hearing children together: Confronting the challenges of inclusion. In M. J. Guralnick (Ed.), *Early childhood inclusion: Focus on change* (pp. 365–398). Baltimore, MD: Paul H. Brookes.

Antia, S. D., & Metz, K.K. (2014). Co-enrollment in the United States: A critical analysis of benefits and challenges. In M. Marschark, G. Tang, & H. Knoors (Eds.), *Bilingualism and bilingual deaf education* (pp. 424–441). New York: Oxford University Press.

Antia, S. D., Stinson, M. S., & Gaustad, M. G. (2002). Developing membership in the education of deaf and hard-of-hearing students in inclusive settings. *Journal of Deaf Education and Deaf Studies, 7*(3), 214–229.

Avramidis, E., & Norwich, B. (2002). Teachers' attitudes towards inclusion/integration: A review of the literature. *European Journal of Special Needs Education, 17*(2), 129–147.

Bat-Chava, Y., & Deignan, E. (2001). Peer relationships of children with cochlear implants. *Journal of Deaf Studies and Deaf Education, 6*(3), 186–199.

Beni-Noked, S., Ingber, S., & Ringwald-Frimerman, D. (2014). Challenges in integrating preschool children with hearing loss in Israel. In T. Most & D. Ringwald (Eds.), *Theoretical and applied aspects of the rehabilitation and education of hard-of-hearing and deaf children and adolescents* (Vol. II, pp. 49–97). Tel Aviv: Mofet Institute. [In Hebrew]

Blum-Kulka, S., & Hamo, M. (2010). *Kids talk: Peer talk patterns of communication.* Tel Aviv: Center for Educational Technology. [In Hebrew]

Boothroyd, A. (1995). Speech perception tests and hearing-impaired children. In G. Plant & K. E. Spens (Eds.), *Profound deafness and speech communication* (pp. 345–371). London: Whurr Publishers.

Bronfenbrenner, U. (2001). Bioecological theory of human development. In N. J. Smelser & B. P. Baltes (Eds.), *International encyclopedia of the social and behavioral sciences* (Vol. 10, pp. 6963–6970). New York: Elsevier.

Connor, C. M., Craig, H. K., Raudenbush, S. W., Heavner, K., & Zwolan, T. A. (2006). The age at which young deaf children receive cochlear implants and their vocabulary and speech-production growth: Is there an added value for early implantation? *Ear and Hearing, 27*(6), 628–644.

DeHart, G., Sroufe, L. A., & Cooper, R. (2004). *Child development: Its nature and course* (5th ed.). New York: McGraw-Hill.

Dromi, E., Fux, O., Ringwald-Frimerman, D., & Tzohar, N. (2003). Implementation of the "Kesher" language program in kindergarten frameworks. Tel Aviv: Maalot. [In Hebrew]

Dromi, E., & Ringwald-Frimerman, D. (1999). *From communication to language: An Israeli intervention program for hearing impaired children and their families*. Paper presented at the Symposium on Recent Trends in Early Deaf Education: An International Perspective. The 9th European Conference on Developmental Psychology, Spetes, Greece.

Eleweke, C. J., & Rodda, M. (2000). Factors contributing to parents' selection of a communication mode to use with their deaf children. *American Annals of the Deaf, 145*(4), 375–383.

Fischer, S. D. (1998). Critical periods for language acquisition: Consequences for deaf education. In A. Weisel (Ed.), *Issues unresolved: New perspectives on language and deaf education* (pp. 9–26). Washington, DC: Gallaudet University Press.

Guralnick, E. (1995). *Guralnick screening test for Hebrew speaking children at preschool age*. Unpublished master's thesis, Tel Aviv University. [In Hebrew]

Guralnick, M. J. (2001). An agenda for change in early childhood inclusion. In M. J. Guralnick (Ed.), *Early childhood inclusion: Focus on change* (pp. 531–541). Baltimore, MD: Paul H. Brookes.

Guralnick, M. J. (2005). An overview of the developmental systems model for early intervention. In M. J. Guralnick (Ed.), *The developmental systems approach to EI* (pp. 3–28). Baltimore, MD: Paul H. Brookes.

Guralnick, M. J. (2017). EI for young children with developmental delays. In H. Sukkar, C. J. Dunst, & J. Kirkby (Eds.), *Early childhood intervention* (pp. 17–35). Oxford: Routledge.

Hamo, M., & Blum-Kulka, S. (2007). Apprenticeship in conversation and culture: Emerging sociability in preschool peer talk. In J. Valsiner & A. Rosa (Eds.), *The Cambridge handbook of sociocultural psychology* (pp. 423–443). New York: Cambridge University Press.

Humphries, T., Kushalnagar, P., Mathur, G., Napoli, D. J., Padden, C., Rathmann, C., & Smith, C. R. (2012). Language acquisition for deaf children: Reducing the harms of zero tolerance to the use of alternative approaches. *Harm Reduction Journal, 9*(16), 2–9.

Inan, H. Z. (2009). The third dimension in preschools: Preschool environments and classroom design. *European Journal of Educational Studies, 1*(1), 55–66.

Ingber, S. (2004). *The philosophy and practice of parental involvement in EI for children with hearing impairment in Israel*. Unpublished doctoral dissertation, Tel Aviv University. [In Hebrew]

Ingber, S., Al-Yagon, M., & Dromi, E. (2013). Mothers' involvement in EI for children with hearing loss: The role of maternal characteristics and context-based perceptions. *Journal of Early Intervention, 32*(5), 351–369.

Israeli Ministry of Education and Culture. (2002). The Inclusion Act for children with disabilities. Jerusalem: Ministry of Education and Culture. Retrieved from http://cms.education.gov.il/EducationCMS/Units/Zchuyot/ChukimVeamanot/Chukim/HockKhinuhMeuhad.htmm

Kaiser, A. P., & Hancock, T. B. (2003). Teaching parents' new skills to support their young children's development. *Infants & Young Children, 16*(1), 9–21.

Kirchner, C. J. (1994). Co-enrollment as an inclusion model. *American Annals of the Deaf, 139*(2), 163–164.

Kishon-Rabin, L., Taitelbaum, R., Elichai, E., Maimon, D., Debait, N., & Hazan, N. A. (1994). Questionnaire to assess auditory skills of hearing impaired infants. *DASH: Dibur ve'Shmia, 23*, 12–22. [In Hebrew]

Kluwin, T. N., Stinson, M. S., & Colarossi, G. M. (2002). Social processes and outcomes of in-school contact between deaf and hearing peers. *Journal of Deaf Studies and Deaf Education, 7*(3), 200–213.

Knoors, H., & Marschark, M. (2012). Language planning for the 21st century: Revisiting bilingual language policy for deaf children. *Journal of Deaf Studies and Deaf Education, 17*(3), 291–305.

Kovach, H. L. (2015). *Teacher language in oral deaf and hard-of-hearing kindergarten classrooms.* Unpublished doctoral dissertation, University of Colorado, Boulder.

Kreimeyer, K. K. H., Crooke, P., Drye, C., Egbert, V., & Klein, B. (2000). Academic and social benefits of a co-enrollment model of inclusive education for deaf and hard-of-hearing children. *Journal of Deaf Studies and Deaf Education, 5*(2), 174–185.

Kristoffersen, A. E., & Simonsen, E. (2014). Teacher-assigned literacy events in a bimodal, bilingual preschool with deaf and hearing children. *Journal of Early Childhood Literacy, 14*(1), 80–104.Kuhl, P. K. (2004). Early language acquisition: Cracking the speech code. *Nature Reviews Neuroscience, 5*(11), 831–843.

Lane, H. (2005). Ethnicity, ethics, and the deaf world. *Journal of Deaf Studies and Deaf Education, 10*(3), 291–310.

Lang, H. G. (2003). Perspectives on the history of deaf education. In M. Marschark & P. E. Spencer (Eds.), *The Oxford handbook of deaf studies, language, and education* (Vol. 1, pp. 6–17). New York: Oxford University Press.

Lieber, J., Wolery, R. A., Horn, E., Tschantz, J., Beckman, P. J., & Hanson, M. J. (2002). Collaborative relationships among adults in inclusive preschool programs. In S. L. Odom (Ed.), *Widening the circle: Including children with disabilities in preschool programs* (pp. 81–97). New York: Teachers College Press.

Luckner, J. L., & Cooke, C. (2010). A summary of the vocabulary research with students who are deaf or hard of hearing. *American Annals of the Deaf, 155*(1), 38–67.

Luterman, D. (2003). Counseling parents about cochlear implants. *The ASHA Leader, 8*, 6–7.

Maital, S., Dromi, E., Sagi, A., & Bornstein, M. H. (2000). The Hebrew communicative development inventory: Language-specific properties and cross-linguistic generalizations. *Journal of Child Language, 27*, 43–67.

Marschark, M. (2007). *Raising and educating a deaf child: A comprehensive guide to the choices, controversies, and decisions faced by parents and educators.* New York: Oxford University Press.

Marschark, M., Knoors, H., & Tang, G. (2014). Perspectives on bilingualism and bilingual education for deaf learners. In M. Marschark, G. Tang, & H. Knoors (Eds.), *Bilingualism and bilingual deaf education* (pp. 445–476). New York: Oxford University Press.

Marschark, M., Lang, H. G., & Albertini, J. A. (2002). *Educating deaf students: From research to practice.* New York: Oxford University Press.

Marschark M., & Spencer, P. E. (2011). What we know, what we don't know, and what we should know. In M. Marschark & P. E. Spencer (Eds.), *The*

Oxford handbook of deaf studies, language, and education (2nd ed., vol. 1). New York: Oxford University Press.

Marschark, M., Tang, G., & Knoors, H. (Eds.). (2014). *Bilingualism and bilingual deaf education.* New York: Oxford University Press.]

Martin, M. P., Balanzategui, M. V., & Morgan, G. (2014). Sign bilingual and co-enrollment education for children with cochlear implants in Madrid, Spain. In M. Marschark, G. Tang, & H. Knoors (Eds.), *Bilingualism and bilingual deaf education* (pp. 368–395). New York: Oxford University Press.]

Mayberry, R. I. (2007). When timing is everything: Age of first-language acquisition effects on second-language learning. *Applied Psycholinguistics, 28,* 537–549.

Mayberry, R. I., & Lock, E. (2003). Age constraints on first versus second language acquisition: Evidence for linguistic plasticity and epigenesis. *Brain and Language, 87*(3), 369–384.

McGonigel, M. J., Woodruff, G., & Roszmann-Millican, M. (1994). The transdisciplinary team: A model for family-centered EI. In L. J. Johnson, R. J. Gallagher, M. J. LaMontagne, J. B. Jordan, J. J. Gallagher, P. L. Hutinger, & M. B. Karnes (Eds.), *Meeting EI challenges: Issues from birth to three* (2nd ed., pp. 95–131). Baltimore, MD: Paul H. Brookes.

Ministry of Education, Special Education Department, Supervision of Education for DHH Students (n.d.). Retrieved September 1, 2017, from https://sites.google.com/a/lakash.tzafonet.org.il/main/demograf

Mitchell, R. E., & Karchmer, M. A. (2004). When parents are deaf versus hard of hearing: Patterns of sign use and school placement of deaf and hard-of-hearing children. *Journal of Deaf Studies and Deaf Education, 9*(2), 133–152.

Moeller, M. P., Carr, G., Seaver, L., Stredler-Brown, A., & Holzinger, D. (2013). Best practices in family-centered early intervention for children who are deaf or hard of hearing: An international consensus statement. *Journal of Deaf Studies and Deaf Education, 18*(4), 429–445.

Moores, D. F. (2001). *Educating the deaf: Psychology, principles, and practices* (5th ed.). Boston: Houghton Mifflin.

Most, T., Ingber S., & Heled-Ariam, E. (2012). Social competence, sense of loneliness and speech intelligibility of young children with hearing loss in individual inclusion and group inclusion. *Journal of Dead Studies and Deaf Education, 17*(2), 259–272.

Most, T., & Ringwald-Frimerman, D. (2014). Introduction. In T. Most & D. Ringwald (Eds.), *Theoretical and applied aspects of the rehabilitation and education of hard-of-hearing and deaf children and adolescents* (Vol. I, pp. 1–18). Tel Aviv: Mofet Institute. [In Hebrew]

Most, T., Weisel, A., & Ezrachi, S. (2009). Deaf education in Israel. In D. F. Moores & M. S. Miller (Eds.), *Deaf people around the world: Educational and social perspectives* (pp. 101–118). Washington, DC: Gallaudet University Press.

National Academies of Sciences, Engineering, and Medicine. (2016). *Ensuring quality and accessible care for children with disabilities and complex health and educational needs: Proceedings of a workshop.* Washington, DC: National Academies Press.]

Newport, E. (2006). Critical periods in language development. In L. Nadel (Ed.), *Encyclopedia of cognitive science* (pp. 737–740). Hoboken, NJ: John Wiley

& Sons. Retrieved September 9, 2012, from http://www.bcs.rochester.edu/people/newport/Newport-ECS-A0506.PDF

Nishimura, H., Hashikawa, K., Doi, K., Iwaki, T., Watanabe, Y., Kusuoka, H., Nishimura, T., & Kubo, T. (1999). Sign language "heard" in the auditory cortex. *Nature, 397,* 116.

Nunes, T., Pretzlik, U., & Olsson, J. (2001). Deaf children's social networks in mainstream schools. *Deafness & Education International, 3*(3), 123–136.

O'Leary, C. C. (2001). *The early childhood family check-up: A brief intervention for at-risk families with preschool-aged children.* Unpublished doctoral dissertation, University of Oregon.

Plaut, A. (2007). *What has changed? The history of educational frameworks for students with hearing impairments in Israel, 1932–2005.* Tel Aviv: Mophet Institute Publications [In Hebrew].

Post, J., Hohmann, M., & Epstein, A. (2011). *Tender care and early learning: Supporting infants and toddlers in child care settings* (2nd ed.). Ypsilanti, MI: High Scope Press.

Reiter, S., & Schalock, R. L. (2008). Applying the concept of quality of life to Israeli special education programs: A national curriculum for enhanced autonomy in students with special needs. *International Journal of Rehabilitation Research, 31*(1), 13–21.

Sandberg, A., & Ottosson, L. (2010). Pre-school teachers', other professionals', and parental concerns on cooperation in pre-school—all around children in need of special support: The Swedish perspective. *International Journal of Inclusive Education, 14*(8), 741–754.

Smith, R. M., & Erevelles, N. (2004). Towards an enabling education: The difference that disability makes. *Educational Researcher, 33*(8), 31–36.

Spencer, P. E. (2003). Parent–child interaction: Implication for intervention and development. In B. Bodner-Johnson & M. Sass-Lehrer (Eds.), *The young deaf or hard of hearing child: A family-centered approach to early education* (pp. 333–368). Baltimore, MD: Paul H. Brooks Publishing.

Spencer, P. E., & Marschark, M. (2010). *Evidence-based practice in educating deaf and hard-of-hearing students.* New York: Oxford University Press.

Steinberg, A., Bain, L., Li, Y., Montoya, L., & Ruperto, V. (2002). *A look at the decisions Hispanic families make after the diagnosis of deafness.* Washington, DC: Gallaudet University, Laurent Clerc National Deaf Education Center. Retrieved June 15, 2017, from http://www.gallaudet.edu/documents/clerc/hispanicfamilies-english.pdf

The national legislation database of the State of Israel (2018). The Inclusion Act for children with disabilities (amendment no. 11). Jerusalem: the Knesset. Retrieved from https://main.knesset.gov.il/Activity/Legislation/Laws/Pages/LawPrimary.aspx?t=lawlaws&st=lawlaws&lawitemid=2000664

Theilheimer, R. (2006). Molding to the children: Primary caregiving and continuity of care. *Zero to Three, 26*(3), 50–54.]

Tubul, L. G., Lapidot, M., & Whole, A. (1995). Test of phonological awareness as a predictor tool for reading acquisition. *Helkat Lashon, 19,* 169–188. [In Hebrew]

Uhler, K., Thomson, V., Cyr, N., Gabbard, S. A., & Yoshinaga-Itano, C. (2014). State and territory EHDI databases: What we do and don't know about the hearing or audiological data from identified children. *American Journal of Audiology*, 23(1), 34–43.

Waltzman, S. B., & Roland, J. T. (2005). Cochlear implantation in children younger than 12 months. *Pediatrics*, 116(4), 487–493.

Westwood, P. S. (2009). *What teachers need to know about students with disabilities*. Australian Council for Educational Research. Camberwell, Victoria: ACER Press.

Yoshinaga-Itano, C. (2014) Principles and guidelines for EI after confirmation that a child is deaf or hard of hearing. *Journal of Deaf Studies and Deaf Education*, 19(2), 143–175.

Zimmerman, I. L., Steiner, V. G., & Pond, R. E. (2002). *Preschool language scale* (4th ed.). San Antonio, TX: The Psychological Corporation.

7

Bilingual, Inclusive, Mixed-Age Schooling in Vienna

Silvia Kramreiter and Verena Krausneker

BIMODAL BILINGUAL EDUCATION IN AUSTRIA: HISTORY AND EXPERIENCES

Until 1990, there was little to no documentation of using Austrian Sign Language (ÖGS) in education, and there were no publications on the topic. Bimodal bilingual education was a concept unknown in Austrian deaf education. Similarly, co-enrollment was unknown and—as far as we know—had never been practiced. Yet, despite this, two experimental bilingual classes were set up in Austria in the 1990s: one in the school for the deaf in Klagenfurt (Pinter, 1992) and one in Graz (Bortsch & Tischmann, 1996). Both pilot schemes lasted about five years but were not extended by the educational authorities. The reasons for this are unknown. Although these two pioneer trials were not co-enrollment models, they paved the way for bimodal bilingual education in Austria and will be described here briefly.

Klagenfurt 1990: The Pioneers

The bimodal bilingual class that pioneered the use of ÖGS in schools was opened in 1991 in a school for the deaf with four pupils aged 14 to 16 who had until then been taught using and learning spoken language. ÖGS was used as the medium of instruction by a hearing teacher and a deaf pedagogue, while German was a subject. The effects were impressive: massive improvement in literacy, growth in vocabulary, heightened motivation to learn language, communicative joy, curiosity, and eagerness were obvious. Within the first school year, the passive written German vocabulary of pupils grew by 50% (Pinter, 1992). Pinter also noted the importance of having a deaf adult as a role model; for some of the pupils, this was the first deaf person they had met in their lives. The Klagenfurt experiences were documented by one of the teachers (Pinter, 1992) and an "evaluation" was put together by Pöllabauer (1992), but the trial was terminated in 1995. In 1996, the educational team transferred to a local school (VS 1 Klagenfurt) and a mixed-age, bimodal bilingual classroom was started. The pupils would visit the local elementary or secondary school for specific lessons (English, sports, religion) while being accompanied by one of their three sign language-competent (deaf and hearing) teachers to either explain or interpret in ÖGS. Krausneker and Schalber (2007) conducted a three-day participant observation and wrote a detailed and enthusiastic portrait of this "positive and unique" practice (p. 45), which was, for more than a decade, the only educational setting in Carinthia (southern Austria) that gave ÖGS a fixed and undisputed place in classroom education and everyday communication. In 2015, another elementary school started a bimodal bilingual class with a deaf teacher (VS St. Leonhard bei Siebenbrünn),[1] and in 2016 a hearing ÖGS-competent teacher was transferred to a lower secondary school (NMS Klagenfurt Waidmannsdorf) in order to accompany one deaf pupil, so the use of ÖGS in mainstream settings has continually expanded.

Graz 1995–1999: Deaf–Hearing Team Teaching

In 1995, a bilingual elementary school class was opened at the school for the deaf in Graz. Five pupils were taught by a hearing and a deaf teacher, though this team teaching was practiced for only seven lessons per week; the other lessons were taught by either one of them. German and ÖGS were contrasted and the room and even the blackboard were neatly divided by language, but the speaker and the signer used all their language competencies and did not strictly stick to only one language for teaching. They considered this important in order to be role models for multilingual children. Especially in grade 1, the focus was on communicative competencies and on mastering dialogue, which was considered the basis for conveying content and knowledge. The two teachers documented their subjective experiences, and thus we have one publication on the program (Bortsch & Tischmann, 1996).

Vienna 2000–2004: Co-Enrollment and Deaf–Hearing Team Teaching in a Regular School

At the turn of the century, an elementary school in Vienna pioneered bimodal bilingual co-enrollment: for four years (2000–2004), the first bilingual class with both deaf and hearing pupils and teachers took place in Volksschule Bilgeristraße. This model was documented in great detail in a longitudinal participant-observation study (Krausneker, 2004) and summarized in an English publication (Krausneker, 2008). The bilingual experiment started in grade 1 (with pupils aged 6) and ended in grade 4, when all the pupils moved on to the next level of schooling. Throughout all four years of their elementary education, the languages of instruction for all subjects were both ÖGS and German. One deaf teacher, one hearing teacher, and one interpreter taught as a team. Teaching was either done by one teacher in her first language (spoken or signed language) and was simultaneously interpreted and related to the other language group; alternatively, a parallel teaching method was used, with both the speaking and the signing teachers using their respective languages. Deaf and hearing children were all taught at the same pace. The materials were adapted for the deaf children, but in general, no exceptions were made. Based on the essential conviction that all the children must receive all the information, the teachers gradually built up a bilingual team approach based exclusively on their own experiences.

A distinguishing feature of this class was that the deaf pupils were required to master all school subjects in accordance with the standard Austrian elementary school curriculum (not that of a special school) within the same timeframe as hearing pupils. The Vienna bilingual class showed that

> Deaf children can be educated according to the standard curriculum of elementary schools. The Deaf children had no difficulty keeping up with the academic content and met the intellectual challenges just as well as the hearing rest of the class. The academic success rate (with the Deaf pupils acquiring marks and results above the class average) proves that Deaf children are capable of coping with a standard curriculum. (Krausneker, 2008, p. 216)

The bilingual co-enrollment ended with the pupils successfully finishing primary school, but the program was not continued with a new group. Krausneker (2008, p. 216) stated, "In conclusion, Austria's policy of maintaining low standards in schools for the deaf is questionable." Nevertheless, the substantial documentation (Krausneker, 2004, also contains a DVD with three hours of video clips that explain literacy teaching and bilingual classroom practice) was decisive for further development of bilingual co-enrollment in Austria.

Vienna 2005–2009: Co-Enrollment in a Regular School

In this Viennese mainstream classroom, 11 hearing and 6 deaf and hard-of-hearing (DHH) pupils were co-enrolled for the four years of their elementary schooling. The regular curriculum and materials were used, and the languages of instruction of the two teachers were German and ÖGS. A deaf teacher came in for a few hours every week and was part of the team. Austrian law granted the DHH pupils accommodation, so they had a few extra lessons per week to study with their teacher. One of the teachers conducted research over the course of three years (see Kramreiter, 2016) by applying various methods, all rooted in Grounded Theory: observation, participant-observation, interviews, pupils' well-being profiles (Krause, Wiesmann, & Hannich, 2004), and a research diary. The teacher-researcher focused on social and communicative interaction, educational-linguistic teaching processes, identity development/formation, and well-being in the context of the classroom.

Results of her research show that this bilingual co-enrollment worked excellently with regards to social inclusion (see Yiu et al., this volume). With regards to academic performance the DHH pupils did well: they were highly motivated and liked to study (see Hennies & Hennies, this volume). The DHH pupils compared themselves to their hearing peers and were proud that they were fit to study at a *Gymnasium*, the prestigious and more challenging version of secondary education. Their extraordinary effort was sustained by discipline and self-responsibility. When asked how they did in school, the pupils mostly answered: "It is demanding, but I like going to *Gymnasium*" (Kramreiter, 2010, p. 174, our translation). After eight years of co-enrollment, it became obvious that this kind of inclusive co-enrollment had positive effects on their motivation, and the placement in a *Gymnasium* did raise their self-worth. Recognition, positive grades, and feedback from teachers, parents, and friends strengthened their trust in their own capabilities and helped to free more resources.

Salzburg: Co-Enrollment and Team Teaching in the Special School

The co-enrollment in Salzburg is special in that it takes place in a special school for the deaf. Since 1996, hearing students have come into this school on the primary school level (years 1–4) with a maximum of 16 pupils per class. It was always a goal to include ÖGS in this model, so in the teams one teacher needed to be competent in sign language. After this innovative trial "fulfilled expectations," it was extended to secondary school. This also brought change in the approach: whereas previously the school had asked which pupils "needed" ÖGS, they now offered ÖGS for all, and it became an asset as opposed to a workaround. Finally, in 2014–2015 ÖGS was implemented as a foreign language (compulsory subject). This is noteworthy insofar as there was, as of 2018, no official Austrian school curriculum for ÖGS, so the Salzburg school had to invent its own curriculum. The problems the school faces are—like in so many instances—too few native signing teachers and, even though the approach is supported by the hearing teachers, scarce knowledge of ÖGS and Deaf culture. Unfortunately, there are no publications available yet about this model.[2]

CO-ENROLLMENT IN AUSTRIA: LEGAL AND IDEOLOGICAL CONTEXT

Before describing the bilingual mixed-age co-enrollment practice that is taking place in a school in Vienna today, we would like to sketch the context within which it takes place.

As stated earlier, bimodal bilingual approaches and co-enrollment were concepts unknown in deaf education in Austria until the 1990s. Typically, the Deaf community and linguists were (even this early) well aware of the need to create a stable situation for ÖGS and promoted the use of ÖGS in schools (see Krausneker, 2006). The National Assembly of Austria was handed a petition in 1991 and again in 1997 (and again in 2017) with regard to the legal recognition and educational use of ÖGS. While ÖGS achieved official recognition in the Austrian constitution in 2006, its use in schools has remained a matter of good will and individual grassroots action.

Krausneker and Schalber (2007) conducted a study on the status of ÖGS in Austrian schools and at University of Vienna. Their data, gathered in 38 different classroom settings in special and mainstream schools, made it evident that reforms were needed. At this point (2006–2007) the use of ÖGS for bilingual education was the exception nationwide, especially in mainstream schools. Most mainstreamed pupils had access to only a few hours per week of extra teacher support. Krausneker and Schalber noted that pupils as well as teachers suffered from lack of access to resources and competencies, and "co-enrollment" with DHH pupils was put to practice in less-than-ideal situations with great compromises. They concluded their study with 86 concrete suggestions for innovation.

In a more recent study on bimodal bilingual school education that spanned 39 European countries, the participating experts from Austria stated their perception of obstructive and supportive factors and offered recommendations for the future.[3] They stated that attitudes (strong oral tradition; one influential, negative individual in school management; school management has no knowledge and little interest) and politics (educational policy responds too slowly; members of expert working groups lack deep understanding) were most obstructive, while both attitude and politics were also named as most helpful in implementing bimodal bilingual education. For more detailed results and contextualization of the Austrian data within the other 38 countries, see Becker, Audeoud, Krausneker, and Tarcsiová (2017) and Krausneker, Garber, Audeoud, Becker, and Tarcsiová (2018).

Legal foundations for co-enrollment have been in place for a long time in Austria. Currently, the relevant laws[4] frame inclusive co-enrollment. DHH pupils in Austria may be schooled according to the regular curriculum or according to the special school curriculum, irrespective of their actual placement. At present there is no curriculum available for ÖGS as a compulsory subject, so making room for the language during the school day is complicated. For a description of the current legal situation of ÖGS and its users in Austria, see Krausneker (2013). For an analysis of the relevance of the United Nations Convention on the

Rights of People with Disabilities on the legal foundations of bimodal bilingual education, see Krausneker, Garber et al. (2018).

CO-ENROLLMENT IN VIENNA TODAY: BIMODAL BILINGUAL MIXED-AGE INCLUSION AT NMS PFEILGASSE

We are now going to summarize one model practiced in Vienna today that we consider innovative and exceptionally successful. A detailed description was published based on the perceptions and documentation of one teacher who taught there for four years (Kramreiter, 2015). Another portrait of this school compared it with seven other bimodal bilingual good-practice schools in Europe (Becker et al., 2017; Krausneker, Becker et al., 2018). The concept describes inclusion, bilingualism, and mixed-age groups as the pillars of co-enrollment, with a progressive teaching philosophy/approach as a fourth important characteristic.

Mixed Ages: Eight Grades, Three Groups

2012 saw the start of the cooperation between the mainstream school NMS Pfeilgasse and the local school for the deaf Bundesinstitut für Gehörlosenbildung. Qualified teachers of the deaf and pupils joined a fifth-grade group at the public school. Every year, more DHH pupils joined until the model encompassed altogether eight grades. By 2016–2017 it had grown to three groups consisting of 15 DHH and 60 hearing pupils between the ages of 6 and 15. Group I consists of preschool and three grades of elementary school, group II consists of pupils in grades 4 to 6, and group III consists of grades 7 and 8.

In group I, three teachers are present in all lessons: two hearing mainstream teachers plus a deaf teacher of the deaf and a hearing teacher of the deaf who take turns. This unusually big team of teachers is necessary due to fact that four grades are schooled together (in a group of 27) and that one ÖGS-competent teacher needs to be present at all times. In middle school, all lessons are taught by a team of two teachers. All lessons take place in the mainstream school, with DHH pupils being offered several additional hours per week including ÖGS practice, articulation, cochlear implant practice, and other therapy.

This model, with eight grades, guarantees that hearing and DHH pupils can seamlessly transfer from elementary school to lower secondary school. Studying together and spending free time together creates a social space and learning space characterized by new forms of schooling and of grading, in which each pupil receives individualized support.

Bilingual School Life

Teachers from the mainstream school work together with qualified deaf and hearing teachers sent by the school for the deaf, similar to the model of 2005–2009 described earlier. Hearing mainstream teachers speak and write German without exception; hearing teachers of the deaf use ÖGS and Sign Supported German (LBG). The deaf teachers of the deaf use written German and ÖGS. Thus, both German and ÖGS are actively put to use at all times during class, either simultaneously by both teachers or separately, for example when explanations or teamwork requires a differentiated didactic strategy. LBG is only used while reading and writing.

Deaf-appropriate didactics are employed during exercises or for additional explanations for the DHH pupils. After a while, some of the hearing pupils joined these activities because they appreciated some extra information; ever since, it has become practice that the whole class comes together when the teacher of the deaf starts her additional explanation activity. Especially for those hearing pupils who do not speak German as a first language, the "deaf-specific didactics" have turned out to be very useful.

All pupils perceive all their teachers as equally competent, and hearing pupils consult with deaf teachers just as DHH pupils address questions to the hearing teachers (see De Klerk et al., this volume). When addressing them, hearing pupils usually speak German. Bilingual practice in this setting is not two language domains next to each other, but bilingualism employed by all, depending on their language competencies. Hearing teachers and pupils experience their DHH peers as linguistically different. If there were any notion of a "deficit" in anyone, it would be the limited ÖGS competence of the hearing mainstream teachers and some hearing pupils. Communication strategies employed with them are writing, mime, and fingerspelling. Deaf pupils see that the deaf teachers are competent, equal, and fully respected, and this has positive effects on their self-esteem and identity development. They are proud of their young, groundbreaking deaf teachers and look up to them. That the deaf teachers really are role models becomes evident in pupils' conversations about their career aspirations (see Baker, Miller, Fletcher, Gamin, & Carty, this volume).

Deaf teachers are consulted by hearing teachers when it comes to appropriate communication strategies with the DHH pupils and when they need to reflect on a specific situation that occurred during class. This is enriching and important for the whole team, because issues are seen from different perspectives, misunderstandings are reduced, and solutions and compromises are found much more quickly together. Deaf teachers are a bridge to the Deaf community, and access to Deaf culture is guaranteed by bringing in cultural events such as Deaf theater. These events very much shape the everyday life in this school.

As mentioned earlier, there is currently no official Austrian school curriculum for ÖGS, but in this class hearing pupils receive one lesson a week (the maximum possible within the school's autonomy in lesson planning). Hearing teachers have the possibility of studying ÖGS with a deaf teacher at the teacher training college. Deaf pupils receive one ÖGS lesson per week in order to reflect on grammar of their first language. This is minimal, but at present it is the only option there is. (In 2017, the ministry for education commissioned a project to develop a curriculum for a school subject ÖGS that covers all grades and takes deaf learners as well as hearing learners of ÖGS as a foreign language into account. The project was completed in autumn 2018, but the implementation is expected to take several years.)

Inclusion

Seating order in the three classrooms is adjusted for work on individual week plans and for non–teacher-centered learning. Pupils sit together around big round desks that can be divided if necessary if smaller groups or partner work is wanted. The classrooms are situated next to each other and are joined by doors and one common lobby. During breaks and sometimes during class time, there is lively contact between the age groups. In addition, there is one extra room that can be used if needed. The spaces and rooms heavily influence social dynamics and pose a relevant positive factor for linguistic interaction possibilities between older and younger pupils. Break times for all groups have been arranged to take place at the same time and are used for joint play, informal tutoring, and generally the older ones looking for the younger ones. In summary, it is obvious that rooms and a sensible concept of spaces can strongly support a mixed-age project.

Progressive Teaching Approach

At the heart and core of the progressive teaching approach are individual weekly study plans. Each pupil has his or her individual workload clearly laid out in a weekly study plan. The teachers' time is not tied by "chalk and talk," but they are free to individually support all the pupils with their questions and needs or to explain content. Sometimes this is initiated by pupils walking up to the teachers' table or by teachers joining the pupils at their big round tables. Teachers walking around and making themselves actively available usually takes place after new content has been introduced.

Weekly study plans have a number of advantages and benefits for the pupils. They study at their own pace, choose topics and content as it suits them, critically assess their own work, and learn to manage themselves and their own studying with regards to timing, interest, and correctness. In a mixed-age group the older pupils become resources for the younger ones. The younger pupils observe their habits and strategies of managing their workload. Thus, highly disciplined and self-guided learning but not "teaching" is at the core of everyday activities in this class.

Pupils learn how to learn and they learn to cooperate, to manage their own time resources, their interests, and their energy (see Ringwald-Frimerman, Ingber, & Most, this volume). Furthermore, they learn self-guided learning and various formats (individual, tandem, group study). Mixed-age group work means that experienced pupils can serve as role models for the younger or slower ones. Pupils have been observed explaining concepts and other matters in the most intuitively child-appropriate manner and with immense patience. Co-learning around the big round desks is characterized by joy and eagerness to acquire new knowledge and find the right answers.

It is an additional incentive that pupils who were efficient in class do not have to take home any work. Everyone in the group is interested in finishing his or her work in school, so the group becomes a self-regulating unit, where a quiet, focused atmosphere and work ethos are demanded by (mostly the older) pupils. The work ethos includes not only oneself but also peers: co-learning and strategies of assisting each other have developed by themselves. Interestingly, an even give-and-take is closely monitored by all peers, and attempts at simply copying someone else's work or only consuming help but not contributing are not tolerated by peers.

In all subjects, the teachers regularly conduct smaller or extended checks on the learning targets (quizzes). These checks are usually put into the semester plan that is available to all so that pupils can prepare. Sometimes, the teachers offer additional exercises before the quizzes. Conventional written class tests are offered as scheduled in the curriculum, with the class tests in German divided into the three domains of grammar, spelling, and free writing.

Austrian law allows for individual placement of pupils in different curricula if needed (and thus different grading standards in a subject). DHH pupils can be graded according to the mainstream curriculum or—for example, in the subject German—according to the curriculum for DHH. It gives DHH pupils more time to reach the goals, but they are not stuck there because teachers can decide anytime that they are ready to be graded in the framework of the mainstream curriculum. When this seems appropriate, it is discussed openly with the pupils and their grades according to both curricula are made available to them, thus achieving complete transparency about the effects and consequences of a possible new placement.

Parallel grading in both curricula is done for a while so that both pupils and teachers know where they are heading and when a change into another curriculum seems appropriate. Exams and quizzes are calculated in percentages (as common in the Anglo-American world but not in Austria) so that achievements can be calculated more accurately than usual (Kramreiter, 2015, p. 87).

Program Challenges

This model of bimodal bilingual co-enrollment has many obvious advantages but also poses challenges.

Linguistic Diversity Among Pupils

Altogether there are over 15 different primary languages present in the three groups. DHH pupils who have deaf parents or who have attended a bilingual elementary school often have excellent ÖGS competency. Others do not and need guidance and input, especially to build their vocabulary. German literacy levels are very diverse as well. Interestingly, the hearing status of the pupils is not a safe predictive factor. There are DHH pupils with and without cochlear implants in the three groups, as well as hearing children of deaf parents. The diversity of these pupils does pose a challenge for the teachers as well as for the methods and didactics they employ.

Bilingual Team Teaching

This program consists of eight grades and 14 teachers with various backgrounds or specializations who considers themselves as one team. Special education and mainstream teachers feel responsible for all pupils. The team has one hour per week for their meetings and planning (and one year without this resource of one joint hour for the team showed that tensions, problems, and misunderstandings grew significantly). Since 2014, two deaf teachers and one hard-of-hearing teacher work in the team, and this has changed communication habits toward more discipline and structure as well as including time for interpretation. Until March 2017, this interpretation service was provided by lay interpreters (hearing, sign language-competent teachers), and only since then has the school authority paid for professional interpreter services during team meetings, supervision, teacher conferences, and parent–teacher conferences.

It has become clear that the success of putting an inclusive philosophy into practice is highly dependent on the attitude of the teachers: if they are open, flexible, and interested in languages, cultures, and the specifics of DHH pupils' learning, then inclusion can work (Kramreiter, 2015, p. 90).

Qualified Teachers

Until 2015, there were no systematic and continuous teacher training options for studying ÖGS. Most of the courses that did take place covered lower levels but did not build up to competence levels C1 or C2 according to the Common European Framework of Reference for Languages. The ÖGS competence levels of most hearing teachers (of the deaf) are accordingly weak.[5] Another huge challenge is the lack in training in bilingual didactics. Although these concepts exist internationally and are accessible in the literature, there is no focused training for teachers in Austria, and junior teachers now arrive in schools with some ÖGS competence but without any specialized knowledge on bilingual didactics and methods.

ÖGS as a Subject

The entire classroom is bilingual, and any teaching is done bilingually in German and ÖGS. Teachers pay attention to the quality in both languages. However, German is allocated a dominant place in the weekly lesson plan with many hours and ÖGS is not. Until now, it has only been possible for pupils to choose ÖGS as an elective. DHH pupils have two hours of "therapeutic exercises" in their lesson plan; this period is sometimes used to teach contrastive grammar. An hour of ÖGS per week is far too little and leaves no room for deaf-specific subject topics such as culture, identity, and history.

Supply and Demand

It has become clear the mixed-age groups are constantly growing. Pupils finish the elementary levels and then move on to lower secondary school. In 2019, there will be more DHH pupils than originally planned for, and it will become apparent whether school authorities are flexible and supportive enough to handle this situation appropriately. In Austria, parents do have the right to freely choose a school and placement for their children, so this will be the basis and background for the problem already visible on the horizon.

Cooperation

To offer continuous bimodal bilingual education up to the *Matura* (Austrian A-levels, high school exit exam, prerequisite for higher education), there is a cooperation with another Viennese school. After successfully finishing grade 8, pupils may transfer to *Gymnasium Karajangasse*, accompanied by their ÖGS-competent teacher of the deaf who covers the subjects German and English. In the *Gymnasium*, another teacher fully competent in ÖGS and appropriate professional interpreter services enable linguistic access. With sign language-competent high school teachers and a school that embraces the co-operation, DHH pupils are fully supported in their advances into higher education. Every year, a small number of DHH pupils graduate and go on to universities. Obviously, the cooperation of several schools and over a dozen teachers with diverse specializations requires a certain amount of attention. In effect, bureaucratic and organizational challenges are all manageable if all partners want to cooperate constructively.

BENEFITS OF BILINGUAL CO-ENROLLMENT

There is a steady level of interest by parents as well as Deaf clubs/associations in bimodal bilingual education for DHH children. The benefits of bimodal bilingual, inclusive, mixed-age schooling are manifold for pupils, teachers, and general society.

Pupils

Both deaf and hearing pupils benefit from the neat transfer and closed gap between elementary and lower secondary school (in Austria, this gap is generally still wide and decisions need to be made by parents when their children are only 10). The closed gap is achieved not only academically and structurally but also socially by joint projects and activities.

This co-enrollment project is a cooperation between a mainstream school and a special school and thus has available technical equipment and highly qualified staff resources that can cater to all needs. Grade reports are issued by the mainstream school while indicating which curriculum and grading system was used in which subject. Pupils benefit from a mainstream school grade report because special school reports are still highly stigmatized and associated with reduced academic accomplishment. In fact, DHH pupils show a high motivation to perform above average. They compare themselves with their hearing peers and are fully aware that they need to pay more attention to their German studies and that they will take more time to achieve the same levels as hearing peers. Hearing pupils profit from having access to a diverse learning environment enriched by many methods and the resource of two, sometimes three, teachers. Everyday life is characterized by a quiet and attentive atmosphere, respectful and friendly communication, and peer management of the need to stick to the agreed-upon classroom rules. The cooperative learning environment generates a helpfulness between DHH and hearing pupils that is present all day long and is the source of much pride. Communication is mastered mostly without problems, with all partners employing creative strategies. Both hearing and DHH pupils benefit immensely and build linguistic as well as social competencies by navigating, observing, and negotiating their school life.

Hearing pupils proudly acquire ÖGS, and DHH pupils acquire strategies to live in a hearing bilingual environment that challenges and fosters their bilingual language competencies every day. In this atmosphere, social bonds and friendships are formed across hearing status and linguistic "barriers."

Teachers

Teachers benefit from teaching in a diverse team: they broaden their competencies, challenge their perceptions of the "other," and experience equality in a new way (see De Klerk et al., this volume). Having DHH teachers as part of the team means that sensitive linguistic issues in teaching are reflected by all teachers, and the hearing teachers' experiences with their deaf colleagues mean they are highly aware of their DHH pupils' needs. Working with DHH adults also means that they have the possibility to gain access to a minority community and culture, and experiencing adults outside the deficit paradigm has important effects on the teachers' open and positive attitudes toward DHH pupils. Even other teachers and pupils who are not directly involved in this co-enrollment project benefit from theater and other cultural projects that are brought into this mainstream school.

Society

Society benefits from this project because it constitutes one real and honest realization of the demands as put forward in the UN Convention on the Rights of People with Disabilities (ratified by Austria in 2008). This form of bimodal bilingual inclusion is so obviously successful, with immense benefits for pupils, that it helps to generate visions of inclusive school education.

CONCLUSIONS

In Austria, bimodal bilingual education has been the exception in a traditionally monolingual conceptualization of deaf education. We see few changes in these old structures: there are no deaf headmasters/mistresses and teachers who are fully competent in ÖGS are rare, due to the teacher training. The bilingual, inclusive, mixed-age model practiced in Vienna has become a center of bimodal bilingual practice, but it has generated much international interest from near and far because it is also mixed-age and progressive in its teaching practice. Visitors from the fields of education, social work, and psychology find the didactics and methods inspiring and are eager to understand the adjustments in the administrative framework that allow it to take place. Special appreciation comes for the Austrian Deaf community and from hearing and deaf parents. In fact, pupils from other counties have put up with several hours of train travel daily in order to enjoy their schooling in this Viennese project.

This mixed-age model of bilingual inclusion seems to be the future of bimodal bilingual education in Austria. It circumvents the problem of "too few pupils of the same age group" that has hindered peer inclusion for a long time. It is our vision that this model will be put into practice in other parts of Austria as well. For this to happen, a teacher training program (initial and continuing) is needed that focuses on ÖGS learning and didactics. To work in this kind of mixed-age bilingual inclusive educational program, teachers should ideally (1) be prepared to work in a team, (2) see the benefit of investing time in team meetings, supervision, and joint planning, (3) have adequate language competencies, (4) be flexible and open, and (5) be prepared to cooperate with researchers.

It is crucial that deaf teachers are part of the team, but due to the fact that teacher training has only officially accepted deaf candidates since 2013 (they were banned before), there is a great scarcity of trained deaf teachers. And, of course, it would be helpful if politics would finally create the necessary legal foundations for bimodal bilingual education. For a detailed list of structural, practical, and cultural conditions for successful bimodal bilingual education, see Krausneker, Becker et al. (2018).

NOTES

1. Thanks to Johann Weishaupt for the background information on this.
2. Thanks to Jutta Onrednik for her help in summarizing the Salzburg model.
3. See the online map and double-click on Austria: www.univie.ac.at/map-designbilingual (3.5.2017).
4. See www.cisonline.at/gesetzliche-grundlagen (1.7.2017).
5. Since 2015, one teacher training facility (KPH Wien/Krems) has been offering a continuing education program entitled "Inclusive bilingual sign language pedagogy with a focus on studying ÖGS." Since 2018 there is a cooperation with teacher training facilities in Salzburg and in Graz.

REFERENCES

Becker, C., Audeoud, M., Krausneker, V., & Tarcsiová, D. (2017). Bimodal-bilinguale Bildung für Kinder mit Hörbehinderung in Europa. Erhebung des Ist-Stands. *Das Zeichen*, 105, 60–72.

Bortsch, E., & Tischmann, O. (1996). Unsere ersten Erfahrungen. Ein Bericht zum zweisprachigen Unterricht in Graz, Österreich. *Das Zeichen*, 37, 322–332.

Kramreiter, S. (2010). Integration gehörloser Schüler in einem Wiener Gymnasium—Probleme und Perspektiven. *Hörgeschädigte Kinder Erwachsene Hörgeschädigte*, 4(10), 171–174.

Kramreiter, S. (2015). Inklusiv-Bilingual-Mehrstufig: Das Wiener Schulmodell. *Das Zeichen*, 99, 82–93.

Kramreiter, S. (2016). *Bilingualer inklusiver Unterricht bei hörbeeinträchtigten und hörenden Schülern—Ein innovatives Unterrichtskonzept*. Heidelberg: Median Verlag.

Krause, C., Wiesmann, U., & Hannich, H.-J. (2004). *Subjektive Befindlichkeit und Selbstwertgefühl von Grundschulkindern*. Lengerich: Pabst Verlag.

Krausneker, V. (2004). *Viele Blumen schreibt man „Blümer" Soziolinguistische Aspekte des bilingualen Wiener Grundschul-Modells mit Österreichischer Gebärdensprache und Deutsch*. Hamburg: Signum Verlag.

Krausneker, V. (2006). *Staubstumm bis gebärdensprachig. Die österreichische Gebärdensprachgemeinschaft aus soziolinguistischer Perspektive.* Klagenfurt/ Celovec: Drava.

Krausneker, V. (2008). Language use and awareness of Deaf and hearing children in a bilingual setting. In C. Plaza-Pust & E. Morales-Lopez (Eds.), *Sign bilingualism. Language development, interaction, and maintenance in sign language contact situations* (pp. 195–221). Amsterdam: John Benjamins Publishers.

Krausneker, V. (2013). Österreichische Gebärdensprache ist anerkannt. In E. Vetter & R. de Cillia (Eds.), *Sprachenpolitik in Österreich. Bestandsaufnahme 2011* (pp. 127–141). Reihe Sprache im Kontext. Switzerland: Peter Lang Verlag.

Krausneker, V., Becker, C., Audeoud, M., & Tarcsiová, D. (2018). Bimodal bilingual school practice in Europe. In K. Reuter (Ed.), *UNCRPD implementation in Europe—A deaf perspective. Article 24: Education.* (pp. 154–171) EUD Publications.

Krausneker, V., Garber, D., Audeoud, M., Becker, C., & Tarcsiová, D. (2018). Legal foundations supporting the use of sign languages in schools in Europe. In K. Reuter (Ed.), *UNCRPD implementation in Europe—A deaf perspective. Article 24: Education.* (pp. 68–85) EUD Publications.

Krausneker, V., & Schalber, K. (2007). *Sprache Macht Wissen. Zur Situation gehörloser SchülerInnen, Studierender & ihrer LehrerInnen, sowie zur Österreichischen Gebärdensprache in Schule und Universität Wien.* Retrieved May 3, 2017, from www.univie.ac.at/sprachemachtwissen

Pinter, M. (1992). Klagenfurter Unterrichtsprojekt: Bilinguale Förderung hörgeschädigter Kinder in der Gehörlosenschule. Bericht über das 1. Schulversuchsjahr. *Das Zeichen, 20*, 145–150.

Pöllabauer, M. (1992). *Pilotprojekt „Gehörlosenkultur", Endbericht 1990–1992.* Unpublished, University of Klagenfurt.

United Nations. (2006). *Convention on the Rights of People with Disabilities.* Retrieved July 12, 2017, from www.un.org/development/desa/disabilities/ convention-on-the-rights-of-persons-with-disabilities.html

8

Establishing a Bimodal Bilingual Co-Enrollment Program in Germany: Preconditions, Policy, and Preliminary Data

Johannes Hennies and Kristin Hennies

Germany has a long tradition in deaf education. It is home of one of the first schools for deaf in the world, founded by Samuel Heinicke (1727–1790) in Leipzig in 1778, which has influenced deaf education in other countries. Most notably, it is the self-proclaimed motherland of the "German Method." This purely "oral" approach to deaf education has dominated the schools for the deaf from the 1880s to the 1980s internationally and the German schools for the deaf even until the 1990s, when the first bimodal bilingual program was developed. To understand the circumstances of the establishment of the first bimodal bilingual co-enrollment program, as outlined in the second part of this chapter, it is useful to understand the basics of the educational system for deaf and hard-of-hearing (DHH) students in Germany.

THE EDUCATIONAL SYSTEM FOR DHH STUDENTS IN GERMANY

The educational system for DHH students in Germany is characterized by the following aspects with regard to, respectively, early intervention, schools for DHH students, and inclusion in regular schools (for a concise overview of the history and state of deaf education in Germany, see Günther, Hennies, & Hintermair, 2009).

Early Intervention in Germany

Traditionally, the educational system for DHH students in Germany has focused mainly on school and offered little support for very young children. This started to change in the 1960s, when the first pedagogical audiological counseling centers were established. These centers offered diagnostics and educational support for toddlers and preschoolers (Löwe, 1992). Since that time, almost all schools for the deaf have established early intervention centers, with a variety of names and organizational structures (Große, 2003; Renzelberg, 2008). In most regions in Germany, early intervention for DHH children is offered by centers that are closely associated with a school for DHH students, but there is an increasing diversity of early intervention centers for DHH children that are not part of schools. The aim and scope of early intervention for DHH children in Germany has changed fundamentally in the last years. The main reason lies in the establishment of the universal newborn hearing screening (UNHS) in 2009 (Bundesministerium für Gesundheit, 2008). Finckh-Krämer, Spormann-Lagodzinski, and Gross (2000) presented data from the German registry for hearing loss in children before the UNHS, when deafness was diagnosed on average at the age of 1;9 (year; month), severe hearing loss at the age of 2;5, and moderate hearing loss at the age of 4;4. Rohlfs, Wiesner, Drews, Müller, Breitfuß, Schiller, and Hess (2010), in contrast, were able to show that for Hamburg, after the establishment of UNHS, a hearing loss of 35 dB (HL) or higher was detected at a median age of 0;4 and early intervention began at a median age of 0;5. This opens new opportunities for the field of early intervention in DHH children but also changes the way these intervention centers are able to work. They have to gain a deeper understanding about how early cognitive and linguistic development functions and how to support parents and families with very small DHH children (Günther & Hennies, 2012).

However, even under these improved conditions, large-scale assessments have shown that a significant number of deaf children, even with early cochlear implantation, do not reach age-equivalent spoken language abilities (Diller, Graser, & Schmalbrock, 2000; Szagun, 2001, 2010). Thus, these children are in danger of not catching up with their hearing peers and might face long-time consequences in their personal and academic development. Therefore, a growing number of early invention centers started to include the use of signing in their programs, most often accompanying spoken language in the form of simultaneous communication (SimCom) (for an overview, see Hennies, 2010; see also Ringwald-Frimerman, Ingber, & Most, this volume). There is a growing literature advocating a bimodal bilingual early intervention approach for a larger number of DHH children in Germany (Becker, 2013; Günther, Hänel-Faulhaber, & Hennies, 2009; Günther & Hennies, 2012; Hofmann & Hennies, 2015). These authors argue that the inclusion of both a natural sign language and spoken language might be the safest way to ensure an unimpaired language acquisition in at least one language, and they offer suggestions on how even with two hearing parents, a complete language input in spoken and sign language can be ensured. Although this is an emerging field in German deaf education, the number of early intervention centers offering bimodal bilingual education and employing deaf professionals as part of their team is still very small (Deutscher Gehörlosen-Bund, 2016; Renzelberg, 2008).

Schools for DHH Students in Germany

In Germany, there are established schools for the deaf that have a very stable number of students. There are currently about 60 schools for DHH students and 10 specialized centers for vocational training. Contrary to the almost unanimous prediction of experts in the field of deaf education (Große, 2003; Günther, 2002; Hartmann-Börner, 2006), there has been no decline in the number of students in these schools over the last 15 years. Germany's official census bureau has registered only a small fluctuation in the total amount of 10,500 to 11,200 students in these schools during this period (Statistisches Bundesamt, 2001–2016). Against the background of a decreasing general population of students, this qualifies as an increase of 15%. However, the student populations in these schools have become more heterogeneous, with a wide range of hearing loss and remaining auditory abilities (including an increasing number of children with central hearing loss), language preferences with regard to spoken and sign language, learning abilities, and social and ethnic background (see Große, 2003). There is a similar shift in this group as in other Western countries, because the classic core population in schools for DHH students (i.e., bilateral sensorineural deaf to severely hard-of-hearing students with little access to auditory information and spoken language) is decreasing due to modern hearing technology, widespread cochlear implantation, and UNHS.

Germany has held on to a purely spoken language approach in schools for DHH students longer than most other countries. The first change was marked by a consensus paper by different experts in the field, among them the leaders of the German Deaf Association and the Association of German Teachers of the Deaf, in 1982, which officially allowed the use of SimCom in the schools (Braun, Donath, Gast, Keller, Rammel, & Tigges, 1982). The first explicit bimodal bilingual school program was established at the Hamburg School for the Deaf in 1992; the first students in this program left school in 2005. The main characteristic of this program was the equal amount of time spent on sign language and spoken/written language in the classroom, because a large part of the lessons was co-taught by a deaf and a hearing teacher. The program was also the first to employ deaf professionals as fluent signers for instruction in all subjects. Because bimodal bilingual education was heavily criticized by the overwhelming majority of German teachers for the deaf and academic professionals in this field, the program could only be realized under the condition of a scientific survey, examining the work of the teachers and documenting the development of the deaf students until they were leaving school. The studies within the survey showed a very favorable language development in

German Sign Language and in written German and higher academic results compared to other groups with DHH students (Bizer & Karl, 2002; Günther, 1999; Günther & Schäfke, 2004). These results have led to the decision by the Hamburg School for the Deaf to adopt the bimodal bilingual concept for all students and by other schools to start similar programs. In 2000, Große (2003) already counted 19 bimodal bilingual classes with deaf and hearing teachers or—in the absence of deaf colleagues at the school—two hearing teachers working as a team. This represents 1.9% of all classes in the study. An additional 55% of all classes used "manual communication" to a lesser degree.

In a second bimodal bilingual school project at the Berlin School for the Deaf, which ran from 2001 until 2010, the research team could verify the findings from the first project in Hamburg. There was the additional observation that some DHH students in this group with modern hearing aids and cochlear implants also showed good spoken language development (Günther & Hennies, 2011; Hennies & Günther, 2015). Mainly because of the positive experience in these two projects, an increasing number of schools have developed bimodal bilingual programs. This development correlates with the sharp increase in deaf teachers in schools for the deaf. There were almost no deaf teachers in German schools for most of the 20th century; Schumann (1929) only found one deaf teacher for drawing and handicrafts in the 1920s. This started to change in the 1970s, when Rehling (1981) documented the employment of 5 deaf und 13 hard-of-hearing teachers in German schools. Twenty years later, Große (2003, p. 52) reported 16 deaf und 12 hard-of-hearing teachers. When the latest study on this subject was conducted in 2011 by Wozniak (2013), there were 151 DHH teachers. About 50% of these teachers were deaf and 50% were hard of hearing.

Another result of the bimodal bilingual projects is the increasing openness of state governments to introduce German Sign Language as a regular subject in the schools for DHH students. The weekly television magazine program for DHH people in Germany conducted a survey in 2015, reporting that 6 of the 16 German states declared that they include the subject German Sign Language in the curriculum of schools for DHH students (Bayerischer Rundfunk, 2015). Although bimodal bilingual education is still only offered for a minority of DHH children, it can be seen as an established educational concept in Germany. This trend seems to go in a different direction than in other Western countries, where bimodal bilingual programs sometimes seem to be in decline because of the lack of evidence for better outcomes than achieved in other programs (Marschark, Tang, & Knoors, 2014). Günther and Hennies (2015) address these discrepancies and suggest that one reason for the different results between most of the studies cited by Marschark et al. (2014) and the results of the two German programs lies in the actual concept of bimodal bilingualism itself. According to Marschark et al. (2014), an obstacle to an evidence-based perspective on bimodal bilingual deaf education is the absence of a concise definition of what qualifies as a bimodal bilingual approach. This makes them conclude that "bilingual deaf education" can be described as "use of both signed language/signed system and the written/spoken vernacular in educating DHH youth" (Marschark et al., 2014, p. 449). Arguably, this definition is too broad to enable the evaluation of the efficiency of an educational program. Many international programs, however, are modeled after the Swedish example, which was developed in the 1970s as a successive-bilingual model with sign language as a first language and written language as second language (Heiling, 1995). This approach did not include the use of spoken language because deaf children at that time could be characterized by the simple fact "that they cannot hear" (Svartholm, 1994, p. 63). However, since the advent of UNHS and the possibility for DHH children to receive modern hearing aids and cochlear implants at a very young age, a successive-bilingual model no longer seems to be the right concept for all children. Svartholm (2007, p. 137) describes the dilemma for the Swedish schools when she argues that deaf children without cochlear implants "must be guaranteed continuing Swedish Sign Language and written Swedish proficiency, the kind of bilingual program that has been successful in developing these skills in the past" but also wants the schools "to combine this kind of bilingual program with an education for deaf children for whom speech and hearing are important."

Günther and Hennies (2015, p. 505) argue that the different concept of the bimodal bilingual programs in Germany has helped avoid the backlash that can be seen in some other countries with regard to sign language in deaf education. The programs in Hamburg and Berlin, which have been the blueprint for bimodal bilingual education in German-speaking countries, have followed a simultaneous bilingual model from the beginning, offering equal access to German Sign Language and spoken and written German from primary school (and in some cases preschool). The choice for such a program can also be explained against the background of a long oral/aural tradition in German schools, because a successive-bilingual model would just not have been possible at the time of the first program. However, this concept could be more adaptable to the needs of an increasingly diverse population in schools for the DHH with opportunities for every child to develop individual language preferences and could be responsible for more robust findings regarding the outcome of these programs in Germany.

Inclusion in Regular Schools in Germany

Despite the fact that the idea of mainstream education of deaf children already started in the 19th century in Germany with the work of Johann

Baptist Graser (1766–1841), deaf children remained almost exclusively in special schools for the deaf until the 1960s (Leonhardt, 2001; Löwe, 1985). Change in the subsequent four decades, however, was slow. The first year the census bureau provided data on the number of DHH students in special schools and mainstream programs in Germany was 2001. This survey showed that 80% of these students were educated in schools for the deaf and 20% in mainstream schools (Statistisches Bundesamt, 2001). With the ratification of the Convention of the United Nations on the Rights of Persons with Disabilities (UNCRPD, United Nations, 2006) in 2009, the debate on special educational needs and the recommended school settings changed rapidly in Germany. From 2001 to 2016, the national census bureau found a continuous increase in German DHH students enrolled in regular schools, while the total number of students in special schools for DHH students remained roughly the same. These results, compared to the census of 2001, show a different ratio, with 61% of DHH students in special schools and 39% in regular schools. The association of the headmasters of schools for the deaf in Germany and neighboring countries conducted an internal survey and found that there are additional DHH children who are supported in regular schools but do not appear in the official statistics. This could mean that there are as many DHH children enrolled in regular schools as there are in schools for the DHH (D. Schleicher, personal communication, January 27, 2014). This increase in enrollment in regular schools can be explained best by two factors. First, Günther (2002) already suggested that a large number of mainly hard-of-hearing children have always attended regular schools without being recognized and therefore without support by specialized educators. It seems that with the early identification of a hearing loss and increased awareness, these children are getting more help than 15 years ago. Second, it seems that more DHH children are now eligible for education support for whom schools for DHH students would not have felt responsible a few years ago, such as students with unilateral hearing loss in regular schools. There are no official census data on the demographic characteristics of DHH children in regular schools, but studies suggest that they are not fully comparable to DHH students in special schools. DHH children in the mainstream display better hearing and spoken language abilities, they rarely have additional handicaps, and they usually do not communicate in German Sign Language (Hennies & Hintermair, 2015). A deaf student using sign language interpreting in mainstream schools is a relative new phenomenon in Germany, which until recently could only be found in a pilot project or as part of individual solutions (Appelbaum, 2008; Latuske, 2004). Since the ratification of UNCRPD, however, German courts have consistently ordered the state and local authorities to pay for sign language interpreting for deaf children wanting to attend regular schools. As a result, the number of these children has increased to about 35 DHH children attending regular schools with interpreters in recent years (Marquardt, 2014). There is only limited information about the academic success, social integration, and general well-being of these children.

Becker and Meinhardt (2013) interviewed five interpreters in these settings and found different attitudes toward their job. Two of them concentrate just on being an interpreter and would not help with smaller tasks within the classroom, like assisting the teacher or other students. The other three see themselves as part of a team and therefore would engage in educational tasks besides interpreting. Both groups, however, describe conflicts between the professional attitude as an interpreter and the necessities in interacting with DHH children in an educational context. This echoes the international discussion on education interpreting. Marschark, Sapere, Convertino, and Seewagen (2005) present findings that even high-quality interpreting does not allow DHH students to participate fully in lessons in mainstream settings. The authors conclude that these students actually need additional educational assistance that is rarely provided by sign language interpreters, partly because it does not fit their professional role and partly because of a lack of awareness of these needs. In summary, both of these articles stress that direct instruction by a competent teacher can be expected to be more beneficial to DHH children than sign language interpreting.

In Germany, the vast majority of DHH children in regular schools are the only DHH children in their class. A study by Baldzun and Hintermair (2009) among teachers visiting DHH students in regular schools revealed that only 4% of these children have contact with other DHH children in their class or school. Hennies and Hintermair (2015) found, in a study incorporating 154 DHH adolescents in regular schools in three states, that over 90% do not meet other DHH students. There are just a few programs in which a group of DHH and hearing children learn together. Some of these programs are situated within the school for the deaf. Große (2003) reports that 10% of German schools for the deaf include hearing children without diagnosed learning difficulties. This reverse integration was established more than 30 years ago for the first time (Pfalzinstitut für Hörbehinderte, 2008). Co-enrollment programs that are situated in regular schools can only be found in some states or regions (Jacobs, 2014). These co-enrollment programs proved to be beneficial, but they only include DHH children who use spoken language. There have been only a few attempts to include deaf students using sign language in a co-enrollment program with hard-of-hearing and hearing students. Bredehöft (2017) described a secondary co-enrollment program that ran from 2014 to 2017 where one deaf student was educated together with a group of hard-of-hearing and hearing peers in order to reach a general higher education entrance qualification ("Abitur," which allows entrance to university). In this program, a secondary school teacher and a teacher for the DHH offered bimodal bilingual instruction for the whole class. The author described that bimodal bilingual instruction worked well and to the benefit of all students. However, despite the best intentions by teachers and students, some of whom also learned the basics of German Sign Language, the social integration between the deaf student on one side and the hearing and hard-of-hearing students of the other side was troublesome because of the language barrier. This points to the necessity to start a bimodal bilingual co-enrollment program in primary school in order to give the students time to interact and to learn to communicate from the start, similar to the only permanent co-enrollment program in a German-speaking country, in Vienna (Kramreiter 2016; Krausneker & Kramreiter, this volume).

THE BIMODAL BILINGUAL CO-ENROLLMENT PROGRAM IN ERFURT

Establishment of the Program

The co-enrollment program in Erfurt started as an initiative of parents of DHH children, just like the bimodal bilingual school programs in Hamburg and Berlin. In Erfurt, parents were considering the best school choice for their children who had received bimodal bilingual early intervention but also had been visiting regular kindergartens. These families were supported by the early intervention center of Erfurt (ECC). The parents started to discuss with the center's specialist the options, most of them initially preferring the use of a sign language interpreter. When it became clear in 2014 that there was a whole group of parents of DHH children and some deaf parents with hearing children (CODAs) who were about to start school in 2016 and 2017, the specialist suggested a bimodal bilingual co-enrollment program as an alternative model that appeared to be more suitable for the social-emotional and linguistic needs of these children. The ECC started cooperating with the University of Education in Heidelberg to ensure the quality of the suggested program and to initiate a research program to evaluate the progress of the children in school. During the initial contact with the Ministry of Education in Thuringia and the local school authorities, the project team received positive feedback for the idea and started to discuss the program with several regular schools. After two primary schools rejected the request immediately, a Thuringian comprehensive school (TGS am Roten Berg) agreed to participate in the project. In Thuringia, the establishment of comprehensive schools is supported by the state government because it allows all students to learn together and stay in one school during primary and secondary education, in contrast to the traditional school system in Germany, where schools are separated along three graduation levels. The teachers and headmaster of the school were very motivated and eager to participate in the project. They had prior experience with students with disabilities but no specific knowledge about DHH children and German Sign Language.

In October 2015, the project team presented the project proposal, which was subsequently submitted in written form, at a joint meeting with the headmaster of the school, the head of the local school authority, and the representatives of the Ministry of Education. Although the initial reaction seemed positive, the Ministry of Education rejected the proposal half a year later in a meeting with the explanation that co-enrollment programs are not in accordance with state policy on inclusion. However, it was also clarified that these parents had the right to send their DHH children to the comprehensive school and that the school itself was allowed to build a bimodal bilingual program without any interference by the Ministry of Education. After the local school authorities confirmed their support for this project and promised to finance the necessary additional teachers, the project team proceeded to search for suitable teachers with a degree in deaf education who were fluent in German Sign Language and ideally deaf themselves. Because of an extensive search by the project team via personal contacts and social networks, the local school authorities were able to recruit a deaf and a hearing teacher who met the criteria. They are employed at the local school for the deaf, where they also teach some lessons, but they are seconded to the comprehensive school for the duration of project and for most of their weekly hours. There was one further interference by the city of Erfurt, which objected to enrollment of DHH children from other school districts, but this was finally settled because the comprehensive school had the authority to choose its own students.

In August 2016, three DHH children and one CODA started the program and in August 2017 an additional five DHH children and another CODA joined the same year-overlapping class, so that the core group now consists of eight DHH children, two CODAs, and ten hearing children. Since there were substitute teachers for the better part of the school year 2016–2017 and the ongoing political discussion was not completely resolved, the research project really started in the school year 2017–2018. The project will focus on the linguistic and social-emotional development of the DHH children and CODAs as well as on the quality of instruction and educational solutions of the bimodal bilingual lessons.

Preconditions for the Bimodal Bilingual Program

To establish such a program in an at least partly adverse political climate, several conditions had to be met. The first was a close cooperation with the early intervention and counseling center for hearing and communication in Erfurt (ECC). The ECC is an institution independent from the local school for the deaf, under the umbrella of the Herbert Feuchte Foundation Association (HFS). It covers most of Thuringia and offers one or two early intervention visits a week, depending on the funding by the local government granted to an individual family with a DHH child. Early intervention is tailored to the specific needs and circumstances of each family and can be provided at home and at the kindergarten. Following the principles of family-based intervention (Moeller, Carr, Seaver, Brown, & Holzinger, 2013), the ECC is cooperating with parents and all the medical and therapeutic professionals; it also helps in the transition from kindergarten to school. The ECC has been offering bimodal bilingual early intervention for DHH children and CODAs for about seven years. There are a variety of different features in the bimodal bilingual early intervention program, such as sign language classes at home, family gatherings for deaf and hearing parents, and sign language workshops for nursery teachers. Additionally, the ECC provides communication assistance in the kindergarten for DHH children, using sign language dominantly. The communication assistants are educators who are fluent in German Sign Language, because most are DHH themselves. Without the work of the ECC, it would not have been possible to gather the parents and prepare the bimodal bilingual co-enrollment program in time.

The second precondition was the support and the solidarity of the children's parents. The majority of the parents of DHH children and CODAs in this group are DHH themselves and supported the idea very strongly. The parents also founded a local association for bimodal bilingual education and informed the state's ombudsman for persons with disabilities about their wishes and needs. Beside the actual quality of the proposed program, the ability of these parents to stand up for their rights proved to be one of the strongest arguments during the discussion with representatives of the different levels of government.

The third precondition for the realization of the program was the support of a coalition that was as broad as possible, most notably the teachers and headmaster of the comprehensive school, the ECC, the University of Education in Heidelberg, and the local school authority.

The final precondition was the organization of a preschool program for DHH children, as will be outlined in the next section.

Preschool Program

A specific preschool program seemed necessary for several reasons. Usually, a regular kindergarten prepares children for school by providing information to the parents and by training preschool competences in children, such as phonological awareness and working with school material. DHH children might not really be included in these preschool experiences, because most kindergarten teachers are not competent in German Sign Language. Furthermore, DHH children have different needs with respect to preschool education than hearing children; these differing needs are not addressed in most kindergartens. It also seemed necessary for the DHH children and CODAs in the bimodal bilingual co-enrollment program to meet each other before the school started and to become familiar with the specifics of bimodal bilingual instruction, especially the team teaching situation. Therefore, a preschool program was developed that included four one-hour sessions and took place in the ECC. During the sessions, the hearing and deaf parents had time to meet and share their views and experiences. The sessions were organized by the early intervention specialist and a teacher of the bimodal bilingual school.

The preschool program focused on four different aspects. First, the social-emotional well-being of the DHH children in the group was a primary concern. Since they live in different parts of the city and the state, they had seen the others only occasionally before. Also, most of them were the only DHH children in the kindergarten they attended before. The preschool program provided peer contacts with other DHH children and enabled the group to get to know each other before the school, with all its additional challenges, started. Second, the children could get used to the structure of a school day and the lessons. They also became acquainted with different forms of social learning setting (e.g., plenum, working with a partner or in a small group). The sessions provided helpful information for the teacher about the competencies and interactions of the DHH children. Third, since the DHH children depend on sign language input, they should also be familiar with a bimodal bilingual team teaching situation before starting school. Therefore, the early intervention specialist and the teacher used spoken German and German Sign Language throughout the sessions, with each of them representing one language. Fourth, DHH children with sign language skills and CODAs have different prior knowledge of the written language and therefore other early literacy competences compared to other children, specifically because of the use of fingerspelling in everyday conversations in German Sign Language. The preschool program used fingerspelling as a bridge to the first written words and supported the development of an early visual literacy vocabulary. The preschool program was viewed as very positive by educators and parents alike and enabled a smooth transition to school.

Characteristics of the Bimodal Bilingual Program in Erfurt

The bimodal bilingual program has the following characteristics:

1. The school accepts DHH children and CODAs in every school year.
2. The school organizes year-overlapping classes with vertical groups, consisting of students of two grades. This enables the

new DHH children to learn from their older peers and provides them with the opportunity to learn at their own speed.

3. All lessons are taught by a team of teachers, one using spoken language and the other one using sign language as well as SimCom occasionally.

4. The other teachers working in the class take a course providing basic knowledge in deaf education and German Sign Language.

5. The lessons take place in a room with improved acoustics, and the DHH children are connected to a digital wireless transmitting system for spoken language if they choose to.

6. German Sign Language is introduced as a subject of its own for the DHH children, the CODAs, and the rest of the class.

7. The lessons in music are adapted to the specific needs of all children.

8. The lessons in English as the first official second language are accompanied by American Sign Language (ASL) signs for the DHH children and CODAs.

9. Students have the possibility to stay in this school until grade 10, thus receiving a lower general school-leaving certificate after the completion of grade 9 ("Hauptschulabschluss") or a higher general school-leaving certificate after the completion of grade 10 ("Realschulabschluss"). Furthermore, cooperation with a high school will be established for those DHH children who are able to achieve a general higher education entrance qualification.

To support the school in setting up permanent cooperation and structures, a coordinator will oversee the first six years of the program and counsel teachers and other school staff. Furthermore, the program will be evaluated with a focus on the individual development of the DHH children and CODAs, the parents' and teachers' perspectives on the program, and the didactic solutions for the bimodal bilingual classroom. The research team will administer a variety of scientific methods, from standardized tests to structured observations and interviews.

SUMMARY AND CONCLUSION

This chapter explained the current state of the educational system for DHH children in Germany with regard to early intervention, schools for the deaf, and inclusion in regular schools and described the planning and establishment of the first bimodal bilingual co-enrollment program within this system. The school project in Erfurt became possible due to a variety of factors that are outlined, specifically the existence of a bimodal bilingual early intervention center, the solidarity of

parents of DHH children and CODAs, the interdisciplinary cooperation of different institutions, and the cooperation of a regular school
that invested in the program. The evaluation of the program provides
the unique opportunity to collect data on a group of DHH children
who learn under conditions enabling them to choose the language they
prefer to use and promoting learning together with hearing peers. After
the results of the two bimodal bilingual school projects in the Hamburg
and Berlin schools for the deaf, this will be the third research project
collecting data on a bimodal bilingual class from the first grade on in
Germany. If the results prove to be positive, it could be a beneficial example for children, parents, and teachers elsewhere.

ACKNOWLEDGMENTS

The Herbert Feuchte Foundation Association (HFS) supports this project by funding a part-time project coordinator.

REFERENCES

Appelbaum, B. (2008). Integration mit Dolmetscher: Ein Beispiel aus der
    Sekundarstufe I (Klasse 5–10). *Hörgeschädigte Kinder—Erwachsene Hörgeschädigte,*
    45(3), 135f.
Baldzun, B., & Hintermair, M. (2009). Identitätsarbeit hörgeschädigter
    Schülerinnen und Schüler an Regelschulen—eine Studie zur Wahrnehmung
    der Situation durch den Sonderpädagogischen Dienst. *Hörgeschädigtenpädag*
    ogik, 63, 50–62.
Bayerischer Rundfunk (2015, November 14). *DGS als Wahlpflichtfach.* Retrieved
    from   http://www.br.de/fernsehen/bayerisches-fernsehen/sendungen/
    sehen-statt-hoeren/sehen-statt-hoeren-dgs-wahlpflichtfach-100.html
Becker, C. (2013). Bilinguale Frühförderung. In A. Leonhardt (Ed.), *Frühes*
    Hören. Hörschädigungen ab dem ersten Lebenstag erkennen und therapieren (pp.
    209–225). München: Reinhardt.
Becker, C., & Meinhardt, J. (2013). Lernen mit Gebärdensprachdolmetschern.
    Überlegungen und Befunde zur aktuellen Praxis in Deutschland. *Das Zeichen,*
    27(95), 402–415.
Bizer, S., & Karl, A.-K. (2002). *Entwicklung eines Wortschatztests für*
    gehörlose Kinder im Grundschulalter in Gebärden-, Schrift- und Lautsprache.
    Hamburg: Universität Hamburg. Retrieved from http://www.sub.uni-
    hamburg.de/opus/frontdoor.php?source_opus=881
Braun, A., Donath, P., Gast, R., Keller, A., Rammel, G., & Tigges, J.
    (1982). *Kommunikation mit Gehörlosen in Lautsprache und Gebärde.*
    München: Bundesverband der Elternvertreter und Förderer Deutscher
    Gehörlosenschulen.
Bredehöft, J. (2017). Hörend, schwerhörig, gehörlos—Gemeinsam auf dem
    Weg zum Abitur: Schüler der Stadtteilschule Hamburg-Mitte leben den
    Inklusionsgedanken—Ein   Erfahrungsbericht.   *Hörgeschädigtenpädagogik,*
    71(1), 20–25.

Bundesministerium für Gesundheit. (2008). Bekanntmachung eines Beschlusses des Gemeinsamen Bundesausschusses über eine Änderung der Kinder-Richtlinien: Einführung eines Neugeborenen-Hörscreenings. Retrieved from www.g-ba.de/downloads/39-261-681/2008-06-19-Kinder-H%C3%B6rscreening_BAnz.pdf

Deutscher Gehörlosen-Bund. (2016). *Sprachen bilden. Bilinguale Förderung mit Gebärdensprache—Anregungen für die Praxis.* Berlin: Deutscher Gehörlosen-Bund.

Diller, G., Graser, P., & Schmalbrock, C. (2000). *Hörgerichtete Frühförderung hochgradig hörgeschädigter Kleinkinder.* Heidelberg: Winter (Edition S).

Finckh-Krämer, U., Spormann-Lagodzinski, M.-E., & Gross, M. (2000). German registry for hearing loss in children: Results after 4 years. *International Journal of Pediatric Otorhinolaryngology, 56*(2), 113–127.

Große, K.-D. (2003). *Das Bildungswesen für Hörbehinderte in der Bundesrepublik Deutschland: Daten und Fakten zu Realitäten und Erfordernissen.* Heidelberg: Winter (Edition S).

Günther, K.-B. (1999). *Bilingualer Unterricht mit gehörlosen Grundschülern. Zwischenbericht zum Hamburger Bilingualen Schulversuch. Theorie & Praxis 3.* Hamburg: Hörgeschädigte Kinder.

Günther, K.-B. (2002). Veränderungen in der schulischen Betreuung Hörgeschädigter Perspektiven aus dem Förderschwerpunkt Hören. *Hörgeschädigte Kinder—Erwachsene Hörgeschädigte, 39*(1), 5–13.

Günther, K.-B., Hänel-Faulhaber, B., & Hennies, J. (2009). Bilinguale Frühförderung hochgradig hörgeschädigter Kinder—Entwicklungstheoretische Grundlagen und frühpädagogische Bildungspraxis. *Frühförderung Interdisziplinär, 28*(4), 179–186.

Günther, K.-B., & Hennies, J. (Eds.) (2011). *Bilingualer Unterricht in Gebärden-, Schrift- und Lautsprache mit gehörlosen SchülerInnen in der Primarstufe: Zwischenbericht zum Berliner Bilingualen Schulversuch.* Hamburg: Signum.

Günther, K.-B., & Hennies, J. (2012). From pre-symbolic gestures to language: Multisensory early intervention in deaf children. In A. Foolen, U. Lüdtke, J. Zlatev, & T. Racine (Eds.), *Moving ourselves, moving others: (E)motion in the making of consciousness, intersubjectivity and language* (pp. 369–382). Amsterdam: John Benjamins.

Günther, K.-B., & Hennies, J. (Eds.) (2015). Stand und Perspektiven einer bimodal-bilingualen Erziehung und Bildung für gehörlose und schwerhörige Kinder: Eine diskursive Auseinandersetzung mit dem Sammelband Bilingualism and Bilingual Deaf Education, hrsg. von Marc Marschark, Gladys Tang & Harry Knoors. *Das Zeichen, 29*(101), 498–508.

Günther, K.-B., Hennies, J., & Hintermair, M. (2009). Trends and developments in deaf education in Germany. In D. Moores & M. Miller (Eds.), *Deaf people around the world: Educational, developmental, and social perspectives* (pp. 178–193). Washington, DC: Gallaudet University Press.

Günther, K.-B., & Schäfke, I. (2004). *Bilinguale Erziehung als Förderkonzept für gehörlose SchülerInnen: Abschlussbericht zum Hamburger Bilingualen Schulversuch.* Hamburg: Signum.

Hartmann-Börner, C. (2006). Im Gespräch: Christiane Hartmann-Börner [interview]. *Hörgeschädigtenpädagogik, 60*(2), 73–74.

Heiling, K. (1995). *The development of deaf children—Academic achievement levels and social processes.* Hamburg: Signum.

Hennies, J. (2010). Frühförderung hörgeschädigter Kinder: ein aktueller Überblick. *Hörgeschädigte Kinder—Erwachsene Hörgeschädigte, 47*(1), 3–5.

Hennies, J., & Günther, K.-B. (Eds.) (2015). Abschlussbericht zum Berliner Bilingualen Schulversuch. *DFGS Forum, 23*(1) [Supplement].

Hennies, J., & Hintermair, M. (2015). Die Bedeutung von gleichbetroffenen Peers für die Entwicklung hörgeschädigter Kinder in inklusiven Settings. *DFGS Forum, 23*(1), 10–30.

Hofmann, K., & Hennies, J. (2015). Bimodal-bilinguale Frühförderung: Ein Modell zur Evaluation von Input, Sprachnutzung und Kompetenz (EvISK). *Hörgeschädigtenpädagogik, 69*(5), 138–144.

Jacobs, H. (2014). Von der Außenklasse zur Klasse mit inklusivem Bildungsangebot für Schüler mit Hörschädigung. In U. Horsch & S. Bischoff (Eds.), *Inklusion konkret. Wissen aus Forschung und Praxis* (pp. 61–88). Heidelberg: Median.

Kramreiter, S. (2016). *Bilingualer inklusiver Unterricht bei hörbeeinträchtigten und hörenden Schülern—Ein innovatives Unterrichtskonzept. Dokumentation einer wissenschaftlichen Untersuchung in einer inklusiven/integrativen Klasse in Wien.* Heidelberg: Median.

Latuske, M. (2004): *Modellprojekt: Gehörlose Kinder an der Regelschule mit Gebärdensprachdolmetscherinnen.* Retrieved from http://gehoerlosekinder. de/Ebene02/infos_zub_02/projekt_regelschule/Projekt_Lat_komplett. pdf?nach_id=480

Leonhardt, A. (2001). Gemeinsames Lernen von hörenden und hörgeschädigten Schülern: Historische Aspekte und aktuelle Sichtweisen. In A. Leonhardt (Ed.), *Gemeinsames Lernen von hörenden und hörgeschädigten Schülern: Ziele—Wege—Möglichkeiten* (pp. 11–21). Hamburg: Verlag Hörgeschädigte Kinder.

Löwe, A. (1985). *Hörgeschädigte Kinder in Regelschulen.* Dortmund: Geers-Stiftung.

Löwe, A. (1992). *Hörgeschädigtenpädagogik international, Geschichte, Länder, Personen, Kongresse: eine Einführung für Eltern, Lehrer und Therapeuten hörgeschädigter Kinder.* Heidelberg: Schindele.

Marquardt, E. (Writer & Director) (2014). Inklusion an Regelschulen [Television series episode]. In I. Wiemer (Executive Producer), *Sehen statt Hören.* Munich: Bayerischer Rundfunk.

Marschark, M., Knoors, H., & Tang, G. (2014). Perspectives on bilingualism and bilingual education for deaf learners. In M. Marschark, G. Tang, & H. Knoors (Eds.), *Bilingualism and bilingual deaf education* (pp. 445–476). New York: Oxford University Press.

Marschark, M., Sapere, P., Convertino, C., & Seewagen, R. (2005). Educational interpreting: Access and outcomes. In M. Marschark, R. Peterson, & E. A. Winston (Eds.), *Sign language interpreting and interpreter education. Directions for research and practice* (pp. 57–83). New York: Oxford University Press.

Marschark, M., Tang, G., & Knoors, H. (Eds.) (2014). *Bilingualism and bilingual deaf education.* New York: Oxford University Press.

Moeller, M. P., Carr, G., Seaver, L., Brown, A. S., & Holzinger, D. (2013). Best practices in family-centered early intervention for children who are deaf or hard of hearing: An international consensus statement. *Journal of Deaf Studies and Deaf Education, 18*(4), 429–448.

Pfalzinstitut für Hörbehinderte (Ed.) (2008). *30 Jahre Präventive Integration: Theorie und Praxis am Pfalzinstitut für Hörbehinderte in Frankenthal/Pfalz.* Heidelberg: Median.

Rehling, B. (1981). Hörgeschädigte Lehrer von Hörgeschädigten. *Hörgeschädigt enpädagogik, 35*(5), 266–279.

Renzelberg, G. (2008). Die Beratungsstelle für Pädagogische Audiologie—Von der Vision zur Realität. *Hörgeschädigte Kinder—Erwachsene Hörgeschädigte, 45*(4) [Supplement].

Rohlfs, A.-K., Wiesner, T., Drews, H., Müller, F., Breitfuß, A., Schiller, R., & Hess, M. (2010). Interdisciplinary approach to design, performance and quality management in a multicentre newborn hearing screening project: Introduction, methods and results of the newborn hearing screening in Hamburg (Part I). *European Journal of Pediatrics, 169,* 1353–1360.

Schumann, P. (1929). Taubstumme Lehrer [Kleine Mitteilungen]. *Blätter für Taubstummenbildung, 42*(17), 317.

Statistisches Bundesamt. (2001–2016). Fachserie 11—Reihe 1: Bildung und Kultur: Allgemeinbildende Schulen.

Svartholm, K. (1994). Second language learning in the Deaf. In I. Ahlgren & K. Hyltenstam (Eds.), *Bilingualism in deaf education* (pp. 61–70). Hamburg: Signum.

Svartholm, K. (2007). Cochlear-implanted children in Sweden's bilingual schools. In L. Komesaroff (Ed.), *Bioethics and cochlear implantation* (pp. 137–150). Washington, DC: Gallaudet University.

Szagun, G. (2001). *Wie Sprache entsteht; Spracherwerb bei Kindern mit beeinträchtigtem und normalen Hören.* Weinheim: Beltz.

Szagun, G. (2010). Einflüsse auf den Spracherwerb bei Kindern mit Cochlea Implantat: Implantationsalter, soziale Faktoren und die Sprache der Eltern. *Hörgeschädigte Kinder—Erwachsene Hörgeschädigte, 47*(1), 8–36.

United Nations. (2006). *Convention on the Rights of Persons with Disabilities and Optional Protocol.* Retrieved from http://www.un.org/disabilities/documents/convention/convoptprot-e.pdf

Wozniak, L. (2013). Hörgeschädigte Lehrer für hörgeschädigte Schülerinnen und Schüler!? *Sonderpädagogik in Berlin, 1,* 12–16. Retrieved from http://www.vds-in-berlin.de/Heft%201_2013/Beitrag%20Wozniak.pdf

9

Include to Grow: Prospects for Bilingual and Bicultural Education for Both Deaf and Hearing Students

Lucrezia Di Gregorio, Vincenzina Campana, Maria Lavecchia, and Pasquale Rinaldi

Historically, in Italy, as in many other countries, deaf children were enrolled in special schools, most of them residential ones. These students stayed in dormitories during weekdays, and only children whose families lived in the school's neighborhood went home on weekends while others went home only on holidays. Sign language was used in these schools on a daily basis not only to teach but also to establish and maintain social interactions. In 1977, the Italian government passed Law 517 (Law 517/1977) allowing families to enroll their deaf children (as well as children with other disabilities) in mainstream schools along with hearing children. Only since 1992, with Law 104 (Law 104/1992), have children's families had the right to request the presence in the classroom of a teaching assistant who could also use Italian Sign Language (LIS). Nowadays, deaf children in Italy are provided with different types of schooling, but in most cases, there is only one deaf child per class of hearing children (see Caselli et al., 2006; Meristo et al., 2007; Rinaldi et al., 2015). Very few public schools offer bilingual curricula that involve a consistent use of Italian and LIS in the classroom. Among these, the Tommaso Silvestri–State Institute for Specialized Education for the Deaf (ISISS) Magarotto School, located in the center of Rome, Via Nomentana 56, offers a bilingual bicultural curriculum for both deaf and hearing pupils.

HISTORY

The Tommaso Silvestri–ISISS Magarotto School was the first public school for deaf people in Italy and has a long history that began in 1700 with the journey of Father Tommaso Silvestri (the person who the school was named after), who had been to Paris to "learn the art of teaching to the deaf and dumb" from the famous Abbot l'Épée. On his return to Rome, Tommaso Silvestri opened a school for deaf children—with only eight pupils attending—at the home of lawyer Di Pietro, who had funded his trip to Paris. In the following years, the school changed its location several times until 1889, when the building where it is currently located was finally built. As shown in the manual *A Way of Teaching the Deaf and Dumb to Speak Fluently* written by Tommaso Silvestri (Maragna & Vasta, 2015), the proposed model of education was the bilingual model, written and spoken Italian and sign language. After the Second International Conference of Educators of the Deaf (ICED) in Milan in 1880, the school in Rome also abandoned the bilingual model, choosing rigid oralism instead. In reality, signs that had been banned in classrooms were used in daily life inside the school premises for internal communication, for confession, and even during Mass, when communication had to be learned without any misunderstanding. The Institute accommodated up to 300 pupils per year, and, in 1939, a school for the specialization of teachers was created; it was self-financed and operated until a few years ago.

Starting from the Unification of Italy (1861), the school came under the jurisdiction of the Ministry of Education and became, together with schools based in Milan and Palermo, one of the three state institutions for the deaf, under the name of the Royal Institute for the Deaf and Dumb. Subsequently, two important events that changed the life of the school occurred: the drastic decline of the number of students due to the abovementioned Law 517 and the arrival, in the same building of the school, of a team of researchers belonging to the Institute of Psychology of the Italian National Research Council (today Institute of Cognitive Sciences and Technologies [ISTC-CNR]). In this context, ISTC-CNR offered its scientific supervision in transforming the kindergarten (1990) and the primary school (1992) located in Via Nomentana. At that time, the schools were annexed to the State Institute of Deaf. However, since September 1, 2000, they have been legally detached from the State Institute of Deaf and aggregated with the ISISS Magarotto, a group of specialized schools for the deaf. The school, which previously was a special school, attended exclusively by deaf pupils, started enrolling hearing children living in the neighborhood and has become an integrated school where a bilingual Italian/LIS education program is implemented in a co-enrollment model (Maragna, 2004; Rinaldi et al., 2014).

EVOLUTION FROM SPECIAL SCHOOLS TO SCHOOLS SPECIALIZED IN DEAFNESS

The Tommaso Silvestri School was previously named 173rd Circolo Didattico at the Rome State Institute of Deaf. In September 2000, with the inclusion of this school in the ISISS, there was a further change as it was no longer a special school but rather a specialized school that adopted didactics (teaching and learning strategies) aimed at overcoming learning difficulties related to deafness. ISISS Magarotto in fact created a state-run school complex that combined the former special schools for deaf people in Italy: the State Professional Institute for Industry and Crafts (IPSIA) and the Magarotto Applied Sciences High School in Rome, Padua, and Turin; the Severino Fabriani secondary school with two locations in Rome; and the Tommaso Silvestri kindergarten and primary school. Actually, the evolution from special school to specialized school and above all the experimentation that had started in the 1990s with the inclusion of hearing students made the Institute flourish once again, becoming the School Complex of Excellence for the education of deaf students and practice of innovative didactics. The school received an award on May 27, 2014, from the President of the Italian Republic (at that time), Giorgio Napolitano.

The Co-Enrollment Aspect

The formerly mentioned experimentation put in first place bilingual education: LIS was introduced in the school curriculum in 1990 within the projects named "Bilingual Education in a Model of Integration Among Deaf and Hearing Children" and "Culture of Image and Culture of Words: From a Special School for the Deaf to a Path for Everyone Beyond Diversity" and subsequently within the project "New Methodologies and Technologies in the Education of Deaf Children."

The positive elements that emerged from this experience led to the evolution of experimentation, transforming it into a real educational project made possible by the Law on School Autonomy (No. 440/1997, Implementing Directive No. 238 of 19/5/1998). Thus, under the supervision of ISTC-CNR in Via Nomentana, primary and secondary schools ultimately adopted an inclusive co-enrollment model called "upside down." It involves a reversal of didactic activities: didactics designed for deaf pupils and offered to hearing pupils as well. The training is based on the ministerial guidelines and is characterized, in addition to daily teaching lessons, by labs in which bodily expression and play are a means for learning (ludic-expressive). Children play and learn in an environment designed for visual education. LIS is taught to all pupils, deaf and hearing, since childhood, thus becoming an opportunity for cognitive and cultural growth for all. This approach represents the beginning of an educational process that will bring about real integration between deaf and hearing children. In addition, the above-mentioned Law on School Autonomy allowed LIS to be the second language for all students. Because it is now a subject to study, it is included within the evaluation document. All children, deaf and hearing, also receive a mark in the evaluation document for the degree of integration with their classmates.

The innovative aspect includes the didactics concerning a bilingual perspective with a bicultural outcome, and a co-enrollment model for small groups of deaf and hearing pupils. The special experiences of the kindergarten and primary school have allowed for the development of a didactic system that was organized and modified according to pupils' needs. To this purpose, the presence in the school of experts who are either deaf and hearing is foreseen for some activities. The aim of research and comparison is to analyze and overcome the difficulties of conveying information to deaf pupils, to ensure the full implementation of their right to study, and to promote the development of deaf children's cognitive potential. For all teaching activities, computer technologies such as the multimedia interactive whiteboard (LIM) connected to the Internet and supplied in each classroom are also used, allowing for searching for images or downloading real-time insights (Caselli et al., 2015).

In the kindergarten, classes are attended by a maximum of 15 pupils, with the number of deaf students ranging from 2 to 5. From the primary school onward, classes consist of a maximum of 12 pupils, with the number of deaf students ranging from 2 to 4. The enriched relationships that stem from this approach can be an essential premise for a new culture of diversity, which leads children to see others who are different from them as a source of personal enrichment, a process that works also when there are students from other countries. Deaf children are not seen as "sick" or "disadvantaged," and the potentialities and the cultural and linguistic enrichment dimension evolved and in evolution within the Deaf community therefore becomes valued (Sacks, 1990).

The beginning of the co-enrollment program from early childhood allows for early intervention in a vertical curriculum context, leading the students to achieve excellent educational and schooling results. Vertical curriculum means developing a unique didactic program across three consecutive school grades (kindergarten, primary school, and secondary school). Thanks to the vertical curriculum, teachers from different school grades can share information about programs, class groups, and individual pupils, thus allowing didactic and methodological continuity not only between the different classes of the same school grade but also between consecutive school grades.

SCHOOL ORGANIZATION

Italian public schools are directed by the school director who manages, organizes, and is responsible for the financial and structural resources of schools' organization. Inside the school, the director uses the support of teachers who also function as the head of campus. The head of campus, in addition to being a classroom teacher like other teachers, coordinates work and the external experts and is responsible for the relationships with families and administration. Table 9.1 shows how the Italian school system is structured.

The ISISS Magarotto follows students throughout their course of study from the age of 3 to 19. Currently, the Tommaso Silvestri School, in Via Nomentana, has three kindergarten classes, eight primary school classes, and three secondary school grades. All classes are co-enrolled. Altogether, 500 pupils are enrolled in all the ISISS Magarotto campuses. About 200 of them are deaf. The campus of Via Nomentana hosts 100 children; 50 of them are deaf.

Seven teachers work in kindergarten, 17 teachers work in the primary school, and 12 professors teach in the secondary school of the first degree. All teachers, in addition to holding qualifications for teaching in ordinary schools, hold a Specialization Degree in deafness or have attended LIS courses. At Tommaso Silvestri, there is no support teacher (a professional who usually works in ordinary schools in those classes that enroll children with special needs). Instead, the class teacher is usually helped by a teaching assistant, a professional working in schools to support the learning, socialization, and inclusion of deaf students in accordance with Law 104. Pupils with other disabilities in addition to deafness are supported also by a cultural education assistant.

Although, in Italy, primary schools have gone back to a Main Teacher Master Method, where one teacher teaches almost all disciplines, at Tommaso Silvestri there is a modular structure that best suits the Didactics Teaching Method and Open-Method classes. In the modular organization, the school has a full-time schedules from 8:30 a.m. to 4:30 p.m., Monday to Friday, and several teachers are present, each of whom teaches one or more subjects. This organization, more similar to that of secondary schools, makes the student's transition to the next grade more gradual and serene. School subjects are assigned to individual teachers respecting certain criteria, including didactic continuity and are as follows: (a) Italian, English, and LIS (languages);

Table 9.1. Structure of the Italian School System

Nursery School 3 School Years	Kindergarten 3 School Years	Primary School 5 School Years	Secondary School, First Degree 3 School Years	Secondary School, Second Degree 5 School Years	University Minimum 3 Years
Until 36 months	3–6 years	6–11 years	11–14 years	14–19 years	From 19 years
Not mandatory			Mandatory	Mandatory until 16 years of age	Not mandatory

(b) mathematics and sciences (logical-mathematical field); (c) history and geography (anthropological field); (d) arts and image, technology, physical education, and music; and (e) Catholic religion or alternative subject. The school also collaborates with deaf experts for LIS and arts lessons and with external hearing or deaf experts for sports activities.

Team Collaboration

The organization of all activities takes place through weekly programming meetings. Once a week, the teams of each class of the primary school meet after school to plan the work to be carried out. Programming requires an optimal organization of lessons and must be shared with the whole teaching team and the teaching assistants. The programming is structured as follows: the student's starting situation is analyzed; the goals to be reached are decided on; and the learning units are prepared.

During the meetings, teachers share strategies and methodologies, exchange information, and organize educational fieldtrips, theatrical performances, and so forth. Every 15 days, all teams meet to discuss the overall course results of individual classes. Once a month, the primary school teachers meet the kindergarten teachers to share the projects common to the vertical curriculum. Twice a year, there are interclass meetings between teachers and parents who are elected as class representatives. The ordinary or extraordinary teaching staff meetings that are organized several times during the year give all teachers the opportunity to share experiences, plan activities, and discuss the didactics to be implemented.

This co-enrollment project requires teachers specialized in teaching to the deaf; teaching assistants, both deaf and hearing, able to communicate with children who do not know LIS; and a well-balanced class composition as far as the number of deaf and hearing students with, at most, one pupil with other disabilities. In addition, in the context of bilingualism, the role of deaf teaching assistants is fundamental to all pupils, because these assistants serve as proof that deaf people can do everything that hearing people can.

TOMMASO SILVESTRI PRIMARY SCHOOL

Following this overview on the ISISS Magarotto School organization, this section will concentrate on the experience gathered in the primary school, located on the first floor of the Institute, extending along a corridor overlooking the colorful classrooms decorated by the work done by the students themselves. The small and cozy classrooms are characterized by the semicircular arrangement of desks, which guarantees a clear view to all and makes communication easy. The limited number of pupils per class promotes learning and facilitates the teacher–student relationship. Pupils change classrooms according to the schedule of the subjects: on one side of the corridor there are classrooms dedicated to languages and anthropological subjects and on the other side there are classrooms dedicated to logical-mathematical subjects. The different environments are functional and already organized for the respective disciplines with thematic billboards. An accessible didactic program is implemented, which also includes technological support, adaptation of teaching activities to the class group, and a didactic laboratory in which the pupil plays an active role in a deliberately designed learning environment.

Didactic Strategies

Education is based on the use of various methodologies and strategies for participatory and inclusive didactics. In particular, the school adopts the following techniques:

- *Preparatory classroom lecture*: This is expository and intended as an active and participatory lesson that allows for sharing of content.
- *Guided discussions*: These start with a topic proposed by the teacher. Each pupil shares his or her point of view on the subject.
- *Flipped classroom*: In this reversed teaching experience, the pupil is the active protagonist of knowledge building by looking for research material that will become a classroom-based study topic. Children work individually or in small groups.
- *Brainstorming*: This creative group technique is used for generating ideas, troubleshooting, and starting discussions from a particular topic.
- *Cooperative learning*: In this methodology, students learn in small groups by helping each other.
- *Problem solving*: Pupils learn the cognitive process to solve problems.
- *Peer tutoring*: Knowledge is transferred between pupils or between peer groups.
- *Modeling*: Based on observational-imitative learning, pupils learn from a reference model.
- *Mastery learning*: Students take responsibility for their own learning while respecting everyone's pace of learning.
- *Participatory heuristic method*: Pupils are gradually led to ask questions about the cause of things.
- *Circle time*: Circle time facilitates communication, allows for sharing of mutual knowledge in groups, and serves as a tool for conflict prevention and management.

- *Learning by doing* and *learning by thinking*: Learning through actions that need to be internalized and mentally executed to acquire awareness.
- *Guided discovery*: Free exploration in which the teacher proposes the new activity and the pupil learns by discovering alone through direct manipulation or through observation of facts and events.
- *Dramatization*: Used in various disciplines to internalize the presented content and increase self-esteem.

These methodologies and intervention strategies are accompanied by the use of audiovisual and multimedia tools. The LIM becomes a notebook for the class on which the teachers and students save the course of the lesson, the pedagogical sequence with the intervention, integration, and the observations made by both teachers and pupils. Additionally, older students use e-readers and sometimes tablets and laptops for lexical enrichment, as reading approaches, or to jot down written text. During the school year, the teaching assistants or pupils make videos related to lessons in both oral and sign language to support the learning process. The presence in the classroom of the teaching assistant facilitates the application of the activities proposed by the teachers and makes the content of the various disciplines more accessible. This educational organization also offers pupils a stimulating educational context useful to learn another language, LIS, and also to learn through another language.

The methodology chosen by the school gives the student a central role and provides for active involvement for participatory and inclusive didactics in a welcoming class atmosphere. The methodologies adopted emphasize gaining knowledge from experience. Using these methodologies, teachers recognize the different cognitive styles and the different forms of intelligence of the students in the classroom. The purpose is to reach interdisciplinary, social, individual, and metacognitive goals.

Programs and Organization of Didactics

The Tommaso Silvestri School is a public school that, like every Italian school institution, follows the National Guidelines for the Kindergarten Program and the First Cycle of Education (www.indicazioninazionali. it), in which the disciplinary areas to be developed within the school context are explained. The conceptual basis of the disciplinary programs in this school is common to that of other schools, but the difference consists in how the didactics are presented and carried out in a co-enrollment context.

The entry of a deaf pupil in a class is preceded by an observation of an interaction of the deaf pupil with a teacher and/or with peers. It is important to know whether the pupil comes from a deaf or hearing family, whether he or she receives speech therapy, and whether he or she already knows LIS. It is also necessary to view all medical records, including the Functional Diagnosis, a document issued by the local healthcare provider, who analytically describes the student's functioning in different areas (e.g., autonomy, cognitive skills, social skills, linguistic skills, hearing loss, motor skills, and neuropsychological profile). This document constitutes the fundamental basis for analyzing and structuring a didactic pathway for each pupil. When deafness is associated with intellectual disabilities, a functional dynamic plan along with an individualized educational plan is then drawn up to be shared during meetings of the operative working group for the student with special needs. The school director, the teachers, the teaching assistant, the cultural education assistant, the family, and the therapists who deal with the pupil attend these meetings.

Teaching Principles

The true strength of teaching is the awareness that there is no single and infallible method to use in the co-enrolled class and that it is necessary to know how to work in teams, to be versatile, and to remain constantly updated on and open to experimenting with new methodologies.

The school's teaching aims to transmit through a visual modality whatever cannot be passed on through the auditory channel. It starts from the assumption that teachers structure the lesson with information ranging from concrete to abstract. Depending on educational goals set, access to disciplinary content in the school is done by using two languages, often at the same time, or by preferring one to the other. During the LIS lesson time and during the arts and theater laboratories with external deaf experts, LIS is the main language used to teach. Great efforts are made to ensure that communicative messages reach recipients. Therefore, inclusive principles and approaches are followed, including the following:

- Arranging classrooms so that every student can have a thorough view; this is why a semicircular layout of the desks is preferred;
- Agreeing on the appropriate position of the teacher and the teaching assistant so that deaf students can access all information, whether scholastic or relational, thus guaranteeing communicating and learning;
- Maintaining frequent visual contact with the deaf students to obtain feedback about their level of attention to and understanding of communication;
- Ensuring good acoustic and visual conditions within the classroom;

- Being always proactive and highlighting the positive characteristics of every pupil rather than emphasizing problematic aspects;
- Having all pupils participate in what is happening in the classroom, including noneducational activities.

To enhance some educational aspects where deaf pupils have particular difficulties, such as written texts in Italian, activities aimed at approaching reading through adapted texts and the extension of vocabulary are implemented. In addition, the use of images and the construction, together with pupils, of conceptual maps is fundamental. The difficulties shown by children are not always related to one subject only, or to the way that a subject is presented. Often the deaf pupil does not understand the teacher's request or the written text. The presentation of the activities in Italian and LIS guarantees the understanding of content to all pupils. For every discipline, the preparation of visual material is essential. In the classrooms, the material is labeled with drawings and signs; the walls are covered by billboards depicting the main concepts taught.

In Italy, there is no school textbook specially intended for deaf pupils; therefore, for some years now, digital textbooks have been made accessible to students at home to offset this situation. These digital textbooks contain extra content with respect to the printed book and offer the pupils the possibility to add digital notes to the text.

Another common and interdisciplinary element is that each pupil creates his or her own lapbook with the supervision of the teacher. Lapbooks are easy-to-read, captivating working tools, containing simple texts and conceptual maps. Lapbooks (Fig. 9.1) are suitable for everyone: they enhance memorization, creativity, and manual skills and activate other learning channels.

Learning in Different Disciplines

The first approach to the Italian language is through short and simple sentences, accompanied by signs and illustrations. During the first year of primary school, after the beginnings of the syllabic-writing processes, there are linguistic games where every word or phrase is associated with its meaning, and the teacher constantly monitors the child's comprehension by requesting answers of the pupils using questions of various types. Italian books are chosen by taking into account the type of illustration and the correspondence between written text and images; if necessary, they are adapted to be more accessible. Also useful is the creation of digital lessons using the LIM (Fig. 9.2), where pupils write down new terms learned and their meaning. All children learn English as third language. The study of English is mainly done through the use of flashcards, the retrieval of images through

Figure 9.1. Example of lapbook realized during a history lesson.

the LIM, the combination of English words in drawings made by the pupils, and short dramatizations of classroom texts.

Logical-mathematical activities are carried out through a playful approach, using practical and manipulative experiences, in addition to the traditional way. For example, we start from experiences and objects that are common in everyday life to better write the text of math problems. During science lessons, scientific experiments are carried out. These require actively involving pupils and feeding their curiosity. For example, the study of the plant cycle takes place through the experience of sowing, care, growth observation, and finally fruit harvest.

Figure 9.2. Teacher-pupil using the LIM during a lesson of Italian language.

History topics are presented starting with the pupil's personal life and then placing the main historical events on a visual timeline built together with the students in class. In addition, civilization visual maps are drawn—visual summaries that analyze the main aspects of a people or society according to common indicators such as social organization, religion, and so forth. In particular, by using these civilization visual maps, students can make comparisons between different periods and see how change occurred. Theoretical study is integrated through visits to museums or archaeological sites in Rome. Geography is taught with an interactive approach, involving pupils in games and activities that make them protagonists: puzzles, quiz games, outdoor excursions, thematic charts, or orienteering. The study of technology takes place through an approach to the use of computers and communication media and to the basic notions of computational thinking with coding and exploration of both simple objects of everyday life and more complex devices.

Musical activity is offered through the experience of the "Little Choir of White Hands," a heterogeneous group of pupils and school teachers who study, learn, and sign songs, performing with white gloves. The rhythm is learned through vibrations and in-depth study of the texts. The support of teaching assistants, in particular the deaf assistants, helps the children to learn in a natural way. Music education, a discipline often considered inaccessible to deaf students, is provided through LIS videos allowing pupils to review the texts of the songs studied at school. These videos are also available at their homes.

The school employs a psychologist to monitor class dynamics and provide support to pupils, teachers, and families. In Italy, speech therapy services are provided by the national health service rather than by the school system; therefore, deaf children usually receive speech therapy in special facilities far from the school twice a week on average. As a consequence, they miss much of the school day. To overcome this disadvantage, the Tommaso Silvestri School signed an agreement with two external cooperatives who, even though their offices are not on the school campus, send their speech therapists directly to the school's premises. In this way pupils do not miss as many school hours and are less tired and less stressed. Thanks to an agreement with another external cooperative, deaf children can also attend lessons, either during or after school time, aimed at supporting and enhancing comprehension and production of written texts.

EVALUATION

Teaching, in addition to transmitting knowledge, developing motivation, using appropriate methodologies, and tailoring pupils' cognitive styles, also has an important function: assessing student skills. In school, teachers, using a number from 0 to 10, where sufficiency is represented by 6, attribute value to activities aimed at assessing the learning of a given subject. Verification tests are structured and administered at different times: at the beginning of the school year through entrance tests (prerequisite assessment); during the teaching-learning process at the end of the teaching units (training evaluation); at the end of each quarter (midterm evaluation); and at the end of the year (summary assessment).

The teachers structure verification tests in an objective way so that the results are reliable and calibrated on the level of the individual pupils. For pupils with an Individualized Educational Plan, the choice of evaluation tests to be used depends on the didactic objectives. Verifications are also carried out at informal times, such as during classroom meetings for teachers to see whether a concept has been internalized and to propose further insights. Testing takes place in a serene atmosphere to allow the student to express his or her best potential.

To evaluate deaf students, multiple-choice tests are designed, with some open-answer questions. It is important to consider the communicative-language skills of the pupil, with tests suitable to the student's age and cognitive development, taking into account the amount of time the student has been exposed to the Italian language. During the correction of the tests, it is important to be objective and not to point out too many mistakes. When students face a page full of corrections, they get discouraged and cannot focus on the most serious mistakes. The teacher must also explain the mistakes made by the student, thus helping the student to internalize the correct form.

When the assessment is not aimed at assigning marks but rather on determining the skills acquired and the student's cognitive transfer ability, the evaluation is more oriented to an informal method through tasks concerning a real-life environment. In this situation, the student's ability to make decisions and act and react in a pertinent and valid way in contextualized and specific situations is evaluated by linking the contents of the didactic program to the real world.

In Italy, at the end of the school year, the National Institute for the Evaluation of the Education and Training Education System (INVALSI), an agency supervised by the Ministry of Education, creates tests on Italian language and mathematics and English for all Italian primary and secondary school students. The school, thanks to a team of specialized teachers, has collaborated for years with INVALSI in adapting these tests to deaf students.

RELATIONSHIPS WITH OTHER AGENCIES

In the school context, special attention is dedicated to relations with families and external associations, and in the bilingual context, this attention requires even greater care because two cultures must be taken into account: the Deaf culture and the hearing culture. Generally, the teachers are all able to communicate in sign language so they can directly interact with families who have deaf members. In official situations (PTA meetings, technical meetings, didactic seminars, moments of project sharing, open days), a professional LIS interpreter is used. The interpreter is a professional who guarantees a relationship with the deaf community and ensures equal dissemination of information and true integration between the two cultures. Some formal communication to families is sent via email or video calls, while news and official communications are posted on the school's website.

The school is supported by parents who have founded a committee called Fiorire ("to bloom") as a growth metaphor for children who, if well cared for, blossom into beautiful flowers. In addition, the school collaborates in various educational projects with external associations dealing with deafness in order to have deaf professionals who can better understand the needs of the deaf learners. The school's strategic position has allowed for a collaborative network with the surrounding territory and the associations operating in the Institute. Therefore, there are various standing collaborations with the following:

- The 2nd Town Hall of Rome, which offers a project for the enhancement of sports activities and ensures the cultural education assistants;
- The Lazio Region, which through the association "Segni di integrazione" manages the service of teaching assistants;
- The association Kiasso T.I.S. (International Tourism for Deaf);
- The Intercammini Foundation, which has proposed several intercultural paths;
- CABSS, a nonprofit organization that offers early intervention programs for deaf and deaf-and-blind children between the ages of 0 and 6. CABSS also provides support to schools in which deaf-and-blind pupils are enrolled;
- The Group for Study and Information on Sign Language (SILIS), which organizes LIS courses for pupils and offers interpreting services for family–school meetings;
- The cooperative Treno33, which organizes bilingual activities for children during extracurricular time;
- The Zero Laboratory, a theatrical company formed by deaf people who provide occasional collaboration for dramatization activities;
- The cooperatives Le Farfalle and Capodarco, who are engaged in providing speech therapy services during school hours;
- The Logogenia cooperative, which is engaged in supporting comprehension and production of written texts.

Other extremely important collaborations are with the Institute of Cognitive Sciences and Technologies of the Italian National Research Council (ISTC-CNR), which supports the school with counseling and evaluations, and with the Institute for Deaf in Rome (ISSR), which offers some spaces such as the library, the computer room, the seminar room, and the filming room.

CONCLUSION AND FUTURE PERSPECTIVES

Changes in our society are increasingly calling for recognition and respect for diversity. Schools are homes to cultural integration, which increases the awareness of diversity and possible marginalization in order to prevent and counter prejudice. In the education of deaf children, a bilingual method emphasizes the spoken language and reevaluates the Deaf culture. It is worth noting that the Italian government has not yet legally recognized LIS as a language. The educational project of the school, thanks to a multiyear experience, has enabled us to understand that LIS is not an obstacle to the acquisition of the Italian language as many people still think today. In fact, informal observations (which must be confirmed by research) showed that deaf students attending this school appeared to be more competent in Italian than deaf children attending ordinary schools. Strong encouragement also comes from the research carried out by ISTC-CNR on the effects of LIS acquisition on (deaf and hearing) children's cognitive development (Capirci et al., 1998). Some of these results have recently been replicated in a study involving deaf and hearing students of the Tommaso Silvestri primary school.

In our experience, we often observe that deaf students, who come from ordinary schools, have low self-esteem and autonomy; however, in a few months' time, a real metamorphosis takes place: the peaceful and nonjudgmental context, the comparison with other deaf children, the communicative exchange with hearing students, and the presence of a positive deaf adult model transform the pupil into a more serene, motivated, and self-confident child. In this school, co-enrollment is essential to carry out interdisciplinary teaching that, by stimulating curiosity, is the basis of learning. This activates all communication channels and develops pupils' innate potentials. This co-enrollment project, born as a timid experiment, has become a real educational model that could be summarized in the following motto: "Include to grow."

In the realization of such a complex project, however, there are obstacles of both bureaucratic and economic nature. Among the main difficulties is that there are few teachers who are specialized in deafness. The school suffers from a periodic turnover of teachers, thus not guaranteeing continuity of teaching. Furthermore, there is no specific funding for the bilingual project, something that would allow the implementation of all the actions planned for the good functioning of the school since the beginning of the school year. It would be desirable to start each school year with full-time teaching staff and the appropriate hours of teaching assistants and cultural education assistants to ensure an optimal start of the entire school program.

The strength of the school lies in the philosophy of inclusion, which leads to great attention to all children, a condition made possible by having classes with few pupils. This situation allows a strong relationship to develop among pupils and teachers and among pupils themselves by paving the way to an open, curious, tolerant class able to see an added value in each child. The true richness of this educational project comes from trained, flexible, and highly motivated teachers; constant updating of the entire school team; the presence of proactive, attentive leadership; and the involvement of deaf adults in teaching activities. A school where the pace of learning is decided by its students and not by the programs, a school that patiently waits for results, a school that unites instead of dividing and lays the foundation for deep relationships that go beyond any barrier is not utopian. It is not utopian to see pupils entering the classroom happy and having in their eyes the spark of curiosity and the joy of learning, who are not afraid of making mistakes, to grow up becoming adults preserving friendships born among the school desks. Educating children to respect others and to see an added value in other people means that schooling has not failed.

REFERENCES

Capirci, O., Cattani, A., Rossini, P., & Volterra, V. (1998). Teaching sign language to hearing children as a possible factor in cognitive enhancement. *Journal of Deaf Studies and Deaf Education*, 3, 135–142.

Caselli, M. C., Maragna, S., & Volterra, V. (2006). *Linguaggio e sordità. Gesti, segni e parole nello sviluppo e nell'educazione* [Language and deafness. Gestures, signs and words in development and education]. Bologna: Il Mulino.

Caselli, M. C., Rinaldi, P., Onofrio, D., & Tomasuolo, E. (2015). Language skills and literacy of deaf children in the era of cochlear implantation: Suggestions for teaching through e-learning visual environments. In H. Knoors & M. Marschark (Eds.), *Educating deaf learners: Creating a global evidence base* (pp. 443–460). Oxford: Oxford University Press.

Maragna, S. (Eds.) (2004). *L'Istituto Statale dei Sordi di Roma Storia di una trasformazione* [Rome State Institute of Deaf: History of a transformation]. Rome: Edizioni Kappa.

Maragna, S., & Vasta, R. (Eds.) (2015). *Il manuale dell'abate Silvestri. Le origini dell'educazione dei sordi in Italia* [The Abbot Silvestri's manual. The origins of the education of the deaf in Italy]. Rome: Bordeaux edizioni.

Meristo, M., Falkman, K. W., Hjelmquist, E., Tedoldi, M., Surian, L., & Siegal, M. (2007). Language access and theory of mind reasoning: Evidence from deaf children in bilingual and oralist environments. *Developmental Psychology*, 43, 1156–1169.

Rinaldi, P., Caselli, M. C., Onofrio, D., &Volterra, V. (2014). Language acquisition by bilingual deaf preschoolers: Theoretical, methodological issues and empirical data. In M. Marschark, G. Tang, & H. Knoors (Eds.), *Bilingualism and bilingual deaf education* (pp. 85–116). New York: Oxford University Press.

Rinaldi, P., Di Mascio, T., Knoors, H., & Marschark, M. (2015). *Insegnare agli studenti sordi. Aspetti cognitivi, linguistici, socioemotivi e scolastici.* [Teaching deaf learners: Cognitive, linguistic, socio-emotional and educational aspects]. Bologna: Il Mulino.

Sacks, O. (1990). *Seeing voices: Journey into the deaf world*. New York: HarperCollins.

10

The Best of Both Worlds: A Co-Enrollment Program for DHH Children in the Netherlands

Annet de Klerk, Daan Hermans, Loes Wauters,
Lilian de Laat, Francien de Kroon, and Harry Knoors

The best of both worlds: that was the starting point for the co-enrollment program we established in the Netherlands in 2003. As employees of Kentalis, we were inspired by the ideas of the TRIPOD program of Carl Kirchner in California (Kirchner, 1994, this volume). With those ideas in mind, we found a mainstream partner school that was willing to collaborate with us. We called this unique form of cooperation between mainstream and special education the Twinschool (unique because special and mainstream education were separated systems in the Netherlands at that time).

The best of both worlds: a combination of the specific knowledge, skills, and context of special education for deaf and hard-of hearing (DHH) students and the more general knowledge and context of mainstream education. We combined specific didactic and pedagogical knowledge about language and reading education, attention to Deaf culture, and identity formation with a normal pace of instruction, a bigger social group, and, perhaps the most important, an attitude of looking at the strengths of students. That was what we then called the best of both worlds and still do after all these years of experience.

Now we operate in a completely different educational landscape, a landscape that has been created by the Dutch Appropriate Education Act of 2014. One of the goals of this act is to reduce the referral of students with special educational needs to special schools (European Agency for Special Needs and Inclusive Education, 2017) and thus to include as many students with special education needs as possible in mainstream education.

We are also in a completely different landscape because we collaborate with a different partner school than we did at the start of our co-enrollment program. Since 2013, we have been cooperating with OBS de Bolster, a primary school in Sint-Michielsgestel, the Netherlands.

Currently, 27 DHH students are enrolled in their educational program, together with 330 hearing students in this primary school. This is 30% of the total DHH population we support in our part of the country. Other DHH students are either individually mainstreamed in various schools or attend the special school for the deaf. The program is unique because we are the only co-enrollment program in primary education for DHH students in the Netherlands. Because of the outstanding quality of education provided, both partners in the Twinschool, Kentalis Talent (since 2014) and OBS de Bolster (since 2015), have been awarded the distinction "Excellent School" from the Dutch government.

In this chapter we will highlight the structure of the co-enrollment program and the achievements of our students. We will describe the key components that, in our experiences, are necessary to ensure that the program is sustainable and successful with respect to student achievement and satisfaction of parents and professionals. We also describe the main challenges that we have encountered and taken up throughout the years, some of which we still have not completely overcome. The chapter is a co-production of authors working at Kentalis Talent, the special school for the deaf with a support team for DHH students in mainstream, at primary school de Bolster and at the Kentalis Academy. The Kentalis Academy is involved in the monitoring of achievements and the scientific evaluation of the program.

ESTABLISHING A CO-ENROLLMENT PROGRAM

Establishing a qualitatively good co-enrollment program is not easy and takes time. After more than 10 years of experience, we are still learning and optimizing the program. As the type of co-enrollment program we envision is actually a co-creation between special and mainstream education, the first step is to find a mainstream partner school that is the best match for the program. Several issues play a role in the decision process of choosing the most appropriate partner school. Important issues are the educational policy and the willingness of the professionals to cooperate; perhaps the most important is the commitment of all parties involved, including the board of administrators (Antia & Metz, 2014). In this chapter we will discuss each aspect that plays a role in establishing a co-enrollment program and outline the context of our program.

The Appropriate Education Act

The Netherlands has a long history of two separated educational systems. Mainstream and special education operated relatively independently, under different educational laws, until 2014. DHH students either were in special schools or, less frequently, went to a mainstream school on an individual basis, most of them with the support of an itinerant teacher. Until the early years of the 21st century, most profoundly deaf students, up to 90%, were educated in bilingual schools for the deaf. The introduction of universal newborn screening and early cochlear implantation led, over a relatively short period, to an influx of profoundly deaf students in mainstream education.

Despite this separation of the two systems, in 2003 several people from Kentalis Talent saw advantages in combining the strengths of the two systems in a co-enrollment program for students who could profit from this type of educational environment, namely the mainstream educational program and the bigger social group. This option was discussed with parents and led to the start of the co-enrollment program.

In 2017, the program still exists within the context of the Appropriate Education Act of 2014. According to the Department of Education, the goal of this law is to enable all children to attend a school that provides education suited to their talents and capabilities. About one in every five pupils needs extra assistance in primary education. The law introduced a "duty of care" for all schools to offer an appropriate place to children who need additional support (Government of the Netherlands, 2017). Under this policy, every school board has the responsibility to provide adequate education for all students who enroll, regardless of their specific educational needs and the kind of support that they need. By cooperating with other school boards at the regional level, schools are required to arrange educational provisions in such a way that all children can be educated taking into account their special educational needs. Schools are free to decide on how the arrangements are offered, either at a mainstream school or at a school providing special education (European Agency for Special Needs and Inclusive Education, 2017). DHH students or students with developmental language impairment may be referred to a designated special school for support in mainstream education or placement at a special school. This referral has to be formally approved by a committee of professionals that also determines the level of support. After a fixed period of time, the effectiveness of support has to be evaluated by this committee.

By introducing the law on appropriate education, the government seeks to ensure that (1) every child will receive appropriate schooling, preferably at a mainstream school; (2) schools will get more facilities to provide tailor-made education; (3) the focus will be on children's potential and educational needs, not on their impairments or disabilities; and (4) children will no longer spend long periods at home because schools cannot cater to their needs (Government of the Netherlands, 2017).

Primary schools are organized in regional consortia. They have to monitor the achievements of their students. According to the Department of Education, it is possible to tell at an early stage, by testing, observing, and monitoring students, whether a student is lagging behind or failing to make sufficient progress. If a student has learning difficulties, mainstream schools need to intervene by adapting the curriculum or by providing additional support. The school needs to draw up an individual development plan for all students who receive additional support, describing the educational objectives for that pupil. The plan indicates the level that the student can achieve and the support that he or she will need to achieve it. This plan has to be discussed with the parents (Government of the Netherlands, 2017).

The regional consortia receive a budget for support of students with special education needs from the department of education, a budget that in the past went to the special schools and their support services for mainstream education. An exception is made for education and educational support for DHH students, students with developmental language impairments, and students with visual impairment. The support and education of these students is still financed separately. The budget is allocated to the four organizations that provide special education and support services in mainstream education for DHH students. For these students, there are three educational options depending on their educational needs. The first option is a support program in a special school for the deaf. This special school offers an intensive-support program in relatively small classes exclusively for DHH students. The second option is a medium-support program in mainstream education. An example of this medium-support program is the co-enrollment program. Several DHH students follow the mainstream educational program together with hearing students in a primary school. The third option is a minimum-support program for DHH students in mainstream education. These are students who are enrolled in a mainstream school, most of the time on an individual basis, in their hometown. An itinerant teacher of the deaf visits the student and the school. Placement in a special school or in a co-enrollment program is usually linked to a larger budget than the budget available for individual support in mainstream education.

Educational Policy

The educational policy of the mainstream school involved in the co-enrollment program is an important issue and fundamental for the success of the program. We started our program in a primary school physically close to the school for the deaf. We thought such proximity was an advantage because it was only a five-minute walk between schools. Gradually, it became clear that we had overlooked the effect of the specific population of the hearing students who attend this school. These are mostly students from economically prosperous backgrounds who learn easily. Consequently, as DHH children grew older and attended the higher grades of primary school, the gap between their educational achievements and those of the hearing peers in their class widened. It became increasingly difficult for DHH students to follow the educational program that was offered because the school uses a predominantly whole-classroom teaching approach with too little acknowledgment of the attainments of the (lower-achieving) DHH students. The accent was on teacher-directed instruction, and teachers were not really accustomed to teaching students with diverse capacities.

In addition, some parents of the DHH students did not feel at home in this school. For too many of them, the world of the parents of hearing peers at this mainstream school was not their world. This eventually led to our decision to look for a different partner school. Based on the experiences with the first school, two criteria were set for the choice of a partner school: the school philosophy had to include all students regardless of their background, and the teachers had to be capable of dealing with educational differences. A recent report of the Dutch government, "State of the Art of the Education," shows that effectively and successfully handling diversity among students in education still is a difficult issue for many mainstream schools and their teachers in the Netherlands (Inspectie van het Onderwijs, 2017).

Commitment

Perhaps the most important aspect of a solid and sustainable cooperation is the commitment of the people involved. Whole-school commitment is, in our opinion, the most important success factor. Every individual teacher should commit to teach DHH students, to treat them equally, and to fully include them in their classroom. It also means the commitment to cooperate closely with their colleagues from special education through co-teaching. The administrators should be committed to facilitate and stimulate the program and to show enthusiasm. When teachers and administrators show their commitment, they function as an example for hearing students and for their parents in accepting DHH peers at school.

A precondition for commitment is the feeling of self-efficacy of the staff involved from special and mainstream education. Confidence in their own and their colleagues' capability to teach in a co-enrollment program is crucial. Therefore, a period of thorough preparation before the start of the program is important. The preparation for our co-enrollment program took seven months. For the mainstream teachers, this preparation consisted of receiving information about what it means to be DHH, the educational and pedagogical consequences of being DHH, and the educational needs of the DHH students. It also means accepting that many DHH students need a sign language interpreter in the classroom. The teachers of the deaf must be prepared for their role as a co-teacher in mainstream school and for their role as an advisor to their mainstream colleagues. Related to commitment is the issue that teaching is based on moral values (Fullan & Hardgreaves, 2016); a match in this underlying pattern of values is important in embarking on a co-enrollment program, as well as a good relationship between people. It is this match that can generate enthusiasm, spirit, and commitment to overcome smaller or bigger bumps in the journey to establish a successful co-enrollment program.

Practical Key Issues

When establishing a co-enrollment program, there are many practical issues to deal with. Handling these issues is as important for the success of a co-enrollment program as is accepting the foundational philosophy or having a good match with colleagues. These practical issues may have profound consequences for the quality or content of the program. In our co-enrollment program, there are DHH students in various classes in the primary school. The number of DHH students varies per class, with a maximum of 20% to 25% of all students in class. In some of the classes, there are also some hearing students with special needs. In the opinion of the teachers, this percentage guarantees a good balance in the classroom between students with and without special needs. The average size of an entire class is 25 to 28 students. In each classroom, there is a teacher of the primary school together with a teacher from the school for the deaf. These two teachers co-teach in various ways. The number of hours or days the teacher of the deaf is present depends on the number of DHH students in the classroom, because the latter number defines the budget available. For example, with six DHH students in a class, the teacher of the deaf will be present for three whole days. In addition, a speech-language therapist and a deaf sign language teacher work in and outside the classroom. Sign Language of the Netherlands (SLN) interpreters are available in the classroom for the whole week.

In this co-enrollment program, the teachers of the deaf and other members of the support team are employed at the school for the deaf. They work in the co-enrollment program on a full-time or part-time basis, but the school for the deaf is their home base. This connection with the school for the deaf is an advantage because it is the place where these teachers of the deaf can share their knowledge and work on their professional development with other teachers of the deaf, enabling them to provide high-quality support in the mainstream environment. It is also an advantage for the school for the deaf to stay up to date with developments in mainstream education. The staff members who work in the co-enrollment program bring their experience and knowledge from mainstream school to their colleagues at the school for the deaf.

Another relevant practical issue is the availability of space in and outside the primary school classrooms. In addition to room for hearing and DHH students and for mainstream teachers and teachers of the deaf, the school also needs to provide space for speech and language therapists who sometimes work outside classrooms, for sign language teachers, and for interpreters. At the moment, approximately 14 different (part-time) interpreters are present during the week. Coordination of the co-enrollment program is another key practical issue. For our co-enrollment program, it has worked well to have two senior members of the staff, one from the mainstream program and one from the special education program, to jointly coordinate the program. Currently, the co-enrollment coordinator of the primary school is a language specialist and the co-enrollment coordinator of the special school for the deaf is a speech and language therapist, but their roles could also be fulfilled by other senior staff members. The coordinators are present in the school on a regular basis. They meet regularly and cooperate intensively. They offer support to their colleagues in the program. Besides these two coordinators, there is also support from educational coaches from mainstream and special education. Together, these coaches monitor the development of the individual students and reflect on classroom practice together with the teachers involved in the program.

At the start of the program, a program script was developed as an outline for all professionals involved, and that has proven to be very helpful; it is still very important for smooth cooperation. The script is drafted annually in the form of a calendar and includes a description of program-specific actions per day, week, and month. All these activities are normally not part of the primary school calendar of activities. These activities include consultation meetings, checking equipment (e.g., hearing aids, FM systems), sign language courses for hearing peers, meetings for parents, writing reports, and special tasks related to our scientific evaluation program. In this script are also incorporated the weekly schedules of the professionals who work together inside and sometimes outside the classroom.

One of the most important practical issues is time. Teachers and other professionals involved need extra time to collaborate effectively. They must plan their lessons together and arrange their roles and tasks. The provision of extra time has been accomplished by giving the staff members involved in the co-enrollment classroom fewer general school responsibilities than their colleagues who are not involved in the co-enrollment program.

Leadership at the start of the program is crucial. Initially, the administrators of the special and mainstream school were intensively involved in establishing the program. School administrators can inspire and stimulate their teams. They can think of possibilities. It is also very important that they are willing to support the staff members involved in the program by providing them time for learning, cooperation, and preparation.

All these investments cost money. The support service of the school for the deaf receives the budget for the additional support for the DHH students. Part of this budget is transferred to the mainstream school so that the mainstream school can pay for the coordination of the co-enrollment program, for the decrease in class size, and for other additional support for the DHH students. The support service of the special school for the deaf uses the other part of the budget to pay the DHH professionals who staff the co-enrollment program. The SLN interpreters are paid from a separate budget that is provided by the government directly to the parents of DHH students. The SLN interpreters are freelancers. The coordinators organize the interpreters and their schedule.

KEY PRINCIPLES

The best of two worlds is what we bring together in this co-enrollment program. One of the advantages for DHH students is a bigger peer group with more possibilities for interaction. Social interaction does not happen automatically but has to be learned and stimulated. Social interaction is explicitly stimulated by the two classroom teachers from mainstream and special education and by the speech and language therapist who sometimes works with mixed smaller groups of DHH and hearing students. The deaf sign language teacher also discusses issues with the DHH and hearing students that have to do with interaction with peers. Because the sign language teacher is deaf, he can bring in his own experiences and can reflect on this issue with the students.

The best of two worlds also includes a normal pace of instruction. One of the pitfalls of special education is the reduction of the pace of instruction because of extensive adaptation for students with complex needs. Of course, there is a critical balance for pace of instruction. The teacher must not talk over the heads of the students and proceed too fast, but in special education, teachers tend to elaborate extensively, repeating instructions time and again, until all students grasp the content. In contrast, teachers of the deaf, when they work in mainstream education, become aware that it is quite normal that not all students grasp the content fully the first time and that there will be subsequent additional opportunities for them to learn.

Another danger that can exist in special education is offering too much support to DHH students. Too often we encounter "learned helplessness." In mainstream classes, students are challenged to act more independently, but independence also has to be learned. Step by step, DHH students from special education who enroll in the co-enrollment program are challenged to become more independent learners. They are challenged to solve their problems independently or through collaboration with their hearing or DHH peers. Adequate executive functioning of DHH students plays an important role in this process (Hermans, Vugs, Van Berkel-Van Hoof, & Knoors, 2015; Vissers & Hermans, in press). Since many DHH students experience problems in this domain, teachers often need to coach DHH students with respect to the organization of their work, their planning, and their problem-solving.

Professionals need to provide DHH students with support in mainstream education that is closely connected to their educational needs. Support includes special didactic strategies to stimulate communication and language development, special attention for learning to read, executive functioning and identity development, accessible instruction, sign language lessons, speech and language therapy including auditory training, and the presence of DHH teachers or classroom assistants who are role models for the DHH students. All these aspects are present in our co-enrollment program. An example regarding the special didactic strategy is the extra and specific attention for vocabulary development. The teacher of the deaf plays an important role with respect to this vocabulary development, but the speech and language therapist and the sign language teacher can also pay extra attention to vocabulary development inside or outside the classroom. The extra attention for vocabulary development is also something the mainstream school profits from. With the support of the speech and language therapist, teachers have started to work on a more structured approach for vocabulary instruction for hearing students as well. For DHH students in grades 1 and 2, there is additional support for learning to read by the teacher of the deaf and by the speech and language therapist. Reading comprehension is one of the most important subjects in higher grades that DHH students need support for, many of them during their whole school career.

Core Components of the Program

Access to Communication and Instruction

The DHH students in the co-enrollment program have very diverse communicative needs. These needs may vary depending on the circumstances, such as whether they are following instruction in a silent classroom or attending the school's weekly closure session. The number of participants involved in the discourse and the complexity of the content also make a difference. Because of the diverse communicative needs, many options have to be available in every co-enrollment classroom. The teachers from mainstream and special education both use an FM system to enable auditory access to their spoken language. There are several table or pass-along microphones available for hearing students and for DHH students who use spoken Dutch in the classroom.

Spoken Dutch (with or without signs) and SLN are available as the languages of instruction. In every classroom with DHH students, a sign language interpreter is present. The teacher of the deaf has not been trained as an interpreter. She is fluent in using signs or sign language when teaching in the classroom or supporting groups or individual DHH students, but her role is not to interpret the mainstream classroom teacher. Thus, the roles of the teacher of the deaf and the interpreter are different. The teacher of the deaf is present to support the DHH students in their learning process. The role of the interpreter is to translate the classroom communication in SLN for the DHH students who prefer this form of communication.

When the mainstream teacher teaches the whole group of DHH and hearing students, the interpreter translates in SLN. The teacher of the deaf uses sign supported Dutch (SSD) when she teaches. Most deaf students have access to a rich form of SSD, a form that includes many grammatical elements of SLN. It can also happen that the teacher of the deaf only uses spoken Dutch and the interpreter translates in SLN. Students were asked what they prefer. In some groups and for more complex topics, they prefer the SLN interpretation. They may find it distracting when the teacher of the deaf uses SSD at the same time. When the teacher of the deaf is not present in the classroom, the interpreter is always together with the mainstream teacher.

Co-Teaching

In the co-enrollment program, co-teaching is the basis for classroom instruction. The mainstream teacher and the teacher of the deaf teach together. For the organization of their co-teaching, they use the model of Clarke and DeNuzzo (2003). This model consists of six forms of co-teaching: (1) one teaches, one observes, (2) one teaches, one drifts, (3) station teaching, (4) parallel teaching, (5) alternative teaching, and (6) team teaching. Depending on the goal of the lesson and the educational needs of both the hearing and DHH students, the two teachers choose the most appropriate form of co-teaching. An example is reading instruction in grade 1. The teachers decide that the mainstream teacher should provide classroom instruction to all students. The teacher of the deaf gives extra support to individual students in the classroom; she drifts. So they choose option two, one teaches, one drifts. In this way, co-teaching is used as an educational strategy to meet the diverse needs of the students. Co-teaching can also be used as an effective form to exchange knowledge and skills between professionals. In the co-enrollment program, the mainstream teacher or teacher of the deaf and the speech and language therapist also teach together. The aim of this form of co-teaching is to transfer knowledge about the most effective ways to teach vocabulary, grammar, and other aspects of language (Hermans, Willemsen, Wauters, & Knoors, 2016).

Bilingual Education

Spoken and written Dutch and SLN are taught as school subjects. Spoken and written Dutch are obligatory for all students in the classroom. Preteaching and reteaching are offered to many DHH students to have better access to the content of these general classroom lessons. Depending on their needs, DHH students may receive extra vocabulary instruction. Some DHH students follow an individually adapted curriculum for Dutch language and/or for reading.

The speech and language therapist from the school for the deaf cooperates with the teacher of the deaf to enable DHH students to meet their individual Dutch language goals. She also works in the classroom either as a co-teacher for Dutch language or to support students in learning to read. Some DHH students, mostly the young ones, also have individual speech and language therapy.

At the start of the co-enrollment program, SLN was taught as a subject for the DHH students 1.5 hours per week. The bottleneck, however, was allocating time to this activity, given the importance of many other subjects taught to the entire class. We aim to have as little as possible pull-out from the general classroom, because this is detrimental to the involvement of the students (Knoors & Hermans, 2010). Besides, some DHH students do not like to leave the classroom because they want to be a full member of the class. This led to a reconsideration of teaching SLN as a subject. Currently, SLN as a subject is taught half an hour per week. The subject Cultural Identity and Diversity for DHH Students (CIDS) is also taught in sign language for half an hour per week. The interpreters, and sometimes the teachers of the deaf, use SLN during the day in the classroom. We monitor the sign language proficiency of all DHH students to see whether there are any effects of this adaptation. Thus far, we do not see significant negative effects. In one of the next sections. the results of the SLN development will be described.

DHH Role Models and Deaf Culture

Deaf adults function as role models for DHH students. There is a deaf sign language teacher in the co-enrollment program who teaches SLN and Identity and Deaf Culture. Deaf Culture and deaf awareness is taught through a specific curriculum called CIDS, as noted earlier. This curriculum has been developed by Leap Forward, a Dutch expertise group for education of the deaf. This group has developed several curricula and materials for DHH students with financial support of the schools for the deaf and the Dutch government (De Klerk, Fortgens, & Van der Eijk, 2015).

Full Members of Class and School

DHH students are full members of their class; most of the time, they are present in the general classroom together with their hearing peers. This means that pull-out of individual DHH students or working in small groups of exclusively DHH students is restricted as much as possible. Antia, Stinson, and Gaustad (2002) point to the importance of membership in inclusive settings. Inclusive education can be successful if DHH students are seen as full members of their class and school. In the co-enrollment program, it is possible to work in smaller mixed groups of DHH and hearing students inside or outside the classroom. There are some activities exclusively for DHH students that take place outside the classroom: preteaching in SLN of content that will later be taught to the whole group, SLN and CIDS lessons, and individual speech and language therapy. Some of these activities take place during the relatively long recess. How much time DHH students spend outside the classroom depends on their individual needs. There are also activities for the whole classroom to become aware of what it means to be deaf. These activities offer hands-on experience of deafness. Hearing students can listen to speech perceived and processed through a cochlear implant, try speechreading, and try to understand signs. There is instruction about the characteristics of being DHH and information about the FM system used in the classroom. There is a listening game, and they can interview a deaf teacher. DHH students explain to their classmates what it means to be deaf and how interaction can be optimized. Hearing students also have the opportunity to take a sign language course as an extracurricular activity. This course contains ten lessons of 45 minutes. These activities are very important to stimulate cohesion and to foster interaction between hearing and DHH students.

THE DHH STUDENTS IN THE PROGRAM

As we pointed out earlier, legally there are three educational options for DHH students: special education, co-enrollment in a mainstream school, and mainstream education on an individual basis. A multidisciplinary team of parents and professionals discusses the most appropriate educational environment for the DHH student. The basis for this multidisciplinary discussion is the assets and risks as mentioned by Antia (2015): motivation, quality of communication, functional hearing, curriculum access, classroom participation, contact with peers, social-emotional development, and the amount of support from the family. On the basis of these assets and risks, we describe the educational needs of the student and the most appropriate educational environment and support program. A formal and independent committee of professionals reviews the motivation for this choice.

As pointed out before, we see DHH students with diverse needs in the co-enrollment program. This is also true for their hearing status and their devices. Of the 27 DHH students currently in the program, 4 wear one cochlear implant, 9 have bilateral implants, 8 wear both an implant and a hearing aid, and 6 wear two hearing aids. To illustrate the diversity of the students enrolled in the program, three of the DHH students are introduced in the next section.

Case Studies

The three students who are described have all been enrolled in the co-enrollment program from grade 1 on. This is not the case for all DHH students. Some of them started in kindergarten at age 4. Other students have been enrolled in grade 3 or 4. The age of enrollment is rather diverse and depends on the individual development of the children.

Marc

Marc started his school career in the co-enrollment program in grade 1. Before that, he was at the school for the deaf in a bilingual program in preschool and kindergarten. Marc was born deaf in a Deaf family. He wears a cochlear implant. At home, the main language is SLN. Marc's nonverbal cognitive potential is average. At the special school, Marc had a positive but also relatively passive attitude toward learning and did not have a very good relationship with peers. He occasionally behaved manipulatively. His auditory development with his cochlear implant was not optimal, which may be related to the restricted amount of auditory input in the home environment. The motivation to enroll him in the co-enrollment program was twofold. The positive influence and exemplary (positive) behavior of peers might lead to improvements in his own behavior, and an environment with increased auditory input (compared to the school for the deaf) might lead to better results in spoken language with his cochlear implant. At the start, Marc had a delay of one year in his school subjects.

Marc always needs a rich form of SSD or SLN to have access to the curriculum and to communication. The focus in language development for Marc is on vocabulary extension by establishing a link between the sign, the fingerspelling, the written word, the auditory representation, and the correct articulation.

Currently, Marc is in grade 3. His achievements vary. When he started in the co-enrollment program, his results in SLN proficiency were above average. This is still the case. His delay in the Dutch language was severely below average at the start compared to monolingual and bilingual hearing students. This is also still the case. Marc's educational development increases with his age, but the delay of one year remains. His social-emotional development is positive; he has profited considerably from positive role models in his class, although some concerns with respect to his behavior remain.

Kevin

Kevin also started in the co-enrollment program in grade 1. Before that, he was a student at the special school for the deaf and received bilingual education. Currently, Kevin is in grade 4. Kevin was born deaf and wears a cochlear implant and a hearing aid. He is able to identify small differences in sounds and is able to understand speech in quiet circumstances. In the classroom, he needs the support of an interpreter because the acoustics in a classroom with many students often are challenging. The etiology of Kevin's deafness is the Pendred syndrome. He has an average nonverbal IQ. Kevin communicates predominantly in spoken Dutch. The motivation to enroll Kevin in the program was positive growth in his speech and spoken language development and in his social-emotional development. After enrollment, Kevin was additionally diagnosed with attention-deficit/hyperactivity disorder (since 2015, he has been prescribed medication) and with characteristics related to the autistic spectrum. His working memory is quickly overloaded. Kevin experiences fine motor problems when writing. In the classroom, he uses a computer to write. Kevin shows a positive educational growth. His achievement scores are average or just below average compared to his hearing classmates.

The passive vocabulary and the use of word structures show a positive development, and achievement scores are average compared to hearing classmates. Sentence structures, understanding stories, and active vocabulary show a slight downward trend after a period of growth. Kevin scores just below average in these linguistics domains. This seems to relate to the more abstract and therefore more difficult language that is asked for. His scores in SLN are above average. His passive skills of SLN are better than his active skills.

Maud

Maud started in the co-enrollment program in grade 1. Before, she was a student at the school for the deaf, where she visited the bilingual preschool and kindergarten. Now she is in grade 4. Maud was born deaf. The cause of deafness is unknown, although deafness is present in the family. Maud wears a cochlear implant and a hearing aid. She is able to identify small differences in sounds and is able to understand speech in quiet circumstances. In the classroom, she needs the support of an interpreter because the acoustic circumstances are not optimal in a classroom with many students. She communicates in spoken Dutch and sometimes uses SSD. Her IQ is average. She was placed in the co-enrollment program because of her good scores on general achievement tests. When she started in the co-enrollment program, her results were at age level. Also, there was growth in her speech and language development. Besides this, Maud's parents explicitly preferred a mainstream environment with deaf peers and deaf role models. The co-enrollment program offers both of them.

Maud needs instruction that is supported by signs, visual materials, or written text. Maud still scores at age level for her school subjects. Her sentence development in Dutch is average. Her passive and active vocabulary show a growth from below average to average. The explanation of difficult concepts remains difficult for Maud, more specifically the use of abstract language. When Maud started in the co-enrollment program, her sign language scores were average. Now she scores above average. Her passive scores are better than her active scores. Localization in sign language grammar still needs attention.

Meeting the Diversity of DHH Students

In the preceding section, three DHH students participating in our co-enrollment program have been described. They are fairly representative of the diverse group of DHH students in the program. Besides several similarities in students' needs related to their deafness, there are also many diverse needs to be met. For each student, there is an individual plan with a description of assets and risks and educational needs. The teachers, duos from mainstream and special education, are responsible for meeting these needs in their daily teaching practice. This calls for proactive planning and differentiation of the educational program (Knoors, 2016). Teachers need to plan their lessons carefully. Beforehand, they need to plan what form of co-teaching is going to meet these needs and which students need preteaching or reteaching. Teacher duos plan their lessons differently. Some duos plan every week. Others plan every term. In practice, we see a lot of informal consultation in their work during the week.

The teacher of the deaf also needs to discuss what type of support the language and speech therapist and the sign language teacher can provide and what goals they all have to work on in a certain period. They also need to decide whether this can be realized in the classroom or whether some activities have to be planned outside the classroom.

Twice a year, after students' assessments, the results of all DHH students are discussed. There is a weekly (short) consultation with the speech therapist and sign language teacher about the type of support that is needed in the classroom. The program also provides extra support for new staff members several times a year through information about more general topics that have to do with the co-enrollment program.

PARENT INVOLVEMENT

The parents of the DHH students have intensively been involved in the decision process about the placement in the co-enrollment program. Together with parents, the choice of placement is discussed in a multidisciplinary team of professionals. For many parents, the transition from the school of the deaf to the co-enrollment program is a rather big step; therefore, it is important to discuss their questions. Before the actual placement, parents are invited to visit the co-enrollment program. They can talk with the staff members of the mainstream school and get in touch with parents who have DHH or hearing children who are already in the co-enrollment program. After this visit, the new DHH student is invited to visit the new classroom several times and is introduced to the other deaf and hearing classmates.

At the start of the co-enrollment program, the principal of the mainstream school gave information about the inclusion of DHH students to all the parents of hearing students. However, he deliberately did not give it too much attention because parents of hearing students might get the idea that it could have negative consequences for their child. Thus, it was a deliberate choice of the principal to keep the start of the co-enrollment program "small" because he did not want to overemphasize the changes. Also important was to start with a relatively small group of DHH students and gradually expand the program. This turned out to work very well. Parents accepted the fact that deaf students were enrolled in the school. There were not a lot of questions. Right from the start of the program, parents of hearing students (who all live close to the school) have invited DHH students home to have lunch together with their hearing peer(s). Most deaf students cannot have such at their own home because they live farther away from school than their hearing peers. These lunch invitations of parents turned out to be very helpful for the development of new friendships between deaf and hearing students.

MONITORING THE PROGRAM AND STUDENTS' ACHIEVEMENT

Since the start of the co-enrollment program, the content of the program and the achievements of the students have been monitored. Monitoring takes place in cooperation with researchers from the Kentalis Academy and Radboud University. The results of this monitoring are used to improve the program (Hermans, de Klerk, Wauters, & Knoors, 2014; see Yiu, Tang, & Ho, this volume). Research and practice go hand in hand. In the next section, the research program is described more in detail.

The Research Program

Since the start of the program, Kentalis has initiated several research studies that can be characterized as program evaluations. A wide range of topics has been addressed in these evaluations so far, such as DHH students' outcomes (language, reading, mathematics, social functioning, executive functioning, and well-being), the quality of instruction, and the experiences and perceptions of parents and teachers (see also Hermans, de Klerk, et al., 2014; Hermans, Wauters, de Klerk, & Knoors, 2014; Knoors & Hermans, 2010). In the next sections, we will highlight some of the main findings from these evaluations.

Executive Functioning of DHH Children

One of the domains that we recently have started to address in our evaluations is DHH children's executive functioning (EF). EFs are the cognitive functions that allow us to control and change our behavior to achieve our goals in life. We need those functions especially when it is unwise to follow our (conditioned) automatic behavior or in new situations in which we simply cannot lean upon our experiences (Diamond, 2013). EFs are important for language acquisition (Archibald, 2017), school achievements (Alloway & Alloway, 2010), and, last but not least, social functioning (Nigg, Quamma, Greenberg, & Kusche, 1999). Research studies in the last two decades have shown that, on average, DHH children have delays or deficits in this domain (see for a review Vissers & Hermans, in press).

We assessed DHH children's EF using the Behavior Rating Inventory of Executive Function (BRIEF: Gioia, Isquith, Guy, & Kenworthy, 2000) in the spring of 2017. Note that there was a lot of variation in the amount of time that DHH children had been enrolled in the co-enrollment program at that time (0;8 to 3;8 years). Both the special education teacher and the mainstream teacher independently filled in the questionnaire. The BRIEF consists of eight separate subscales (Inhibit, Shift, Emotional Control, Initiate, Working Memory, Plan/Organize, Organization of Materials, and Monitor), which are combined to form the Behavior Index (Inhibit, Shift, Emotional Control), the Metacognition Index (Initiate, Working Memory, Plan/Organize, Organization of Materials, and Monitor), and the Global Executive Composite (all eight scales). Scores above the average are indicative for EF problems. The results are shown in Table 10.1.

Inspection of Table 10.1 reveals that the average T-score for this group of DHH children was descriptively generally below the average (mean = 50) of their hearing peers in the normative sample, which seems to indicate that they have fewer problems in their EF. However, analyses (one-sample t-tests, criterion 50) revealed that the DHH children's scores did not significantly deviate from the norms for hearing children

Table 10.1. DHH Children's Scores on the BRIEF

Executive Function	Special Education Teacher			Mainstream Teacher		
	Mean	Min–Max	T ≥ 65	Mean	Min–Max	T ≥ 65
Inhibit	47.8	38 66	3.8%	47.9	38 69	3.8%
Shift	48.7	38–65	3.8%	49.9	40–65	3.8%
Emotional control	49.4	39–68	8.7%	49.9	39–71	8.7%
Initiate	50.7	36–62	0%	51.6	36–63	0%
Working memory	47.7	36–64	0%	49.8	36–63	0%
Plan/Organize	46.6	35–58	0%	49.0	39–64	0%
Organization of materials	48.3	40–63	0%	48.3	40–63	0%
Monitor	48.3	37–63	0%	48.2	37–63	0%
Behavior Index	48.1	38–66	3.8%	48.7	37–67	3.8%
Metacognition Index	48.5	35–63	0%	49.6	35–63	0%
Global Executive Composite	47.6	36–60	0%	48.5	35–60	0%

Table shows average T-scores, the minimum (Min) and maximum (Max) scores, and the percentage of the children with elevated scores (T ≥ 65).

(all p's > .1), with the exception of the children's scores on the subscale "Plan/Organize" given by the special education teacher (t $_{(25)}$ = −2.85, p < .01). On this subscale, DHH children actually scored significantly lower than their hearing peers from the normative sample, indicating that they had less difficulty in this EF area than their hearing peers.

We also computed the percentage of DHH children with elevated scores, the percentage of children with T-scores equal to or larger than 65. These percentages reflect how many DHH children have severe EF deficits or delays. Note that the percentage of hearing children with elevated T-scores in the normative sample is approximately 7%. As shown in Table 10.1, the percentage of DHH children with elevated scores was close to zero. To illustrate, none of the DHH children had elevated scores on the Metacognition Index and the Global Executive Composite, and only one child (3.8% of the children) had elevated scores on the Behavior Index.

The results obtained with the BRIEF are obviously positive but, at the same time, quite puzzling as they are inconsistent with the literature on DHH children's EF (Vissers & Hermans, in press). For instance, Hintermair (2013) found, in a large-scale study in Germany with DHH children and adolescents using the BRIEF questionnaire, that the prevalence of EF deficits or delays (T-scores ≥ 65) among DHH children is approximately four times higher than the prevalence of EF deficits or delays among hearing peers. In our group of 26 DHH children, no such deficits or delays were observed.

How can we account for this finding? Enhancing (DHH) children's EF requires a delicate balance between adjusting the child's environment (exemption/compensation) and subsequently training the child's EF skills. In our view, this is exactly the point where the "best of both worlds" may have met. For instance, special education teachers can use various didactic strategies to compensate for DHH children's verbal (auditory) working memory deficits during instruction (e.g., visualization, repetition, linking new information to existing knowledge). That is clearly part of their expertise. The mainstream school that we are working with has a strong focus on enhancing children's independence and 21st-century skills (to which EFs are central). In other words, teachers from the mainstream schools have expertise in enhancing children's EF skills and (DHH) children are challenged throughout the day in their EF development. We think that the expertise from both sides creates the fine and necessary balance that is needed to enhance children's EF skills. Further research obviously is needed to corroborate our claim.

Social Functioning of DHH Children and Their Well-Being

Children's social functioning has been a (undisputed) research topic in all evaluations that we have conducted since the start of the co-enrollment program (see also Yiu et al., this volume). We have chosen to monitor DHH children's social functioning every year as we know that DHH children's social position is at risk in mainstream schools (Kluwin, Stinson, & Colarossi, 2002; Musselman, Mootilal, & MacKay, 1996; Stinson & Antia, 1999; Stinson & Kluwin, 2003) and children's social functioning has a major impact on children's well-being, both in the short and long term (e.g., Shaffer, 2005).

When the co-enrollment program was initiated in 2003, we assumed that this program would strengthen DHH children's social position in the classroom in comparison to DHH children who are individually enrolled in mainstream education. Theoretically, co-enrollment programs provide opportunities for intensive contact between DHH children and their hearing peers in an environment where they are not the only DHH child (Antia & Kreimeyer, 2003; Kirchner, 1994). In other words, our positive expectations regarding DHH children's social functioning in co-enrollment programs originate from the idea that DHH children will find support in the presence of other DHH children in the classroom. These positive expectations have predominantly been supported by the empirical data we have collected throughout the years.

In our evaluations, we have mainly used two sociometric tasks to assess children's social functioning. In the peer nomination task, children nominate three classmates they like the most (positive nominations) and three classmates they like the least (negative nominations). In the peer rating task, children indicate on a three-point scale how much they like to play with a particular classmate (a happy face [3 points], a neutral face [2 points], and a sad face [1 point]).

Over the years, we have consistently found that that DHH children's social position is significantly less positive than the social position of their hearing classmates. However, although these significant differences seem to be quite robust, the size of the differences between DHH children and their hearing classmates is actually really small (z-score differences between DHH and hearing children's scores is about 0.25 across all studies and tasks that we have conducted; see also Hermans, de Klerk, et al., 2014). Furthermore, the percentage of children with average scores on the sociometric tasks that we consider to be problematic (scores more than 1.5 standard deviations below the mean) is the same for DHH children (7.4%) as for hearing children (6.5%).

Finally, in the sociometric studies, we have also found that DHH and hearing children have a preference for peers with the same hearing status. To illustrate, in the current evaluation (2013–2017), we have found that DHH children give significantly more positive nominations (31.1%) and a higher rating (mean = 2.45) to DHH classmates than to hearing classmates (respectively, 9.0% and 2.32). This pattern is observed for hearing children as well. This finding supports our assumption that DHH children do find support in the presence of other DHH children in their class.

Children's social functioning affects their well-being, both in the short term and in the long term (Shaffer, 2005). We also assessed children's well-being at school on several occasions using teacher reports (grade 1 to grade 6) and self-reports (grade 4 to grade 6) from ZIEN! (Broer, Haverhals, & de Bruin, 2012). ZIEN! is a norm-referenced student achievement tracking system for children's social skills and well-being in primary education. The percentile scores from the teacher reports (mean = 65) and the self-reports (mean = 62) were descriptively above average (mean = 50) on the ZIEN! well-being scale. One-sample t-tests revealed that the difference between DHH children's well-being scores and the hearing norms (test value = 50) was significant for the teacher reports ($t_{(14)} = 2.25, p < .05$) but not for the self-reports ($t_{(7)} < 1$).

In sum, our evaluations have shown that there are differences between DHH children's and hearing children's social functioning. Nevertheless, the differences between DHH and hearing children are generally quite small, there is no overrepresentation of DHH children among the group of children who score in a range that we consider problematic, and DHH children indeed find support in the presence of other DHH children in the classroom. Our studies have also revealed that DHH children's well-being at the co-enrollment school is comparable or even slightly better in comparison to hearing children's well-being. Therefore, we think that these results have corroborated our positive expectations of DHH children's social functioning and wellbeing in the co-enrollment program.

Language Development in SLN and Spoken Dutch

Another research topic that we have addressed in our evaluations is DHH children's language development. The DHH children in the co-enrollment program are proficient in SLN and in spoken Dutch (and occasionally in a second spoken language as well). Our main interest was in the level of proficiency of DHH children in both languages and, more importantly, in the variability in their language scores. When we analyzed the DHH children's language proficiency, we found that the variability in their proficiency in both languages was quite large. Let us illustrate this point with the vocabulary assessments that were made in the spring of 2017. The DHH children's scores on a receptive and an expressive test in SLN (T-NGT, Hermans, Knoors, & Verhoeven, 2009) were, respectively, 0.9 and 0.4 standard deviations above the norm for DHH children. T-tests revealed that these differences were significant ($t_{(25)} = 5.74, p < .001$ and $t_{(24)} = 2.40, p < .05$). The variability in the scores was quite high, ranging from –0.6 to +3.0 standard deviations for the SLN receptive vocabulary test and from –1.2 to +2.5 for the SLN expressive vocabulary test. The DHH children's average scores on a receptive and an expressive vocabulary test in spoken Dutch were, respectively, –1.28 and –1.66 standard deviations below the norms for hearing children. T-tests revealed that these differences were significant ($t_{(26)} = -6.60, p < .001$ and $t_{(25)} = -10.55, p < .001$). Again, the range in the scores was quite large, ranging from –3.0 to +1.3 standard deviations for the receptive vocabulary test and from –3.0 to 0.0 standard deviations for the expressive vocabulary test.

In other words, on average, the DHH children's vocabulary scores in SLN are above the DHH children's norms, whereas DHH children's vocabulary scores in spoken Dutch are below the hearing children's norms. More importantly, the variability in children's scores in both languages is very large. Some DHH children have excellent skills in SLN, whereas others score well below the normative means for DHH children. Similarly, some DHH children acquire age-appropriate skills in spoken Dutch, whereas other DHH children fall behind their hearing peers. These results stress the necessity of the availability of both languages, spoken Dutch (the teachers) and SLN (special education teacher/SLN interpreter), in the classroom to make instruction accessible for all DHH children.

School Achievement

The school achievements of DHH children are a topic that we have addressed in all of our evaluations. That should by no means be a surprise because it is known that many DHH children fall behind their hearing peers in their achievements at school (Karchmer & Mitchell, 2003; Qi & Mitchell, 2012; Wauters, van Bon, & Tellings, 2006). As we pointed out earlier, the co-enrollment program allows us to combine the strengths of special education (e.g., special didactic strategies to stimulate communication and language development, special attention for learning to read, accessible instruction) with the strengths of mainstream education (fast pace of instruction, high expectations, enhancing children's independence, and stimulating their 21st-century skills).

In the Netherlands, children are assessed by tests that classify children's achievement into one of five categories: I, good (percentile scores 81–100); II, above average (percentile scores 61–80); III, average (percentile scores 41–60); IV, below average (percentile scores 21–40); and V, weak (percentile scores 1–20). Thus, in the normative sample of hearing children, each category includes 20% of the children.

Table 10.2 depicts the percentages of DHH children across these categories in the spring of 2017 for word decoding, comprehension, mathematics, and spelling. Inspection of Table 10.2 reveals that DHH children are underrepresented in the "good" and "above average" categories (especially in reading comprehension and mathematics), whereas DHH children are overrepresented in the "poor" category (especially in reading comprehension and mathematics).

The present results show that DHH children in the co-enrollment program fall behind their hearing peers in word decoding, reading, and mathematics. However, it also is clear that 52% of the DHH children obtained average or above-average scores on word decoding, 27% on reading comprehension, 26% on mathematics, and 39% on spelling. Although we don't know yet whether these percentages will be sustained by the time the DHH children will finish primary education, these figures give rise to some optimism in trying to bridge the gap in the school achievement of DHH children and their hearing peers. But there is also room for improvement, for instance by increasing the

Table 10.2. Percentage of DHH Children in Each of the Five Percentile Intervals for Word Decoding, Reading Comprehension, Mathematics, and Spelling

Category	Word Decoding	Reading Comprehension	Mathematics	Spelling
I (Good)	8.7%	6.7%	4.3%	13.0%
II (Above average)	17.4%	13.3%	13.0%	8.7%
III (Average)	26.1%	6.7%	8.7%	17.4%
IV (Below average)	13.0%	6.7%	17.4%	13.0%
V (Poor)	34.8%	66.7%	56.5%	47.8%

Distribution normative hearing sample is 20% in each category.

amount of time for school subjects such as reading or by enhancing the teachers' didactic skills.

Experiences of Teachers

In the end, it is mainly up to the teachers to successfully implement the co-enrollment program, but that is easier said than done. Working together in the classroom requires excellent interpersonal communications skills, compatibility in teaching philosophy, mutual trust, and perceiving each other as equals with complementary skills (Antia & Metz, 2014; Kreimeyer, Drye, & Metz, this volume). As teachers are central to the co-enrollment program, their perceptions and experiences are an essential part of the evaluation. How do they experience the benefits and challenges of the co-enrollment program for the pupils and for their own professional development? We have collected the teachers' experiences through questionnaires we administered at the end of several school years. All in all, these questionnaires have sketched a predominantly positive view on the co-enrollment program.

All the teachers indicated that working in the co-enrollment program requires extra time (e.g., fine-tuning in preparation, consulting about pupils, dividing the work). In addition, the teachers from the special school indicated that they needed good communicative skills, excellent coaching skills, and an appropriate and flexible attitude (see also Antia & Metz, 2014).

Regarding the benefits for pupils, Antia and Metz (2014) have pointed out that teachers indicate that the lowered student–teacher ratio allows for more attention to the needs of each student, DHH or hearing. This was unanimously corroborated by the teachers in our co-enrollment program. They also indicated that the faster pace of instruction, the richer (spoken) language environment, and the presence of hearing peers as social role models were the main benefits for DHH children. The teachers also indicated there were disadvantages for hearing and DHH children. The turmoil in the classroom (e.g., the sign language interpreters), causing distraction for DHH and hearing students, and the decrease in the pace of instruction (in comparison to classes without DHH children) were named by some of the teachers as disadvantages for children.

With respect to their own professional development, all the teachers indicated that their professional development has been boosted by the co-enrollment program. Knowledge of classroom management, pace of instruction, and a positive attitude toward differences between children were named by the special education teachers. Teachers from the mainstream school indicated that they had acquired knowledge about DHH children and had learned valuable new didactic (visualization) techniques.

Experiences of Parents

An essential part of parental involvement is their endorsement of the school's policy and educational system (Kohl, Lengua, & McMahon, 2000). This endorsement is vital, as parental involvement is a variable that is known to affect children's achievements (Fan & Chen, 2001). In the evaluations we have conducted throughout the years, we have collected parental perceptions on a variety of issues related to the co-enrollment program (e.g., the impact of the presence of children with a different hearing status on their child's well-being, social functioning, and school achievement; the impact of the co-teaching system on their child's development) through questionnaires. These questionnaires have revealed that parents of DHH and hearing children are predominantly very positive about the co-enrollment program. Although some parents have raised some concerns ("too much money, attention and time is spent on DHH children" and "my child is distracted by the interpreter"), most of them (88%) were satisfied with the co-enrollment program and expressed no concerns. Nevertheless, we will continue to collect parental perception in the years to come.

SUMMARY AND CONCLUSIONS

In our view, the added value of our co-enrollment program for DHH students is as follows:

- A maximum academic challenge, combined with adequate specialized support;
- The presence of DHH role models;
- The opportunities that the DHH students have to increase independence and self-efficacy;
- A challenging and safe environment to practice EF skills;
- A rich social context at school.

This requires from members of staff at school:

- A commitment to co-enrollment of all primary school teachers and other professionals involved;
- Finding ways to make sure that the parents of all children, hearing and DHH ones, are committed to co-enrollment;
- An attitude among school personnel and students that celebrates diversity;
- Structural provision of extra planning and consulting time for teachers;
- Availability of sufficient and adequate options for the coaching of special education and mainstream teachers;
- Willingness of administrators and teachers to welcome DHH staff and sign language interpreters;

- Willingness to learn and apply relevant didactic strategies, including practicing co-teaching;
- Flexibility of teachers in their planning and teaching.

A co-enrollment program for DHH and hearing students is definitely not easy to establish and sustain. It requires a lot of effort from all teachers and other professionals involved; parents need to accept the program and its objectives, and serious practical issues have to be resolved. A co-enrollment program stretches legal and financial conditions to the limits, certainly in a country like the Netherlands with its historically very segregated systems of mainstream and special education. And yet, we have succeeded in continuing a co-enrollment program for over 13 years; the program has become an example for other schools in the Netherlands trying to include DHH students and students with specific language impairments.

The success of the co-enrollment program may certainly be ascribed to the determination of the founders of the program, all members of staff, and the parents, but, most of all, the flourishing of the hearing and DHH students explains the success. True, our co-enrollment program does not accomplish miracles. Not all DHH students profit from the program in all respects as much as we hoped for. Not all DHH students achieve academically at age-appropriate levels. But many DHH students do progress tremendously in learning and achievement even though there continues to be a huge variation in academic outcomes. Socially, our co-enrollment program has succeeded over the years in creating a community in a mainstream school where hearing and DHH students not only feel welcome but manage to interact socially with each other and with the teachers in ways that, on the one hand, in many respects a hearing loss does not seem to matter much anymore, while, on the other hand, being deaf as a characteristic of some students is appreciated by all. It is, indeed, the best of both worlds.

REFERENCES

Alloway, T. P., & Alloway, R. (2010). Investigating the predictive roles of working memory and IQ in academic attainment. *Journal of Experimental Child Psychology, 106,* 20–29.

Antia, S. D. (2015). Enhancing academic and social outcomes: Balancing individual, family, and school assets and risks for deaf and hard-of-hearing students in general education. In H. Knoors & M. Marschark (Eds.), *Educating deaf learners: Creating a global evidence base* (pp. 527–546). New York: Oxford University Press.

Antia, S. D., & Kreimeyer, K. H. (2003). Peer interactions of deaf and hard-of-hearing children. In M. Marschark & P. E. Spencer (Eds.), *The Oxford handbook of deaf studies, language, and education* (pp. 164–176). New York: Oxford University Press.

Antia, S. D., & Metz, K. K. (2014). Co-enrollment in the United States: A critical analysis of benefits and challenges. In M. Marschark, G. Tang, & H. Knoors (Eds.), *Bilingualism and bilingual deaf education* (pp. 424–444). New York: Oxford University Press.

Antia, S. D., Stinson, M. S., & Gaustad, M. G. (2002). Developing membership in the education of deaf and hard-of-hearing students in inclusive settings. *Journal of Deaf Studies and Deaf Education, 7*(3), 214–229.

Archibald, L. M. D. (2017). Working memory and language learning: A review. *Child Language Teaching and Therapy, 33,* 5–17

Broer, N. A., Haverhals, B., & De Bruin, H. L. (2012). Verantwoording pedagogisch expertsysteem ZIEN! Voor het primair onderwijs. Driestar Onderwijs advies, Gouda.

Clarke, A., & DeNuzzo, D. (2003). *Co-teaching in inclusive classrooms: Practical practice.* Paper presented at the International Conference on Inclusion, the Netherlands.

De Klerk, A., Fortgens, C., & Van der Eijk, A. (2015). Curriculum design in Dutch deaf education. In H. Knoors & M. Marschark (Eds.), *Educating deaf learners: Creating a global evidence base* (pp. 573–593). New York: Oxford University Press.

Diamond, A. (2013). Executive functions. *Annual Review of Psychology, 64,* 135–168.

European Agency for Special Needs and Inclusive Education. (2017). *Netherlands. National overview special needs education.* Retrieved May 22, 2017, from www.european-agency.org

Fan, X., & Chen, M. (2001). Parental involvement and students' academic achievement: A meta-analysis. *Educational Psychology Review, 13,* 1–22.

Fullan, M., & Hargreaves, A. (2016). *Bringing the profession back in: Call to action.* Oxford, OH: Learning Forward.

Gioia, G., Isquith, P., Guy, S., & Kenworthy, L. (2000). *Behavior Rating Inventory of Executive Functions.* Lutz, FL: Psychological Assessment Resources.

Government of the Netherlands. (2017). *Appropriate education at primary school.* Retrieved June 1, 2017, from https://www.government.nl/topics/primary-education/contents/appropriate-education-at-primary-school

Hermans, D., De Klerk, A., Wauters, L., & Knoors, H. (2014). The Twinschool: A co-enrollment program in the Netherlands. In M. Marschark, G. Tang, & H. Knoors (Eds.), *Bilingualism and bilingual deaf education* (pp. 272–291). New York: Oxford University Press.

Hermans, D., Knoors, H., & Verhoeven, L. (2009). Assessment of sign language development: The case of deaf children in the Netherlands. *Journal of Deaf Studies and Deaf Education, 15,* 107–119.

Hermans, D., Vugs, B., van Berkel-van Hoof, L., & Knoors, H. (2015). Deaf children's executive functions: From research to practice? In H. Knoors & M. Marschark (Eds.), *Educating deaf learners: Creating a global evidence base* (pp. 231–260). New York: Oxford University Press.

Hermans, D., Wauters, L., De Klerk, A., & Knoors, H. (2014). Quality of instruction in bilingual schools for deaf children: Through the children's eyes and the camera's lens. In M. Marschark, G. Tang, & H. Knoors (Eds.),

Bilingualism and bilingual deaf education (pp. 272–291). New York: Oxford University Press.

Hermans, D., Wauters, L., Willemsen, M., & Knoors, H. (2016). Vocabulary acquisition in deaf and hard-of-hearing children: Research and interventions. In M. Marschark & P. E. Spencer (Eds.), *The Oxford handbook of deaf studies in language* (pp. 161–180). New York: Oxford University Press.

Hintermair, M. (2013). Executive functions and behavioral problems in deaf and hard-of-hearing students at general and special schools. *Journal of Deaf Studies and Deaf Education, 18,* 344–359.

Inspectie van het Onderwijs. (2017). *De Staat van het Onderwijs 2015–2016.* Utrecht: Inspectie van het Onderwijs.

Karchmer, M. A., & Mitchell, R. E. (2003). Demographic and achievement characteristics of deaf and hard of hearing students. In M. Marschark & P. E. Spencer (Eds.), *Oxford handbook of deaf studies, language, and education* (pp. 21–37). New York: Oxford University Press.

Kirchner, C. J. (1994). Co-enrollment as an inclusion model. *American Annals of the Deaf, 139,* 163–164.

Kluwin, T. N., Stinson, M. S., & Colarossi, G. M. (2002). Social processes and outcomes of in-school contact between deaf and hearing peers. *Journal of Deaf Studies and Deaf Education, 7,* 200–213.

Knoors, H. (2016). Language use in the classroom: Accommodating the needs of diverse deaf and hard-of-hearing learners. In M. Marschark, V. Lampropoulou, & E. K. Skordilis (Eds.), *Diversity in deaf education* (pp. 219–246). New York: Oxford University Press.

Knoors, H., & Hermans, D. (2010). Effective instruction for deaf and hard-of-hearing students: Teaching strategies, school settings, and student characteristics. In M. Marschark & P. Spencer (Eds.), *The Oxford handbook of deaf studies, language, and education* (Vol. 2, pp. 57–71). New York: Oxford University Press.

Kohl, G. O., Lengua, L. J., & McMahon, R. J. (2000). Parent involvement in school conceptualizing multiple dimensions and their relations with family and demographic risk factors. *Journal of School Psychology, 38,* 501–523.

Musselman, C., Mootilal, A., & MacKay, S. (1996). The social adjustment of deaf adolescents in segregated, partially integrated, and mainstreamed settings. *Journal of Deaf Studies and Deaf Education, 1,* 52–63.

Nigg, J. T., Quamma, J. P., Greenberg, M. T., & Kusche, C. A. (1999). A two-year longitudinal study of neuropsychological and cognitive performance in relation to behavioral problems and competencies in elementary school children. *Journal of Abnormal Child Psychology, 27,* 51–63.

Qi, S., & Mitchell, R. E. (2012). Large-scale academic achievement testing of deaf and hard-of-hearing students: Past, present, and future. *Journal of Deaf Studies & Deaf Education, 17,* 1–18.

Shaffer, D. R. (2005). *Social and personality development.* Belmont, CA: Wadsworth.

Stinson, M. S., & Antia, S. D. (1999). Considerations in educating deaf and hard-of-hearing students in inclusive settings. *Journal of Deaf Studies and Deaf Education, 4,* 163–175.

Stinson, M. S., & Kluwin, T. N. (2003). Educational consequences of alternative school placements. In M. Marschark & M. E. Spencer (Eds.), *The Oxford handbook of deaf studies, language, and education* (pp. 52–64). New York: Oxford University Press.

Vissers, C. T. W. M., & Hermans, D. (in press). Social-emotional problems in DHH children from an executive and theory of mind perspective. In H. Knoors & M. Marschark (Eds.), *Evidence-based practice and deaf education*. New York: Oxford University Press.

Wauters, L. N., Van Bon, W. H. J., & Telling, A. E. J. M. (2006). The reading comprehension of Dutch deaf children. *Reading and Writing, 19*, 49–76.

11

Conditions for Effective Co-Enrollment of Deaf and Hearing Students: What May Be Learned from Experiences in Belgium

Magaly Ghesquière and Laurence Meurant

Since 2000 in Namur, a town in the French-speaking part of Belgium, Sainte-Marie, a mainstream school, has been running bilingual classes for deaf and hard-of-hearing (DHH) pupils. The parents of a deaf child were at the origin of this setting. They wished to make it possible for groups of DHH children to be provided with a level of schooling similar to that offered to their hearing peers, through bilingual education in both sign language and spoken language, and in a context of inclusion within groups of hearing pupils. Although they developed a setting that was first believed to have no counterpart and still remains unique in Belgium, these guiding principles later appeared to meet the characteristics that define the inclusive model known as "co-enrollment" by Kirchner (1994).

After more than 15 years of experience, this setting has revealed different issues related to the variety of profiles among deaf learners, the search for an appropriate bilingual pedagogy, the co-teaching approach, and the complementarity between bilingual teachers and interpreters. After a brief presentation of the context in which the bilingual classes emerged and the way they are organized in practice, this chapter will develop these issues and show how they are essential conditions for ensuring that DHH pupils can benefit efficiently from the expected advantages of a co-enrollment setting.

AT THE BEGINNING

In 1998, the so-called Immersion Decree was approved in the Fédération Wallonie-Bruxelles, namely the political authority responsible, among others, for education in the French-speaking part of Belgium. It enabled schools to organize instruction by immersion in a language other than

French. Thanks to the joint efforts of the Deaf Association and the Association of Parents of Deaf Children, French Belgian Sign Language (LSFB) was recognized as one of the languages offered in immersion by the decree. This legal context paved the way for the hearing parents of a 1-year-old deaf child to imagine a new education setting for all DHH children, where the main defining features were related to linguistic issues rather than being focused on disability.

In 2000, together with another parent, they created a nonprofit association, *École et Surdité*, aimed at gathering funding to launch the project and waiting to get it recognized and then funded and organized officially by the government. *École et Surdité* started looking for an ordinary school that would welcome the project, in a town rather than a village in order to be attractive to more families. The director of the elementary section of the Sainte-Marie school, in the center of Namur, agreed to take on the project. Sainte-Marie provides general elementary education, including preschool (ages 2.5 to 6 years), primary school (ages 6 to 12), and secondary education (ages 12 to 18). The elementary section has a mean enrollment of some 600 pupils for the nine class levels, while the secondary section enrolls around 1,000 pupils distributed over the six levels. This means that each level comprises several (three to nine) classes with a mean of 25 pupils.

Starting from the first level of preschool, a bilingual teacher was hired to open the first bilingual class in September 2000. First only one child was included, but after a few months, a small group of three DHH children aged 2.5 to 3 years was included in the class with hearing peers. The regular French-speaking teacher who kept teaching the hearing pupils as before saw a bilingual teacher joining her class and teaching the DHH group. The instructions given to the bilingual teacher were to ensure the DHH pupils were included in the class, to perform the same activities as the co-teacher in order to follow the same curriculum and the same objectives, and to make the class fully accessible to the DHH pupils in LSFB and in French. The hearing pupils who were enrolled in the bilingual class rather than in one of the other classes of the same level experienced the presence of two teachers and two languages in the class, rather than one. The hearing peers are not expected to, but neither are they prevented from, acquiring LSFB: the bilingual immersion setting is intended only for the DHH pupils.

The expected advantages of the setting under construction were threefold. First, at an academic level, it was aimed at providing DHH pupils with a completely accessible education, where they are guided toward understanding and learning just as hearing pupils do, rather than being occupied with the effort of listening. As the curriculum and the requirements are the same for all, the aim is to provide the DHH pupils with the same schooling level and the same opportunities in higher education as their hearing peers. Second, at a psychological level, it was hypothesized that the DHH pupils would benefit from interacting with, rather than being isolated from, their hearing peers. In such a context of inclusion, DHH children are given a better opportunity to become aware of and accept their personal characteristics in comparison with other DHH peers as well as with hearing ones. Third, at an ethical level, as this form of teaching was not based on hearing and speech competences, it was open to all profiles of DHH pupils, be they from hearing or DHH families, and regardless of the quality of their access to sound and speech.

THE SETTING

The project grew up with the older pupils, one additional class having been opened each year, replicating the functioning of the first class. To be recruited, the bilingual co-teachers must have a teaching degree and a certified level of UF12 in the official LSFB education, which corresponds to a C1 level on the scale of the Common European Framework of Reference for Languages. In addition, they must pass a recruitment assessment for which they are put in a teaching situation and evaluated on both their pedagogical skills and their linguistic competences in LSFB and in (at least written) French.

As for all pupils, the main objectives of preschool are acquisition of autonomy, socialization, and first learnings. But for the DHH pupils, special attention is paid to the development of the two teaching languages of the program, namely LSFB and French. Therefore, depending on the age of children, times of inclusion alternate with moments where the DHH pupils are grouped separately for specific activities. On a regular basis, in particular, DHH groups take part in bilingual activities in French with cued speech and LSFB.[1] The signing teacher and a good cued speech coder coordinate between themselves to provide the whole linguistic content of the session in both languages. The main objectives of these bilingual activities are to provide immersion in spoken French made visually accessible, to help pupils distinguish between the two languages and install bilingualism in their consciousness, to create interest in French through fun activities, and to give them access to the phonology of the French language for the purpose of supporting their emerging literacy development.

From the first grade of primary school onward, all nonlinguistic classes (e.g., math, history, geography, the sciences, physical education, art education) as well as all extracurricular activities (e.g., museum, cinema, sports center) are organized in inclusion and through co-teaching, while for linguistic classes (LSFB, French, English, and the so-called bilingualism class), DHH pupils are taught separately by their bilingual teacher. Indeed, it appeared that, for linguistic subjects, it was inappropriate to follow the same lesson plans and rhythm for hearing and DHH pupils because of the differences in their linguistic background. Therefore, inclusion proved not to be appropriate for language learning at school.

Interpreters also take part in the setting. Their role is to facilitate communication between signing and nonsigning interlocutors, be it within or outside the class, in order to foster inclusion. Teachers may call interpreters into their class when a collaborative work exercise among pupils is scheduled, or to make a theatrical play accessible in sign language, for instance. Interpreters are also essential during class councils or to make communication possible between the school director or any nonsigning member of the school and DHH pupils, parents, educators, or teachers.

From 2004 onward, when the first pupils were about to enter primary school at the age of about 6 years, École et Surdité established a collaboration with the linguists of the University of Namur, who at that time had just started research on LSFB. The idea came from the teacher who was about to engage herself for the first time in bilingual education at the level of primary school (children aged 6 to 12). She anticipated her need for linguistic support to teach all school subjects in LSFB, as it had probably never been done before and no cases had been documented. This collaboration took the form of continuous training based on the principle of offering the teachers a place to address their daily questions to linguists, to signers of different ages and profiles, and to interpreters who were invited to collaborate in this training (Meurant and Zegers de Beyl, 2009).

While École et Surdité was established to launch the project and sustain it during its very first years, it took nine years before the government recognized the specificities of this bilingual setting for elementary school. The decree approved in 2009 specified, for example, the number of pupils needed for a full-time teacher to be hired by the government; this number had to be negotiated down in comparison with the general rules in mainstream schools because of the demography of deafness. It also described the required qualifications to be hired in such a bilingual setting for DHH pupils and mentioned the creation of specific training (which, unfortunately, has not yet been implemented).[2] This legal recognition did not entail full financial support, since the number of pupils was not sufficient to cover the needs in teachers, because not all members of the team had the required diploma to be hired by the ministry (i.e., a teaching degree as a preschool teacher, as a primary school teacher, or as a secondary school teacher in one of the class subjects), because the decree did not cover the requirements for interpreters nor for continuous training, and because it only concerned elementary school. It was in 2011 and in 2016 that the decree was extended to the first cycle of secondary education, and then to the whole secondary school.

Currently, 50 DHH pupils are enrolled in the bilingual classes of Sainte-Marie in Namur, from preschool and primary school (a total of 35 pupils) to the end of secondary school (15 pupils). *École et Surdité* still plays an important role in supporting the program, in recruiting and training teachers and interpreters, in coordinating the bilingual classes and their inclusion within the school community, and in funding the project. In 2012, when the whole primary cycle had been completed for the first time, *École et Surdité* decided to take a step back to reflect on the experience gained in teaching DHH pupils included in ordinary classes bilingually, with a focus on pedagogical issues. The most experienced teacher from the program has been dedicated to putting down in writing all the specificities and good practices that were worth describing and passing these on to the current and future members of the team.

A CO-ENROLLMENT SETTING?

This descriptive work (Ghesquière and Meurant, 2018) resulted in bringing to light the relationship between the bilingual classes of Sainte-Marie and the principles of co-enrollment described by Kirchner (1994, this volume). A majority of the features shared by existing co-enrollment experiments, as pointed out by Antia and Metz (2014, p. 439), also fit with Namur's program: (1) the classes include DHH students among mainly hearing students in a mainstream education system; (2) they are co-taught by a general education teacher and a teacher in charge of DHH students; (3) qualified sign language interpreters are available as necessary for all classes; (4) both speech and sign language are valued and used in the classroom; and (5) all students have the necessary visual and auditory support or accommodations to fully access classroom teaching.

However, other features pointed out by the same authors do not correspond exactly to the experience described in this chapter. First, Antia and Metz (2014) mention that the presence of a critical mass of DHH students within the class, namely 20% to 50%, usually defines co-enrollment settings. In this case, the proportion of DHH pupils within the bilingual classes averages 15%. However, the school includes several nonbilingual classes at each grade, from preschool to secondary school. When compared with the total number of students in the school community, the proportion of DHH pupils falls to 3%. The fact is that in French-speaking Belgium, parents are free to register their DHH child in any mainstream school (where, with only a few hours per week of support, he or she will be exposed to an education in French only) or in special schools for the deaf. Practical constraints such as travel distance from home to school definitely play a role in the choice parents make. Therefore, taking into account the support of political and medical professionals in favor of spoken-language-only education, as well as the recent legal recognition of the bilingual setting of Namur, it is understandable that the proportion of DHH pupils within this setting is not higher. It reflects more or less the proportion of DHH people in the entire population in Western countries.

Second, despite the fact that it is planned in law, no specific teacher training exists in the French-speaking part of Belgium for educating DHH students. Internal training is provided by *École et Surdité*, and especially in collaboration with the University of Namur, but it is mostly based on the transmission of competences from more experienced teachers to less experienced ones. The same can be said about interpreters since the first training started in 2014: the professionals involved in the project either have been trained abroad and in an sign language other than LSFB or have been trained on the job. No specific training exists for interpreters working specifically in the context of education.

Third, hearing teachers and students of the school community, whether they are involved in the co-enrollment classes or not, are offered classes in LSFB but are not forced to accept. The bilingual LSFB/French setting, pedagogy, and objectives are addressed only to the DHH pupils enrolled in the school. It follows that only a small proportion of the hearing students and professionals of the school community has basic skills in LSFB. Hence, DHH pupils and members of the staff depend on LSFB interpreters for sustained conversations with other children and adults. But this unbalanced multilingualism stimulates some of the DHH pupils to develop friendly relationships with hearing peers and therefore to strengthen their use of French in informal situations.

Marschark, Tang, and Knoors (2014, p. 462), when synthesizing the fundamental principles underlying co-enrollment programs, suggest that, even if it is most often the case, the sign-language-versus-spoken-language bilingualism used in the classes is not a defining necessity; according to the authors, a co-enrollment program for DHH pupils could involve spoken language instruction only. In Namur's program, however, LSFB/French bilingualism is a central feature, and it is seen as contributing to the ethical aim of the project, which is to make the mainstream level of schooling accessible to all DHH students, regardless of their access to sound and their linguistic profile. This choice to include all profiles of DHH students has important implications for the way of conducting bilingual pedagogy.

WELCOMING ALL PROFILES OF DHH STUDENTS

The profiles of DHH students who are co-enrolled in the classes are as varied as they are in society. They are related to the variety of family contexts and linguistic environments, to the degree of hearing loss of each individual, as well as to the way communication was established with each child before entering school. From the beginning of the program, three main profiles were included in bilingual classes, but they have been recently supplemented with a fourth profile. For convenience, they will be referred to as A, B, C, and D and represented in some details by the fictive figures and stories of Andrew, Brianna, Chloe, and Daniel. Beyond the inevitable reduction made by these fictive portraits, the experience showed that it is very important for a teacher to differentiate the pupils and identify their respective needs in order to guide their pedagogical actions. That is why we devote quite a large space here to describing these four profiles, as details are expected to help the teacher's analysis.

Profile A: French as First Language, LSFB as Second Language

Profile A includes DHH pupils like Andrew who have French as a first language and who have developed LSFB at school. Andrew was born in a hearing family who knew nothing about deafness before. He benefitted from a bilateral cochlear implant from an early age, and his family got into the habit of making their speech in French visually complete and accessible, thanks to the use of cued speech. Because they were advised by medical staff to avoid contact with sign language, Andrew's parents were hesitant but finally enrolled Andrew in Sainte-Marie when he was 4 years old. At that time, he was able to speak and understand French when the speaker was using cued speech, but he was discovering LSFB and was in contact with it only at school. Until the age of 12, Andrew's dominant language was French, but he progressively acquired a more and more balanced mastering of French and LSFB and, at age 15, he became aware that he was a bilingual student who could comfortably express himself in both languages.

In regard to academic skills, Andrew was what is called a brilliant student with high intellectual capacities (like many of his peers with the same profile), but he developed problematic behavior toward others from the age of 8: he needed to control everything and everybody and could not accept any negative remark, frustration, or failure. In fact, Andrew needed psychological support. He had to accept that he had severe hearing loss, which he could experience when he was not wearing his cochlear implants, and needed to stop thinking and acting under the illusion that he could hear normally. The pressure he had undergone about his hearing capacities, from adults around him and from himself, combined with the fact that it was impossible for him to compare the quality of his hearing with that of others, had progressively made him oversensitive and produced his problematic behavior.

Andrew and his peers are a minority of the DHH students enrolled in Sainte-Marie. They developed linguistically and cognitively without any delay or subsequent disorder. Their first language is the majority spoken language and they have fluently mastered it. Logically, their education will need to be based on this language. Being co-enrolled and immersed in sign language, they will be offered access to all aspects of their schooling, not limited by their hearing capacities, by the acoustic conditions of the class, or by their capacity to concentrate on speech perception. Students with Andrew's profile in this co-enrollment setting explicitly underline that being taught in sign language is highly comfortable for them, even if it is not their first language. Moreover, experience suggests that the process of their identity building is made more serene thanks to the group inclusion and the bilingualism of the co-enrollment setting.

Profile B: No First Language when Entering School

Profile B includes pupils like Brianna who have a severe delay in their linguistic development at the age of entering school. They have almost no language at the age of 3. Brianna lives in a hearing family and received a cochlear implant, but some of her peers in profile B live with deaf parents and wear hearing aids or no aids at all. Brianna entered a bilingual class when she was 5 years old, after her first regular school advised her parents that she was not progressing well. She could produce some words in French and could understand simple injunctions in LSFB, but she answered "yes" with her head and her voice to any question and mimicked any behavior she thought appropriate for the situation. In fact, she was unaware that she had hearing loss and that some others did not. At home and generally out of school, all conversations and linguistic inputs were escaping her. When she arrived in Sainte-Marie, she was not able to communicate; she could not answer or follow others' communication. LSFB was totally unknown to her, but it has been used by the teachers to make her emerge from her shell. Their urgent task was to educate her to use her gaze for communication and to involve her in first communicative exchanges. They first used sign language to ensure the complete accessibility of the linguistic input, but they progressively taught her to "listen with her eyes," both in sign language and in spoken language, to detect visual cues such as facial expressions, lip movements, and cued speech keys.

Students of Brianna's profile represent the majority of the DHH students who are co-enrolled in bilingual classes at Sainte-Marie. Many of them received one or two cochlear implants early, but one can hypothesize that they did not receive a sufficient or adequate linguistic input, be it in spoken language, in spoken language completed with cued speech, or in visual communication in general. In fact, it often happens that before they even have time to realize the consequences of hearing impairment on the daily life of their child, parents start to expect the possibility to cure deafness and hope for a miraculous effect of cochlear implants. They are not conscious of the lack of passive linguistic input their child is facing and of its devastating consequences on his or her development. Moreover, since they are often told that they will need to "wait for a couple of years" before they can see the results of the operation and are advised to avoid contact with sign language, parents may be not alarmed by the signals of communication disorders shown by their child. In such a context, it may well be that parents of children like Brianna did not feel necessary to make their spoken language visually accessible. Due to inappropriate placement or a poor vigilance to the use of shared gaze, for example, Brianna and her peers had probably not received sufficient addressed language and communication during the first years of their life. Delay in acquiring a first language has more or less harmful effects on the cognitive and psychological development of those children (Dammeyer, 2018).

Thanks to the vigilance of the teachers, in close collaboration with the families and professionals such as speech therapists and psychologists, pupils like Brianna will develop some competences in at least one of the two languages used in the class, even if they will retain linguistic and cognitive specificities. With time, some of them may tend to resemble their profile A peers, while others will lean more toward profile C. Teachers will have to watch out for this evolution, in combination with potential cognitive delays, and adapt their pedagogical actions to them.

Profile C: LSFB as First Language, French as Second Language

Profile C groups together students like Chloe, whose first language is LSFB, French becoming a second language during schooling. Like the majority of her family members, Chloe has a significant hearing loss. When she entered school at age 2.5, she had a level of sign language similar to the spoken language level of hearing children of the same age, since her deaf parents communicated in LSFB with her from birth, and her cognitive development was also perfectly equivalent to that of her hearing peers. She rarely wore her hearing aids, her parents allowing her to choose whether to wear them or not. She discovered the existence of spoken language at school. French was foreign to her, notably because it is inaccessible without adaptation. In her family, for several generations, French has been considered by analogy as the language of "the others": people who prohibited the use of sign language, want to "repair" deafness, and predict the disappearance of sign languages (Meynard, 2003). Her family considers itself to be a member of a misunderstood linguistic minority. In Chloe's family, French language takes only a utilitarian function for the unavoidable contacts with the hearing majority, but it does not receive any place or prestige in the daily life of the home. Chloe will therefore only come into contact with this language at school, and mainly in its written form. This will certainly affect the evolution of her French language learning.

With students of Chloe's profile, the role of the teachers is to make them meet the requirement and develop the desire to learn French—to make them consider they are affected by this language too. Support for homework must be provided to families that do not have the required mastery of French.

Profile D: LSFB and French Bilingual

After 15 years, the school started to welcome children with a profile that is different again. Profile D refers to pupils who, like Daniel, were bilingual upon arrival. Daniel has DHH parents who naturally use French or LSFB according to daily situations. He is autonomous in the use of his hearing aids and wears them regularly. At the end of preschool, he was comfortable with both languages and switched from one to the other with ease. He could also already decode small written words and could write some words too, based on his auditory perception of the word. For example, he wrote <opeupa> for <on ne peut pas> ("one cannot"), or <avil> for <avril> ("April").

Since pupils like Daniel are very young, and there are few of them at the school, it would be risky to draw conclusions or to comment on educational methods related to the needs of this profile of students. However, it already appears from the portraits we have presented here that teachers' concerns will be focused on different elements depending on whether they are working with students like Andrew, Brianna, or Chloe.

Pedagogical Adaptations to the Variety of Profiles

From preschool, with a child of Andrew's profile, the main challenge lies in helping him and his parents realize and accept that he has hearing loss. Brianna's profile calls for urgent action when entering school, namely to help her develop a first language in order to minimize her linguistic and cognitive delays. To convey a completely and naturally accessible language, sign language will be the priority during this crucial period. In the case of a child like Chloe, the challenge for her teachers is to help her enjoy the French language and to sustain her first achievements in French in order to prepare for the acquisition of reading and writing.

When it comes to the first stages of learning to read in primary school, pupils belonging to profiles A, B, and C obviously cannot progress in a similar way, since they have different relationships to the oral language they are expected to read. Andrew and his peers will follow the same path as most hearing pupils with similar stages of development. French is their first language, and they will have to understand the regular (and irregular) relationships between the written code (graphemes), the sounds they refer to (phonemes), the recognized words, and their meaning. Pupils of this profile will experience specific difficulties related to their hearing loss: their incomplete perception of a spoken word can obstruct the recognition of this word, even after a correct decoding. A consistent use of cued speech is an essential way to disambiguate these problems and refine the phonological understanding of French for those children.

In the case of a child like Chloe, learning how the alphabetic system functions cannot be based on the grapheme–sound relationship. But it would also be impossible to make her learn correspondences between written French words and LSFB signs by heart, without giving her the key of the productive system of alphabet. However, and even in preschool, it is possible to rely on the competences that Chloe spontaneously developed in lip reading and in articulating more or less accurate mouth movements while signing. Starting from the child's mouth movements (shown, for example, in a pocket mirror, or via a video recording of the child) associated with a sign like MAMAN ("mom"), PAPA ("dad"), or POMME ("apple"), the teacher can make the link to the cued speech form and to the fingerspelling of the corresponding French word, before referring to the written form. Anyway, Chloe will not be able to avoid the necessity of learning French vocabulary as a foreign vocabulary in order to be able to read autonomously. The development of her vocabulary will take several years, and the teachers must be aware of that to support her efforts. They can also help her in using methods developed for the acquisition of French as a second language, namely the explicit study of morphemes or the use of functional reading and all kinds of play.

Pupils of Brianna's profile face the difficulty that they cannot rely with certainty on their knowledge of French, nor on their knowledge of LSFB to infer a meaning from a written form. In all instances, Brianna has to check whether to resort to one language or the other, but she is never sure she will be able to solve a problem on her own. In other words, the paths used by Andrew and by Chloe are often a dead end for her. Besides that, the main obstacle lies in the fact that she is used to not understanding; she does not even seek the meaning of phrases, texts, events, or situations. Brianna represents the typical pupil who is able to decode an entire text, being convinced that she has read it, but is unable to infer any meaning from what she decoded, in the same way as she is unable to realize that she did not understand something she was just taught. Teachers must be permanently vigilant to bring her out of this.

Most of the time, teachers face a mix of these student profiles in their class. As we illustrated here with a brief focus on preschool and on the first stage of learning to read, pedagogical approaches must be differentiated and adapted to the needs of the different linguistic profiles of DHH pupils. In close association with this consideration for the heterogeneity of learners' profiles, teachers also need to conduct their pedagogy in two languages. The reflective work recently undertaken to document the teaching experience acquired in Namur offered the opportunity for the pedagogical team to clarify the nature of such a bilingual pedagogy addressed to DHH pupils (Ghesquière and Meurant, 2018).

BILINGUAL PEDAGOGY

The program described in this chapter is referred to as bilingual. This does not mean that the use of two languages is reduced to a tool to support learning, but rather that in addition to the school curriculum, teachers are expected to enable all DHH pupils, regardless of their linguistic profile, to become bilingual in LSFB and (at least) written French by the end of secondary school. The idea is to ensure they acquire equal ease and fluency in the two languages, even if each individual will probably have a greater affinity with one of the two (Grosjean, 2010).

To reach this objective, the basic condition is that both languages are considered equally rich and respected by all parties, and notably by all teachers, be they hearing or deaf, bilingual or not. However, the experience demonstrated that immersion in LSFB and French alone, even when made visually completely accessible, is not sufficient to make DHH pupils bilingual. The use of the word "immersion" in the decree in which this program originates (see the first section of this chapter) probably blinded teachers. This decreased their awareness that, due to the implications of hearing loss and due to the visuo-gestural modality of LSFB, both languages must be permanently articulated in the same way as oral and written language are permanently articulated in any course, and even explicitly compared. Even more, this articulation defines and affects the pedagogical actions for all school subjects.

The fact of the matter is that, on the one hand, LSFB, like all sign languages, has no written tradition and, on the other hand, French is only partly accessible to DHH students. For some, it is only accessible in its written form, and for others, it is accessible in its written form and to a varying extent in its spoken form. Therefore, LSFB and French are impossible to separate in class, where spoken and written language constantly intertwine through explanations, on the blackboard, through interactions, and on books and worksheets. Neither one of the two languages in itself is able to comfortably fulfill all the communication requirements for all DHH students.

Spontaneously and from the beginning, teachers and pupils alternated between the two languages, during every class on every subject. This first occurred unconsciously but then became embarrassing and was even concealed because it raised many questions and apprehensions. Teachers' actions were implicitly influenced by Grammont's "one person, one language" rule dating from the early 20th century in the field of multilingualism (Ronjat, 1913). In the light of this rule, even if it is now largely nuanced, they tended to avoid language alternation. Alternation was confused with language mixing and associated with a kind of signed-supported French, if not with oralist oppression of sign language. Time and experience resulted not only in relieving teachers' feelings of guilt but also in making them realize that it was important to make this alternation explicit and thoughtful, in line with what Swanwick (2016) describes about translanguaging in bilingual classes with DHH students, or what Coste (2003) describes about language alternation in the bilingual education of hearing students. Translanguaging or language alternation is a constitutive dimension of multilingual education that is aimed not only at learning but at the same time at linguistic knowledge (Coste, 2003, p. 14; Ormel & Giezen, 2014). Language alternation should not be confused with "total communication" practices in which the spoken language is punctuated with signs borrowed from sign language and keys from cued speech system.

Language alternation in bilingual pedagogy focuses on teaching all concepts by presenting them in two languages and by making explicit the relation between both ways of explaining, defining, and using them. The students are taught to be able to reuse concepts in both languages and to be aware of the correspondences between the linguistic structures they use for that purpose in each language. For example, learning the digestive system in sciences implies that students can understand and explain what this body function does and how it does so. From the bilingual perspective, it means that they have to work on this subject through several converging axes: by reading French texts on it, by understanding equivalent LSFB discourse on it, and then by describing and explaining how the digestive function works in LSFB and in written French themselves. Students who are able to do so will also practice similar comprehension and expression skills in spoken French.

The triangular links between the concept and each language are progressively and overtly built and trained by the bilingual teacher by combining explanation and interactions, terminology comments, texts and syntheses, reading and writing. In doing so, teachers must keep in mind that some topics are easier to teach in one language, while other topics are easier in the other due to their specific structures. For instance, geometry and geography will be easier to make understandable in LSFB, while comparisons in general, and the concepts of more, less, equally, and so forth, will be easier to make clear using the French structures that are used to express them (Duverger, 2009; Ghesquière and Meurant, 2018).

The bilingual teachers will have to choose an accurate path depending on which language they use to introduce a new concept. For example, it will be more efficient to elicit the notions of pair, even, and odd (*paire, pair*, and *impair* in French) by classifying a mix of socks, hats, gloves, and scarves than by making pupils reflect on the common points shared by shoes, glasses, binoculars, and so forth. The latter option relies on associations that are spontaneous in French (in the same way as in English: a pair of shoes, of sunglasses, of binoculars) but that do not converge with a common sign in LSFB. On the contrary, commenting on why they put hats and scarves aside when classifying clothing, children will spontaneously produce signs with the appropriate meaning of duality and its contrary in LSFB, just like French-speaking children will spontaneously use the term pair (*paire* in French) in phrases like pair of gloves, pair of socks, and so forth when commenting on their action. And since the clothing classification seems to be appropriate to address the notion in LSFB and in French, this entry should certainly be preferred in order for the co-teachers to take as much advantage as possible of inclusion, offering DHH and hearing students the opportunity to interact, and spoken French and LSFB to be connected in a spontaneous situation.

CO-TEACHING

As the example of "pair" revealed, co-teaching a group of hearing students in French and a group of DHH students in LSFB and French in parallel within the same classroom cannot be efficiently achieved without good coordination. As already mentioned, the languages used may affect the logic and the path of the course construction. But co-teachers are also confronted with the fact that DHH students use eyesight to perceive interactions in LSFB, while hearing students following oral interactions keep their eyesight available for other purposes. DHH students are developing their learning in two languages, while hearing students do so monolingually. All this forces co-teachers to anticipate the way they will conduct the lessons and to manage the inevitable differences in rhythm between both groups.

In terms of achievements and needs, both groups also differ on several elements. The lack of linguistic input caused by their hearing loss greatly affects the level of general awareness of DHH pupils (Convertino et al., 2014). For example, by not having been exposed from an early age to the informal conversations of adults about weight, size, temperature, banknotes, and coins, DHH pupils do not share the same background as their hearing peers when starting to work on quantities and measures. In such situations, it is up to the co-teachers to evaluate whether they can count on the knowledge of the hearing group to feed the exchanges (through the bilingual teacher who makes communication possible) and fill in the gaps the DHH group has, or whether it is necessary to separate the DHH students for part of the teaching sequence on the tricky subject in order to catch them up efficiently.

These remarks emphasize that the role of a bilingual teacher requires a set of varied qualities and skills. In the linguistic domain, in addition to having good competences in LSFB and in French (written French at least), a bilingual teacher is expected to be able to switch easily from one language to the other, and even more precisely to have the meta-linguistic ability to compare the two languages. In other words, he or she needs to rely on a fluent mastery of both languages, on contrastive linguistic competences, and on translator/interpreter-like skills. In the pedagogical domain, bilingual teachers are of course specialized in questions related to deafness. They must be able to analyze the linguistic and cognitive needs of the DHH students, not only to adapt the pedagogical approach accordingly but also to identify potential disorders, be they related or unrelated to the pupil's hearing loss, and accurately act to the benefit of the harmonious development of the student, possibly in collaboration with the student's family and with professionals outside the school. On a daily basis, because of the variety of pupil profiles in the class, the teacher has to juggle differentiated teaching methods. And, last but not least, as one of the pivots for inclusion of DHH pupils within the class, the teacher must be able to collaborate closely with his or her co-teacher to anticipate the different needs of both groups and evaluate the best answers to give.

For the teaching tandem to function smoothly, it is recommended that the two co-teachers make a habit of overtly discussing a series of concrete questions in order to prepare the collaboration, including:

What is the objective of the lesson?
Is the same methodology adapted to each group and each profile of students, or is it necessary to conduct the lesson in different ways?
Will we work in parallel during the entire lesson, or only at times? If so, when?
Which tools will be used?
Who will prepare the material?
Who evaluates whom?
Are there different levels of requirements addressed to different groups of students?
Who will write on the blackboard?
How will we guide the group, and how will we manage the questions and answers from the group?
How will we manage the time and rhythm differences?

The experience revealed that special attention must be paid to each new tandem. During a period of two years, the new co-teachers are coached by a more experienced tandem. In the case of a tandem made up of a DHH teacher and a hearing teacher, this coaching requires even more vigilance, above all if the hearing partner does not know anything about being deaf, about the way to behave with a DHH person, and about sign language. This is one of the reasons why interpreters are an integral part of the educational team.

THE ROLE OF INTERPRETERS

Interpreters are one of the primary facilitators of inclusion in a bilingual education setting such as the one described in this chapter. Indeed, they ensure communication within the school community and between the variety of actors it includes.

Inclusion outside the classroom would not be possible without the intervention of interpreters in all institutional situations that involve hearing and DHH actors meeting, such as the director, teachers, educators, psycho-medical service, and parents. Their role is crucial upstream and downstream of any class situation, and in particular when hearing and DHH teachers meet for pedagogical consultations or for coordination between co-teachers, and during meetings between teachers and parents. Interpreters are essential for DHH teachers to participate in the life of the educational team at a schoolwide level, since only a small proportion of the people involved in the school use sign language. For instance, they enable all meetings between teachers, class councils, pedagogical days, and meetings with internal or external actors.

Although they are considered facilitators, or a tool to improve accessibility and equity, interpreters can also provide added value in classroom situations, for the benefit of teaching and education in general. This does not mean that the teacher is replaced by the interpreter. The teacher keeps his or her pedagogical responsibility, and it is within this framework that he or she has the opportunity to call in an interpreter as pedagogical support. This is particularly relevant when co-teachers want students to be involved in discussions or debates, or when they elicit exchanges between students, as in teamwork, oral presentations, or collective discussions. Different elements must be taken into consideration in order to evaluate the relevance of involving an interpreter in the class: the pedagogical objective, the age of pupils, or the density of the information to be interpreted. But, in any case, the intervention of interpreters can be integrated in the pedagogical approach taken by the co-teachers.

Recently, the team of interpreters in the bilingual classes of Namur developed their collaboration with DHH teachers so they could fully assume their pedagogical function. For example, the interpreter ensures that the DHH teacher has access to any support that makes use of auditory information, both during course preparation and during the course itself. But even within the classroom, interpreters remain in the background of the pedagogical relationship, in compliance with the ethical principles of their profession. Their role and the role of the bilingual teachers are complementary in the setting and cannot be confused.

The first ethical principle of an interpreter concerns fidelity to the source discourse. He or she is expected to translate accurately, without omissions or additions, and respect the intention of everyone. Therefore, an interpreter could not step away from the running discourse in order, for instance, to correct the linguistic production of a pupil in LSFB, to comment on the difference between a structure in LSFB and its counterpart in French, or to check whether all students have a sufficient linguistic level to understand the message interpreted in LSFB. Rather, all these actions are part of the mandate of the bilingual teacher, who has to make explicit the linkages between both languages and the concepts at stake and ensure the students' understanding.

The second ethical principle is about neutrality. Interpreters do not intervene in their personal capacity, they do not give their opinion on what is said, nor do they comment on the way interlocutors are expressing themselves. This principle of neutrality often is difficult for students and the co-teacher to understand. For students, any adult represents authority and can be called on to help or to answer questions. For the teacher, an adult coming into the classroom should collaborate and help. And for the interpreters themselves, neutrality is difficult to assume. For example, they cannot intervene if they note that one pupil has lost the thread of an explanation, nor if they remark that the pedagogical choices made by the speaking teacher are not adapted to DHH students and leave them confused. These tasks fall to the bilingual teachers; unease and ambiguity can result if they are implicitly or explicitly entrusted to an interpreter.

The third ethical principle is professional privacy. Interpreters do not disclose the messages they interpret. This principle is also incompatible with a pedagogical responsibility, since, for example, it prevents interpreters from discussing what is happening in class with parents, or participating in meetings focused on the situation of one student.

The bilingual and inclusive setting of Namur represents a microcosm of society where future DHH adults will also be a minority, and where they will make use of the services of interpreters. It is then important that pupils learn at school when and how to use their services, and that the position of the interpreters they meet at school be as representative as possible of the professionals working outside the school. In that sense, the scope of interpreters' and bilingual teachers' actions are not to be confused. They are complementary when seeking the combined objectives of bilingualism and inclusion. Interpreters are at the service of teachers, of students, of the institution, of parents, and of the educational missions of school in general, for the purpose of inclusion and equity.

BENEFITS AND CHALLENGES

From the beginning of the program, political authorities, parents, physicians, and speech therapy centers have demanded results, facts, numbers, and success rates. It remains impossible, however, to measure the impact of this setting on the educational development of DHH students. First, because only 50 students are currently co-enrolled in the bilingual classes of Sainte-Marie, representing such heterogeneous profiles, no specific number or mean could be considered valid or informative. Second, during the first years of the program, teachers made errors, but they have gained experience and have tested and improved new methodologies. This means that the older students have not received the same teaching model as the younger ones. Third, not all students follow the whole curriculum from preschool until the end of secondary school. Therefore, all the numbers would be skewed. Finally, the program population is not representative of the entire DHH community in French-speaking Belgium. Many hearing parents are still concerned by the relative youth of the program and above all by sign language, which makes them prefer exclusively oralist settings. And even though several families have moved to Namur in order for their child to be enrolled in a bilingual and inclusive education system, not all families can do so, and therefore the population is geographically filtered.

For all these reasons, it would be misleading to pretend that this setting could be proven to be beneficial to the education of DHH students. The educational team constantly reflects on whether they are acting in the right way, but until now they have not had the opportunity to compare with colleagues from counterpart co-enrollment settings.

Benefits?

The expected advantages of the program, as stated at the beginning of the chapter, lie on three levels: academic, psychological, and ethical. At the academic level, the aim was to offer the same schooling level to DHH and hearing students. The co-teaching function is a constant safeguard against all temptations to lower the content of the curriculum and to soften the requirements for DHH students. In the same way, all students of the school, whether hearing or DHH, are subject to the same official assessments organized by the education department (at the end of primary school, at the end of the second year of secondary school, and at the end of sixth year of secondary school). The results at the end of primary school (based on 17 DHH children who represent seven cohorts of pupils having passing the exams between 2010 and 2017; Table 11.1) show that achievements of DHH students are on average comparable to those of hearing students at the school (i.e., 558 children during same period of seven years). It is worth mentioning, however,

Table 11.1. Average Results on the Official Assessment Test at the End of Primary School, Hearing versus DHH Students, Sainte-Marie in Namur, 2010–2017

2010–2017	French (and LSFB for DHH Students)	Mathematics	Sciences	Geography/History
Hearing students	80.9%	80.6%	82.1%	84.6%
DHH students	70.2%	78.2%	78.8%	75.9%
All students	80.6%	80.5%	82%	84.4%

that the numbers appearing in the first column of Table 11.1 must be approached with caution when comparing hearing and DHH students. Indeed, this column presents without distinction the scores achieved by hearing pupils on spoken and written French exams on the one hand, and the scores achieved by DHH pupils on written French and on LSFB examinations on the other hand, since DHH pupils' skills in spoken French are not evaluated.

Two issues related to the academic development of DHH students, however, deserve mention. First, the targeted schooling level is the same as for hearing students, but in addition to what is expected from hearing peers, DHH students must acquire all competences in two languages and not just one, which is more demanding. And second, as mentioned earlier, not all DHH students start school with the same linguistic profile; most of them (profile B) show an important linguistic and cognitive delay at an early age, which has a significant impact on the efforts they have to make and the pace of their learning. Those students would certainly not be able (or welcome) to pursue their schooling if they were integrated into an ordinary school without bilingual pedagogy. This is an additional reason why the impact of this setting cannot be compared with other existing structures welcoming DHH students in the French-speaking part of Belgium. It is closely related to the ethical position underlying the program, which is that all DHH students are welcomed and cared for according to their needs.

At the psychological level, it was hypothesized that the group inclusion would help pupils to become aware of and accept their hearing loss and to avoid feeling isolated. Again, it is difficult to measure the well-being of children and young adults and impossible to evaluate the impact of the setting on the psychological state of an individual. An indicator that may be considered is that the external psychosocial services with which the educational team is collaborating observe that the identity questions of DHH students related to the acceptance of their hearing loss emerge earlier in the bilingual and inclusive program than in other cases of isolated integration. However, it remains tricky to draw general conclusions from this observation. What is certainly observable in Sainte-Marie is that regardless of the degree of their hearing loss, DHH pupils have the opportunity to create links with hearing pupils, in French and in LSFB. Being bilingual in LSFB and French is considered to be achievable by all, DHH and hearing students.

At a schoolwide level, the educational team has observed beneficial effects from the existence of the bilingual setting that were not expected at the beginning. Welcoming DHH students induced more tolerance and openness to differences among hearing students as well as among hearing (co-)teachers, who, for example, engaged in getting more attention toward students with learning difficulties. Forced to collaborate with their bilingual teaching partner, teachers in charge of hearing students often had the opportunity to test new pedagogical approaches and to reflect on their practices and change them.

Remaining Challenges

Maintaining the principle of bilingualism itself remains a challenge for the program, because sign language and spoken language continue to be fundamentally seen as in competition in society. Otolaryngologists and audiologist services often see sign language as an obstacle to the development of spoken language by DHH children, which affects the conscious and unconscious position of hearing parents toward sign language and bilingual education for their child (Grosjean, 2010). For many DHH parents, on the contrary, French language and above all the use of cued speech causes mistrust and evokes defensive reactions against what is explicitly or implicitly considered as oppression and discrimination toward the DHH community. It is a great challenge for bilingual teachers, who are torn between these opposing monolingual tendencies, to maintain the bilingual objective and to practice systematic and unbridled language alternation to reach it.

In their concern to practice language alternation and to make explicit the comparison between LSFB and French, bilingual teachers face a tremendous lack of scientific and pedagogical support. Sign languages in general and LSFB in particular are far less documented than spoken languages and particularly French. The situation is even worse in terms of contrastive studies between sign languages and spoken languages, and notably between LSFB and French. Existing contrastive studies are scarce and in any case not yet at the stage of practitioner outreach. Teachers cannot count on any handbooks or reference material to sustain their own metalinguistic analysis, which makes their work remarkable and challenging. The partnership between the school program and the LSFB Lab of the University of Namur provides a stimulating and valuable opportunity to make up for this lack of knowledge. Many questions and ideas are shared between the field and research, to the benefit of both partners. But it remains the case that the state of knowledge about LSFB and about LSFB versus French comparison is unbalanced in comparison with all that is known, described, and available for teachers about French language.

On a daily basis, bilingual teachers face the difficulty of combining the main principles of the program, namely bilingualism and inclusion. Three main reasons explain the complexity of their task. First, DHH students are expected to learn all the concepts in two languages, while hearing students are taught only in French. This entails at times differences in the pedagogical approaches. Second, hearing loss affects DHH students' ability to benefit from all informal information that circulates in the environment. This produces a difference between the acquired knowledge of DHH and hearing students that the bilingual teacher must make up. Third, the teaching and learning pace of DHH students is affected by the fact that they can only rely on eyesight to receive information, while hearing students can simultaneously combine hearing and eyesight.

In view of these specific needs, it becomes evident that bilingualism and inclusion are at times impossible to combine, or may even seem incompatible. Teachers have the liberty and the responsibility to make thoughtful choices when necessary and to balance both objectives on a weekly, yearly, or two-yearly cycle, and by using interpreters with relevance. In the same vein, it was decided after several years to separate DHH and hearing students for linguistic courses (French, LSFB, English) because the needs of each group were not met in inclusion. It appeared afterward that these moments outside the main class greatly benefit DHH students, who meet together with peers sharing the same needs, the same pace, and the same relationship to the world: it contributes to the identity building of the students.

The bilingual and inclusive program offered at Sainte-Marie in Namur is certainly not a miracle solution to all the challenges posed by the issue of teaching DHH learners. The 17-year-long experience of this setting has enabled the specific needs of DHH learners to be better taken into account, in the variety of their profiles, the nature of bilingual pedagogy addressed to DHH students to be clarified, and the complementary roles of the different actors of the educational team to be better defined, namely the co-teachers and interpreters.

Following general schooling is a great challenge for all DHH students and remains more demanding than for hearing learners. The setting presented in this chapter does not avoid the difficulties but offers a coherent proposal that takes into account the implications of hearing loss and the urgency for DHH young adults to be better included in society. The challenge is at least as great for teachers. Their task is tricky and not given enough support by appropriate training, exchanges with counterpart colleagues, scientific knowledge, or pedagogical supports.

Nevertheless, these students and teachers, together in a tightrope performance,[3] show that it is possible to make school and quality education accessible to all DHH students.

NOTES

1. Cued speech is a manual system that makes use of visual information from speechreading combined with hand shapes positioned in different places around the face in order to deliver completely unambiguous information about the syllables and the phonemes of spoken language. In the case of French, it has been proven to help DHH children learn to read and write (Leybaert & LaSasso, 2010).
2. The training that had been conceived, in particular in collaboration with linguists from the University of Namur, has not been implemented until now because of a lack of financial means at the level of the government and due to the difficulty in recruiting people with qualifications and experience in this domain, able to involve as a trainer. The consequence of this absence of specific training is that teachers are trained on the job, especially in differentiating their pedagogy according to the variety of DHH pupils' profiles and in comparing French and LSFB.
3. A documentary on the bilingual classes of Sainte-Marie was produced by Volon (2015) entitled *Les Funambules de Sainte-Marie* ("The tightrope of Sainte-Marie"). More than 1,000 people attended the premiere. This event contributed greatly to the understanding of the program by politicians, parents, and the deaf community. The film is available on YouTube: https://www.youtube.com/watch?v=kxQISAMN01A.

REFERENCES

Antia, S., & Metz, K. K. (2014). Co-enrollment in the United States: A critical analysis of benefits and challenges. In M. Marschark, G. Tang, & H. Knoors (Eds.), *Bilingualism and bilingual deaf education* (pp. 424–441). New York: Oxford University Press.

Convertino, C., Borgna, G., Marschark, M., & Durkin, A. (2014). Word and world knowledge among deaf learners with and without cochlear implants. *Journal of Deaf Studies and Deaf Education, 19*(4), 471–483.

Coste, D. (2003). Construire des savoirs en plusieurs langues. Les enjeux disciplinaires de l'enseignement bilingue. *Santiago de Compostelle*. Retrieved from http://www.adeb.asso.fr/archives/problematique/dnl/Coste_Santiago_oct03. pdf

Dammeyer, J. (2018). Mental health and psychosocial well-being in deaf and hard-of-hearing students. In H. Knoors & M. Marschark (Eds.), *Evidence-based practices in deaf education*. New York: Oxford University Press.

Duverger, J. (2009). *L'enseignement en classe bilingue*. Paris: Hachette.

Ghesquière, M. and Meurant, L. (2018). *École et surdité. Une experience d'enseignement bilingue et inclusive*. Namur: Presses universitaires de Namur.

Grosjean, F. (2010). Bilingualism, biculturalism, and deafness. *International Journal of Bilingual Education and Bilingualism, 13*(2), 133–145.

Kirchner, C. J. (1994). Co-enrollment as an inclusion model. *American Annals of the Deaf, 139*(2), 163–164.

Knoors, H., & Marschark, M. (2014). *Teaching deaf learners: Psychological and developmental foundations.* New York: Oxford University Press.

Leybaert, J., & LaSasso, C. J. (2010). Cued speech for enhancing speech perception and first language development of children with cochlear implants. *Trends in Amplification, 14*(2), 96–112.

Marschark, M., Tang, G., & Knoors, H. (2014). Perspectives on bilingualism and bilingual education for deaf learners. In M. Marschark, G. Tang, & H. Knoors (Eds.), *Bilingualism and bilingual deaf education* (pp. 445–476). New York: Oxford University Press.

Meurant, L., & Zegers de Beyl, M. (Eds.). (2009). *Dans les coulisses d'un enseignement bilingue (langue des signes—français) à Namur. Le groupe de réflexion sur la langue des signes française de Belgique (LSFB)* (Vol. 11). Namur: Presses universitaires de Namur.

Meynard, A. (2003). Accueil des enfants Sourds: les langues signées vont-elles disparaître?: Langue des signes française (LSF): Enjeux culturels et pédagogiques. *La Nouvelle Revue de l'Adaptation et de la Scolarisation, 23*, 101–111.

Ormel, E., & Giezen, M. (2014). Bimodal bilingual cross-language interaction: Pieces of the puzzle. In M. Marschark, G. Tang, & H. Knoors (Eds.), *Bilingualism and bilingual deaf education* (pp. 74–101). New York: Oxford University Press.

Ronjat, J. (1913). *Le développement du langage observé chez un enfant bilingue.* Paris: Honoré Champion.

Swanwick, R. (2016). Scaffolding learning through classroom talk: The role of translanguaging. In M. Marschark & P. Spencer (Eds.), *The Oxford handbook of deaf studies in language* (pp. 420–430). New York: Oxford University Press.

Volon, R. (Director). (2015). *Les Funambules de Sainte-Marie* [Documentary]. Belgium: University of Namur.

12

Four Co-Enrollment Programs in Madrid: Differences and Similarities

Mar Pérez, Begoña de la Fuente, Pilar Alonso, and Gerardo Echeita

In recent years, the implementation of co-enrollment models in the education of deaf and hard-of-hearing (DHH) children has proved a prototypical example of the general need *to think and act in different ways*. The traditional separation of special and mainstream schools now is changing for deaf students, but there is still a basic requirement to achieve the goal of inclusion, a goal all education systems are committed to formally (United Nations, 2006, 2016; UNESCO, 2008).The *medical model* has been the predominant pattern in educational organizations for students regarded as having any disability (Barton, 2002). Therefore, deaf students had to attend special education schools where specialized teachers, using mostly an oral approach, were responsible for education. Official recognition that sign languages are actual languages valid for communication and instruction did not, at first, change the conception that a specialized education in schools different from the mainstream was necessary. Thus, what we know as *dual models* were created: mainstream schools for "normal students" and special schools for students regarded as "special."

For many years, most teachers, specialists, and academicians, as well as families, thought that providing instruction using two languages simultaneously in the same school context was impossible. And it certainly *was* impossible if the old "school grammar" (Tyack & Cuban, 1995) of one teacher per group of students was to be maintained, no matter whether the teacher was competent in both oral and sign languages. The present chapter will show that we can and we must "think in a different way" (Ballard, 2011) if progress toward more inclusive education is to be made. Development of co-enrollment models in several schools demonstrates that it is not only possible but also positive from several perspectives.

First, this chapter describes briefly the process through which four educational schools located in Madrid, Spain, developed successful models of co-enrollment. They did so thanks to their serious commitment to this model and despite their diverse educational traditions, histories, and contexts: among them, we find academy/charter schools and state-funded schools. In Spain, academy schools (*colegios concertados*) are privately established schools that are partially funded by the state. They are subject to the same regulations applying to state-funded schools. Several academies have a long tradition in teaching DHH children. Second, we will not just provide a mere description of what these schools do but will also analyze the conditions facilitating a major change in education that allows the schools to continue the process, without forgetting the multiple challenges they face. Taking into consideration what these schools have in common, yet without ignoring their differences and singularities, enabled us to deduce some lessons learned during the past few years that may be useful to other schools and education teams who want to (and should?) follow this approach.

The authors of this chapter have deep knowledge of this field. The first three work at what is called in our region an Educational and Psychopedagogical Team (EOEP is the Spanish acronym), in this case specialized in the education of DHH students. The main task of the EOEP consists in advising and supporting DHH students' diagnostic and educational processes from infant school to upper secondary school in the entire region, the Autonomous Community of Madrid. They collaborate closely with other professional advisors, schoolteachers, families, and deaf people's associations to ensure the quality of the education these students are entitled to by law. The fourth author is familiar with the educational reality regarding DHH students and is considered an expert in the analysis of inclusive education policies and practices.

When writing this chapter, we bore in mind that it was crucial to listen to the voices and experience of those who are the real protagonists of this process: the professionals carrying it out. That is why several strategies were used to collect the analyses and evaluations of the teachers working in the schools in question. We designed a questionnaire asking about the implementation and functioning of their respective educational projects or vision. We planned and conducted two focus groups[1] (Barbour, 2013) with members from the management teams of the four schools in order to analyze and discuss two important matters in this model: the roles and tasks of the two teachers present in the classroom and the use of two languages for instruction, spoken and signed.

Preparing this text, together with the work dynamics we adopted to do so, provided us with the opportunity to create a "resting point along the way"—in other words, a pause that allowed us a moment of group reflection both on the work we are carrying out in the field of DHH children's education and also on the challenges we will face in the next years, especially with regard to the complex and, in the light of ongoing technological and societal changes, surely uncertain context we are immersed in (Noah, 2015).

WHAT ARE WE REFERRING TO WHEN WE SPEAK OF "CO-ENROLLMENT" IN OUR CONTEXT?

While legislation allowing DHH children to be integrated in schools with hearing peers varies in every country, we have observed that the same terminology is being used to define different practices. Even though these practices certainly share some elements, there exist several nuances as pointed out by Marschark, Tang, and Knoors (2014). The word "co-enrollment" is used chiefly to describe educational programs such as TRIPOD in the United States (Kirchner, 1994, this volume), Twinschool in the Netherlands (Hermans, Wauters, & Knoors, 2014), and Sign Bilingualism and Co-enrollment (SLCO) in Hong Kong (Yiu & Tang, 2014). In our context, the equivalent to the word "co-enrollment" would be "shared education." Nevertheless, it is important to distinguish between this "shared education" program and other options for schooling DHH students (in our country and especially in our Autonomous Community) derived from the legislation on education currently in force (LOMCE organic law): *school integration* and *special education* (Fig. 12.1).

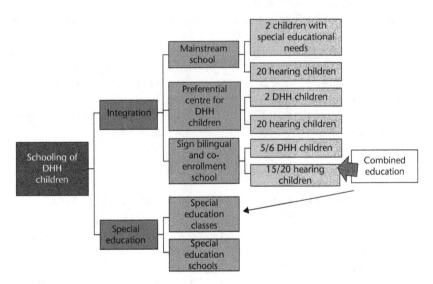

Figure 12.1. Models of integration for DHH learners.

There are two main options for deaf students: integration/ mainstreaming and special education. The *integration* of DHH children is implemented in mainstream schools under the denomination *preferential schools for* (the integration of) *DHH students*. Behind the idea of creating preferential schools lies the criterion of gathering together the additional human resources (i.e., specialized teachers) considered necessary for teaching DHH children.

In these preferential schools, DHH children attend mainstream lessons with hearing students of the same age. Because the number of DHH students within the school population is small, the tendency is to have one or a maximum of two DHH students in groups with an average of 20 hearing students. In the last 15 years approximately, another option has emerged that could be included in the term "integration." This new option increases the ratio of DHH students in mainstream classrooms to five or six, grouping them with 15 to 20 hearing classmates. In the context of our Autonomous Community, we call this option *shared education* (i.e., shared between DHH and hearing students). We would like to clarify that Anita & Metz's (2014) concept of "co-enrollment" is named "shared education" by us, since the term in Spanish defines better the real meaning and purpose of the experiences to be described in this chapter.

Under the "special education" option, students can also attend mainstream schools where there are specific separate groups of DHH children only, typically DHH children who tend to have other associated disabilities. The special education option appertains to what, in the Spanish current legislation, is called the Compulsory Basic Education (CBE), for students aged 6 to 18 years.

Finally, the Spanish legislation also allows the development of "combined education" projects. These programs are different from co-enrollment programs. There are two possibilities: (1) children can go to two different schools where they can do different activities; one of the schools offers special education and the other is a mainstream school; and (2) the special education and the mainstream activities are offered in the same school. The second option is how DHH students with other disabilities are educated in Madrid.

FEATURES OF CO-ENROLLMENT

Why and How Do Co-Enrollment Projects Appear in Our Autonomous Community?

Co-enrollment projects in our region emerge from three differentiated and relevant sources. First, we had some experiences of bilingual education (Spanish and Spanish Sign Language [LSE]) carried out in special education schools (Alonso, Rodríguez, & Echeita, 2009; Pérez,

Valmaseda, & Morgan, 2014). It is pertinent to point out that these originated thanks to the dissemination of bilingual experiences in Northern European countries (Lewis, 1995) as well as a growing interest in sign languages and their study (Ahlgren et al., 1994). Other contributing factors were the families' urge for development of these type of sign language projects in an effort to improve their deaf children's low academic achievement, especially in written language, and the impact of neurologist and writer Oliver Sacks's visits to several DHH special education schools (Sacks, 1989). All of these, together with the demands of the deaf community worldwide, helped intensify the struggle for the recognition of the linguistic status of sign languages.

The second source of influence was the advance of school integration policies as a result of the international guidelines on education of children with special educational needs (UNESCO, 1994), which questioned segregated schooling practices for children with disabilities and, therefore, for DHH students also. The third decisive factor came with the use of cochlear implants (CIs) as technology for hearing and spoken language development support. Thanks to CIs, many families (most of them hearing) of DHH pupils considered more attractive the possibility of educating their children in mainstream settings without giving up the shared use of LSE and spoken Spanish.

It is also important to stress that these co-enrollment projects did not develop from top-down planning promoted by the administration; rather, they were initiatives created from the bottom up (Morales López, 2008) and *allowed* by the administration. Furthermore, the motivation behind the co-enrollment initiatives was survival since some of the special schools were losing many DHH pupils. Another influence was a quest for more inclusive teaching practices for DHH students (Domínguez & Alonso, 2004).

Three of the four schools we analyze in this chapter—the CEIP El Sol and the Academies Ponce de León and Gaudem[2]—used to be special education schools for DHH children. In the years 1998, 2004, and 2008, respectively, these schools started to make changes in their educational projects by incorporating hearing students. A merger between the "specialty" of specific schools and the "normality" of mainstream schools was conceived. These changes were initiated with hope and excitement but also with effort, dedication, and enthusiasm by the management teams, teachers, and families involved. The EOEP (to which the first three authors of the chapter belong) have supported and participated in the project throughout. The fourth school included in this chapter is the Piruetas Nursery School.

What Features Define These Projects of Co-Enrollment?

The fact that these projects originated from bilingual programs is the reason they have maintained two fundamental characteristics. One is the *cultural approach* applied when designing the programs—in other words, the conviction that acquiring a sign language will help develop the pupil's Deaf identity and culture. Second is the essence of signed bilingualism in Spain: the simultaneity in the use of both languages. From the first moment the DHH child joins the co-enrollment program, he or she starts learning the spoken language immediately, without waiting for the signed language to be developed. It would not have been possible to begin with successive bilingualism (Pérez, Valmaseda, & Morgan, 2014) when we consider the strength that spoken language has always had in the education of DHH pupils in Spain. Nowadays, these schools reinforce this model of simultaneous bilingualism, even though each of them has evolved differently; indeed, we could say, in colloquial terms, that some are "more bilingual" than others depending on the emphasis and use of LSE and spoken Spanish in their linguistic planning.

The four schools have in common the following features regarded as fundamental in co-enrollment education programs:

- All students are part of the same class, with a proportion of five to seven DHH students per 15 to 20 hearing pupils.
- The same curriculum applies for DHH and hearing students.
- Two teachers work together in the classroom where the project is being implemented. One is a specialist in the educational stage (nursery or primary) and the other in deafness—that is, a teacher specialized in speech and language with training in LSE.
- There is "dual" linguistic input: spoken language and LSE in the classroom both for communication and learning.
- Deaf professionals native in LSE (specialists in LSE) are present in all classrooms where LSE is taught and/or where support for learning curricular content in LSE is needed.

How Many DHH Students? What Is Their Profile?

In the Madrid region, during the academic year 2016–2017, the total number of DHH students enrolled in schools from nursery to secondary education was 974. Out of them, 31% (304) have a CI and 26% (257) have, in addition, another associated disability. Table 12.1 shows the number of children in each of the four schools by age. During the academic year 2016–2017, 178 DHH pupils were enrolled in the four co-enrollment schools—that is, 18% of the total number of 974 deaf children in the region. The school with the greatest number of DHH students (68) is El Sol (state-funded school) owing to the fact that families do not have to bear any economic cost. In total, there are 86 children with CI, which is 48% of all children in the four schools. This indicates that many families whose DHH children received a CI choose the co-enrollment option.

Table 12.1. Number of Students Enrolled in the Four Sites

Name of School/ Number of Children	0–3 years (Infant School)		3–6 Years (Preschool)		6–12 Years (Primary)		12–16 Years (Secondary)		Total		Deaf with Other Disabilities	With Cochlear Implants
Deaf/ Hearing	D	H	D	H	D	H	D	H	D	H		
Piruetas	11	114	-	-	-	-	-	-	11	114	5	5
Sol	-	-	19	109	49	443	-	-	68	552	1	38
Ponce	-	-	12	45	29	90	16	63	57	198	21	17
Gaudem	2	62	13	212	17	452	10	285	42	1011	6	26
Ttotal	13	176	41	366	95	985	26	348	178	1875	31	86

Altogether, 31 (17%) of the total DHH students enrolled in these schools have other disabilities as well, but these students are not equally distributed across all four schools (see Table 12.1).

Early schooling is a common practice in our country, and both DHH and hearing children begin attending these bilingual co-enrollment programs at an early age. The choice of school is made by the families and advised by the EOEP. In the case of DHH students, the school is determined not by proximity to their home but by the quality of education provided. Similarly, in the case of families with hearing children (a significant number, as indicated in Table 12.1), the choice of school is determined by the parents' positive views on the linguistic projects and the innovative nature of the teaching methodology. Unfortunately, it often occurs that many deaf children's families, who would enroll their children in these schools, are unable to do so due to lack of vacant seats or for economic reasons. There is a decline in the number of DHH students enrolled in compulsory secondary education, due mainly to the fact that the state school El Sol only has nursery and primary education stages. After finishing the primary stage, some students continue their studies in state secondary schools nearby, while others are referred to a special education option.

Management teams do not determine whether children with hearing loss should or should not enroll in their schools. On the contrary, they pride themselves on considering their schools' capability of responding to a great variety of children. This variety is due to the currently existing diversity in relation with accessibility to spoken and signed languages, and by the different ages at which some children have exposure with a first language. Thus, in these co-enrollment education classrooms, it is possible that a profoundly deaf child with neither a CI nor any auditory functionality for speech and a DHH child with a very good auditory functionality and who has received one or two early CIs can both learn at the same time. The variety is also due to DHH children with school failure coming from mainstream schools who enroll in the co-enrollment classrooms at more advanced ages hoping to regain the academic, linguistic, and in many cases emotional levels corresponding to their ages.

What Changes Had to Be Made to Schools' Organizational Structure and Resources to Adapt to Co-Enrollment?

Implementation of co-enrollment programs entails organizing a complex and expensive structure. It requires more personnel (two co-teachers per classroom, LSE specialists, speech and language therapists, interpreters, school counselors) and some changes in organization. Schools had to create new structures or strengthen some already existing ones such as the levels and cycles[3] so that all professionals, including LSE specialists, could be included in classroom planning meetings (held between the two co-teachers of each group), LSE department meetings, and other meetings held in order to plan and organize different workshops related to the languages.

All these changes and initiatives have been facilitated by the major role that the management teams from these four schools have played. The teams included three people coming from special schools for DHH children. Hence, they are professionals with training and knowledge about DHH children's education who have a clear perspective on the purposes and functioning of co-enrollment projects. Due to their excellent job, DHH students attending their schools feel like active members with the same rights as their hearing equals, but also deaf professionals feel the same sense of belonging inside the teachers' group.

Little could have been achieved if these management teams had not supported the project by means of a solid policy of permanent in-service training for the staff. During these years, school staff have gone through continuous training in aspects related to language learning in bilingual contexts, DHH and hearing children's written language learning, knowledge of complementary systems to speech, knowledge of psychological developmental stages and processes of bilingual education, inclusive methodologies, and many others.

ARE THESE SCHOOLS INCLUSIVE?

"The only sense in which we would wish to claim a school as 'inclusive' is when it is committed to a development journey guided by inclusive values" (Booth & Ainscow, 2011, p. 28). If we follow this criterion, we can conclude that these schools are indeed inclusive. Certainly, along that journey, some have reached farther than others have, due to their own singular circumstances and characteristics. Yet, as Booth and Ainscow (2011, p. 28) state: "Schools are always changing; children and staff arrive and move on; new forms of exclusion arise; new resources are mobilised or lost." In this regard, it is important to highlight a difference that has become significant when analyzing the similarities and disparities among the four schools. El Sol is a state school, which means it is constrained by limitations imposed from the administration—for instance, regarding recruitment of new staff. Their staff are civil servants and their recruitment follows rigid procedures that cannot be adjusted to the specific requirements needed for this type of project. The other three schools are private (academy/charter) schools having full authority to select their staff according to their values, principles, and needs (e.g., they can select nursery or primary teachers with good command of LSE). This issue influences the stability of teaching teams and, hence, project consistency over time. State-funded education in our country needs to face the arduous task of improving pedagogical and management autonomy if the challenge of student diversity in inclusive contexts is to be addressed with some honesty.

The common values across the four schools, though, are undeniable. This includes a strong and genuine commitment to student *equity*, meaning that specific educational needs of DHH pupils do not become educational disadvantages. Furthermore, there is a clear commitment to innovation and improvement, thus ensuring that the right of all DHH students to quality education is not a mere formal statement. These schools are participative as well; teachers and families have some power for decision-making with regard to the future of the project. Educational teams are guided by core values; they are honest, thoughtful, and critical toward their policies and practices; they are always questioning what they do and how results could be improved. This constant questioning attitude might show a need for a better understanding of the linguistic, educational, and social beliefs implicit in their practices. Yet it is through this ongoing reflection/action process that features of high-quality education schools are strengthened and maintained over time.

This attitude of honest reflection about their job manifested itself once again when they agreed to participate in this analysis, both answering the proposed questionnaire and collaborating in the focus group sessions. Such reflection is what made policies and practices in terms of co-enrollment become evident. In particular, there are two major matters we wanted to analyze in detail. The first was how to define and organize the roles and characteristics of co-teaching. The second was the status and functioning of the two languages (spoken and signed) used in teaching. As expected, other relevant issues related to school conditions that make this model possible arose, as well as some challenges and pressing needs required for its successful implementation.

ASPECTS RELATED TO TEACHING AND LEARNING PROCESSES

How Is Co-Teaching Organized?

Co-teaching DHH students raises many important questions. First, all co-teachers, both in nursery and primary stages, must have a good command of LSE. As stated before, this requirement is not compatible with the restrictions that apply to the El Sol state school on staff recruitment, since teachers arrive there through a procedure that does not always guarantee they have the training for teaching DHH students. Nevertheless, successful co-teaching depends greatly on teachers' attitudes and collaborative work. Both are recognized as equal teachers; in other words, there is not a main tutor teacher accompanied by an assistant teacher for helping or supporting DHH pupils, but two co-teachers with full and shared responsibility in planning and providing education to all their students, deaf and hearing. In many accounts of the focus group participants, we found clear references about the importance of empathy and forming a close bond between the two teachers, which is usually stronger when this model of co-enrollment with DHH students is fully shared. In nursery education, criteria for organizing the co-teaching pairs are established based not solely on the teachers' own characteristics but also on the need of younger children (0 to 3 years old) to forge an emotional bond with their teachers. The management and teaching staff from the Piruetas School develop an emotional link to all their students.

Concerning whether to maintain co-teaching pairs every year or vary them regularly, the schools have different policies. For instance, in the Ponce de León School, pairs change every year with the purpose of better adjusting to every new group of students, whereas the other three schools tend to maintain the same pairs once they have proven they work well together. In any case, a constant common to all four is carefully supervising co-teaching pairs' performance and adjustment. The co-teachers say that they need more time to self-reflect on their practices—for example, how they evaluate, how they adapt their linguistic input, and how much attention to spend on each student. Unfortunately, although this is a matter of great importance, this task is often carried out under time pressure.

One clear distinction between our co-enrollment models and others (Mastropieri & Scruggs, 2006) is that the two co-teachers have the same role (teachers) and status (tutors) inside the classroom, and they make these roles explicit to ensure students understand this early. This is not incompatible with each teacher being the reference for one of the languages (spoken Spanish and LSE) for all hearing and DHH students. Furthermore, co-teachers are at all times aware they have to be flexible to adapt to the multiple and unpredictable circumstances always surrounding the teaching activity, especially since pupils have a very diverse access to the languages.

Spoken Language and Sign Language in the Classroom: A Matter of Quantity or Quality?

Language use and distribution in this co-enrollment model is a fundamental issue. Originally, when the model was implemented, it was characterized by the following aspects:

- Each co-teacher was the exclusive reference for one of the languages and tried to communicate either with DHH or hearing students solely in that language.
- Both co-teachers were continually present in all teaching/learning activities carried out in the classroom.

This initial "rigidity" became progressively more flexible to better adapt to the specific communication needs of every student and of the groups formed each year. There was a significant advance toward a better individualization concerning which language to use in what moment. In this regard, we cannot ignore that the development of CIs has raised a new set of questions in which deaf children are becoming more able auditorily and, thus, the balance between sign and spoken language needs to be adjusted. Yet every child, in every group, in every stage and every year has different needs; for instance, when, in a group, there is a signing DHH child with few possibilities of learning speech, it is evident that LSE acquires more importance than the spoken language:

> In one classroom LSE may be present 100% together with speech, whereas in other group there are by coincidence three auditory able students who does not need LSE that much, so it is used in a smaller proportion there. That is, these decisions are made based on educational needs of each child, within the group. (Headmistress of a charter school, focus group 2)

This adjustment or linguistic adaptation to the child is especially important in nursery education. In planning the teaching of language for young children, teachers begin with actions that are aimed at the development of auditory and visual skills. In the infant period, several types of activities are attempted:

1. Developing hearing (e.g., identifying silence, localizing sounds, and recognizing sounds)
2. Developing a visual communication (e.g., looking at an object and then the signing person [divided attention]) or following

visual information in the classroom, like a flashing light signaling that someone is entering.

In any case, an evolution toward more flexible practices with regard to the use of two languages is clear. However, there are differences between the schools. In preschool, some schools, like Piruetas, always use spoken language and sign language in the classroom at the same time; one of the co-teachers uses spoken Spanish, the other LSE. In El Sol, difficulties occur in relation with finding and recruiting enough teachers to form stable co-teaching pairs with adequate training in LSE. Therefore, LSE tutors have to teach different groups of children during the school day; they are not tutor teachers of a single group. Consequently, LSE is used to teach only some subjects, particularly those that have greater linguistic and content demands, such as science and mathematical problem-solving.

Management teams from these schools informed us that this adjustment process toward a more flexible model in relation to the use of languages has been done without any formal systematized and rigorous evaluation. Instead, changes occurred based on multiple actions such as observations of live or video-recorded classroom sessions, frequent meetings with education teams, or guidance and support provided by the EOEP.

This linguistic adjustment is also a result of the necessities inherent in the teaching methodologies applied in some of the schools analyzed here. As claimed by experts (Echeita, Sandoval, & Simón, 2016), a more inclusive education is possible only if we abandon the "one size fits all" framework for teaching and assessment and progress toward more diversified and varied manners of providing education content, motivating students, and recognizing what they have learned. Two schools in particular (Ponce de León and Gaudem) are implementing teaching methods based on research projects in diversified space organization and student grouping (corners/zones and workshops), using a variety of materials and rich visual and technological aids. The advantage of this working structure in zones/station or workshops is that it makes possible to have one language and one teacher as linguistic reference in each of them. For example, in the mathematics zone, only LSE can be used by all students, DHH and hearing, but in essay projects, speech is used together with programmed cued speech if necessary.

This manner of working is causing teachers to collaborate in order to better respond to student diversity in their classrooms. We can frequently find two or three teachers in a classroom—the two co-teachers plus the specialist in LSE or deaf consultant, who need to coordinate efficiently with each other in order to carry out the planned tasks.

We noticed that, more and more, the traditional teacher role is also changing from having full responsibility for everything to having students become, according to their age, more autonomous, cooperative, and strategic regarding their own learning. In addition, students become capable of better discussing with each other to reach decisions, resolve conflicts, and interact properly without the need for an adult to mediate in all processes and situations. This is why these schools attach great importance to having hearing classmates learn LSE, to having written language teaching materials accessible to DHH students, and to speech being adjusted to the individual needs of each deaf student.

This model meets an irresistible need of all children, which is a key motivational factor: the possibility of selecting what to learn at every moment and which language to use—something they learn to decide early. Over time and as they acquire good command of both languages, they become able to differentiate when using either one or the other is appropriate.

How Is Language Education Provided?

Language planning for teachers and specific teaching of spoken language and LSE directed at children are regular activities in these schools. These happen during different school activities (e.g., routines, assemblies, presentations of curriculum content) in which access for all deaf children has to be facilitated. To guarantee learning of both languages, schools organize different language workshops for the pupils. These workshops include prerequisites (visual or auditory) for each language and comparison between languages. Grouping (large/small groups) and composition (deaf and/or hearing children) of the workshops may vary depending on the workshop purpose and school staff availability. Another level of planning is the individual linguistic planning that the teachers and specialists design for each DHH student. The aim is to better adjust to the child's competences and difficulties.

Figure 12.2 is an example from the Piruetas School showing different workshops for all children (DHH and hearing). Below the workshops,

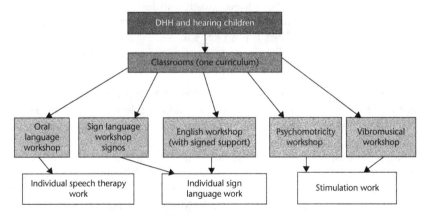

Figure 12.2. Example from the Piruetas School showing different types of workshops.

we specify the individual work that is done with the DHH children. All of them receive individual speech therapy and individual sign language instruction. The objective of these individual sessions is to make an intervention adapted to the communicative and linguistic level of each DHH child.

LSE has become important in these schools since it is accessible to all children and enables them to communicate and speak with each other regardless of auditory abilities. The strong presence of LSE has motivated most of the schools to create LSE departments composed of deaf professional specialists in LSE who are responsible for watching over LSE education planning, ensuring that co-teachers and other members of the staff use LSE correctly as well as conveying the values and culture of the Deaf community. Experience and reflections within these LSE departments have generated several proposals, including:

- Some schools, like El Sol, have been developing for years what is designated as an *LSE vocabulary bank*. Faced with the necessity of setting signs to teach the basic contents of the curriculum to deaf children by means of this language, training has been provided by the school through four academic years with the purpose of adapting LSE vocabulary to the curricular subjects of language, mathematics, and natural and social science at all levels of primary education. Terms in this vocabulary bank have been agreed on and included in the website of the European Sign Languages Centre via programs such as *Spreadthesign*,[4] a collection of signs from many different countries all around the world.
- Gaudem School has recently taken the initiative of implementing LSE as a compulsory subject in primary grades, both for hearing and DHH students. This subject is taught by professionals from the LSE department within school hours; thus, it is a subject planned, taught, and assessed just like any other. It guarantees that all hearing children learn and can communicate in LSE. It is a very interesting initiative, although there are still problems of lack of experience, resources, and regulations to implement it properly.

Concerning the Spanish language, it is clear that the shared teaching context helps to provide deaf students exposure to the language, since they have multiple chances to participate in communicative exchanges. The presence and use of LSE does not pose an obstacle to spoken language development (Pérez, Valmaseda, De la Fuente, Montero, & Mostaert, 2013). Learning LSE enables DHH children with different hearing devices (CI, hearing aids) to continue linguistic exchanges even when these devices fail or break down. In an educational context of signed bilingualism, the fact that a child has any technical problem with his or her hearing aid does not affect his or her access to communicative interactions or learning content as dramatically as in a context of monolingualism or unimodal bilingualism. Nevertheless, all schools are concerned that this advantage can easily turn into a disadvantage if it causes carelessness concerning auditory conditions and access to spoken language.

This concern has lately presented an important challenge in the schools: accessibility to spoken and written Spanish language. Teachers often make spoken language more visible by using these systems:

- *Cued speech (CS)*: This is used in conjunction with speech. There are eight hand positions with three positions near to the mouth. The deaf student watching a speaker using CS is aided in seeing "invisible" phonemes disambiguating lip patterns.
- *Visual phonics*: This a technique for making phonemes more visible. The speaker indicates visually a particular characteristic of the sound he or she is making (e.g., throat vibration). It is used in speech therapy.
- *Simultaneous communication or Sign-Supported Speech*: This is a combination of speech and sign from LSE following the grammatical structure of the spoken language.

In addition to these systems, we use technologies such as sound field frequency-modulated systems (FM).

The fact that spoken Spanish is available in the classroom does not imply that it is accessible to DHH learners; thus, a child with moderate hearing loss in a noisy classroom would not have access to the information provided by the co-teacher using spoken Spanish unless he or she has an FM system or the co-teacher uses CS. To make spoken language more accessible to DHH students, in three of the co-enrollment schools, CS is used as support, while simultaneous communication is not used as much at the present time. Teachers consider that CS is still useful and that it should be used uniformly from early ages. However, use of CS in these schools is not yet systematic but variable, because it requires proficiency and thoughtful planning by the co-teachers who use spoken language.

Sometimes, there are specific teaching sessions outside the classroom for the deaf children to work on spoken language skills such as use of CS, the phonological skills program, or special exercises required to improve the usefulness of the CI. Teachers specialized in speech and language organize these sessions, always with the criterion that occasions in which DHH children need to leave their classroom should be minimized.

A point shared by teachers and managers from these schools is the formal recognition that the two languages have equal status. That is, both are used as a means of communication and social interaction and as a means of instruction and learning. Certainly, this desire and conviction are on occasions faced with the reality of one language predominating over the other, for example in those groups where the DHH students have achieved a very good competence in spoken language. The task of not favoring one language over the other causes a constant tension in the teams. As there is not a definitive and sole solution, teachers' capability for reflection and shared analysis comes into play once again.

This discussion about the status of the two languages present in the classrooms drew attention to a complex and controversial issue: how to incorporate a third language, English. In Spain, like in most countries, the consideration of English as the lingua franca has resulted in education authorities strongly developing Spanish/English bilingualism policies in state and academy/charter schools at all educational stages that did not take into consideration the situation of more vulnerable students such as DHH students, among others. Faced with the challenge of "trilingualism," some of these schools are seeking ways of making this third language accessible to DHH pupils as well.

The arrival of CIs has enabled many children with severe to profound hearing loss to develop spoken language to levels unimaginable until now (Boons et al., 2013; Geers, 2009; Niparko et al., 2010). This is why teachers from many schools as well as the families are contemplating the possibility that these children may be capable of learning a second spoken language. One of the four schools, Gaudem School, has participated in these Spanish/English bilingual programs from the Madrid Autonomous Community since the academic year 2009–2010. External evaluators assess these programs, in this case the Franklin Institute of the University of Alcalá. This challenge means preparing individualized linguistic plans for each child that include the child's characteristics (e.g., audition and cognition), the child's and family's motivation toward learning a third language, and school and families providing the best opportunities they can offer to facilitate English learning (Kohnert, 2008).

In summary, we can conclude that regarding exposure to a third language, what schools need to bear in mind is that quantity and quality is very important. The following are some strategies to achieve this (also valid for spoken Spanish): (1) preteaching the content to be taught by the English teacher, using either LSE or spoken Spanish, depending on the child; (2) paying attention to the acoustic conditions and quality of auditory reception when using FM systems; and (3) using strategies such as repetitions and/or linguistic expansion and extension. These strategies often require one of the co-teachers to stand next to the English teacher, transforming the latter into an actual co-teacher and producing a "change of pair." This English teacher is providing 10 hours a week of English input and therefore is also considered a co-teacher.

Close monitoring of the third language experience could serve to generalize and extend this proposal to other co-enrollment projects. Although it is clear that acquiring another language is extremely complicated for DHH children, we cannot turn our back on this option, especially when considering that having a good command of a language such as English is nowadays a determining factor in matters like employment.

IS CO-ENROLLMENT BENEFICIAL OR DETRIMENTAL?

All four schools from Madrid Autonomous Region implementing this co-enrollment model are convinced of its relevance and benefits for DHH students. Although these schools come from diverse realities and histories—there are state and public schools, large and small, newly established or with a long tradition in education of DHH children—all of them agree that "it is the model to follow" if we want to provide a quality education for DHH pupils without detriment to the quality of education for their hearing classmates. Reasons and evidence supporting this judgment vary according to students, teachers, families, the Deaf community, and our own team, too.

First, the model is beneficial because the presence of two teachers in the classroom is an indispensable means of better addressing all students' diversity in educational needs. Second, the presence of hearing and deaf pupils, with or without other specific educational needs, constitutes a constant call for school improvement and innovation in teaching and assessment methods as well as in new ways of organizing and managing the classroom. Third, the project contributes to enhance teachers' professionalization, as it strengthens their reflective and collaborative competencies (Perrenoud, 2007; Schön, 1983). Fourth, students learn positive attitudes and values, such as mutual support or respect for differences (e.g., the languages one needs to communicate, interact, and think in). The teachers and children work in contexts and practices in which diversity is the rule and not the exception.

Furthermore, throughout the years, the model has also benefitted the Deaf community and helped many teachers "of the deaf," who for years have lived distant from the Deaf community, to better understand it. The model was beneficial because those who could and should teach LSE were deaf people from the community. Educational schools for the deaf and the Deaf community began together, for the first time, a path to LSE training including how to introduce LSE in schools. Multiple courses, seminars, and conferences on sign language organized over the years were propitious not only for learning the language itself but also for many hearing people getting involved with the Deaf community. In addition, the interest in placing value on both languages, especially LSE, has led our team to collaborate in the development and/or adaptation of several tests to evaluate LSE,[5] as there did not exist any assessment tools before.

It could be argued that benefits we describe may not be enough without a confirmed improvement in DHH pupils' learning of curriculum key competencies. We are obtaining evidence pointing in this direction as well. A study to assess LSE and the Spanish language development in a group of children with early CI use attending these four schools began in 2009 (Pérez, Valmaseda, & Morgan, 2014). We followed these children, and, in 2017, a sample of 15 early implanted children in these co-enrollment schools was examined. Preliminary results show that these children, assessed at two different ages (5 and 7 years old), obtained an average achievement in spoken language (vocabulary and grammar) within age-adequate levels with respect to hearing peers (in preparation).

The results from the school achievement examination carried out by the Madrid Community at the end of primary education (12 years old) evaluates several key competencies: linguistic competence in Spanish and English, mathematics, and Science and Technology. Schools could choose not to send their DHH students to participate in this exam, as these students are exempted due to being considered as having special educational needs. Nonetheless, all the schools analyzed here send increasing numbers of children to sit for this examination. In the academic year 2016–2017, nine DHH children took the test; six obtained positive results, particularly in mathematics and Science and Technology. We will pay close attention in future years to see whether these good academic achievement rates are continued.

We are also following up and evaluating the spoken languages of children with CI participating in the Gaudem School's trilingual project. This evaluation helps schools make important decisions concerning not only the quality and quantity of exposure to each language, but also with regard to sending these students to take official English tests together with their hearing peers. To date, four DHH children have had the opportunity to take these external tests that take place in the second and fourth year of primary education for levels A1 and A2, respectively. Three of the four children have passed the exams in both required skills (listening and speaking), whereas one of the students passed only one. It is important to note that two of these four pupils are native in LSE and, thus, the school makes a remarkable effort to ensure spoken languages have greater presence in their personalized plans, since they lack opportunities for spoken interaction in contexts other than the educational one.

In conclusion, we are clear that these and others are the reasons behind many families with deaf or hearing children opting for this model, committing themselves to it, and supporting these educational teams. Yet we have to highlight that the cost of these achievements is, at the present time, very high for these educational teams, especially when human and material resources are insufficient, as is the case. If the state administration lent a more determined support for these co-enrollment education projects, schools could have a greater selection of qualified teachers, training, review, follow-up, and accompaniment indispensable for the attainment of their objectives without requiring tremendous personal effort from teachers.

This model of co-enrollment has been developed mainly at nursery and primary education stages. Similar proposals for secondary education have yet to be achieved. In our country, as may also be the case in others, it is very difficult to find teachers of secondary education core curricular subjects (e.g., mathematics, language, history) who have proficiency in LSE. Pressures for a more "academic" curriculum and requirements derived from the diploma to be obtained at the end of the stage pose serious obstacles to the development of more innovative teaching practices in secondary schools like the ones implemented by the schools studied in this chapter. Finally, it is also less likely to find secondary teachers willing to engage in collaborative work inside the same classroom, which is the essence of this approach. While it is true that the presence of LSE interpreters and support teachers in secondary education guarantees, to some extent, access to curricular contents, at this moment co-enrollment education in secondary schools is different from the experiences in nursery and primary education presented here.

The schools analyzed in this chapter are not equal, and any comparison between them would be unfair. We want to focus on the important factors they have in common: they are "moving schools" driven by values of equity and recognition of diversity, and they are schools committed to providing their DHH and hearing learners with the best education possible.

ACKNOWLEDGMENTS

We would like to thank and recognize the support given by Piruetas, El Sol, Ponce de León, and Gaudem Schools in the writing of this chapter. We would like to thank the Specific Education Counseling Team for Deaf and Hard of Hearing Students in the Community of Madrid, Spain.

NOTES

1. The in-depth analysis of the focus groups conducted is part of a Master Final Project by student Laura Martín and her academic tutor, Nacho Montero: "A resting point in the co-enrollment and sign bilingual education journey: School management viewpoints," Madrid, Master's Degree in Educational Psychology, Faculty of Psychology, Universidad Autónoma De

Madrid (unpublished, 2017). We would like to express our gratitude and acknowledge her participation and support in this chapter's preparation.

2. In Spain, *colegios concertados* are privately established education schools that are partially funded by the state—hence the name "concerted schools" and the fact that they are subject to the same regulations applying to state-funded schools. These schools are similar to the "academies" in the United Kingdom and the "charter schools" in the United States. In most of them, all compulsory education stages are taught (primary education and compulsory secondary education), plus preschool and different upper secondary education specialties. As for Spanish state-funded schools, they are divided in stages: CEIPs (infant and primary education school, ages 3 to 12) and IESS (secondary education school, ages 12 to 16 for compulsory secondary education and 16 to 18 for upper secondary education and vocational training).

3. Level is the equivalent to grade or year (e.g., first, second, third). The primary education stage has six levels. *Cycle* is an "unofficial" organizational structure established with the idea of programming the teaching task with a longer perspective than that of a mere academic year. Again, unofficially, we often divide primary education into three cycles: first cycle (first and second levels/grades), second cycle (third and fourth levels/grades), and third cycle (fifth and sixth levels/grades). Depending on the size of the school, it is possible that there are one, two, three, or even more different groups studying the same level. In this sense, a *level meeting* is that of all tutors from the respective groups in the same level. Similarly, a *cycle meeting* is that including all tutors from every group in the levels of the same cycle.

4. https://www.spreadthesign.com/gb/

5. EOEP website: https://www.educa2.madrid.org/web/centro.eoep.auditivas.madrid/evaluacion

REFERENCES

Ahlgren, I., Bergman, B., & Brennan, M. (Eds.). (1994). Perspectives on sign language usage. Papers from the Fifth International Symposium on Sign Language Research. Durham: ISLA.

Alonso, P., Rodríguez, P., & Echeita, G. (2009). El proceso de un Centro Específico de sordos hacia una Educación más Inclusiva. Colegio Gaudem, Madrid. *Revista Latinoamericana de Educación Inclusiva, 3*(1), 167–187.

Antia, S., & Metz, K. (2014). Co-enrollment in the United States. A critical analysis of benefits and challenges. In M. Marschark, G. Tang, & H. Knoors (Eds.), *Bilingualism and bilingual deaf education* (pp. 424–441). New York: Oxford University Press.

Ballard, K. (2011). Thinking in another way: Ideas for sustainable inclusion. *International Journal of Inclusive Education, 17*, 762–775.

Barbour, R. (2013). *Los grupos de discusión en investigación cualitativa.* Madrid: Morata [*Doing Focus Group.* Londres: SAGE, 2007].

Barton, L. (Ed.) (2002). *Disability, human rights and society.* Buckingham, UK: Open University Press.

Booth, T., & Ainscow, M. (2011). *Index for inclusion. Developing learning at participation in schools* (3rd ed.). Bristol, UK: CSIE.

Boons, T., De Raeve, L., Langereis, M., Peeraer, L., Wouters, J., & van Wieringen, A. (2013). Expressive vocabulary, morphology, syntax and narrative skills in profoundly deaf children after early cochlear implantation. *Research in Developmental Disabilities*, 34(6), 2008–2022.

Domínguez, A. B., & Alonso, P. (2004). *La Educación de los alumnos sordos hoy. Perspectivas y respuestas educativas.* Málaga: Ediciones Aljibe.

Echeita, G., Simón, C., & Sandoval, M. (2016). Making the right for inclusive education to come true for all students: Inclusive pedagogy in the classroom. *EU Project TDiverS*. Retrieved from https://www.dropbox.com/s/hygoozzkp4xr5iu/Making%20the%20right%20to%20inclusive%20education%20come%20true%20for%20all%20students.%202docx.pdf?dl=0

Geers, A., Nicholas, J. G., & Sedey, A. L. (2003). Language skills of children with early cochlear implantation. *Ear & Hearing*, 24(1), 46–58.

Hermans, D., Wauters, L., & Knoors, H. (2014). The Twinschool: A co-enrollment program in the Netherlands. In M. Marschark, G. Tang, & H. Knoors (Eds.), *Bilingualism and bilingual deaf education* (pp. 646–691). New York: Oxford University Press.

Khonert, K. (2008). Second language acquisition: Success factors in sequential bilingualism. *The ASHA Leader*, 13, 10–13.

Kirchner, C. (1994). Co-enrollment as an inclusion model. *American Annals of the Deaf*, 139(2), 163–164.

Lewis, W. (1995). Bilingual teaching of deaf children in Denmark. Description of a project (1982–1992). Aalborg, Denmark: Dove Skolernes Material Center.

Marschark, M., Tang, G., & Knoors, H. (2014). Perspectives on bilingualism and bilingual education for deaf learners. In M. Marschark, G. Tang, & H. Knoors (Eds.), *Bilingualism and bilingual deaf education* (pp. 723–772). New York: Oxford University Press.

Mastropieri, M. A., & Scruggs, T. E. (Eds.) (2006). *The inclusive classroom. Strategies for effective instruction* (3rd ed.). New York: Prentice-Hall.

Morales López, E. (2008). Sign bilingualism in Spanish deaf education. In C. Plaza-Pust & E. Morales López (Eds.), *Sign bilingualism: Language development, interaction, and maintenance in sign language contact situations* (pp. 223–276). Philadelphia: John Benjamins Publishing.

Niparko, J. K, Tobey, E. A., Thal, D. J., Eisenberg, L. S., Wang, N., Quittner, A. L., & Fink, N. D. (2010). Spoken language development in children following cochlear implantation. *Journal of the American Medical Association*, 303(15), 1498–1506.

Noah, Y. (2015). *Homo deus. A brief history of tomorrow.* Israel: Kinneret Zmora-Bitan Dvir.

Pérez, M., Valmaseda, M., De la Fuente, B., Montero, I., & Mostaert, S. (2013). Desarrollo del vocabulario temprano en niños con Implante coclear escolarizados en centros con bilingüismo oral-signado. [Early vocabulary development in deaf children with cochlear implants educated in oral signed bilingual schools in Madrid.] *Revista de Logopedia, Foniatría y Audiología*, 34(2), 85–97.

Pérez Martín, M., Valmaseda, M., & Morgan, G. (2014). Sign bilingual and co-enrollment education for children with cochlear implants in Madrid, Spain: A case study. In M. Marschark, G. Tang, & H. Knoors (Eds.), *Bilingualism and bilingual deaf education* (pp. 602–645). New York: Oxford University Press.

Perrenoud, P. (2007). *Desarrollar la práctica reflexiva en el oficio de enseñar.* Barcelona: Graó [*Développer la pratique réjlexive dans fe métur d'enseignant.* París: ESF éditeur].

Sacks, O. (1989). *Seeing voices. A journey into the world of the Deaf.* New York: Vintage Books.

Schon, D. (1983). *The reflective practitioner. How professionals think in action.* London: Routledge.

Tyack, D., & Cuban, L. (1995). *Tinkering toward Utopia: A Century of Public School Reform.* Cambridge: Harvard University Press.

United Nations. (2006). *Convention on the Rights of Persons with Disabilities.* Retrieved from http://www.un.org/disabilities/convention/conventionfull.shtml

United Nations. (2016). *General comment No. 4 (2016). Article 24: Right to inclusive education. Convention on the Rights of Persons with Disabilities.* Retrieved from http://www.ohchr.org/EN/HRBodies/CRPD/Pages/CRPDIndex.aspx

UNESCO. (1994). *The Salamanca statement and framework for action on special needs education.* Adopted by the World Conference on Special Needs Education: access and quality. Retrieved from http://www.unesco.org/education/pdf/SALAMA_E.PDF

UNESCO. (2008). *Inclusive education: The way of the future. International Conference on Education, 48th session.* Retrieved from http://www.ibe.unesco.org/fileadmin/user_upload/Policy_Dialogue/48th_ICE/CONFINTED_48-3_English.pdf

Yiu, K. C., & Tang, G. (2014). Social integration of deaf and hard of hearing students in a signs bilingual and co-enrollment environment. In M. Marschark, G. Tang, & H. Knoors (Eds.), *Bilingualism and bilingual deaf education* (pp. 342–367). New York: Oxford University Press.

13

Willie Ross School for the Deaf and Partnership Campus: A Dual-Campus Model of Co-Enrollment

Louis Abbate

As the chapters in this volume make clear, co-enrollment education for deaf and hard-of-hearing (DHH) students takes various forms. Perhaps most generally, co-enrollment involves having a critical mass of DHH students in a fully inclusive academic environment with hearing peers that is sensitive *and responsive* to their diverse needs socially, linguistically, and academically. Several of the best-known co-enrollment programs (described in other chapters) include two teachers working together in the same classroom, co-teaching in sign language and spoken language. Other programs, however, utilize primarily (or only) one communication modality. Some programs have only a single teacher supported by an interpreter, a children of deaf adults (CODA) teaching partner, or other staff. A program may have deaf and hearing teaching partners, although there are never enough certified deaf teachers to go around (both teaching partners therefore may or may not hold formal teaching credentials). Although most co-enrollment programs are unique in one way or another, what they all have in common is a commitment to educating cohorts of DHH and hearing students together in fully inclusive settings where the DHH students are members of the class and not just "visitors" (Antia, Stinson, & Gaustad, 2002).

The Willie Ross School for the Deaf and Partnership Campus offers what appears to be a unique approach to co-enrollment. As noted earlier, it includes (but is not limited to) a setting with a critical mass of DHH students in a fully inclusive academic environment that is sensitive *and responsive* to their needs socially, linguistically, and academically. From some perspectives, this might be an ideal approach to co-enrollment, because it can support essentially any DHH student. But, in some sense, the program is more a horizontal one, focused on educating DHH students across a continuum of classrooms, rather than a vertical one, in which all features of co-enrollment are in a single classroom. To understand the vision, mechanics, and goals for this program, first, some context.[1]

FOUNDED BY PARENTS

Willie Ross School for the Deaf (WRSD), located in Longmeadow, Massachusetts, was founded in 1967 by a group of parents whose children had been born deaf as a result of the rubella epidemic that had swept the Eastern Seaboard of the United States in the early 1960s. Maternal rubella (German measles) used to be the single most frequent cause of hearing loss in U.S. children. The rubella epidemic of 1963–1965, in particular, led to 30,000 to 40,000 babies being born deaf, many of them with secondary disabilities. A rubella vaccine was developed in 1969, and rubella now accounts for only about 2% of the congenital hearing loss in the United States. But the situation was very different back then.

As children of the "rubella bulge" (as the cohort is known) approached school age, the deaf education infrastructure in the United States was ill prepared to handle either the number of children or the heterogeneity of their needs. When the WRSD founding parents started exploring educational options for their DHH children, they found that residential placement was the prevailing option for deaf education. There was a residential school for the deaf within an hour's drive, but the parents wanted their children to live at home and attend a day program. When the existing programs that they contacted did not welcome their vision, they were undaunted by the rejection of their requests. Confident of their beliefs and with the goal of having their children receive educations that would prepare them to enter their communities as full and participating members, the parents decided to move ahead and establish their own day school. The result was the innovative dual-campus model of WRSD, which was designed to recognize the diversity among their children and meet the unique needs of each one. The resulting Willie Ross School for the Deaf and Partnership Campus was established as a nonprofit entity (501(c)(3) in U.S. parlance) licensed by the Massachusetts Department of Elementary and Secondary Education (DESE).

WRSD opened its doors in 1967 and was named in honor of the son of one of the founding parents. The founders purchased a closed public school building and a vacant house. Over the years, construction of new buildings, renovation of existing buildings, and purchase of additional acreage led to the establishment of a comprehensive center-based campus typical of day schools for the deaf.

The dual-campus model consists of a center-based campus, what most people think of as WRSD, located in Longmeadow and known as the Longmeadow Campus, and a Partnership Campus embedded in the East Longmeadow Public Schools (ELPS), located a few miles from the Longmeadow Campus. For the first 20 years of their existence, partnership programs were sited in different schools in different communities around Longmeadow. The programs ran well enough, but they lacked the continuity and collaboration that would come from having one partner in one district with a consistent curriculum. Predictability, continuity, and possibilities for students, teachers, and parents were improved when these programs were embedded in the ELPS in 1987.

TWO SCHOOLS IN ONE—OR IS IT FOUR SCHOOLS IN ONE?

The Longmeadow Campus

The Longmeadow Campus was established as the placement of choice for all children who are admitted at ages 3 to 5 into the early childhood program. This part of the program was based on the belief that the center setting was best positioned to assist in preschoolers' communication development, to maximize the use of their residual hearing, and to provide the foundational skills necessary for their future academic success. Beyond the preschool and kindergarten years, the Longmeadow Campus was designed to serve students whose needs required a small teacher-to-student ratio, relatively intensive or continuous related services, and a completely accessible communication environment. The traditional and important contribution made by schools for the deaf thus is recognized at the Longmeadow Campus.

The Longmeadow Campus offers an academic program at elementary through high school levels that comports with the standards set by DESE. The subject offerings are the same as those at the Partnership Campus at the elementary, middle, and high school levels. At the beginning elementary level, a transitional classroom was established. The students in the transitional classroom are assessed throughout the year to determine which campus placement would be best as they continued their elementary experience. Options are placement at the Partnership Campus, remaining at the Longmeadow Campus, or, in some instances, a combination of both settings.

In addition to academic offerings, vocational opportunities are available to students for whom it was appropriate. From its inception, WRSD embraced the notion that inclusion was not restricted to placement in general education classrooms but should include the community as well. To that end, the vocational program offered work-study opportunities with employers in the local community. Students were transported by WRSD to the various worksites. A WRSD staff member was on site to facilitate the integration and assist with implementing whatever modifications were necessary. The process of selecting an appropriate work-study placement was similar to the preparation conducted when including a WRSD student at the ELPS. The requirements were the same as regards student access and full participation. The goal, in many instances, was for a WRSD student participating in the work-study program to achieve employment upon graduation. Importantly, just as the Partnership Campus would recognize that not all WRSD students would receive inclusion services (discussed further later in the chapter), the Longmeadow Campus recognized that not all students would be prepared for a community placement. In order to respond to this desire for work-study placements to offer an array of services and options, on-campus worksite internships were available as well.

As WRSD grew, there was a growing recognition that a range of instructional approaches were needed. In addition, an essential component of the WRSD vision was that placements should be flexible and possess to capacity to change and adapt to student needs over time. This thinking led to the notion that a center-based campus might not be able to serve all student needs and to the consolidation of partnership programs and establishment of the Partnership Campus in ELPS in 1987.

The Partnership Campus

The Partnership Campus actually consists of three partner schools. When ELPS welcomed the elementary, middle, and high school departments in 1987, WRSD now had two campuses, the center-based campus in Longmeadow and a permanent home for a Partnership Campus in the ELPS. At that time, the Partnership Campus consisted of six classrooms. Two classrooms each at the elementary, middle, and secondary levels were embedded in the corresponding grade structure at ELPS. WRSD leased the classrooms from ELPS. The classrooms are staffed by WRSD faculty, and various service providers for the DHH students from the Longmeadow Campus travel to each of the Partnership Campus classrooms on a daily basis or as needed. The Partnership Campus thus offers support services to DHH students in a public school environment and offers inclusion as an additional service. At its core, the WRSD dual-campus program offers deaf education based upon the recognition of the value of integrating approaches to enhance instruction, offering alternative models in the same school, if not the same school building.

The "integration of approaches" in the WRSD dual-campus model involves both inclusion (ELPS classrooms) and immersion (WRSD classrooms), or in some instances, a combination of both approaches. Moreover, this integrated approach includes the adoption of different communication strategies based on the student's needs in a particular setting. The teaching strategies in the WRSD classrooms comport with the mission of WRSD, which recognizes the unique learning needs of

DHH children. Inclusion into the ELPS classrooms does not include any modifications in the teaching strategies on the part of the ELPS faculty. That criterion is in place in order to ensure that genuine inclusion occurs, that the WRSD student is a full and participating member of the classroom.

DHH students in the six WRSD-leased classrooms are taught by WRSD teachers using the modes of communication appropriate for each student (signed, spoken, or both) while supporting assistive listening technologies, methods, and materials matched to students' needs and strengths. At the same time, being embedded in the Partnership Campus provides opportunities for WRSD students to have access to the general education offerings in the ELPS classrooms. The process, referred to at WRSD as "incremental inclusion," is overseen by WRSD. This availability of alternative academic settings in the same building (elementary, middle, or high school), means that beyond the Longmeadow Campus, WRSD students are able to receive specialized instruction in WRSD classrooms within the ELPS setting and instruction in general education classes in the same setting—that is, without having to travel from one school to another. The offering of both immersion (specialized instruction in the WRSD classrooms) and inclusion (instruction within general education classrooms) ensures that several types of instructional environments are available to WRSD students, together with the option of moving between them.

The Partnership Campus provides multiple approaches and student services in part to address the isolation factor that DHH students were reported to experience when they were the sole deaf student in a public school setting (e.g., Kluwin, Stinson, & Colarossi, 2002; Stinson & Antia, 1999). Not only are there WRSD staff at each level (elementary, middle, and high school) but, consistent with the original co-enrollment philosophy (see Kirchner, this volume), there is a critical mass of DHH peers available to all WRSD students in the leased classrooms. At any given time across the six classrooms of the Partnership Campus, there are between 25 and 30 students. The number depends on which students would do best in that setting, given their Individualized Education Programs (IEPs). Further, the actual number of classrooms at the Partnership Campus has varied from year to year, depending on enrollment.

The students enrolled at WRSD are fully enrolled in a school for the deaf. Full enrollment means that regardless of their classroom placement, they are full-time WRSD students. The elementary, middle, and secondary WRSD classrooms embedded in ELPS are an extension of the Longmeadow Campus. The classrooms are not considered to be self-contained or in any way sponsored by ELPS. Further, the classrooms do not operate in isolation from the Longmeadow Campus. Therefore, WRSD students are not co-enrolled within ELPS. Rather, the WRSD Partnership Campus is embedded in the respective school buildings at the elementary, middle, and secondary levels—thus the description earlier of the WRSD Partnership Campus as involving co-enrollment horizontally, across classrooms, rather than vertically, within classrooms. Inclusion into the ELPS classrooms is overseen by WRSD and conducted in conjunction with ELPS. Thus, even when WRSD students are fully included in ELPS classrooms, it does not alter the status of their enrollment at WRSD.

The Deaf Education Continuum in One Program

The integration of WRSD with the ELPS was an important goal for WRSD. However, of equal importance was the capacity of WRSD to maintain its identity as a school for the deaf. This has been achieved through a variety of methods. On the administrative side, a five-year renewable lease arrangement was developed in 1987 with ELPS. The lease delineated both the responsibilities of WRSD as the lessee and ELPS as the lessor. For example, the lease specified that the WRSD classroom space followed the protocols of the center-based Longmeadow Campus, including using the communication methodology. The leased classrooms were clearly designated through appropriate signage as the WRSD Partnership Campus. The two campuses were not viewed as independent entities. In exchange for a consistent lease rate, WRSD provides consulting services, audiological assistance, and sign language classes for ELPS students and staff at no charge, regardless of their involvement with WRSD.

The establishment of a formal relationship between WRSD and ELPS provided extremely flexible opportunities for incremental inclusion. Importantly, inclusion opportunities for selected WRSD students are considered a service offered by WRSD and not a goal. The partnership campus therefore offers both specialized instruction in the WRSD classrooms (immersion) and instruction within general education classrooms (inclusion) with the goal of maximizing student outcomes; DHH students can move into and out of WRSD and ELPS classrooms as needed. As a result, the continuum of special education has been redefined at WRSD from a linear perspective to a systemic one—the horizontal co-enrollment model alluded to earlier. That is, the model challenges the normal assumption in deaf education that each step on the placement continuum can only offer a single, discrete instructional environment. Placement in this model is seen in terms of services, not a specific location.

To ensure coordinated programming between WRSD and ELPS, there is a WRSD lead teacher in each Partnership Campus school. The lead teacher serves as the liaison to the ELPS faculty members who have WRSD students in their classrooms. The WRSD Education Director works closely with both Partnership Campus principals and guidance departments to ensure appropriate class placement and management of student behavior (discussed further below). A variety of considerations are reviewed in making this determination. Consistent with the "full membership" goal of co-enrollment and all truly inclusive placements for DHH students (see Antia et al., 2002), the placement decision ultimately turns on the likely effectiveness of the setting for facilitating WRSD students' full academic and social participation in the classroom, including access to other students and the ability to engage in all aspects of classroom functioning.

In short, access for all WRSD learners is ensured by the Partnership Campus's offering instructional environments based on the needs of the student at the time, with flexibility to change instructional environments (as well as classrooms) as necessary. The underlying assumption is that when immersion and inclusion are viewed not as distinct placement offerings but as points on a continuum, access to instruction and academic success are enhanced. A bridge can be constructed from immersion to inclusion by offering both settings while recognizing the value of each for different students, and perhaps at different times for the same student.

WHO GOES WHERE? ASSESSMENT OF INDIVIDUAL STUDENT NEEDS

A DHH student can be placed at the Partnership Campus as the result of one of several different assessment processes. One source of such a placement decision is a recommendation from the teachers of the transitional class for 6- to 8-year-olds, located at the Longmeadow Campus. Another source for Partnership Campus placement is a recommendation by staff working with a student enrolled at the Longmeadow Campus, based on the student's changing needs (a process that also can work in reverse, with a student moving from the Partnership Campus to the Longmeadow Campus). A third source of the placement decision might be a determination made at the time of initial WRSD admission by the intake staff. Regardless of its source, all placement decisions are based on the full diagnostic data available, and consultation with the family and the student. The determination of the placement, either at the center-based Longmeadow Campus or at the Partnership Campus, is based on the capacity of the placement to respond to currently assessed student needs and strengths.

The offering of both a center-based campus and a Partnership Campus is fully explained to parents at the time of admission or when a recommendation is made for a transition from one campus to another during the academic year. Parents are informed and assured that they are part of the decision-making team. This is not just an issue of compliance with the Individuals with Disabilities Education Act (IDEA) but is essential to the original vision of the parents who founded WRSD and those who are part of it day to day. Decisions regarding any campus placement for individual children always includes the parents' perspective. In addition, it is made clear to parents that, regardless of the classroom they are in, their children are enrolled at WRSD. It can be confusing for parents, especially those new to the dual-campus model, when their child is in a public school six miles from the Longmeadow Campus and at the same time enrolled in WRSD. To assist families with understanding the notion of incremental inclusion and the opportunities (and potential challenges) of placement at the Partnership Campus, family tours are provided of both campuses when a child is being considered for admission to WRSD. The WRSD Education Director explains the nature of the relationship between WRSD and ELPS, and the campuses are presented to the parents as options, neither of which is superior to the other. Rather, it is explained that the campuses and their connection (i.e., the flexibility to move across sites and classrooms) have been designed to meet their child's needs at the time of admission and for their entire enrollment. Again, the opportunities offered by this horizontal co-enrollment help to ensure that the individual strengths and needs of each child are recognized and appropriately matched to the educational placement.

When it is determined that the Partnership Campus placement is best for a particular student, the ELPS staff and their counterparts at the Longmeadow Campus work closely together. As all of the students are technically enrolled in WRSD, it is WRSD's responsibility to ensure fidelity to the WRSD curriculum and to successfully integrate students into the general education setting. Therefore, support for student learners at the Partnership Campus requires the cooperation of faculties and administrations of both partners.

Ensuring Ongoing Appropriateness of Partnership Placements

When a Partnership Campus placement is made through the evaluation process, a determination also has to be made as to which subjects the WRSD student should take in general education. That decision is coordinated with the team to create the IEP, which includes the subjects to be taught in the WRSD classrooms with DHH peers and the amount of instruction in general education classrooms that include both DHH and hearing peers.

Once a determination is made of which ELPS classes are best for a particular student, the WRSD Education Director works with either the principal or the guidance department of the Partnership Campus school and considers the appropriate general education classroom options. Those recommendations also are reviewed by the WRSD lead teacher and the WRSD classroom teacher; the general education teacher then is consulted to ensure that the classes selected are appropriate from everyone's perspective. Central to this consideration for placement in the incremental inclusion setting is the need to match choices with individual students' goals. Student progress is reviewed regularly, including an extensive annual assessment of the goals on the IEP. The quality of the peer interaction in the general education classroom also is reviewed. This is consistent with the goal of ensuring that each WRSD student has opportunities to participate fully as a member of the class. At the same time, the process ensures that hearing peers have access to the WRSD students. Indeed, the primary area of research emerging from co-enrollment programs is that highlighting the mutual social-emotional benefits to both DHH and hearing students (e.g., Hermans, De Klerk, Wauters, & Knoors, 2014; Yiu & Tang, 2014).

The degree of the inclusion at the Partnership Campus can range from one course to a number of courses. At the high school level, for example, a particular WRSD student might receive inclusion services in science and mathematics classrooms offered by ELPS, and a particular ELPS classroom might include a number of WRSD students. The progress of each student is reviewed annually, and changes for the following year may be recommended. If such changes are recommended, quarterly reviews are held during the following year to ensure that the student and the classroom are appropriately matched. Because assessment information through this review is considered by both the WRSD and ELPS faculty, there is continual assessment of whether the general education classroom is a good "fit" for each WRSD student and what, if any, changes could be made to the classroom to better accommodate the individual's needs.

As suggested earlier, not all WRSD students receive inclusion services at ELPS. Determination of service provision is based on the diagnostic information supporting placement in incremental inclusion in the first place. In some cases, there is recognized value for certain students to be placed in the Partnership Campus with hearing, age-appropriate peers, but it is determined that no inclusion support services are necessary. Because of the availability of WRSD classrooms in each Partnership Campus school, DHH students always have the option of seeking assistance there, and inclusion services can be introduced at any time, as determined by the periodic reviews of student progress and classroom compatibility. WRSD recognizes that, in certain instances, immersion and inclusion need not be offered as a 100% service. Depending on student needs, there is value in both inclusion and immersion being offered on incremental bases.

The regular assessment of student progress includes consideration of a number of domains. The options for placement are many: which campus, what level of inclusion, how much special instruction? As student needs change, so must the assessment process, not just the placement. The right combination of services can change, and, as long as those recommendations are based on current assessment data and the unique needs of each student, the choices will be as effective as possible. This means that the assessment process is best conducted on an ongoing basis and not the more common once-a-year event. Communication between the general education faculty and the WRSD faculty thus has to be ongoing. Ongoing assessments of students' academic and social functioning are dynamic and incremental. For example, a student may have academic success in a Partnership Campus classroom but not be interacting with hearing classmates. Efforts then would be undertaken to support and enhance that aspect of the student's experience. The dynamic assessment process (Mann, in press) allows for new or modified services to be introduced immediately when the need is identified, thereby enhancing the chances for success.

Dynamic assessment of inclusion, like incremental inclusion itself, is considered a service and not a goal. It thus requires the same clinical vigilance as all other support services provided to DHH students. Ongoing assessment has to ascertain that the placement is able to accommodate the needs of the student, builds on the student's strengths, and maintains the student's expected performance level. In so doing, the incremental introduction of inclusion by WRSD, in concert with ELPS through the Partnership Campus, enhances the chances for academic and social success for each student.

By working closely with ELPS for 30 years, a mutual respect and understanding has developed between the two partners. In part, the respect and strength of the collaboration has emerged from recognition of the value of the missions of both campuses and how that mutual respect can enhance student success. The benefits of this understanding also have been demonstrated by the unique contribution that each partner has brought to the education process. Nevertheless, it is the combined efforts of both partners that ensures that all WRSD students in the Partnership Campus are full and productive members of their classrooms. This recognition is a key factor in achieving genuine inclusion for WRSD students.

TEACHING AND LEARNING AT THE PARTNERSHIP CAMPUS

For students at the elementary level placed at the Partnership Campus, the number of classes taken in ELPS is limited to ensure smooth integration into that setting. For example, a WRSD student who is taking only a mathematics course in a Partnership Campus classroom might leave the WRSD classroom (i.e., in the Partnership school) to go to math class with hearing peers. When the math class is over, the student returns to the WRSD classroom. In a case like this, the ELPS math classroom teacher would be responsible for the WRSD student's grade in math The ELPS teacher would submit the grade to the WRSD Education

Director and that grade would be recorded along with other subjects taken in the WRSD classroom for that student. Report cards reflect achievement in both settings.

At the middle and secondary school levels, opportunities for WRSD students to take classes with ELPS students are increased. At the high school level, classes in the sciences and mathematics and at Advanced Placement levels are available, something that is relatively rare in schools for the deaf with their small enrollments. Some middle and secondary school WRSD students, depending on their levels of academic (and social) functioning, may take the majority of their classes in the general education setting. This is not always a simple affair. Considering that the general education setting is an environment designed for hearing students, it can be a complex undertaking to ensure that genuine inclusion with full access to the curriculum can occur. Nevertheless, the challenges of successful inclusion—from both students' and teachers' perspectives—are fewer than when an inclusive placement is an "all or nothing" situation. When inclusion is offered on an incremental basis, along with WRSD oversight and ongoing assessment by WRSD, the chances of success are increased.

This kind of collaboration requires the kind of bridge alluded to earlier between the WRSD classroom (immersion) and the selected general education classroom (inclusion). The WRSD Partnership program and other co-enrollment programs integrate the functions and services of a public school with those of a school for the deaf *before* they integrate students. Similar planning is required for DHH students' instructional opportunities in order to ensure that the placement process is guided by both the appropriate assessment leading to an IEP and agreement of those on the IEP team of the services necessary in different contexts to fully support the WRSD student. This goal requires that placements for DHH students are flexible and that programs and support services are offered based on student needs, not on historical offerings or assumptions based on stereotypes of DHH students.

Communication and Academic Support Services

The inclusion services at the Partnership Campus are intended to reflect accurately recommendations that allow the WRSD student to manage the regular Partnership curriculum as presented. Thus, when WRSD students work with general education faculty and take all their courses in the Partnership classrooms, no modifications are recommended to instructional content or methodologies. This step was taken in order to ensure that the inclusion is genuine and not the *illusion of inclusion*. That is, an essential assumption underlying the dual-campus model is that in order for genuine inclusion to occur, the WRSD student must manage schoolwork as presented and have the capacity to fully engage in the class.

As part of the ongoing monitoring of placement appropriateness, the communication method used by the student is considered in the context of other environmental considerations. Different classes required different levels of coordination. In the WRSD classrooms of the Partnership Campus, direct instruction involves communication directly with DHH students in the most effective mode or modes of communication. For DHH students in the Partnership classrooms, WRSD provides sign language or oral interpreters based on recommendations of student need in the IEP. For some students in some classes (e.g., some students with cochlear implants), there may be no interpreter provided, if so indicated by the IEP. If a classroom has an interpreter, the provision of a clear line of sight for the interpreter to the student is ensured. Classroom acoustics are reviewed by the audiologist, together with consideration of the student's use of hearing aids and cochlear implants, recommendations for FM usage, and related issues (De Raeve, 2015). Teachers in Partnership classrooms always wear lapel microphones for those students who use FM systems. If videos being shown in the classroom are not captioned, the interpreter provides DHH students with access. In short, environmental and audiological issues always are considered and appropriate modifications are taken and/or changed with changes in student need. The content of the instruction, however, is not modified, and the academic expectations for DHH students are the same as for their hearing classmates.

When the students are placed at the Partnership Campus and included in ELPS general education classrooms, tutoring services provided by WRSD faculty are available on an as-needed basis. In addition, WRSD service staff, including counselors and audiologists, meet with the students to monitor amplification devices. The audiological services become especially important when a WRSD student has one or more general education classes with hearing peers. Often these classes are larger, and ELPS teachers may be less aware of when students' devices are not working properly. WRSD audiologists therefore evaluate the general education classrooms in an ongoing manner to ensure that no obstacles have been introduced into the classroom that might disrupt signal transmission. Often, these obstacles are not readily apparent to the general education teachers. After all, their classrooms were originally designed for hearing students, and the challenges of ensuring universal access in the classroom for students with hearing loss (or others with disabilities) may not be familiar or obvious.

Having audiologists regularly conduct assessments to assist with implementing environmental modifications is minimally intrusive. Initially, however, the presence of an interpreter sometimes can be of concern to ELPS teachers, as it is to teachers anywhere who find DHH students in their class. With the assistance of the Partnership Campus, however, the introduction of another person into the classroom, the role (real or imagined) of that person, and the relationship of the interpreter to the student is reviewed prior to the inclusive placement. Over time and with familiarity with the dual-campus model, this process has become smoother, and the advance planning allows WRSD and Partnership staff to respond to whatever questions teachers might have about interpreting and interpreters. As with other aspects of the inclusive placement, support to the student provided by the interpreter is reviewed regularly to ensure appropriate understanding of the interpreter's role by all parties.

"The Devil Is in the Details"

At the elementary level, it frequently is the case that only one ELPS classroom and one ELPS teacher is selected to provide inclusive instruction for WRSD students. Beginning at the middle school level, inclusion usually involves more than one general education classroom and more than one ELPS teacher. Finally, at the high school level, there may be a number of general education classrooms available, including a number of different courses taught by different ELPS faculty. The coordination process in higher grades is more complex but vital. The WRSD lead teacher usually serves as the coordinator between faculties (teachers in WRSD classrooms and Partnership classrooms) and with the team as a whole.

The embedding of one school into another or initiation of a co-enrollment program in any school raises administrative and related issues that may appear mundane but that are critically important to maintaining the integrity of the fully inclusive setting that can provide maximum benefits to DHH students. For example, instruction guidelines for students with IEPs are different from those of hearing, general education students. In the case of the Partnership Campus, a fair and regulatory appropriate standard needed to be created and consistently administered. The ELPS, as host of WRSD, has a reasonable expectation that its rules will be followed by all students. But, as noted earlier, the WRSD students at the Partnership Campus are still WRSD students. The capacity to discipline students has to be in the purview of WRSD, but determination of details—how and what that discipline consists of—has to be decided by the host. At the same time, given acknowledged differences between DHH and hearing children, especially in early socialization (Marschark, 2018), it is important to ensure that the ELPS discipline is appropriate but does not have an impact on the DHH child greater than it would on a hearing child. Therefore, student infractions that occur on the Partnership Campus are responded to by WRSD in conjunction with ELPS.

In the event that a WRSD student behaves in some way that normally would require suspension for an ELPS (hearing) student, the WRSD student is removed from the Partnership Campus and returns to the Longmeadow Campus. The temporary transfer prevents the loss of academic progress but signals to the student that his or her behavior is not acceptable in the public school classroom. The mutual respect and understanding that develops over time between WRSD and Partnership staff provides real benefits to the WRSD students. Because the partners work together, they get to know the WRSD students as individuals and can make decisions with regard to behavioral issues just as appropriate as those that they make with regard to academic issues.

The roles of both WRSD and Partnership Campus clearly are vital to the success of the partnership. Within each of the buildings where WRSD is located, the principal is a key participant in the partnership. That principal has students from many different communities who are also enrolled in another school. This unique situation recognizes that certain details need to be agreed on in advance. To facilitate this process, the Education Director for WRSD and the respective principals meet regularly. The goal of these meetings is to assess administrative and operational issues such as:

1. Supervision of staff
2. Student discipline issues
3. Administration of high-stakes testing
4. Monitoring of attendance
5. Access to extracurricular and athletic services
6. Access to the school nurse
7. Scheduling of inclusion classes
8. Drop-off and transportation management.

By separating academic issues from administrative matters, faculty are permitted to focus on inclusion and the student while recognizing the importance of the roles each partner plays in maintaining the school's integrity. The success of many of the WRSD graduates is testimony to the effectiveness of that process.

More broadly, the extent of the efforts of both faculties and administration demonstrates how complex the inclusion process is to achieve. The partnership of the two systems addresses these challenges in order to develop instructional opportunities that are of maximum benefit to the WRSD students. Once again, however, the ultimate responsibility for all WRSD students rests with WRSD. Therefore, achievement in general education courses is transmitted to WRSD for inclusion in report cards and transcripts. There is not a distinction on the report card as to which were general education ELPS classrooms or WRSD classrooms. The lack of distinction in where the grades were earned, reflecting only the student's achievement in courses, whether taken in the WRSD classroom or ELPS classroom, might be considered a secondary level of inclusion.

WHERE DO WRSD AND SIMILAR PROGRAMS GO FROM HERE?

The evolving needs of DHH children have been driven by advances in technology, early identification, and improved instructional methods. Cultural, linguistic, and socioeconomic factors, as well as the increasing presence of secondary disabilities either associated with or concurrent with hearing loss, have contributed to the growing heterogeneity of the population of DHH students. These changes also have challenged the capacity of a single approach to deaf education to be effective. The limitations of a single instructional environment or a single educational philosophy unduly restrict both the breadth and depth of benefits that can be provided to a population as heterogeneous as DHH learners.

The establishment of the WRSD dual-campus model promoted the delivery of educationally appropriate, clinically sound, and economically advantageous programs for DHH students, recognizing and in some sense embracing their individual differences. School partnerships and other models of co-enrollment will not replace the need for schools for the deaf or endow the public schools with the capability to meet the needs of all DHH students. We believe, however, that the WRSD Partnership Campus approach can serve as a model for integrating the larger educational system and specialized educational settings, as well as combining the respective skills of teachers of the deaf and general education teachers in order to maximize the educational opportunities for DHH in a public school setting. The least restrictive environment (LRE) provision of IDEA that requires students with disabilities to be educated alongside students without disabilities to the greatest extent possible is met by partnerships like this one.

The Partnership model recognizes that specialized instruction will always be necessary in order to meet the needs of some DHH students. At the same time, inclusion, with the accompanying opportunity to fully experience the curriculum and the classrooms in general education, is a laudable goal. Underlying both the vision of the parents who founded WRSD and WRSD's continuing mission is the belief that these environments need not be viewed as mutually exclusive. The Partnership Campus permits both instructional settings to be available to WRSD students, with opportunities for instructional settings to change as students' strengths and needs change. In addition, the program recognizes that DHH students are at least as diverse and heterogeneous as any other group of students. As a result, they require the opportunity to be involved in both immersion and inclusion opportunities within settings that can provide a range of academic and extracurricular opportunities. This can only happen when services are made available based on individual student needs.

The cooperation between WRSD and ELPS faculties and administration has been conducted with mutual respect for both the specialized instruction and general education instruction. The main focus is on the student and ensuring that both environments are providing the needed services. To achieve this goal, the staffs meet regularly to review academic progress and the "fit" of the WRSD student in the current placement. Along with this assessment, the general education classroom's capacity to respond to the needs of the student is reviewed.

ACADEMIC AND SOCIAL OUTCOMES

The Department of Elementary and Secondary Education (DESE), as part of its licensing process, requires private special needs schools to have their curriculum approved. That was part of a standardization process designed to ensure that publicly funded students in the state receive instruction that would comport with, and therefore prepare them for, high-stakes testing.

WRSD students who successfully complete the WRSD curriculum, including, when appropriate, general education courses, and pass the Massachusetts high-stakes testing are awarded a diploma. The diploma is recognized by DESE as having been issued by WRSD, which is an approved school. However, those classes were delineated on the WRSD student's IEP. The outcomes were considered when developing a new IEP along with recommendations for inclusion services. Therefore, the grades on the WRSD student's transcript reflect the student's achievement regardless of his or her campus placement. The final determination of any grade for a WRSD student is determined by the teacher who taught the course (ELPS or WRSD) to the WRSD student. Some students, for a variety of reasons, are unable to achieve success on the state tests. Many, however, perform at the level needed to be successful in their goals. As the WRSD curriculum was approved by DESE, in these cases, students receive a certificate indicating their success.

As noted earlier, the goal of the WRSD academic program is to have all WRSD students who graduate go on to college, independent employment, or supervised employment. Some graduates have returned to WRSD to teach or work in some other capacity as staff members. When educational reform in the mid-1990s was adopted by the state, the route to a diploma was changed. Prior to that time, a WRSD student who completed the course requirements could receive a diploma from WRSD and ELPS. After educational reform, with the introduction of standardized curriculum and high-stakes testing, only the school where the student was enrolled was eligible to grant the diploma. Thus, the approval of the WRSD curriculum—which includes both the Longmeadow and Partnership Campuses—is essential. If not approved by the state, a diploma could not be granted to WRSD students regardless of whether they attend the Longmeadow or the Partnership Campus. Students also have to pass the high-stakes testing at the appropriate level rather than having the option of a variety of testing levels (frequently well below grade level) as occurs in some schools for the deaf. These requirements made integration with the Partnership schools more complicated, but it also helps to ensure fidelity of our standards with those of the public schools.

Finally, it is important to note that social-emotional functioning is one of the areas of student progress reviewed on a regular basis. For some students, the Partnership Campus environment is difficult, and adjusting to the "hearing setting" is a challenge. WRSD thus has social workers working with students to address such issues. Although we do not have empirical data, it appears that WRSD graduates who have spent some or most of their time at the Partnership Campus have found it a bit easier to manage the hearing world. This is particularly true for students who engaged in work-study activities or internships in community (hearing) settings. At the same time, another aspect of the partnership, one no less vital, is the opportunity offered to hearing students to engage with WRSD students. The mutual understanding that has developed between the two student bodies over the history of the partnership has been remarkable. In many instances, long-term friendships have developed and continued well after graduation.

CONCLUSION: INCLUSION IS NOT A PLACE

Given the increasing diversity in the population of DHH learners, educational programming for them increasingly needs to have the capacity to offer both inclusion and immersion on an incremental basis. DHH students' strengths and needs are evolving and are becoming less amenable to being responded to by a single approach, instructional environment, or communication modality. As a result, the value of offering both immersion and inclusion is becoming more apparent for many students, and hence we are seeing a variety of co-enrollment–like programs emerging around the world. Partnership programs provide the capacity to bring together the expertise of two systems, schools for the deaf and public schools, in order to develop a third model combining the benefits of each, leading to an array of programming options that neither system could provide on its own.

When inclusion is considered a service and not a particular educational setting, the opportunities for students, both those with hearing loss and those with normal hearing, increase. As the staffs in the WRSD Partnership program have developed a deeper understanding of the goals of the ELPS, they have been better able to concentrate on improving outcomes for both WRSD students and ELPS students.

At the Partnership Campus, general education teachers who have WRSD students regularly meet with parents along with the WRSD faculty. Open houses are held at both campuses, and parents of WRSD students are welcome to attend both. Parents are shown the benefits of both schools for their child. Parents are welcomed by both schools whether or not their child received inclusion services. We believe this builds a stronger community and a better understanding of DHH individuals by a cross-section of society.

Cooperation at all levels, ongoing communication between the partners, and respect by each party for the other has served as the touchstone of the WRSD Partnership Campus model. The partners have worked together to advance the academic success of their students and found opportunities for personal growth (see Hermans et al., 2014; de Klerk, Hermans, Wauters, de Laat, de Kroon, & Knoors, this volume). As one of WRSD senior faculty based at the Partnership Campus once said,

> We are not special. We are not hidden. We are not on display. We just ARE. We ARE part of the school. All staff look to us as part of the same school in which they work. By the time students get up to the high school, they have seen WRSD students, teachers and interpreters in classes, lunch, recess, assemblies, events. The students, too, do not see us as special, hidden, or on display. They see us as just part of the same school in which they attend. I really believe the success of the partnership is because ELPS fully includes us in classes, programs, technology, and events. There is not an "us" and "them" mindset; it is more a "we all" train of thought.

The founding parents of WRSD had a vision for their DHH children. They wanted their children to receive an education comparable to those of their hearing peers and to have access to their families and to their community. As proud heirs to that legacy of the founding parents' vision, WRSD has continued to expand its offerings. The dual campus recognized that one size does not fit all. The evolution of the programmatic offerings also has recognized the value of historical approaches to deaf education. Meanwhile, the thinking continues to focus on moving beyond just integrating students (i.e., placing them together) to integrating approaches (i.e., immersion and inclusion). If truly inclusive integration can be achieved, the obligation to accept students as individuals by offering them what they need will be met. Those goals can only be accomplished by having dedicated staff and enlightened board members. WRSD and ELPS are both so endowed. The students also should be applauded for their efforts to be in the hearing world, while at the same time maintaining their identity as deaf persons.

Several years before she passed away in 2016, Willie Ross's mother, Bobbi, visited WRSD along with other founding parents to celebrate the 40th anniversary of the school. She was living in California, where she had established the Willie Ross Foundation, which provided services to deaf adults, including Willie. She noted that she was proud of the WRSD and all it had accomplished since its opening in 1967. She said that the goals that the founders imagined for WRSD had been met, and she was confident that they would continue to be into the future. One could conclude that WRSD and the Partnership Campus offer the opportunity for all DHH children to be educated in a least restrictive environment. In our view, the dual-campus model offers an environment that is most enabling for most DHH children.

NOTE

1. This chapter describes the Willie Ross School for the Deaf and Partnership Campus at the time of the author's retirement as President of WRSD in 2013. He has no doubt that the program will continue to evolve as it has over the last 40 years.

REFERENCES

Antia, S., Stinson, M., & Gaustad, M. (2002). Developing membership in the education of deaf and hard of hearing students in inclusive settings. *Journal of Deaf Studies and Deaf Education, 7*, 214–229.

De Raeve, L. (2015). Classroom adaptations for effective learning by deaf students. In H. Knoors & M. Marschark (Eds.), *Educating deaf learners: Creating a global evidence base* (pp. 573–593). New York: Oxford University Press.

Hermans, D., De Klerk, A., Wauters, L., & Knoors, H. (2014). The Twinschool: A co-enrollment program in the Netherlands. In M. Marschark, G. Tang, & H., Knoors (Eds.), *Bilingualism and bilingual deaf education* (pp. 396–423). New York: Oxford University Press.

Kluwin, T. N., Stinson, M. S., & Colarossi, G. M. (2002). Social processes and outcomes of in-school contact between deaf and hearing peers. *Journal of Deaf Studies and Deaf Education, 7*, 200–213.

Mann, W. (in press). Measuring deaf learners' language progress in school. In H. Knoors & M. Marschark (Eds.), *Evidence-based practice in deaf education*. New York: Oxford University Press.

Marschark, M. (2018). *Raising and educating a deaf child* (3rd ed.). New York: Oxford University Press.

Stinson, M., & Antia, S. (1999). Considerations in educating deaf and hard-of-hearing student in inclusive settings. *Journal of Deaf Studies and Deaf Education, 4*, 163–175.

Yiu, K.-M., & Tang, G. (2014). Social integration of deaf and hard-of-hearing children in a sign bilingual and co-enrollment environment. In M. Marschark, G. Tang, & H. Knoors (Eds.), *Bilingualism and bilingual deaf education* (pp. 342–367). New York: Oxford University Press.

14

The Growth and Expansion of a Co-Enrollment Program: Teacher, Student, Graduate, and Parent Perspectives

Kathryn H. Kreimeyer, Cynthia Drye, and Kelly Metz

HISTORY OF THE CO-ENROLLMENT PROGRAM

A co-enrollment program for students who are deaf and hard of hearing (DHH) was initiated in 1982 under the direction of Carl J. Kirchner in the Burbank Unified School District in California (see Kirchner, this volume). Kirchner (1994) wrote about this program (TRIPOD), coined the term "co-enrollment," and proposed this model as an alternative to traditional models of inclusion in which a single DHH student is placed in a general education classroom, receiving fractured services from itinerant support personnel. Kirchner's article sparked interest in the program, which resulted in various other co-enrollment programs being established (Metz, 2013).

The co-enrollment program described in this chapter is within an individual school that is part of a large urban school district in the Southwestern United States. An interview with the individual who served as principal at the time the co-enrollment program was initiated provided insight into the multiple changes occurring at the school as the program began, as well as initial concerns about the co-enrollment approach.

Prior to the co-enrollment program, DHH students at this school received instruction within a self-contained classroom. Federal and district-level initiatives to support inclusion of students with special needs within the general education classroom, as well as concern over the low academic expectations and performance of DHH students, prompted the principal and a small group of teachers to explore alternative service delivery models. In the spring of 1994, the group visited the TRIPOD co-enrollment program in Burbank and received strong encouragement from the staff and parents there to initiate a co-enrollment program at the school. In the fall of 1995, nine DHH students moved from their self-contained classroom into a second-, third-, and fourth-grade classroom with 19 hearing students co-taught by a certified teacher of DHH students and a general education teacher.

As the co-enrollment model was being initiated, other schoolwide changes were occurring. In her interview, the principal noted that she assumed her position in the middle of a school year and spent half a year observing in classrooms and learning about the expectations teachers held for their students and the instructional approaches they used. She began talking with teachers about changes to be implemented during the next school year: (1) increasing the academic expectations for all students, (2) supporting full inclusion of all special needs students within the general education classroom and moving delivery of most support services into that setting, (3) increasing strategies to promote student engagement, (4) using integrated thematic instruction, and (5) moving to multi-grade/multi-age classrooms across the school (see Kramreiter & Krausneker, this volume). By the end of this year, most teachers elected to transfer to other schools following more traditional models of instructional delivery and classroom configuration. Incoming teachers were those attracted to engaging in new learning, to working collaboratively, and to participating in a fully inclusive environment.

Some special educators and parents expressed concern that the special needs of DHH students would be neglected in a large classroom with typical peers and that they would not receive the comparable level of attention that can be provided within a self-contained classroom. To address this concern, staff examined results of the program by looking at student progress. Data collected from the Stanford Achievement Test Series, 9th edition (Stanford-9, 1996) during the second and third year of the co-enrollment program demonstrated that the DHH students in the 3/4/5 classroom performed comparably to the hearing and DHH normative sample in reading vocabulary and above the DHH normative sample, but below the hearing sample in reading comprehension (Kreimeyer, Crooke, Drye, Egbert, & Klein, 2000). A multiyear comparison of the academic achievement of hearing students in the co-enrollment classroom to hearing students not in co-enrollment classrooms showed no significant differences, removing concerns that the presence of DHH students might impede curriculum delivery and thus the academic achievement of hearing students. McCain and Antia (2005) provided descriptive academic data for three fourth-grade and two fifth-grade DHH students in the 3/4/5 classroom after the program had been in operation for seven years. Measures included three consecutive years of performance in reading, math, and language on the Stanford-9 (1996) and teacher perception of academic performance in comparison to classmates as rated on the academic competence scale of the Social Skills Rating System (SSRS, Gresham & Elliot, 1990). Normal curve equivalent scores on the Stanford-9 for DHH students were below their same-grade hearing classmates, with a slightly smaller gap between DHH students and their grade-mates across the school. The gap was larger for reading than for math and language. When data were compared to the DHH normative sample, DHH students in the co-enrollment classroom scored above the 50th percentile in reading comprehension, math procedures, and math problem-solving, with the exception of one student on one subtest. Teachers rated the academic competence of the DHH students in the low-average range on the SSRS. These data encouraged the principal, the teachers, and the parents to continue the co-enrollment program, and it has now been operating for slightly more than 20 years.

DESCRIPTION OF THE CURRENT PROGRAM

Over the past 20 years, the co-enrollment program has expanded from the small group of nine DHH students to include 49 DHH students during the 2016–2017 school year. The school is an open enrollment school, meaning there are no children assigned to the school but all apply for enrollment. The school has become so desirable that typical students are selected through a lottery. DHH students within the district can enroll in the co-enrollment program without going through the lottery. A total of approximately 390 students in preschool through grade 8 were enrolled during the 2016–2107 school year. Ethnic minority students compose 72% of the student body, and 32% of students at the school qualify for reduced-price/free lunch. The 49 DHH students at this school represent slightly less than one-third of the total 130 DHH students in the district. Classrooms continue to be multi-age/multi-grade, typically encompassing three grade levels. Each elementary level co-enrollment classroom continues to have a certified general education teacher and a certified teacher of DHH students working together to meet the needs of all students. DHH and hearing students are educated together following the general education curriculum. Accommodations and modifications are made for students on an individual basis. There currently is a kindergarten, first-grade, and second-grade (K/1/2) co-enrollment classroom (kindergarten students are 5 years of age); a first-, second-, and third-grade (1/2/3) co-enrollment classroom; and a third-, fourth-, and fifth-grade (3/4/5) co-enrollment classroom. There are three additional elementary multi-age/multi-grade classrooms that are not designated co-enrollment classrooms, but students interact across classrooms while addressing reading, math, and social studies and engaging in field trips.

While there has been a designated co-enrollment preschool classroom for the past four years, the teacher and student configuration of this classroom differs from that of co-enrollment classes at the elementary level. The four-day-a-week preschool program enrolls 18 to

20 children, and approximately half of these children have some type of special need. The classroom teacher has a graduate degree in early childhood special education, is fluent in American Sign Language (ASL), and has two years of experience as a teaching assistant in a self-contained preschool program for DHH children. Two special education teaching assistants with some sign skills and an additional teaching assistant are in the classroom on an ongoing basis. An itinerant teacher of DHH provides consult support, and a school-based speech-language therapist, who is also a certified teacher of DHH, works in the classroom three of the four days for approximately an hour a day. The program was full day in previous years, but during 2016–2017 it split into two half-day sessions. One child who is hard of hearing attended the morning session and two children who are deaf attended the afternoon session. DHH children who participate in the preschool program typically move into the K/1/2 co-enrollment classroom.

Upon completing the elementary level, students with hearing loss may continue to receive services and supports within the middle school level, grades 6 through 8, in an inclusive setting incorporating resource classes. The middle school enrolls approximately 103 students and included 19 DHH students in 2016–2017. Due to school district cuts in full-time positions, there is currently one certified teacher of DHH and two special education resource teachers supporting the middle school inclusion program. Classes include students in grades 6, 7, and 8, except for mathematics, which is grade-based. Certified sign language interpreters and teaching assistants provide support as needed.

Co-enrollment classrooms are equipped with a sound field amplification system, and students may also use individual FM systems connected to hearing aids and/or cochlear implants. The school offers related services based on each student's individual needs as documented on the Individualized Education Program (IEP). Speech therapy, occupational therapy, physical therapy, adapted physical education, and audiology are available as needed. Services for students who are English Language Learners are also provided. Some service providers and school staff are fluent in sign language. The school offers music, art, and physical education for all students. Enrichment classes are offered after school in a variety of areas such as gardening, dance, ASL, and arts and crafts. The school staff also emphasize character instruction, using common vocabulary to instill character traits such as kindness, perseverance, and integrity (see Yiu et al, this volume). High academic expectations are established for all students.

Communication Philosophy

Faculty and staff implement a flexible communication philosophy. Multiple communication modalities are used to meet the individual communication needs of each student (Kirchner, this volume). The modalities include ASL, simultaneous communication (sign and spoken English together), spoken English with sign support, or spoken English alone. All instruction is delivered in spoken English and ASL/ sign language with one person typically speaking and a second, often an interpreter, signing. All students and staff are expected to develop sign language skills, and many hearing students do become proficient in sign language. Students who sign thus have a large social/communication group and a rich, dynamic social circle in which to develop peer relationships.

PERSPECTIVES OF DIFFERENT STAKEHOLDERS

To obtain teacher, interpreter, current and graduated student, and parent perspectives on the benefits and challenges of the co-enrollment setting, the chapter authors interviewed individuals using a set of questions specific to each group. Interviews with current students were no longer than 10 minutes. Interviews with teachers, interpreters, parents, and young adults who graduated from the program ranged from 20 to 50 minutes in length. Interviews were recorded, transcribed, and analyzed for common patterns and themes. Perspectives of current students are accompanied by descriptive data on their academic performance. To preserve confidentiality, pseudonyms or reference to an individual's position are used when presenting stakeholder perspectives.

Teachers

Interviews were conducted with 12 teachers who currently or previously taught in the co-enrollment classrooms. These 12 teachers included a special education preschool teacher, two general education elementary teachers, two teachers of DHH students currently working with elementary students, and two other teachers of DHH students currently working with middle school students. Four teachers previously taught in the elementary co-enrollment classrooms; two were teachers of DHH students and two were general elementary teachers. Finally, the teacher of DHH who provides services at the high school attended by a high percentage of the program students was interviewed. One of the elementary-level teachers of DHH is deaf, one is the child of deaf parents, and one has a deaf sibling. Teachers were asked to share the benefits and challenges of teacher collaboration, the greatest benefits that DHH and hearing children experience in a co-enrollment setting and a multi-grade setting, the greatest challenges they face teaching in this setting, use of amplification in the classroom, and characteristics of children for whom the co-enrollment setting may not be appropriate.

Preschool/Elementary Teachers

As teachers work in teams, multiple teachers at this level stated that supporting and respecting one another was essential to a strong functioning classroom. They felt it was beneficial to have teachers select or agree to work as teammates as opposed to assigning teachers to work with one another. Teachers noted that it can take several years of working together to jointly determine classroom routines and expectations, discipline procedures, equipment monitoring for DHH children, and instruction and grading responsibilities and procedures. While it can feel challenging to give and receive feedback from a co-teacher, maintaining a focus on learning and growing together facilitated the process of becoming a cohesive team. Almost all interviewed teachers noted that a benefit of working with a partner is that the workload is shared and that co-teachers bring different perspectives and knowledge of children to the teaching situation. Additionally, as ideas are exchanged during joint planning, creative and engaging lessons evolve in a way that would rarely occur if a single individual planned and prepared them.

Multiple teachers stated that working collaboratively in the co-enrollment program has made them better teachers. General education teachers learned specific strategies to address the needs of DHH students, including integrating more visual strategies into instruction, thinking carefully about and structuring lessons to promote language development, making use of sound field systems and FM systems, and working with interpreters. Teachers of DHH noted that they learned the general education curriculum and standards in significantly greater depth as well as a variety of strategies to organize, manage, and engage large groups of students. Working daily with a general education teacher and general education students helped teachers of DHH raise and maintain the academic and social expectations they held for DHH students. Several teachers commented that students often appreciate having multiple adults in the classroom to assist them and to connect with their individual needs and learning styles. Teachers also stated that if they had experienced a particularly exhausting day or were butting heads with a student, they could call on their co-teacher to step in and assist in specific situations.

A key point made across interviews was that all adults in the classroom (i.e., teachers, interpreters, and instructional assistants) assume responsibility for all children in the classroom (see Baker, Miller, Fletcher, Gamin, & Carty, this volume). For this to occur, all adults must be able to communicate with all children. General education elementary teachers noted that over time, they learned to sign with children. In some cases, these teachers participated in formal sign language classes, but most felt skill development occurred primarily within the classroom through interactions with the teacher of DHH, the classroom interpreters, and the DHH children who sign.

Teachers in the elementary co-enrollment classrooms identified multiple benefits of multi-grade classes. The number of DHH children at individual grade levels can vary year by year. When there are small numbers of DHH students at a specific grade level, a multi-grade setting provides classmates with a range of skill levels. Since most students remained within the same classroom for a period of three years, teachers knew students and their families intimately. Teachers of DHH and general education teachers talked about the benefit of having a group of students who knew the classroom expectations and procedures from the first day of school and could serve as role models to new classmates. Working with a student over several years means that teachers know where to begin academically with the student at the beginning of a new school year. Karla, the teacher of DHH in the K/1/2 class, stated:

> First of all, the idea that we have kids over a period of years rather than just one year is amazing. We form these really tight bonds with families and we get to know the kids really, really, really well. So, when they come back after a first year here, we know right where we left off, we know right where to start with them. We know who they are, we know what their behavior quirks are, so we've got a handle on that from the beginning, which is nice.

Janine, the teacher of DHH in the 3/4/5 class, expressed similar thoughts when asked about working in a multi-grade classroom:

> I love that. I love having that relationship with the kids for two or three years and the families. You can see this progression and you're not trying to figure out a kid for six months and then they're leaving you. It's great because there's so much time at the beginning of the year you're figuring out the kids. And even when a kid is a pain, it's really nice because you know you have to do something and build a relationship because you've got them for three years. It's not like, "I've only got, like, four months more and then I can pass it off to the next teacher."

Teachers at this school felt that family involvement is essential to the success of all students. The multi-grade classrooms allow teachers to develop in-depth relationships with families that extend over several years and facilitate parental involvement and support.

While multi-grade classrooms demand knowledge and juggling of three levels of curriculum, teachers felt that such classrooms provided for flexible groupings that allowed students to work and progress at individual skill levels. Students can work on content at higher or lower grade levels without being viewed as "behind" or "ahead" by classmates. Multiple teachers commented that several students had repeated first grade to strengthen skills and that retention in the multi-grade setting did not seem to result in the stigma students might experience in single-grade settings.

All teachers talked about the benefit of the peer support or teaching that they observe within their multi-grade classrooms. They noted that it is especially beneficial when students with higher language skills mentor or assist peers with limited language. Jackie, a general education teacher, said that providing students with instruction on how to teach a concept to a classmate may be necessary, as she has observed an initial tendency to do the work for the peer rather than to explain what needs to occur. To help students learn to share instructional strategies, she reminds students to think about how they learned a specific skill or concept.

> "How did you learn it? What was your next step? First you did this and second you did that." And that takes a little bit of time, but once they have it and then they go and help somebody sound out the word, Ca-li-for-nia, for their journal writing and they remind them, "Oh, it's a state, it's gotta start with a capital C" and you've got the best tutor ever right next to them and they're remembering all those conventions they need to remember. Or that second grader might know, "I know where to look up the word California. Let's find the conventional spelling instead of just having to sound it out."

All teachers at this level identified multiple benefits of the co-enrollment program for DHH and hearing students. DHH students have the continual presence of hearing students who are producing typical language and engaging in grade-level academics. Both general education and DHH teachers stated that their DHH students are highly motivated to read the same types and levels of books as their hearing classmates and to produce written work with sentences and paragraphs of a comparable length and complexity. Karla, the K/1/2 teacher of DHH who taught in self-contained, resource room, and itinerant settings prior to working in a co-enrollment classroom, noted, "I'm a total convert to the co-enrollment, and I was after that first year because the exposure to real-world models who are achieving at grade level is a bigger motivator than anything I could ever say to my students, anything, ever."

Hearing students can bring richer background knowledge and more varied experiences to the classroom, and these are shared with DHH classmates during large- and small-group activities as well as during individual conversations. Multiple teachers stated that after having been in a co-enrollment classroom, DHH students view themselves as capable of doing the same things that their hearing classmates do. Hearing students in co-enrollment classrooms learn to sign, and multiple teachers noted that watching the interpreters and seeing, as well as hearing, the content presented facilitates the academic achievement and especially the vocabulary development of many hearing students.

DHH children educated within self-contained classes may have a very small number of classmates. While all children within the setting may effectively communicate with one another, the small numbers may mean a limited number of peers with similar academic levels and with similar interests, or even a limited number of peers within a specific age span or of a specific gender. Within typical mainstream settings, there may be only one DHH child, or very few DHH children, within the same school. The co-enrollment classes at this school enroll approximately equal numbers of children at each of the three grade levels within the multi-grade classes and strive to have a ratio of one-third DHH students and two-thirds hearing students. Classrooms enroll 26 to 30 students so everyone can typically find others with similar interests and skill levels, thus encouraging the social inclusion of all students.

This school includes a high number of individuals able to communicate directly with DHH children and adults who sign. A former office manager, the parent of a deaf child, was fluent in ASL, as was a former computer teacher who was hard of hearing, and the current principal is a former teacher of DHH. DHH teachers and multiple general education teachers sign, there are multiple interpreters, and all children within co-enrollment classrooms develop sign skills. After teaching in the 1/2/3 co-enrollment classroom for 12 years, Lauren, the Deaf teacher of DHH, stated that deaf parents found many individuals at the school willing to communicate with them and considered the school culturally friendly toward them. This encourages Deaf parents to enroll their hearing or DHH children in the school and to fully participate in the Parent Teacher Association, school fundraising efforts, and classroom field trips and to volunteer at the school. The presence of deaf children of deaf adults immediately provides both hearing and DHH students with high-level sign skills to emulate. Additionally, these children and their parents bring understanding of Deaf culture to the classroom that benefits hearing peers as well as DHH classmates, who typically have hearing parents.

Many DHH students use amplification, either hearing aids, cochlear implants, or both. Within the co-enrollment program, use of amplification is not considered unusual, and some young hearing students, particularly kindergarten age, asked if they could have hearing aids and/or FM systems. One mother who is an audiologist and had a particularly insistent child "created" a hearing aid for her daughter to wear, which she did for half of her kindergarten year. When asked by hearing children why they couldn't have a hearing aid or why some of their classmates did wear hearing aids or cochlear implants, teachers explained that some people need to wear glasses to help them see better and some people need hearing aids to help them hear better. Teachers repeatedly noted that the ongoing opportunities to play, work, and learn together result in hearing and DHH students who do not view themselves as different from one other, but rather consider everyone to have similarities and differences.

Use of FM systems is relatively consistent at the elementary level as elementary teachers can easily remind students about and monitor use of the FM system. Teachers at all levels expressed frustration with equipment breakdowns. Budget cuts at the district level resulted in only a single audiologist to serve the approximately 130 DHH preschool to high school students across the school district. While all teachers stated that the audiologist is outstanding, there are delays in getting equipment evaluated and repaired. These issues are not unique to a co-enrollment program but are experienced in a variety of educational settings.

When asked about the characteristics of students who might not fit a co-enrollment classroom or for whom this may not be the preferred setting, teachers typically hesitated before providing a response. Karla noted:

> We've had pretty much the gamut. We had a student that was multi-handicapped in a wheelchair, deaf/blind, to someone who barely had a hearing loss and would pass as hearing if you didn't know, so we've had the whole gamut. I will say that we have some students that have had some difficulty if they can't maintain visual attention to a signed message because this is a really busy room.

This teacher described some DHH students with significant visual attention issues and noted that she initially thought they might benefit more from a smaller setting. However, she observed that while these students often seemed lost during their first year in the classroom, by the second year, they could follow the interpreters and function appropriately within the classroom. Courtney, the current speech-language pathologist who is also a teacher of DHH, noted that if a DHH student needs to communicate through sign and the parents are not signing or learning to effectively communicate with their child, teachers may suggest a setting where everyone communicates exclusively in sign to provide more intensive language support.

Middle School Teachers

The middle school component of this school (grades 6, 7, and 8) includes approximately 103 students, of whom 19 are DHH. While most of the DHH students within the middle school program have completed kindergarten through fifth grade within the co-enrollment classes, each year there are typically several students who transfer from the state school for the deaf, which is located within the same city. Middle school students receive instruction in four required content subjects (science, language arts, social studies, and math) and six elective course options. Each course is taught by a specific teacher with five classes operating concurrently, each class including approximately 20 students. At the end of a class period, students move to another class and thus another teacher. To meet our definition of a co-enrollment program, a teacher of DHH would need to co-teach with the general education teacher in at least the four required content courses. The middle school had a strong co-enrollment program in the past, but due to budget cuts, federal changes in teacher certification that required middle school teachers to be certified in a specific content area, and difficulties finding teachers of DHH with additional certification to teach a specific content area, there is currently only a single full-time teacher of DHH, Alison, working at this level. A second teacher of DHH, Pauline, splits her time between teaching the middle school "student court," the sixth-grade ASL elective, and addressing social studies instruction with elementary classes. Alison described the middle school program as a full inclusion program but does not consider it currently to function as a co-enrollment program. The principal and teaching staff are working to increase the number of DHH teachers within the middle school so that a co-enrollment program can again operate at this level. The following describes how Alison provides a full inclusion experience and elucidates challenges when a program has too few teachers of DHH children.

As the only full-time middle school teacher of DHH, Alison feels that she must focus most of her time on DHH students with the most severe needs. She groups these students together and travels with them from class to class. Additionally, she provides a one-hour resource class four days a week that includes most of her DHH students. Within the resource class, she addresses academic content approximately 50% of the time and self-advocacy skills, especially appropriate use of interpreters, the remaining 50% of the time. Alison also helps manage and troubleshoot sound field systems and student amplification and FM systems in the middle school classrooms. The many responsibilities assumed by this single teacher, in addition to writing IEPs for all middle school DHH students, significantly limit opportunities to plan and co-teach with general education teachers.

At the middle school level, multi-grade refers to grades 6, 7, and 8. Alison expressed some concerns about multi-grade classrooms at this level, primarily because she is the only full-time DHH teacher and because the middle school sometimes has a limited number of interpreters. As noted previously, Alison groups students with the highest level of need so that she can accompany this group to their classes. Because the total number of middle school students is small, this grouping can result in close to 50% of students in a specific class being students with a hearing loss. Alison has observed that when close to 50% of the students in a classroom are DHH students with significant academic needs, the pace of the class often slows and the level of academic content being delivered is reduced.

While most of the middle school hearing students come through the elementary program and readily engage in conversational exchanges with their DHH classmates, Alison noted that by eighth grade, content-specific vocabulary and the language associated with advanced concepts make it increasingly difficult for students to directly discuss and work collaboratively on curricular content. Interpreters can facilitate content-based discussions between members of small groups, but a shortage of interpreters can limit skill- or interest-based grouping within classes. Pauline observed that while hearing and deaf students regularly interact with one another both within and outside of the classroom, there is an increase in friendships between individuals with the same hearing status compared to what occurs at the elementary level.

When asked about her students' use of amplification, Alison quickly responded,

> They wear it. There are maybe two or three "frequent fliers" that have an excuse, but I think of the total 19 kids here, because there are so many kids in this building, it's not a "thing" here. If you were at a school that you were one of only two or three, then it may be a thing, but here, it's really not. Really, it's the environment of our school. If you don't have it (amplification), people recognize it and say, "Hey, where's that . . .?" and you actually have to deal with that question as opposed to the alternative.

While students do use their FM systems when they are in the resource class with Alison and when they are with the speech-language therapist, she noted that use of FM systems in other classes is not as consistent. At the middle school level, students change classes and teachers throughout the day. Students must take their personal FM unit to each class and switch to the appropriate channel and then connect with the teacher's transmitter. Alison stated that this can feel cumbersome and daunting for students. When describing the use of FM systems, she stated:

> I definitely think that if the teacher doesn't make it a priority, the kids don't either, and they'll just follow that lead. They know when they come to me they have to have it and we don't have to spend class time on it. Mine's sitting right there [transmitter], so they just connect as they walk in. I don't have to say, "Oh, who's got their . . .?" I don't have to do that. That's because that's the expectation.

To increase use of FM systems in all classes, Alison is encouraging general education teachers to designate time during their initial class bell work for students to connect with teacher transmitters. Establishing this routine across all classes would prompt teachers and students to use the FM system consistently.

At the middle school level, a key self-advocacy focus is learning to use an interpreter appropriately. While interpreters at the elementary level function as instructional assistants and interpreters, both hearing and DHH students at the middle school must learn to work with interpreters in a more adult manner. Pauline noted that both groups of students learn that interpreters involved in student-to-student or student-to-teacher conversations keep shared information confidential. Alison said that within her resource class she makes use of role playing and actual situations she observes in classrooms to help students develop strategies to advocate for appropriate communication access:

> It's a lot of acting, a lot of in-the-moment situations. It's me bringing back what I noticed in class. "I noticed that you walked up to the teacher and you stood there and you looked around because there was no interpreter by your side. In that moment, you needed to say something to the teacher; you expected a human to know what you wanted and to come up to you ready to go, ready to sign for you." It's a fun, safe environment and I just solicit, "OK, raise your hand: what would you have done differently?" and allow them to help each other out. The interpreters are there (present during the resource class) so we can talk to them and say, "Personally, as a professional, how would you like this? You've been at the high school; how does it go there?" and we just have to have a real-life conversation.

The teacher of DHH at the high school noted that she continues to place a strong emphasis on appropriate use of an interpreter and further development of self-advocacy skills. While there are only 103 students in the middle school, the high school that a significant number of these students attend enrolls approximately 3,000 students. This means that the general education high school teachers instruct substantially more students than the teachers at the middle school, so DHH students must assume a higher level of independence to successfully access presented content.

Interpreters

Three of the interpreters working within the elementary-level co-enrollment classrooms were interviewed to learn about their roles and responsibilities and to understand their perspectives on the efficacy, benefits, and challenges of the co-enrollment setting. All three met the minimum education and interpreter certification requirements for the school district. One of these interpreters held an undergraduate degree in educational interpreting.

Two interpreters are assigned to each elementary-level classroom with a floater between classrooms. Classroom teams determine the individual roles each member will assume each day. When asked to describe the responsibilities they assume, all three interpreters stated that in addition to interpreting for teachers and students, they provide language support to both DHH and hearing students in one-on-one as well as small-group situations. Interpreters may repeat or rephrase an instruction, explain a concept, or scaffold language to support comprehension of vocabulary new to a specific student. Interpreters are strong members of the teaching team within each classroom and thus have knowledge of classroom curriculum, procedures, and the educational and social abilities and needs of all students. Interpreters at the elementary level will assume the role of instructional assistant and conduct small-group activities planned by the teachers. Interpreters may also assist with the monitoring of classroom amplification and conduct minor troubleshooting of hearing aids, cochlear implants, and FM systems. As the school is located near a university interpreter-preparation program, classroom interpreters may serve as mentors for interpreters in training. Classroom interpreters may be called on to interpret for students during after-school activities as well as during the school day. Interpreters are available to students during lunch and recess times, but they are infrequently called on in these situations because of the many hearing students at the school who can sign with DHH students.

When asked about their view of multi-grade classrooms, all three interpreters support this approach. Maria felt that the multi-age model boosts the academic performance of all students and motivates them to become independent learners. Both Jamie and Maria commented that they observe the older students serving as strong role models for the younger ones and that younger students are very receptive to the support provided by their older classmates.

All three interpreters believe that the co-enrollment setting is beneficial to both DHH and hearing students, especially in the development of communication and academic skills. Rosie stated that all students, DHH, hearing, and children of deaf adults (CODAs), model and learn language from each other. She feels that in the multi-grade co-enrollment program, there are fewer social problems such as segregation, bullying, racial tension, or negative attitudes about having to repeat a grade. Maria feels that the co-enrollment program prepares DHH students for the real world as they are exposed to the same high expectations as their hearing peers, learn to use an interpreter, and are taught to advocate for themselves. Hearing students learn to accept and support peers of various abilities, communication modalities, and cultures.

Maria stated that both deaf and hearing parents are supportive of the co-enrollment program and that "this is a tight-knit family."

The only concern these interpreters shared about the co-enrollment setting was the inability of most substitute interpreters to understand or assume their roles within the classroom. They commented that substitute interpreters do not always understand the importance of functioning as a classroom team and often do not want to step out of the role of "interpreter" to address the language needs of DHH and hearing students or to work within instructional support situations.

Students

Five students currently participating in co-enrollment classrooms and four students who graduated from the middle school and are now attending college or are employed were interviewed. All students were interviewed by a familiar educator about their experiences within the co-enrollment classrooms. This section presents the results of these interviews as well as data addressing the academic performance of the students currently enrolled in the program.

Current Students

Bradley, who has a hearing loss, was in the K/1/2 classroom; Melanie and Caden, two hearing students who have DHH siblings or parents, were in the 3/4/5 classroom; and Damian and Deidra, two DHH students, were in the middle school (6/7/8 classroom). Students were asked questions such as their feelings about having two teachers in class, how and if they use the interpreters, and strategies they use when they do not understand what is being communicated by peers and staff. Additionally, they were asked to share about their class work groups and recess playmates.

Students liked having two teachers in their classrooms. They stated that having two teachers reduced their wait time when seeking assistance and said that their teachers helped each other. All students said that they used the interpreter to learn word meanings and to improve their understanding of concepts being taught. In addition, all stated that they communicated in spoken English as well as sign language. Regarding access to a sound field system, a student who is hearing replied, "It helps everyone hear better." When asked what strategies they used in class when they did not understand another's communication attempt, students shared the following: asking the person to slow down or repeat, requesting an interpreter, and raising their hand. One student stated that the class rule was, "Ask three kids; then, if they don't know, then ask a teacher."

Four of the five students said they work and play with hearing and DHH students. When asked to identify his friends, one of the students who is DHH listed all students who are hearing. A student in the 3/4/

5 class who is hearing stated, "Deaf people can do what hearing people can do but sometimes they just have a hard time talking."

Of the DHH students who were interviewed, one has two cochlear implants, one has one cochlear implant, and one has two hearing aids. When asked how they took care of their amplification, they unanimously stated they would change their batteries if they were dead, and if they did not have batteries, they would watch the interpreter. Both middle school students kept extra batteries in their backpacks.

Deidra, who is DHH and consistently wears her amplification, explained that she often forgets she has a hearing loss because communication with teachers and classmates is simple. "It's a great school and sometimes I feel like I don't have my hearing aids in 'cuz everyone signs." Students liked having multi-grade classrooms and working with DHH and hearing peers, and they like learning and "learning how to be kind." One of the middle school students stated the importance of having a middle school resource class for the DHH students to deepen their understanding of concepts presented in core academic classes.

The results of the 2017 annual statewide achievement tests in English and math are provided in Table 14.1 for the interviewed students enrolled in grade 3 and above. Results are reported by proficiency levels with four levels possible: highly proficient, proficient, partially proficient, and minimally proficient. Proficiency levels are defined by state-determined cutoff points on scale scores. Deidra is the only student who scored minimally proficient, and it should be noted that she has a learning disability in addition to her hearing loss. Bradley was in second grade, and second-grade students do not participate in the statewide achievement testing. Classroom teachers conduct the Dynamic Indicators of Basic Early Literacy Skills (DIBELS) with students in second grade, and Bradley's end-of-year composite score showed that he was meeting the benchmark for his grade level. His performance was comparable to 77% of the 30 second-grade students at the school. The provided achievement data are not representative of the performance of all students in the co-enrollment classes but provide a context for the statements and opinions expressed by the interviewed students.

Graduated Students

Interviews were conducted with four young adults who had been students in the co-enrollment program and graduated from the middle school. The co-enrollment program extended through middle school when these young adults attended the school. Three of the previous students, Cathie, Jason, and Kelly, are hearing and one, Edward, is DHH. Participation in co-enrollment classes ranged from three years to seven years for this group of students. The three hearing students have completed college degrees and are employed, while the DHH student is in the process of completing his bachelor's degree. These former

Table 14.1. Student Statewide Achievement Test Results

English Statewide Achievement Test Results, Spring 2017

Name/Hearing Status	Grade	State Exam Proficiency Level	Same-Grade Students at School					Same-Grade Students in School District				
			N	%MP	%PP	%P	%HP	N	%MP	%PP	%P	%HP
Damian/DHH	7	Proficient	33	27.3	18.2	36.4	15.2	3292	50.0	18.2	24.8	4.3
Deidra/DHH	6	Minimally Proficient	31	32.3	22.6	45.2	0	3271	50.2	22.3	23.8	1.6
Melanie/hearing	5	Proficient	36	16.7	22.2	38.9	22.2	3696	43.4	23.5	24.8	7.4
Caden/hearing	3	Partially Proficient	29	51.7	10.3	17.2	20.7	3798	52.9	12.1	25	8.7

Math Statewide Achievement Test Results, Spring 2017

Name/Hearing Status	Grade	State Exam Proficiency Level	Same-Grade Students at School					Same-Grade Students in School District				
			N	%MP	%PP	%P	%HP	N	%MP	%PP	%P	%HP
Damian/DHH	7	Partially Proficient	33	51.5	15.2	15.2	18.2	3211	65.1	14.5	11.7	8.8
Deidra/DHH	6	Minimally Proficient	31	38.7	35.5	19.4	6.5	3233	55	24.1	15.4	5.5
Melanie/hearing	5	Partially Proficient	36	27.8	22.2	30.6	19.4	3679	35.1	27.1	26.6	11.2
Caden/hearing	3	Proficient	31	29	35.5	19.4	16.1	3783	29.5	31.7	25.3	13.5

MP = Minimally Proficient; PP = Partially Proficient; P = Proficient; HP = Highly Proficient.

students were asked about the communication approaches used in the program, what they most valued about their co-enrollment experiences, how their experiences influenced what they are doing currently, what they least enjoyed about the program, and their thoughts on the essential components of the program.

All three previous students who are hearing talked about learning and using sign language daily with their DHH classmates, in the classroom as well as on the playground. Cathie and Kelly initially learned sign language by watching adults signing in the classroom and through conversing with DHH classmates. Jason moved to the school as a fourth-grade student but was not part of a co-enrollment classroom until the middle school level. He learned sign language through the ASL classes offered in middle school as well as by observing teachers and interpreters signing during classes and by interacting with DHH classmates. Jason mentioned that it was very acceptable to make mistakes when communicating in sign. Rather than being offended by or critical of mistakes, classmates, teachers, or interpreters simply provided another way to sign the message. This accepting attitude created a safe environment in which to learn and use this new language. Cathie stated that she appreciated that general education teachers were learning to sign along with the hearing students. Everyone in the classroom, adults and students, was viewed as a learner. Edward, a DHH student, commented that he signed with his classmates because everyone in his classes could sign. These former students felt that it is essential for all students and all teachers within co-enrollment classes to learn to sign so that everyone can communicate directly with one another.

The sign competence of the hearing students who began signing during elementary school became quite advanced. The novelty of the co-enrollment program has prompted visits by individuals from many different settings. When a deaf professor visiting one of the elementary classrooms was asked to identify a DHH student, he observed for several minutes and then selected a hearing student. When informed that he'd selected a hearing student, he stated that she must have deaf parents. The teacher needed to call the student over to talk with the professor before he was convinced she had no deaf family members but had learned to sign through the co-enrollment program. This student was Kelly, and when interviewed for this chapter, she shared that as an elementary student, she sometimes understood concepts better in ASL than in English. A short magazine article on the co-enrollment program included a picture of Kelly signing to her teacher. The caption on the picture read, "What was that sign? Kelly, could you please re-sign that?" Kelly remembered asking her teacher, "What does 're-sign' mean?" Her teacher showed her "SIGN + AGAIN," to which she replied, "Okay, that makes sense."

All hearing graduates mentioned that they do occasionally have opportunities to use sign language when interacting with DHH individuals within their employment settings. Cathie also talked about using ASL when she meets with long-term DHH friends from the co-enrollment program. Jason explained that when interacting with DHH individuals, he is careful to face them and watch facial expressions to determine whether the information he is conveying is understood. He attributes use of these communication strategies to his participation in the co-enrollment environment.

When asked about their experiences in multi-grade classrooms, previous students enjoyed being able to work at varying levels and with diverse groups of classmates. They felt the multi-grade setting allowed them to learn at their own pace—to advance and feel challenged in some areas, to move at a "typical" pace in others, or to proceed somewhat slower when addressing a specific skill or area of content they found difficult. It was an accepted part of the classroom that students could work in different ways and at varying levels. Cathie stated, "The program I feel is very well tailored to each student. I thought it challenged me, but at the same time supported me . . . I think having the different grades helps create a better learning atmosphere because of the age span; there is more to pull from." Cathie additionally noted that as students move up in age within a specific classroom, they become confident learners by helping younger peers, something she considered "a really great aspect of multi-age classrooms."

The former students were asked to share what they most valued about their experiences in the co-enrollment program. Cathie, a future elementary school teacher, responded, "Giving students a holistic education, looking at each student as an individual, which I will want to do in my own classroom." Edward shared, "I would say the program prepared me academically for whatever I wanted to do so as a software engineering major, I am thankful to the program for giving me the resources that I needed." Both Kelly and Jason focused on how the program fostered not only acceptance of people with varying abilities but an attitude that people are more like them than different from them. Jason said that it felt very normal for DHH and hearing students to learn together in the co-enrollment program. "There's no separation between this person and that person, kind of the same interaction. I don't think I would have gotten that if I wouldn't have grown up that way through the program." Kelly stated, "It helped me understand different people are in the world and they're not bad or weird, they just are."

Parents

Ten parents of students who are currently attending the school program and parents of students who have attended this school but are now in college and/or graduated from college were interviewed. Four parents have DHH students currently enrolled in the co-enrollment program and one parent has several hearing children enrolled. Two parents (a parent and a grandparent) have hearing children at this school. Three parents have DHH children who are in college or graduated from college but attended the co-enrollment program for all or a portion of their K-8 education, and one parent has a hearing child who previously attended. Parents were asked about their reasons for enrolling their children in this school, what they hoped their children would gain, what they appreciated about the co-enrollment model and school, and what they might say to parents considering this education model for their child who has a hearing loss.

Several parents with DHH children stated that they moved to this city (state) because of the poor educational opportunities within the state where they previously resided. Parents wanted all their children to attend the same school and wanted their children with a hearing loss to have peers who also had hearing losses. Parents commented that this school and its staff demonstrated high academic and social expectations for all students and the school environment was open and welcoming. As one parent stated, "It [is] an intimate place. A welcoming place." Another said, "I love the social and emotional intelligence and the kindness curriculum." Parents hoped their children would make friendships, would have easy access to learning, and would see families that looked like theirs. They hoped their children with a hearing loss would be accepted into the community and, naturally, that their children would improve their academic and communication skills.

By parent report, all students improved their academic skills and increased their level of confidence and ability to communicate with hearing and DHH peers and adults. All children developed friendships with both hearing and DHH peers, and their communications skills improved significantly.

The most frequent response regarding what parents appreciated about the co-enrollment program was the positive community environment and the many ways for family members to be involved. Second, they appreciated the dedicated staff; as one parent explained, "From the outside, it seemed like the staff really worked together as a group and there was a sense that people like working there and then this reflects how they treat the children because they like coming to work." Lastly, a parent of a hearing child valued the focus on individualizing instruction for all students, not just those with IEPs.

When asked how they would respond to parents of a child with a hearing loss who was considering a co-enrollment program, interviewees replied they would encourage the parents to observe the co-enrollment classrooms. These parents stated they would explain the rich diversity of the school and the successful way in which the students, DHH and hearing, effectively learn and communicate with each other.

CONCLUSION

Teachers, interpreters, students, and parents all felt that both DHH and hearing students benefited academically and socially from their participation in the co-enrollment program. In the following section, we offer advice from all stakeholders of this co-enrollment community to others desiring to establish or maintain a successful co-enrollment program.

Establishment and Maintenance of a Co-Enrollment Program

To create a successful co-enrollment program, it is important to identify the motivation for implementing this model, to define educational success within the model, and to be able to articulate these factors in a manner that allows all stakeholders to have a common understanding of co-enrollment and commit to implementing the model. Prior to initiating the co-enrollment program, the principal and interested teachers observed an existing program and talked with the teachers, students, and families involved in the program. This group also sought literature describing optimal programs for DHH students, especially programs that promoted full inclusion. Once a vision of how co-enrollment could occur within this setting was created, the principal and teachers spent considerable time with parents explaining the co-enrollment model, how it would be implemented, and the anticipated benefits for all students.

Now that the co-enrollment model has been operating for more than 20 years, the members of this community have identified some key elements they consider essential to the success of a co-enrollment program:

- A community composed of cohesive and like-minded parents, teaching personnel, and administrative staff at both the school and district level
- A teacher for the DHH and a general education teacher, team teaching in each co-enrolled classroom
- A critical mass of DHH students within the program
- Active parent involvement in the educational process and the school community
- Teaching staff who hold high expectations for all students
- Certified interpreters in each co-enrolled classroom
- Direct communication between all members of the classroom.

Potential Challenges

Over the years that the co-enrollment program has operated, multiple challenges have been encountered. Principals and teachers at this school have repeatedly needed to explain to district-level administrators why both a general education teacher and a teacher of DHH are essential within a co-enrollment classroom and how the co-enrollment team promotes the success of all students at costs that are comparable to or less than having DHH students within self-contained or mainstream situations with itinerant support.

In a few situations, teachers were assigned to work with one another rather than electing to work with one another. Sometimes, these matches were effective; other times, they lasted only a short time. In this school, it is typically either the general education teacher or the DHH teacher that is being hired for a specific classroom. An interview team that includes the existing teacher of a specific classroom, other teachers, and the principal and relevant support personnel facilitates creation of effective teaching teams.

When teachers begin working together, joint planning requires an extensive time commitment. Knowing this in advance can prevent frustration, inadequately prepared lessons, or role confusion within the classroom. Multiple teachers at this school said that after working together for multiple years, the amount of time needed for planning substantially declined. Administrative support for joint planning time can alleviate some of the extended after-school time needed for this process.

Lastly, the endeavor is difficult, but the members of this community feel they have created a setting where both DHH and hearing students thrive, where families are fully involved in the educational process, and where instructional staff are challenged and rewarded daily by those they serve and with whom they work. One comment that was unexpected and repeatedly stated across multiple interviewees was, "This is a magical place." A strong co-enrollment program creates an environment that magically and fully embraces a community learning to encourage and teach one another.

REFERENCES

Gresham, F. M., & Elliott, S. N. (1990). *Social Skills Rating System*. Circle Pines, MN: American Guidance Service.

Kirchner, C. J. (1994). Co-enrollment as an inclusion model. *American Annals of the Deaf, 139*(2), 163–164.

Kreimeyer, K. H., Crooke, P., Drye, C., Egbert, V., & Klein, B. (2000). Academic and social benefits of a co-enrollment model of inclusive education for deaf and hard-of-hearing children. *Journal of Deaf Studies and Deaf Education, 5,* 174–185.

McCain, K., & Antia, S. D. (2005). Academic and social status of hearing, deaf and hard of hearing students participating in a co-enrolled classroom. *Communication Disorders Quarterly*, 27(1), 20–32.

Metz, K. K. (2013). Academic engagement of deaf and hard of hearing students in a co- enrollment program. Doctoral dissertation. Retrieved from ERIC (ISBN: 978-1-3036-2717-0).

15

The Tucker Maxon Story: Mainstreaming in Place

Jennifer M. Hoofard, Glen C. Gilbert, Linda Goodwin, and Tamala Selke Bradham

THE HISTORY OF TUCKER MAXON SCHOOL

The Early Years

If Barbara Ann Boley ("Babs") had not contracted meningitis at the age of 15 months, Tucker Maxon School probably wouldn't exist. Babs's parents, Harvard Law School–educated attorney Paul and Margaret Boley, realized her illness had cost their child her hearing. "It was over Christmas," her mother recalled. "I bought her a music box—she just loved to talk and imitate—and when she came in, I tried to get her attention playing music. No response." The Boleys, of Portland, Oregon, began looking for educational options.

The Boleys enrolled Babs in the preschool program at the Hosford School for the Deaf, where they first met teacher Alice Maxon. Alice's mother, Florence Crandell Metcalf, founded the Hosford School for the Deaf and was principal there until her retirement in 1927. Alice replaced her mother as principal of Hosford that year (Portland Center for Hearing and Speech, 1963). According to Margaret Boley, Alice Maxon declared, "Deaf children can talk!"

Alice Maxon came from a family whose roots in deaf education ran deep. Her maternal grandfather, H. B. Crandell, who was deaf, was the first teacher at the California State School for the Deaf in Berkeley. At the time of Alice's birth, her father was superintendent of the Utah State School for the Deaf and Blind. Her mother's first experience as a teacher of the deaf was at the State School for the Deaf in Salem, Oregon. Alice's mother went on to start the Portland Day School for the Deaf in 1907, with only five students, which later would become Hosford. Starting a school for deaf children was something the Maxons knew how to do.

One summer, Alice volunteered to teach a lip reading class at a hearing center in an old building in downtown Portland where some of what were to become Tucker Maxon's founding families first met. The parents were very impressed, describing Alice Maxon as a "genius." "The kids just loved her," remembered parent Bud Monnes. That fall, Maxon went back to Hosford School. Monnes recalled, "We didn't want them to go to Hosford then because it was all sign; we wanted them to be able to talk" (Stone, 1997). When families felt the classes at Hosford were not doing enough to address their children's needs, Paul Boley set out to do something about it.

In the fall of 1947, Boley researched the few oral deaf schools in the United States, all located in the Midwest or on the East Coast. He was particularly impressed with the Wright School in New York, from where Helen Keller had graduated. But Boley's law practice was in Portland. The distance and difficult admissions policy were obstacles, leading Wright's director to suggest Boley establish his own oral school in Oregon. "The seed had been planted, and it began immediately to grow," Boley remembered (Stone, 1997). Margaret Boley started taking a correspondence course offered through the John Tracy Clinic in Los Angeles to help parents develop oral communication in their children who are deaf. At the same time, another parent of a child who was deaf, Ellen Monnes, was finding similar support through the *Volta Review*, the periodical established in 1899 by Alexander Graham Bell. Margaret Boley remembered, "When we did get this idea of a school started, Mrs. Tracy came up, and she had a meeting up here with a whole flock of people" (Stone, 1997). According to a quote in a 1947 article in *The Oregonian* newspaper, Paul Boley argued the school "must turn out graduates, though profoundly deaf, fully equipped to hold their own in a hearing and speaking world" (Morrison, 1948).

Since other parents were supportive of the idea, Paul Boley set out to raise funds to make a small school in Oregon a reality. To that end, he approached area businessmen he knew in his work as a tax attorney, including Max Tucker, Charles McCulloch, and Herbert Templeton. Max Tucker made an offer to Boley; as Margaret Boley explained, "If we could . . . prove that a deaf child could talk, then he [Tucker] would finance it" (Stone, 1997).

With the challenge set and early funding limited, the Boleys set aside a room in their home in northeast Portland as the first school. The school took up the den, breakfast room, and a bathroom of the Boley home. Alice Maxon's husband, who was a carpenter, helped the Boleys convert the room into a functional classroom. Alice, who had taught all of the same children previously in preschool at Hosford, took a temporary leave of absence to become the school's first instructor, and Margaret Boley made lunches for the children. As Ellen Monnes reminisced, "She [Alice] liked the idea, I think, of teaching the children her way. Oh, she was so good" (Stone, 1997). Indeed, Alice Maxon was one of the first practitioners on the West Coast to employ the "oral method" (*The Oregonian*, 1974).

On January 19, 1948, the Maxon Oral School welcomed its first class, which included Babs Boley, Gordon Burdick, Judy Glenn, Daryl Justice, and Janet Monnes. By the end of that short first term, the children had made tremendous progress. According to Boley's records, the children had mastered an average of 32 of 44 elementary sounds, could say and use 25 different expressions, and had an average lip-reading vocabulary of 100 spoken words (Maxon Oral School, second school brochure). The school doubled its student roster in its second year and continued to grow.

Businessman and philanthropist Max Tucker received the proof he wanted that spring; on his first visit to the school with Charles McCulloch, 4-year-old Judy Glenn spoke her first words: "We were all working out in the rose garden and Mr. McCulloch and Mr. Tucker came to the door, and she jumped up and recognized them. And she, who had never spoken a word in her life, said, 'He is mine,'" remembered Margaret Boley (Stone, 1997). Tucker made good on his pledge with a $250,000 bequest for building a permanent school site. Alice Maxon resumed her teaching duties at Hosford School, and Hattie Harrell joined the school in 1951 as its first executive director. In speeches she gave at local service agencies and at the Seattle Child Hearing League, she said "Please, never say 'deaf and dumb' and never say 'deaf mute.' They aren't dumb and not mute. A deaf child is educationally handicapped." Alice Maxon returned to the school permanently in 1953, and Hattie Harrell was named a "Woman of Achievement" by the Quota Club of the Portland Business Women.

After temporary homes in two rented houses, the school set its sights on building a permanent home. When the founders chose the present site in southeast Portland, they met with some opposition from the neighbors. Ellen Monnes remembered, "They wanted this property, and somebody started a petition [that] they didn't want us with a lot of strange children here." Not taking such resistance sitting down, the founding families mobilized "house to house and knocked on . . . door[s]" to change opinions. Paul Boley wrote a letter to the residents describing the school, addressing the neighbors' concerns, and inviting the neighbors to visit the school at its present location. An excerpt from the letter reads:

> We think you would be amazed if you were to visit the school and see how very bright and keen these little children are, in spite of their great handicap of deafness . . . [P]eople sometimes have the false notion that a deaf child is in some manner mentally retarded or "queer." Nothing could be farther from the truth: the only difference between one of our children and the average child is that our child cannot hear. He cannot speak, either, until we teach him to do so, but in all other respects he is as normal and healthy and alert as any hearing child.

Armed with this letter, a group of Tucker Maxon mothers went door to door to meet the people who had signed the original petition to talk to them firsthand about the school:

> [We] walked through the neighborhood and explained about the school and we . . . talked to the people, and I wrote down all their addresses and wrote down who was against us and who was for us. So many told us: Well, we signed, but we're sorry we did . . . But there was only one person—one man—who voted against it a second time and he said all it would do is raise their taxes to have a school here . . . He wasn't opposed to the school. (Stone, 1997)

The first classroom building opened at 2860 SE Holgate Blvd. to a class of 18 students and was dedicated in January 1954. The school's architect, Pietro Belluschi, would later achieve world-renowned status as the designer of New York's Pan Am building (1958) and the Julliard School (1963–1969). In 1957, Tucker Maxon won an award in an industrial landscaping competition. Landscape architect Robert Walker designed the school's landscape, which was the first time northwestern plantings had received such recognition. A March 1956 storm damaged the building, pulling the roof off at the west end.

The Boley family and board chose to name the school after its benefactor, Max Tucker, and first teacher, Alice Maxon, rather than themselves. Rose Tucker, Max's wife, ran an antique shop from which all proceeds went to fund the school, and though they had no children of their own, the Tuckers were very personally involved in the school. Max Tucker, Charles McCullough, and Mr. Maxon took turns playing Santa at the school's annual Christmas party. As Bud Monnes recalls, "The kids were so . . . excited because their Santa was going to be bringing them something, and they got gifts we never would be able to afford to give those kids—they got spoiled" (Stone, 1997).

In 1960, the Tucker Maxon Oral School ushered in the new decade by graduating its first class from eighth grade: Babs Boley, Judy Glenn, and Ellen Hamaker. In the early days of the school, children who were deaf often boarded with faculty, families of other students at the school, and neighbors so that students from out of state could benefit from the innovative education the school offered. There was initially some talk of making Tucker Maxon a boarding school, and building a dormitory to accommodate deaf children from out of the area. In 1963, a second classroom building containing a gymnasium opened thanks to funds raised by the Hearing League, a group of parents and Tucker Maxon supporters. In 1965, executive director Hattie Harrell was named one of the *Portland Journal's* "10 Women of Accomplishment." Parent Jean Rodway remembered that Miss Harrell expected both parents to attend meetings with her regularly and continue the school's instruction at home: "If you didn't show up for meetings, you got a phone call from

Miss Harrell wondering why . . . You had to have a good reason, and your reason probably wasn't good enough because that was where you needed to be—with that hearing-impaired child, and whatever had to do with that child came first" (Stone, 1997). In 1967, Wallace Bruce became the school's second executive director and board member Tom McCall became governor of Oregon, ultimately serving two terms.

"Reverse Mainstreaming" Begins

When Tucker Maxon was founded in 1947, the school's plan was to educate students in deaf-only classrooms through eighth grade, and then integrate students into their local high schools. From 1963 to 1966, there was a maternal rubella epidemic in the United States, deafening more than 8,000 newborns while they were in utero. According to former executive director Pat Stone, the "Northwest was one of the hardest hit" regions (P. Stone, personal communication, April 13, 2017). In the late 1960s, executive director Wallace Bruce and teachers noticed that some children with good spoken language skills were ready to mainstream into public school classrooms before high school, but some school districts did not feel equipped to take them any earlier. In 1969–1970, Tucker Maxon School received a grant to place four or five children who were deaf or hard of hearing (DHH) into a junior high school in Beaverton (a Portland suburb), allowing teacher Jim Rawlins to take a leave from Tucker Maxon to transfer to that school in order to support the student graduates from Tucker Maxon through junior high (*Tucker Maxon: Celebrating 60 Years*, 2012).

With the success of this program, Tucker Maxon started to explore mainstreaming elementary students sooner. In 1968, the children afflicted with rubella while in utero started entering schools. Students were showing up at Tucker Maxon at ages 5, 6, and 7 who had never been fitted for hearing aids. At that point, the student body swelled to about 75 children, all in deaf-only classrooms ranging from ages 5 to 14 (C. Soland, personal communication, April 14, 2002).

In 1973, Tucker Maxon's first mainstreaming program began, when the school partnered with the private Holy Family School to help support students' transitions to other schools. Two Tucker Maxon teachers transferred to Holy Family School to teach one class each that combined deaf students with typically hearing students and to provide academic, speech, and language support for the classes of students with hearing loss. Later, partnerships with other parochial schools followed, with Tucker Maxon teachers supporting students with hearing loss at All Saints, St. Ignatius, and St. Stephen's schools in Portland. Gail Schiel, who would later run Tucker Maxon's Parent/Infant program, remembers that decisions about when to mainstream a child with hearing loss into a regular classroom were made solely based on academics, with little regard for developing the social skills that would help that child negotiate a new, hearing environment (G. Schiel, personal communication, April 27, 2017). Those transitions to mainstream schools were not always as successful as they might have been without the accompanying social skills needed to navigate a student's new setting.

Adding Early Intervention

The 1970s ushered in the Civil Rights movement in America, including rights for people with disabilities. The U.S. Rehabilitation Act of 1973 was ratified by Congress over President Richard Nixon's veto, prohibiting discrimination in any federal program against people with disabilities (Solomon, 2012, p. 28). In 1975, the Education of All Handicapped Children Act (Public Law 94-142) passed in the United States, mandating free and appropriate education for all children with disabilities, instituting the Individualized Education Program (IEP), and stipulating provision of educational services in the "least restrictive environment" appropriate to the child's needs. That same year, Tucker Maxon became one of the first private schools to be approved and registered by the Oregon State Department of Education. Tucker Maxon added an audiologist that year and began offering free hearing tests to children under 3. One year later, Tucker Maxon lost founding benefactor Rose E. Tucker, who passed away after serving on the board of directors for nearly 30 years. With that ending came a new beginning, as Tucker Maxon began offering early intervention services to families of children under age 4 through the David De Weese Hearing Center at Providence Hospital. The early intervention program for infants and toddlers (known then as the Parent/Infant program) moved to the Tucker Maxon campus two years later in 1978 when Patrick Stone, the son of deaf parents, became the school's new executive director.

Gail Schiel, who would eventually run Tucker Maxon's Parent/Infant program, moved to a new home around this time and her daughter became best friends with a neighbor girl who was deaf and attended Tucker Maxon. Gail joined a book club with the child's mother that was reading Joanne Greenberg's novel *In This Sign*, about a couple who were deaf. The neighbor asked the school's new director, Pat Stone, to speak to her book group about his experience growing up with deaf parents. Stone was upset at the novel's depiction of the deaf couple, believing it did not ring true to his recollections. During the discussion of the novel, Schiel, who was an undergraduate at Portland State University (PSU) at the time, asked Stone if she could visit his classroom. By the time she graduated from PSU, Tucker Maxon had established a graduate teacher training program with Pacific University to educate teachers of the deaf. The primary instructors for the program were all Tucker Maxon teachers, and students fulfilled their practicum requirement at the school. Schiel graduated from the program and was hired by Tucker Maxon as a teacher of the deaf.

During this period, the idea of early identification and intervention started to catch on nationwide. Dr. David Watson, who became director of the Neonatal Intensive Care Unit at Legacy Emmanuel Hospital in Portland, had a son with significant hearing loss and was looking for a neighborhood preschool in which to enroll his son. Schiel evaluated neighborhood preschools but was not convinced they would meet the needs of a transitioning child who was deaf, so she began looking around for better placements. Watson and two other children transitioned into mainstream preschools and did well, but the new placements required a good deal of travel for the Tucker Maxon teachers who supported them. One of the children enrolled at a small private preschool called Childswork, and Schiel was very impressed with a teacher there named Shannon Newmark.

Informal Co-Enrollment Begins

While the move to mainstream deaf children as early as preschool was exciting, it was also concerning from a financial point of view, since students would be leaving Tucker Maxon. In 1984, Childswork was losing its rented space. Newmark's approach was revolutionary at the time, focusing on developing social skills and conflict resolution in children to produce "socially competent" individuals. Michele Volk, who would eventually succeed Newmark at Childswork, called Newmark a "brilliant woman who met children where they were, and believed in the best in every child" (M. Volk, personal communication, April 25, 2017). Schiel remembered Newmark as a wonderful teacher, masterful at instilling problem-solving skills in young children. Stone spent a morning at her school observing how the children related to each other and was so impressed he returned to convince the board to rent space to Childswork at Tucker Maxon. Some on the board were resistant to the idea of bringing a preschool for children with typical hearing onto the Tucker Maxon campus, feeling that the move would take away from the school's mission to educate children with hearing loss. However, Stone ultimately prevailed in convincing the board, and Newmark moved Childswork into the second building on campus. As Schiel remembered, at that time, inclusion programs did not exist at the preschool level.

Schiel recalled that the first experiments with integrating children with hearing loss into the general education classrooms at Childswork did not go well, as children with hearing loss seemed little more than visitors in mainstream classes. Sarah Theberge, a teacher at Childswork at the time, remembered two deaf children (supported by Schiel) coming in for "choice time" in the Childswork classroom of 18 kids. The goal was for the children to belong to the larger group, and staff soon realized the children with hearing loss needed to be there at least two of the three days to achieve a sense of cohesion and belonging in the class, rather than just for "choice time" every day. It was something of a social experiment to see how deaf children would learn to socialize with typically hearing children.

The first real incarnation of the co-enrolled program involved six deaf children who were in a small, segregated classroom on Tuesdays and Thursdays, who integrated into larger Childswork classrooms of 14 to 16 kids on Monday, Wednesdays, and Fridays. Teacher Linda Goodwin, who became the school's principal in 2014, started her career at Tucker Maxon at this time. As a new teacher of the deaf who did not yet have her own children, Linda recalls an enlightening model that helped her realize that her expectations of her students with hearing loss were too low. Linda's realization was prompted by the classroom inclusion of typically hearing peers with whom to compare her deaf and hard-of-hearing students' development. It was a good refresher for teachers of the deaf regarding what typical child development should look like, and it allowed them to adjust their expectations of their students with hearing loss. With co-enrollment, teachers realized they had been coddling their deaf students. As Goodwin remembered, "I thought my expectations of my students who were deaf was high, until I saw what they were capable of!" (L. Goodwin, personal communication, March 15, 2017).

Other teachers were initially more skeptical. Teachers of the deaf were concerned about the noise level in a larger classroom. If a child without good language skills due to his or her hearing loss was placed into a blended classroom prematurely, that acoustic environment would not be conducive to his or her learning. Research shows that high noise levels make it difficult for any child to learn, but this is especially true for a child with hearing loss (Neergaard, 2016). Later classes were co-taught by both a general, early childhood teacher and a certified teacher of the deaf, but it cost a great deal to have two teachers in a classroom with few students. In those early days of blended classrooms, the first class integrated five typically hearing children with two children with hearing loss. Other classes experimented with the ratio, integrating a few hearing kids into a larger group of five deaf and hard-of-hearing children. Not everyone was pleased with how the Childswork model worked for some children. The model worked well for children who did not have behavioral issues, allowing them to better develop spoken language in a less-restrictive environment with hearing peers, but was not as successful for students with behavioral issues or other disabilities (see Baker, Miller, Fletcher, Gamin, & Carty, this volume).

Initially, the motivation for the parents of hearing students to choose to have their child integrated into a classroom with children with hearing loss was the charitable belief that their child would "help" the DHH child. Soon parents realized the underlying benefit of small class size and higher teacher ratios for their typically-developing child and saw that the benefits of co-enrollment were reciprocal to both groups of children. Parents of children who were shy, or perhaps had a learning disability, as well as siblings of children who were deaf and whose families already knew the school, were the first typically hearing children to enroll in the integrated classrooms. Once established, the program would draw typically developing children from the school's working-class neighborhood in southeast Portland (P. Fortier, personal communication, April 5, 2017).

Schiel remembered that by the mid-1990s, Childswork offered eight different classrooms, employed 10 staff members, and integrated 15 children with hearing loss into classes with 100 neighborhood children with typical hearing on Mondays, Wednesdays, and Fridays with a teacher of the deaf, and on their own for specialized instruction on Tuesdays and Thursdays. Eventually, after parents lobbied her, Newmark added a kindergarten component to the program, which worked well, as Portland Public Schools did not offer full-day kindergarten at that time. The kindergarten also provided a bridge for students to continue at Tucker Maxon for elementary school.

Those were heady years at Tucker Maxon. It was a learning experience for everyone involved to see how deaf children would learn to socialize with hearing children. For faculty, the model demanded a great deal. For experienced teachers, it required they not develop tunnel vision and view education solely through the lens through which they had been educated, whether as an early childhood specialist, general education teacher, or teacher of the deaf. The co-enrollment model, as first conceived, was resource intensive, requiring a general education teacher and a teacher of the deaf in a classroom of just seven children. It also required a tremendous commitment from teachers, including continuing education for staff to stay up to date on the latest pedagogical theories and techniques as well as technological advances in amplification. Everyone involved could see how the co-enrollment model held huge potential, but it was also trickier to implement and was not always successful, as different constituencies had different goals and priorities. Should every student at the school be of equal importance, or should the DHH children be a higher priority? Passionate teachers came from both sides, from the early childhood/general education perspective as well as those trained as teachers of the deaf.

As Schiel remembered, training for teachers of the deaf at the time was very teacher-directed and emphasized the primacy of the one-on-one relationship between the teacher and the child. The philosophy informing that intensive work was a belief that individual attention is what deaf children need to develop language. During this period, children were not being diagnosed with hearing loss until age 2 or older and often did not receive amplification equipment sometimes until age 3 or older, whether with hearing aids or by qualifying for an early cochlear implant, so practitioners saw that intensive one-on-one work as necessary. By contrast, this was also the period when research in early childhood education (ECE) was emerging that instructed teachers to follow the child's lead, to make comments instead of asking questions, and to generally be less directive with children in the classroom. Schiel remembers the ECE teachers at Childswork being ahead of the Tucker Maxon teachers in implementing that research into classrooms, making lots of materials available to children, allowing "choice time" during the day for child-directed play, and putting into place other innovations (see Kirchner, this volume; Ringwald-Frimerman, Ingber & Most, this volume). Schiel recalled that, by contrast, the segregated classrooms for children with hearing loss were much more structured, and it was a big adjustment for Tucker Maxon teachers to adapt to the newer classroom model. But soon the schedule of Tucker Maxon classrooms began to mirror that of the Childswork day, with time for snacks, "choice time," cleanup, and circle time. This "child-centered, play-based" approach remains in place to this day at the school.

In addition, teachers trained as ECE specialists needed to learn how to lower their language level to that of the children with hearing loss, or slightly above their level. They also needed to learn to not focus solely on the children with hearing loss in the classroom, which set them apart from the group, calling attention to their disability. While teachers of the deaf were shifting their mindset to become a play partner to children, Schiel reported the hardest part for a mainstream teacher was to adapt her language level to slightly above the deaf or hard-of-hearing child's level. This technique was also something Schiel taught to parents of newly-diagnosed children with hearing loss. She contended it is natural to speak to children at the child's cognitive level, and if the child does not have the language to respond appropriately, to give up and retreat into silence, or to communicate with gestures to a point that leaves little room for language development in the child.

Children with typical hearing also had to learn to adjust their communication for a child with hearing loss by rephrasing things, moving closer, or reducing their language level to that of the DHH child while he or she worked to catch up. Teachers of the deaf, who were used to getting DHH children's attention when working with them one on one, had to teach students with hearing loss to pay attention to the teacher when he or she was not focused solely on them. Children with hearing loss were not trained to pay attention in this way and so would tune out and miss information that could be learned when a teacher was problem-solving with another child. Teachers of the deaf noticed, in less-directive circumstances, that DHH children were learning from other children's interactions with teachers, which effectively served to decentralize the classroom, disrupting the traditional role of the teacher as the sole arbiter of knowledge. Thus, not only did the teachers of the deaf have to learn the less-directive orientation, but they also had to learn to direct the attention of their DHH students to those moments of problem-solving between teachers and other students so that DHH students could benefit.

FM systems, in which the teacher wears a microphone that wirelessly transmits her voice directly into a receiver attached to the DHH child's hearing devices, were first coming onto the market during this period. FM systems certainly helped direct the DHH child's attention to the teacher working with other children, and teachers of the deaf noticed that children with hearing loss were starting to pick up those skills from other children in ways they had not anticipated. Everyone felt it was their task to help all children develop skills for social interactions, integrating strategies that worked for typically hearing kids into teaching children with hearing loss.

For teachers who were willing to negotiate the inherent challenges of blending orientations, and to put the child first, the benefit was a child surrounded by multiple perspectives—but therein also lay the challenge. For newer teachers perhaps not as entrenched in their individual orientations, it was an opportunity to be a pioneer, to see the value firsthand in an inclusive process early in their careers. It was a challenge, particularly for some more experienced teachers of the deaf, who had a mindset about how DHH children should be educated, and how much time was needed with each student, to add children with different needs, and another teacher who was not a teacher of the deaf. Anytime teachers share a classroom, the situation requires excellent collaboration and communication. There was tension in this mix in the early days, but everyone wanted to make it work. Learning to communicate with teachers who had different orientations, and blending expertise, was often very difficult, yet everyone was committed to the model and kept working to make sure that every student was getting the instruction he or she needed to be successful. Pat Stone and his staff were champions of bridging the divides to be able to make a significant difference in children's lives.

With the success of the blended classrooms in the preschool, the faculty started thinking that children with hearing loss would benefit from blended classrooms in the elementary school as well. George Fortier was teaching a combined third/fourth-grade class that he was very interested in getting hearing students to join. He approached the principals at Holy Family and St. Stephen's, and they put out the call in church bulletins. They also contacted some children who had gone to Childswork and were able to get about five or six typically hearing students to join the students with hearing loss in Fortier's class. The children liked it and families were satisfied, but it did require some retooling on the teacher's part to balance the needs of different students and ensure everyone was getting a good education. This success led the administration to believe that the school should be implementing more blended classrooms in the upper grades. In 2002, Tucker Maxon eliminated separate classrooms for DHH children in favor of having only integrated classrooms.

Technological Advances Come to Tucker Maxon

Tucker Maxon has always been an early adopter of technology. In the early 1960s, parents raised money to purchase an oscilloscope, which allowed the children to see the pattern of their voices on the screen. In 1967, students began to benefit from the new "Loop Induction System," allowing them to move freely about the classroom rather than having to plug in earphones to a central unit. Prior to that time, teachers were using a Warren unit, an amplifier as large as two tables, which would separate the teacher's desk from the crescent of students plugged into the device. When students came to school, they would take off their large body unit hearing aids, don headphones, and plug into the Warren unit in order to hear their teachers. In the late 1970s, the full-body hearing aids began to be replaced by behind-the-ear hearing aids, which made students far less self-conscious when integrating into schools with hearing children. The new technology was expensive, though, and Tucker Maxon had to fundraise to provide new hearing aids to students. By the 1970s, children were beginning to be identified with hearing loss at a younger age and fitted with appropriate amplification sooner.

In 1961, Dr. William House performed surgery to put the first cochlear implant in a patient who was deaf. In November 1984, the U.S. Food and Drug Administration (FDA) approved the House Cochlear Implant for implantation in deaf adults, widely celebrated as the first medical device to "replace" a human sense organ. Like Jonas Salk with the polio vaccine, House never sought a patent for his invention: "he . . . felt that anything . . . [they] developed should be shared for the betterment of mankind" (Woo, 2012).

In 1984, Peter Folkestad, a Tucker Maxon student, became the 96th person, and the eighth child, in the world to undergo cochlear implantation surgery. As his mother recalled, "The surgery went really well, and I think we went to Disneyland that afternoon." The success of Folkestad's surgery encouraged Tucker Maxon to get more involved with cochlear implant technology. Chris Soland, the speech-language pathologist at the time, reported that Folkestad returned a different child after his surgery. The next year, the school established the world's first school-based children's cochlear implant center, in conjunction with the House Ear Institute in Los Angeles, and Soland was asked to direct the program. Soland, along with Tucker Maxon's audiologist and executive director, traveled to the House Institute to receive training, enabling parents to receive cutting-edge services in the Portland area. Soland taught parents about the promise the cochlear implant technology held and fought with insurance companies to cover the cost of implants. Schiel remembered when cochlear implants were just starting to come on the market, children with implants who were profoundly deaf started functioning as hard-of-hearing, instead of profoundly deaf, individuals. This significant difference allowed them to have more typical speech and language development.

FM technology also came into greater use in the late 1980s, quite literally putting the teacher's voice in the child's ear to help circumvent distractions in the learning environment. Childswork teacher Michele Volk remembered being a bit intimidated by the technology at first; as a self-described "loud person," she remembered being scared that she would forget to turn it on when giving directions, or off when she wanted students with hearing loss to interact more with peers. Sarah Theberge, also a Childswork teacher at the time, remembered wearing the microphone and modeling language with students with hearing loss, as well as with their families, who would then reinforce at home what she was doing in the classroom. Theberge remembered parents being very involved and recalled that teachers and parents worked as a team to ensure that student's transitions between home and classroom were seamless. Theberge would also have other students in the classroom wear the microphone, providing universal access to whoever was speaking, again effectively decentralizing the classroom, transforming the space from one in which the teacher was the sole source of information into one where children learn from each other (S. Theberge, personal communication, April 17, 2017). According to Chris Soland, parents, with their deep desire to have the best for their children, have always driven advances at the school.

The 1980s were a very successful period in the school's history. In 1987, current principal Linda Goodwin was named "Teacher of the Year" by the International Organization for Education of the Hearing Impaired. In 1988, the Alexander Graham Bell Association published a book detailing Tucker Maxon's conversational development program, *Blueprint for Developing Conversational Competence*, authored by director Pat Stone. Two years later, five members of Tucker Maxon's staff (Arlie Adam, Pam Fortier, Gail Schiel, Margaret Smith, and Chris Soland) co-authored *Listening to Learn: A Handbook for Parents*, also published by the Alexander Graham Bell Association (1990). Also in 1990, the International Organization for Education of the Hearing Impaired named Tucker Maxon its Program of the Year. Interestingly, Dr. House, who pioneered the cochlear implant, wrote a letter in support of Tucker Maxon to be named Program of the Year. Tucker Maxon had established a national reputation for innovation. Also in 1990, board, staff, and parents worked with a production crew to produce *The Voice of a Miracle*, a video explaining Tucker Maxon's mission and programs.

Despite its success, the school faced many challenges. On June 27, 1991, fire damaged the main building, but alumni, families, staff, and supporters came together to rebuild the school in record time.

In 1992, pediatric cochlear implants gained FDA approval, enabling more children to access this technology. Board member Dr. Alexander Schleuning began performing cochlear implant surgery locally, often for free. All third-year medical students from Oregon Health and Science University also came to the school once a week to observe. That same year, Tucker Maxon initiated a model school program providing real-time captioning for students attending junior and senior high school; the program was later expanded to provide the service to fourth- and fifth-grade students attending neighborhood schools. Tucker Maxon parents started an Oregon Chapter of the Alexander Graham Bell Association for the Deaf that year, which sponsored educational programs and advocated for children and adults with hearing loss. In 1995, Tucker Maxon became the first school for deaf children whose classrooms could all access the Internet.

Celebrating its 50th anniversary in 1997, Tucker Maxon established the International Center for Technology in Oral Education, with the mission to develop and disseminate new computer applications for the education of DHH children. In April 1999, universal screening for newborns became law in Oregon, the 14th state to pass such legislation. This legislation meant that infants with hearing loss would be identified much earlier and would be fitted with hearing technology sooner, making early intervention that much more crucial.

CO-ENROLLMENT BECOMES OFFICIAL

In 1996, Tucker Maxon executive director Pat Stone served as a mentor to staff seeking to open a school for children with hearing loss in Seattle. The school, Listen and Talk, recently celebrated its 20th anniversary. In 1997, Tucker Maxon inaugurated a "reverse mainstream" program in its elementary school program, enrolling some hearing students in classes of DHH children. The students had a slumber party to get to know each other. This move extended the broader communication, academic, and social experience the school had instituted in the preschool in 1984 with the advent of Childswork onto campus.

Tucker Maxon ushered in the new millennium with a major change: it said goodbye to Childswork, which relocated to a new facility when it needed more space. During the 2000–2001 school year, the school inaugurated an integrated kindergarten class and, in 2001–2002, an integrated first- and second-grade combination class. On March 13, 2002, Tucker Maxon's board voted to formally establish co-enrollment as a permanent feature at the school. Preschool and elementary classes were co-taught by a teacher of the deaf and a general education teacher, making Tucker Maxon one of the first schools in the country to co-enroll children with hearing loss and typical hearing together. The program evolved from the original model of classes for students with hearing loss to the present model, in which DHH children are always co-enrolled with their typically hearing peers.

Many listening and spoken language programs belong to an association called OPTION schools (www.optionschools.org). Currently more than half (53%) of OPTION schools and programs include at least 10% typically hearing children in their classrooms. In a 2017 survey, 17 of 32 listening and spoken language programs surveyed said they used a co-enrollment model, though the number of typically hearing children enrolled varied greatly (from 10% to 87%). At the time of this publication, 65% of Tucker Maxon students have typical hearing. Approximately 47% of the OPTION member schools and programs are exclusively for children with hearing loss. A few schools or programs may have one or two children with typical hearing, but they do not make co-enrollment a focus of their programs.

In 2010, Tucker Maxon began a three-year self-assessment of the school with OPTION Schools. The Site Review Committee specifically addressed the school's co-enrollment as an Area of Commendation, stating that "the School's co-enrollment model creates daily interaction with typically-developing peers and provides mainstream experiences throughout the school day for children with hearing loss" (Salvucci, 2011, p 6).). In 2013, OPTION Schools concluded that Tucker Maxon exceeded the organization's standards for excellence for Listening and Spoken Language schools, becoming one of only four schools in the nation to do so.

In 2016, the school changed its name to Tucker Maxon School, dropping the term "Oral," an antiquated term that conjured notions for some of oral hygiene. In 2017, Tucker Maxon celebrated its 70th anniversary by beginning a ten-month evaluation process called Project Impact in which the school developed both quantitative and qualitative instruments to gauge the impact it has in the lives of its students. Findings from the Project Impact evaluation revealed that the co-enrollment model provides the added benefit of normalizing disabilities for the hearing students and provides an ideal environment for the teaching of Social Emotional Intelligence. One mother attributed the development of empathy in hearing students to the co-enrollment model itself: "Tucker Maxon taught my daughter to be empathetic."

Tucker Maxon's model is working. Its 2016 Smarter Balanced (State Common Core exam) assessments showed 91% of third- to fifth-graders meeting or exceeding benchmarks in reading and 73% in math. In 2017,

91% of kindergartners taking the School Readiness Test demonstrated readiness for first grade.

On average, DHH students in the United States graduate from high school lagging behind their hearing peers. At Tucker Maxon, 91% of third-graders are already reading at (or above) a third-grade level. A 2017 survey of Tucker Maxon alumni (primarily deaf) showed that 87% went on to college, 77% got a college degree (an AA or BA), and almost 23% earned a graduate degree. By contrast, only 59% of American high school students graduate from college, according to the National Center for Educational Statistics. Despite their disability, Tucker Maxon graduates are outperforming the national average.

CHALLENGES TO THE CO-ENROLLMENT MODEL

When the board voted to include typically hearing children at the school, it did not anticipate that many of the children who would enroll would have other special needs. Tucker Maxon does not always have the capacity or resources to serve children with other special needs; its specialization is working with children with hearing loss. Students with other significant disabilities, such as Attention-Deficit Disorder, Autism Spectrum Disorders, or other communication challenges often take a teacher's attention away from deaf children's needs. And yet, Tucker Maxon's small class size and individual focus have made the school very attractive to parents of children with other special needs. Often, these children have not succeeded in public school classrooms. A few parents of children with hearing loss have expressed that they were looking for a "mainstream" environment for their child and ended up getting more of a "special needs" classroom. Some have been frustrated when their child with hearing loss started to pick up some of the behaviors of children with other special needs. This dynamic challenges the school's intention that children with hearing loss learn good communication skills from being in an environment with typically hearing children. In order for students with hearing loss to benefit most from their typically hearing peers as "language models," the typically hearing peers should have typical development/behavior. Of course, in the last 30 to 40 years, that has become harder to define in both public and private school settings.

Still, other parents appreciate that, in a classroom with so much variety, hearing loss becomes normalized as just one challenge among many. Tucker Maxon teachers help students see that everyone has strengths and weaknesses, and differences. This is part of the school's focus on social and emotional learning.

A situation arose in a classroom that illustrates this dilemma. Of the 13 students in one particular class, only one was deaf. Of the remaining 12 students, the classroom teacher described eight as having other special needs, whether academic or behavioral, which is two-thirds of the classroom population. Three students had the highest behavioral needs, of which the child with hearing loss was one, but another child had significant other issues. The teacher observed the children learning empathy, patience, and tolerance over the course of the school year, but clearly this child took her focus away from the child with hearing loss, since, comparatively, the child with hearing loss was doing well. The teacher admitted she could have pushed the child with hearing loss further academically had her attention and time not been taken up by other children without hearing loss. She argued that having a classroom inclusive of children with special needs provides benefits to the other children, but only if the ratio is lower.

While this was a unique situation, the school recognized that having two-thirds of a class present with special needs was too high a ratio to be successful. While this scenario may be more challenging for a teacher to handle in a public school classroom of upwards of 35 students, public schools also have support staff in place (e.g., school psychologists, counselors, learning specialists) to address these issues when they arise.

The co-enrollment model is also resource intensive, and it is expensive for a small nonprofit. In the 1980–1990s, all classes were co-taught by two teachers, a teacher of the deaf and a general education teacher. With Childswork's departure from Tucker Maxon, classrooms moved to a one-teacher model, using an education assistant in preschool and kindergarten. Students with hearing loss receive a great deal of support, meeting individually with a teacher of the deaf for 100 minutes per week, and with a speech-language pathologist for 60 minutes per week. An onsite audiologist can also troubleshoot equipment needs as needed with students, and they benefit from the audiologist's diagnosis, evaluation, and programming of hearing devices to maximize residual hearing. For almost two decades, Tucker Maxon operated at a deficit, and it nearly went out of business. Part of the problem was the expense of having two teachers per classroom. Since the change in leadership in 2014, the school has been operating sustainably. The two-teacher model proved too expensive to sustain over the long run.

Another challenge is what one could describe as "mission drift." Tucker Maxon School teaches deaf and hearing children to listen, talk, learn, and achieve excellence together. There is a risk that Tucker Maxon could lose focus on its original mission to educate children with hearing loss if the percentage of hearing children becomes too high. This may be more of a concern if the percentage of students with other special needs gets too high.

Tucker Maxon is at an interesting crossroads, with 65% of its students having typical hearing. While the school wants to be true to its original mission as a school for children who are deaf, it also realizes that every student's education is equally important. Tucker Maxon could evolve into a "communication school" and welcome children with other disabilities or learning differences (e.g., Autism Spectrum Disorder, Attention-Deficit Disorder). If it chooses the latter, it will need to hire additional staff with specializations to support a more behaviorally-diverse population (e.g., counselor, school psychologist, occupational therapist, special education teachers, reading specialists). While the organization is not currently discussing this possibility, this challenge infuses the school's daily work and environment. While the bottom line is helping all children succeed, schools like Tucker Maxon need formal criteria and vetting systems to ensure they can serve all children enrolled.

One alumna opted to send her own daughter, who is deaf, to Tucker Maxon. While she was hesitant at first, she ended up being very glad she enrolled her daughter (E. Henry, personal communication. April 5, 2017). She saw her daughter "blossom" at Tucker, learning idioms and slang from her typically hearing peers and correcting the pronunciation of other deaf children, which is empowering and builds her confidence. While this mother taught her daughter to sign, she also opted to undergo cochlear implant surgery for herself as an adult. She initially feared that "the hearing kids might swallow up the deaf kids," but instead she saw her daughter experiencing the blended environment she wished she had when she was a child. Another alumna felt she benefited from integrating on alternate days into a mainstream kindergarten in the pioneering days and did not remember the transition to a mainstream classroom as being hard. This was a child who benefitted from early amplification and intervention in an oral framework; she had never learned to rely on sign language.

BENEFITS OF THE CO-ENROLLMENT MODEL

Children with hearing loss are educated in the "least restrictive environment," as required by the Individuals with Disabilities Education Act (IDEA). This phrase has been widely interpreted to mean the most mainstream-like environment possible (but see Abbate, this volume). But what does that mean? Children with hearing loss are no longer segregated from their hearing peers. As Andrew Solomon (2012, p. 54) observed, the IDEA has "sometimes been interpreted to assert that separate is never equal, and that everyone should attend mainstream schools." Solomon quoted Justice William Rehnquist's argument for the majority in the 1982 U.S. Supreme Court decision in *Board of Education v. Rowley*, in which the court maintained the school district was not required to provide a deaf girl with an interpreter, even though her primary language was American Sign Language, and she only understood half of what was said to her through lip reading, as long as she was passing her courses. Rehnquist wrote:

> The intent of the Act [IDEA] was more to open the door of public education to handicapped children on appropriate terms than to guarantee any particular level of education once inside. The requirement that a State provide specialized educational services to handicapped children generates no additional requirement that the services so provided be sufficient to maximize each child's potential. (cited in Solomon, 2012, p. 55)

Clearly, ideas about "reasonable accommodation" have evolved since 1982, as children with hearing loss are routinely provided sign language interpreters in public schools now. But the fact that the sentiment was codified in a Supreme Court decision that the intent of the IDEA was not to enable children with disabilities to reach their full potential is telling.

All children at Tucker Maxon receive the benefit of the school's strong academics, small class size, and emphasis on social and emotional development and communication. At Tucker Maxon, disabilities are normalized for children who are typically developing by creating an early awareness of differences, fostering a strong sense of empathy for others with communication challenges. "I think it is kind of fun and neat because when I am older, I will be more understanding," asserted Anne, age 8. Her sister Faith, age 12, put it this way: "I have and will have the tools to help others with disabilities and be more accepting." A father of a typically hearing graduate of the school explained how his son left Tucker Maxon "with something that most schools will NEVER be able to teach, and that is treating kids who are different or have disabilities just like you would treat every other kid . . . to have compassion, patience, caring, and the belief that ALL kids should be made to feel accepted" (Buchanan, personal communication, August 18, 2016).

Having peers who are typically hearing in the same classrooms also provides a reference point for speech and language development that keeps expectations high for DHH students. Teachers can integrate typically hearing peers into work with students with hearing loss, connecting and supporting each other. The mother of Anne and Faith quoted earlier described a dynamic she witnessed with her older daughter, who is now in middle school, when she started at Tucker Maxon. Her daughter, who is likely dyslexic, befriended a little boy who was profoundly deaf; as she described it, the two "just embraced each other . . . [and] would help each other. They did not realize the difference." She attributed this interdependence to the culture Tucker Maxon fosters, where children "feel safe to be themselves" (A. Beals, personal communication, April 27, 2017). She also noted that her older daughter receives compliments from a neighbor who notices she always makes eye contact with him during conversations, which he notes is rare in other children her age. The mother attributed this skill to the child's time at Tucker Maxon. She believed the necessity to speak with peers who sometimes need to read lips or talk face to face develops children who are engaged, courteous communicators. Typically hearing peers watch the teachers and the speech-language pathologist and take cues from them on how best to partner with children with hearing loss in their classroom.

An example of a beneficial interaction involving children with other special needs came from the early days of co-enrollment with Childswork. Gail Schiel recalled witnessing a situation in Childswork teacher Michele Volk's classroom involving one of the more challenging children without hearing loss, a boy with severe autism. He had been thrown out of two previous preschools, and his parents wanted to try one last time. He came to the school with an aide, as he could be pretty explosive and aggressive at times, requiring him to be restrained and taken to a quieter place to calm down. Schiel recalled in the spring during circle time, Volk was getting ready to read the children a book, and this child was clearly getting agitated and anxious. She said, "It looks like something is bothering Gus [name changed to protect his privacy]. I wonder what is bothering him?" Volk elicited ideas from the children: "Maybe it is too loud," "Maybe he does not like the story," until one child volunteered, "Maybe we are too close to him? Maybe we should give him more space." The children were learning to "read" Gus, and he was trusting that they would, and he let them know when they arrived at the right issue by visibly calming down when children moved away from him. The children collectively helped problem-solve a solution and were included in de-escalating Gus's behavior. Schiel remembered it making a big impression on her as a masterful teaching moment.

With early identification and amplification followed by successful early intervention, many students with hearing loss are able to transition into their neighborhood schools sooner. This can lead to decreased enrollment and smaller class sizes. Staff note that if Tucker Maxon did not have hearing students in classes, it would have to combine classes (for example, a combined third-, fourth, and fifth-grade class) when it did not have enough children with hearing loss to fill a grade.

A child who is the only student in a mainstream school classroom with hearing loss can become embarrassed by the introduction of new assistive listening equipment that singles him or her out. This may cause the child to become socially isolated and treated as an outlier. In contrast, at Tucker Maxon, teachers and other classmates understand what the child with hearing loss needs, and equipment is normalized rather than stigmatized. Indeed, typically hearing students become comfortable using FM transmitters in class. For children who arrive at the school after they are identified with hearing loss late, often it is their self-concept that needs reinforcement more than their academics or spoken language development. Indeed, Linda Goodwin recalled a few students who did not attend Tucker Maxon after early intervention because staff deemed them ready to go to their neighborhood school. These alumni went on to college and became adults only to come back to Tucker Maxon looking for something missing in their lives—looking for adults like them, people who could understand their hearing loss and relate to them at that level, looking for identity and community.

Despite being integrated in the classroom, children sometimes self-segregate on the schoolyard during recess. This dynamic is less pronounced in preschool, where there is a teacher of the deaf in every classroom who has special training on strategies to integrate all children. Also, listening with a hearing deficit can be very fatiguing and requires high levels of concentration; recess is often a time for children with hearing loss to take a "break" from listening. Recess is also a time when children with hearing loss are not receiving FM transmissions, so it can be challenging for DHH children to concentrate in noisy, outdoor or indoor free-play environments and have quality interactions with groups of children. When staff efforts at relationship-building are successful, children with hearing loss are better integrated into the community, participating in playdates, sleepovers, birthday parties, and extracurricular activities with their typically hearing friends. Because the community is so small, students get to know everyone, which means that everyone becomes an individual rather than being defined by his or her hearing loss.

Identical twin boys, both with hearing loss, who just graduated as valedictorians of their high school with 4.27 grade point averages, were recently admitted to the University of Portland's competitive five-year engineering program with merit scholarships. Their father attributed his sons' success to the confidence they developed at Tucker Maxon interacting with both typically hearing children and those with hearing loss. He remembered a PowerPoint presentation they both gave to a biology class when they first transitioned to middle school in which everyone was impressed with the poise and confidence the boys exhibited. As their dad recalled, the boys did not even falter, since they had been up on stage and presenting to groups since they were in kindergarten at Tucker Maxon (J. Bryan, personal communication, April 6, 2017). Their mother attributed this confidence to the school as well: "We applaud Tucker Maxon for doing such a great job helping our boys to feel as if they can walk into any situation and do well" (B. Bryan, personal communication, July 18, 2015). Another mom reported, "Everyone that meets my son tells me how he has redefined their idea of what it means to be deaf or hard of hearing and I tell them I know ... We have Tucker to thank for that ... With every bone in my body, I believe in this school" (B. Henderson, personal communication, August 14, 2015).

Another parent described her experience with the public school system and explained why she enrolled her daughters with hearing loss at Tucker Maxon:

> Both of my girls have . . . bilateral cochlear implants which offer them hearing at a level equivalent to their [hearing] peers. The public preschool program offers eight hours per week of school in their oral program, 20 minutes per month in a pull-out (in a corner of the classroom) with a teacher of the deaf for one-on-one speech. There is no interaction with hearing peers [in preschool]. Yet they are mainstreamed into a regular classroom at age five. When you visit the classroom, you find children who do not play together and have limited language. And these are kids who have hearing aids, which means they should be speaking almost as well as their hearing peers.

She added:

> In three years [at Tucker Maxon], my first daughter went from no language to testing on par with her hearing peers. When my daughters "mainstreamed," they already knew how to communicate, navigate, and comprehend the mainstream classroom. (H. Leiser, personal communication, July 5, 2012)

A grandfather of a child with bilateral profound hearing loss concurred, using the word *integrated* to describe co-enrollment:

> After only three months, [our grandson] is communicating, reading, and writing confidently and with enjoyment . . . The testing, tutoring, in-house audiologist and speech-language pathologist united under one roof and working together every day with one another and with the children is SO AMAZING! . . . Some families come from across the country for the opportunity to attend. . . . There are few integrated educational options in the world for hearing-impaired children. (B. Moe, personal communication, December 1, 2016)

Tucker Maxon is still evaluating what the ideal ratio of students with hearing loss to typically hearing children should be in the classroom. When the school compares itself with other OPTION Schools programs that co-enroll, Tucker Maxon is on the high end, with two-thirds hearing students to one-third children with hearing loss. This begs the question: At what ratio will a teacher of the deaf be unwilling to work in a classroom under the mainstream model, feeling he or she is not adequately using the specialized skills he or she has learned to best work with children with hearing loss?

A DATABASE FOR LISTENING AND SPOKEN LANGUAGE OUTCOMES

Tucker Maxon is part of a Listening and Spoken Language Data Repository (LSL-DR) (Bradham, Fonnesbeck, Toll, & Hecht, 2018). Educators and researchers have started to use this repository to help improve deaf education. For example, Tucker Maxon plotted two histograms using data from the LSL-DR to illustrate receptive language scores of 4-year-olds who are in an exclusive classroom for just children with hearing loss versus a co-enrolled class. In examining these histograms, the overall average shows children who are enrolled with typically developing children score slightly higher than children who were in classrooms that only had children with hearing loss. This trend was observed across all learning domains (articulation, expressive and receptive vocabulary, and expressive and receptive language). While the receptive vocabulary scores were not statistically significant, any gain can make a big difference in a child and his or her family's life.

WHAT TUCKER MAXON HAS LEARNED

Tucker Maxon celebrated its 70th anniversary in 2017. The school's philosophy is that the more mainstream its environment, the more likely DHH children will successfully integrate into public, private, or parochial schools. Section 504 of the Rehabilitation Act of 1973 "provides for a free, appropriate education in the 'least-restrictive environment,' reasonable accommodations, and a written plan describing placement and services" (https://www.ssdmo.org/step1/laws.html). Tucker Maxon would argue that the "least-restrictive environment" isn't a public school classroom where a child is the only student with hearing loss. By creating a mainstream environment through co-enrollment, while providing all of the supports children with hearing loss need to succeed, this model is helping children reach their full potential in school and life. As an institution, Tucker Maxon is still evaluating the ideal ratio of deaf to typically hearing students. However, the school is committed to co-enrollment as the best way to ensure that students with hearing loss will succeed.

ACKNOWLEDGMENTS

The authors wish to thank the following people for their help during the research and writing of this chapter: Rebecca Archer, Amanda Beals, Maura Berndsen, Jim and Barbara Bryan, Andy Fort, Pam Fortier, Erin Henry, Suzanne Quigley, Gail Schiel, Chris Soland, Pat Stone, Sarah Theberge, and Michele Volk. We'd also like to thank all of the staff at Tucker Maxon, especially Shelby Atwill, Claire Leake, Stacia

Roseneau, and Anne Smyth, who provided feedback on portions of the manuscript. We are also indebted to Emeritus Board member Robert Boley and K. Todd Houston for providing feedback on the manuscript. Finally, we thank all of the past and present members of the Board of Directors for 70 years of volunteer service to Tucker Maxon School.

REFERENCES

Bradham, T. S., Fonnesbeck, C., Toll, A., & Hecht, B. F. (2018). The Listening and Spoken Language Data Repository: Design and project overview. *Language, Speech, and Hearing Services in Schools, 49*(1), 108–120.

Maxon Oral School. (n.d.). Second school brochure.

Morrison, W. (1948, July 25). Parents of deaf children strive for model oral school. *The Oregonian.*

Neergaard, Lauren. (2016, February 26). Background noise makes it harder for kids to listen, learn. *The Oregonian.*

The Oregonian, (May 7, 1974). Obituary of Alice Maxon, p. 39.

Portland Center for Hearing & Speech. (1963, May–June). Profile of Alice Maxon. *Hear Say,* 1(3), 1, 3–4.

Salvucci, D. (2011, October 17–19). OPTION, Inc. Schools Peer Review Team Site Review Report.

Solomon, A. (2012). *Far from the tree: Parents, children, and the search for identity.* New York: Scribner.

Stone, P. (1997, May). Transcript of Tucker Maxon Oral School History Discussion.

Tucker-Maxon: Celebrating 60 years of innovation and commitment to oral education. (2012, July 25). Retrieved from https://www.youtube.com/watch?v=lzZcwCgHYec

Woo, E. (2012, December 12). Dr. William F. House dies at 89; championed cochlear implant. *Los Angeles Times,* p. 15.

16

Visions of Co-Enrollment in Deaf Education

Marc Marschark, Harry Knoors, and Shirin Antia

It is well acknowledged in the field of deaf education that deaf and hard-of-hearing (DHH) learners are far more diverse than their hearing age-mates. DHH learners come into the classroom with all of the same sources of variability that affect hearing learners, but they also vary widely among themselves due to direct and indirect effects of their hearing losses. As a result, deaf education tends to be a more challenging endeavor—for both students and teachers—compared to educating more typical populations of hearing learners. Nelson, Loncke, and Camarata (1993) referred to this as the need for determining the "tricky mix" that accommodates their weaknesses and builds on their strengths, the "converging set of conditions that must cooperate at high levels for high rates of learning to be achieved" (Nelson & Arkenberg, 2008, p. 317). The fact that DHH learners vary so much more than hearing learners means that the tricky mix likely is going to have subtle or not-so-subtle effects on each DHH learner. Knoors (2016, p. 241) thus suggested that in deaf education, "one size fits none." This reality creates particular challenges for the education of DHH learners in mainstream settings, the academic placement of choice for the majority of DHH learners today in most countries. Mainstream classrooms generally are unprepared to accommodate the communication needs of DHH learners and largely unaware that they may have academic needs different from those of their hearing peers (i.e., the tricky mix).

Nowhere in the mainstream are educators as flexible and sensitive to the needs and strengths of DHH learners as in co-enrollment programs. The pioneers of co-enrollment programming for DHH children—many of whom are represented in this volume—reject the one-size-fits-all platitude that still creates barriers to maximizing opportunities and outcomes for this diverse population. The chapters of this volume thus provide guidance, or at least worthy suggestions, for re-envisioning the continuum of placements for deaf learners. The commonalities and differences in the programs described reflect the similarity and diversity of the children they serve and are an implicit recognition of Nelson et al.'s (1993) argument for more options for educating them (see also Knoors & Marschark, 2014, Chapter 11; Marschark & Leigh, 2016; Meadow-Orlans, 2000).

Stories like that of the co-enrollment program in Namur, Belgium, related in Chapter 1 of this volume, are told in different ways, with different beginnings and endings, in each chapter of this volume. In the Belgian story of Ghesquière and Meurant (this volume), as in the stories of others, teachers and administrations in mainstream schools welcomed not only DHH students but teachers of the deaf, sign language interpreters, and other (deaf and hearing) professionals seeking to fully integrate DHH learners with hearing classmates socially as well as academically. Other stories involve programs for DHH learners that welcomed hearing children and teachers into their schools despite the newcomers having little, if any, prior experience with hearing loss. What these and other pioneering programs all had in common was the desire to educate DHH and hearing children together in settings that would allow all children to reach their full potentials (and perhaps make the world a better and more understanding place). How they went about that has varied widely, and therein lies the true tale of this volume.

A ROSE BY ANY OTHER NAME

Upon learning the story of the Namur co-enrollment program (Antia, Knoors & Marschark, this volume), we started searching for co-enrollment programs beyond those with which we already were familiar. Implicitly, it appears that we had a theoretical prototype of what a co-enrollment program was, based primarily on those programs with which the three of us were most familiar, those described in this volume by Kirchner and by Kreimeyer, Drye, and Metz in the United States; by de Klerk, Hermans, Wauters, de Laat, de Kroon, and Knoors in the Netherlands, and by Yiu, Tang, and Ho in Hong Kong. These four programs have four features in common: (1) a desire for full integration of DHH and hearing learners in the classroom, as opposed to what Abbate (this volume) refers to as "the illusion of inclusion;" (2) co-teaching and true teamwork by teachers of the deaf and general education teachers; (3) bilingual education programming; and (4) active involvement of deaf professionals who can serve as role models as well as language models for both DHH and hearing children. Even among just these four programs, however, readers of the corresponding chapters will see considerable variability. Indeed, trying to picture how all of the programs in this volume (and several others that chose not to participate) fit together yielded what looked like a very noisy Venn diagram. Whatever dimensions one considers, the ultimate goal for all of them is to ensure equal access to instruction of DHH and hearing students. The resulting confusion of circles exemplifies suggestions that in deaf education, "one size fits none" (Knoors, 2016) and that "everything works for somebody, but nothing works for everybody" (Marschark, 2018).

Co-enrollment programs are based on recognition and embracing of diversity, striving for a significant proportion of all DHH students to be included as members, not visitors, of the classroom (Abbate, this volume; Antia, Stinson, & Gaustad, 2002). As noted by Antia et al. (this volume), additional characteristics of *most* programs include co-teaching, use of the regular school curriculum, flexibility in mode(s) of communication, and the availability of specialized staff and services for DHH learners. Many also include multi-grade classrooms, bilingual programming, and an emphasis on family involvement. But situations, culture, and population densities (of both deaf students and teachers), in reality, all have had a hand in shaping the programs described in this book. It therefore will be worthwhile considering several of these areas separately, both their benefits and their challenges. These descriptions are not intended to be exhaustive, and one cannot fully appreciate how the various co-enrollment programs have dealt with these issues without actually visiting them. In this sense, the preceding chapters should be considered more a travelogue rather than immersion, with this concluding chapter merely a collection of snapshots.

FOUNDATIONS OF CO-ENROLLMENT

Class Membership

In various descriptions of co-enrollment programming, a DHH student representation of 25% frequently is mentioned as a level at which they no longer "stand out" in the way that DHH learners do in typical main-stream settings. However, programs vary widely. Programs that began as schools for the deaf generally are able to achieve that 25% figure after they have opened their doors to hearing children (e.g., Di Gregorio, Campana, Lavecchia, & Rinaldi, this volume; Hoofard, Gilbert, Goodwin, & Bradham, this volume; Kirchner, this volume; Ringwald-Frimerman, Ingber, & Most, this volume). This is not always possible. The mainstream school described inGhesquière and Meurant, for example, has 900 students at the primary level and 1,000 at the secondary level, but there are only 50 DHH students in their bilingual classes from preschool through secondary school. Recognizing the preferred critical mass of 20% to 50%, Ghesquière and Meurant noted that the proportion of DHH students in their bilingual classes is lucky to average 15%. In some classes, there are fewer, perhaps only a handful of DHH students, but there also some separate classes (e.g., English) consisting entirely of DHH students. DHH students also are greatly outnumbered by hearing students in the Hong Kong program described by Yiu, Tang, and Ho (this volume), but both groups always are taught together.

Ringwald-Frimerman et al. (this volume) describe three different levels of how students in Israel are educated: individual inclusion, co-enrollment classes, and self-contained classes. Only about 15% of Israeli DHH children are enrolled in classes that can be considered co-enrollment. Another 5% are educated in self-contained classrooms, and 80% of DHH children are taught in "individual inclusion" settings, essentially the typical mainstream situation of a single DHH student in a classroom with hearing peers. It is only the co-enrollment classrooms and self-contained classrooms in which signing is common. Individual inclusion classrooms sometimes have sign language interpreters, but DHH pupils and their hearing peers in those classrooms do not share a common language. Thus, less than one-quarter of Israeli DHH children are exposed to the true co-enrollment model with a critical mass of DHH peers.

Similar to the Israeli individual inclusion model, Torigoe (this volume) describes what the author refers to as an "interpreter-prominent" form of co-enrollment in which most DHH children in Japan take courses in mainstream classrooms, sometimes supported by sign language interpreters. Deaf sign language teachers visit schools only periodically, and they teach Japanese Sign Language only to the DHH students. Japanese, mathematics, and English are taught in self-contained classrooms of DHH students in which teachers use both speech and signing (including simultaneous communication). Although the school described in detail by Torigoe is small by Japanese standards (180 students), classes consist of about 40 students with a single general education teacher, and there are only 10 to 15 DHH students in the whole school. The latter situation is similar to programs like those in Madrid schools described by Pérez, de la Fuente, Alonso, and Echeita (this volume), with 5% to 10% of DHH students in "preferential schools for the integration of DHH students."

The chapter by Abbate (this volume) offers another version of co-enrollment programming, one in which co-enrollment can vary from part time to full time, and the number of DHH students in a classroom with hearing peers can vary widely. A partnership between a school for the deaf and local, mainstream elementary, middle, and high schools allows for easy (if carefully monitored) transitions between self-contained classrooms at the school for the deaf, self-contained/resource classrooms in the partnership schools, and full inclusion. Emphasizing that inclusion is determined by the services provided rather than the setting in which they are provided, this U.S. program sees varying numbers of DHH students in mainstream classes with full support not only from teachers of the deaf, interpreters, and other specialized personnel but also from general education teachers and hearing peers. Programs of this sort emphasize that even if the proportion of DHH learners relative to hearing learners is small, as in the Belgian (Ghesquière & Meurant, this volume) and Hong Kong (Yiu et al., this volume) programs, inclusive co-enrollment programming can work when having DHH students in their classes is not an unusual situation for hearing students and teachers, and when all stakeholders are all on board (see Antia, 2015).

Some co-enrollment programs desire larger groups of DHH learners or, when that is not possible, their hearing siblings or children of deaf adults (CODAs) who can help to provide learning environments that are socioculturally deaf (or deaf-friendly) and create an immersive bi-modal bilingual (i.e., sign language and spoken/written language) setting (e.g., Baker, Miller, Fletcher, Gamin, & Carty, this volume; Hennies & Hennies, this volume). Then again, other co-enrollment programs focus more on the integration of groups of deaf and hearing learners with a focus on spoken language with little if any exposure to sign language (Hoofard et al., this volume; Ringwald-Frimerman et al., this volume). Such programs may not match our original prototype for co-enrollment programs, but they clearly meet the goal of educating DHH and hearing children together in flexible, supportive settings that aim to help all children to reach their full potentials to a greater degree than typical mainstream and inclusive programs. Adding further complexity to the co-enrollment picture is determining the point at which an education program initially designed for DHH learners becomes a co-enrollment program (see Hoofard et al., this volume). Acknowledging overlap and variability in program characteristics, the tipping point likely is when the emphasis on language modality is outweighed by other characteristics of co-enrollment such as inclusion, co-teaching, following the regular curriculum, and intensive professional development.

Communication and Language

Unlike "oral" programs such as that of Hoofard et al. (this volume; see also Ringwald-Frimerman et al., this volume) and those in which sign language interpreters support instruction for DHH students in mainstream classrooms, like those described by Torigoe (this volume), most co-enrollment programs assume that both instruction and social interactions among DHH and hearing students ultimately will be optimized by maximizing exposure to natural languages. Other programs, consistent with the original co-enrollment model (Kirchner, 1994, this volume), are not explicitly bimodal bilingual but emphasize the availability of alternative forms of communication in the classroom in order to meet the individual communication needs of each student.

The programs described by Kirchner (this volume), Kreimeyer et al. (this volume), and de Klerk et al. (this volume) incorporate a flexible approach to communication similar to what is often referred to as Total Communication (see also Krausneker & Kramreiter, this volume; Ringwald-Frimerman et al., this volume). Although Total Communication frequently is confused with simultaneous communication (or sign-supported speech, both using sign and speech together), as originally described by Roy Holcomb, it is a communication philosophy rather than a method (Scouten, 1984). Total Communication simply calls for using all available means of communication with DHH children—speech, audition, and sign language—in order to ensure optimal communication and normal language development. Di Gregorio et al. (this volume), Hennies and Hennies (this volume), Baker et al. (this volume), and Yiu et al. (this volume), in contrast, describe programs focused on bimodal bilingual education.

Several of the chapters in this volume explicitly recognize the challenges inherent in asking (or hoping for) teachers and hearing students to acquire a second language when they are not fully immersed in it. The continuum of placements offered by the partnership model described by Abbate (this volume) and the alternative classroom settings described by Ghesquière and Meurant (this volume) and Ringwald-Frimerman et al. (this volume) offer different communication approaches depending on whether a student is attending classes with all DHH students or is included in classrooms with hearing students. More commonly, however, co-enrollment programs expose DHH (and hearing) students to a consistent communication model throughout the school day.

Some co-enrollment programs for DHH learners either depend on sign language interpreting (e.g., Ringwald-Frimerman et al., this volume; Torigoe, this volume), and offer it regularly to facilitate classroom communication (de Klerk et al., this volume; Kreimeyer et al., this volume), or call on interpreters only in special situations (i.e., not for regular instruction, Baker et al., this volume). Co-enrollment programs, especially those that espouse a bilingual approach, understandably have some ambivalence with regard to sign language interpreters in the classroom. Nevertheless, when the interpreters are well qualified, they can ensure DHH students' access to instruction and other aspects of classroom communication. This can be particularly important in settings that lack the resources or critical mass of DHH students in order to implement co-teaching in which one of the teachers always is a fluent signer (e.g., Ghesquière & Meurant, this volume; Kreimeyer et al., this volume).

While potentially valuable contributors to the co-enrollment classroom, interpreters who are not full-time staff often are unfamiliar and uncomfortable with their roles in co-enrollment classrooms, with responsibilities that can vary from day to day. Some interpreters simply are unable or unwilling to step out of the "conduit" role and participate fully in the collaborative activities central to co-enrollment classrooms.

Kreimeyer et al. (this volume), de Klerk et al. (volume), and others emphasize the importance of teachers and co-enrollment classrooms working together, supporting each other, and respecting each other (this will be discussed later). The same kind of teamwork is essential for interpreters in co-enrollment classrooms if they are to contribute to the community atmosphere. Kreimeyer et al., for example, describe the inability of some substitute interpreters to understand the need to work with hearing as well as DHH students. To some extent, such difficulties can be overcome by the use of teacher aides as interpreters when professional interpreters are not available (e.g., Baker et al., this volume). Yiu et al. (this volume) have taken the novel approach, perhaps out of necessity, of creating a Junior Sign Language Interpreter program for hearing children in the co-enrollment program, using their services both in the classroom and in extracurricular settings.

As useful as interpreters are in some situations, their use also contradicts a central goal of co-enrollment programs, that all teachers and students be able to communicate directly with one another. Hennies and Hennies (this volume), for example, describes the assumption of the German model that direct instruction by skilled signing teachers is expected to be of greater benefit to DHH children than sign language interpreting. Sapere, LaRock, Convertino, Gallimore, and Lessard (2005) made a similar argument with regard to mainstream education of young DHH children in the United States. However, as pointed out by Antia et al. (this volume). It may not be realistic to expect that hearing students and classroom teachers will learn to sign fluently, nor is it realistic to expect that the DHH students can be left in some kind of communication limbo while they learn to sign. Thus, interpreters or communication aides may be necessary at times to fill the gaps. Research at the postsecondary level has consistently indicated that direct instruction and interpreter-mediated instruction are equally effective for DHH students with varying sign language fluencies (as well as by hearing classmates), regardless of whether the instructor is deaf or hearing (e.g., Marschark, Sapere, Convertino, & Pelz, 2008). Similar research apparently has not been conducted with younger DHH learners, so we simply do not know whether the presence of interpreters in co-enrollment classrooms adds to ease of communication or not.

While awaiting evidence on the matter, it also should be recognized that interpreters may contradict the philosophical underpinnings of programs that emphasize bimodal bilingual education. For those programs, fluently signing deaf teachers as well as other signing deaf adults—and perhaps older deaf peers—in the classroom provide sociocultural as well as language models for DHH students. Co-enrollment programs vary, however, in the extent to which they support and/or encourage hearing students to acquire sign language skills. Torigoe (this volume) indicates that very few, if any, hearing children in the program described acquire sign language, while the programs described by Kirchner (this volume), Kreimeyer et al. (this volume), and Baker et al. (this volume) are among those that strongly encourage hearing students' acquisition of such skills. Ghesquière and Meurant (this volume) note that hearing students are not expected to learn Langue des Signes de Belgique Francophone (LSFB) but are not prevented from doing so, and with hearing children of deaf adults (CODAs) as well as DHH students in their classes, some eventually do so. Hearing staff in the school are in a similar situation, so that only a small proportion of hearing students and staff can communicate effectively in LSFB. Both groups usually depend on sign language interpreters for extended conversations, although Ghesquière and Meurant note that "this unbalanced multilingualism" contributes to DHH students' skills in spoken French (see also, Hoofard et al., this volume).

Multi-Age, Multi-Grade Classrooms

Several chapters in this volume describe co-enrollment classrooms that include students of different ages and functioning at different grade levels (Baker et al, this volume; Krausneker & Kramreiter, this volume; Kreimeyer et al., this volume). These classrooms include students at two or three grade levels with a wider range of ages and therefore (perhaps) with a wider range of academic and social competencies or skills. Research on the effects of multi-grade classrooms is limited, and results are mixed. Logue (2006), for example, found that disobedience was less frequent in multi-grade than single-grade classrooms, and Frosco, Schleser, and Andal (2004) reported that multi-grade classrooms appear to facilitate cognitive development. Contrasting with both of those reports, a large-sample study by Ansari (2017), using data from the large Early Childhood Longitudinal Study, found no difference in behavioral measures between 5-year-olds in multi-grade and single-grade classrooms, while the former demonstrated poorer performance in academic and executive functioning.

The extent to which studies of multi-grade classrooms including only hearing children can be generalized to the more diverse and frequently language-delayed population of young DHH children is unclear. As noted by Antia et al. (this volume), Bowen (2008) examined social functioning in a multi-grade co-enrollment program involving DHH children in a first- and second-grade classroom and a third- and fourth-grade classroom. Social interactions among children may have been facilitated by what appears to have been a Total Communication environment rather than strictly a bilingual one, but Bowen found that DHH children enrolled in that program demonstrated better sign language skills than peers in a traditional mainstream classroom. A review by Xie, Potměšil, and Peters (2014) concluded that co-enrollment programming can be particularly beneficial for DHH children's social development. Although Xie et al. did not explicitly discuss outcomes from multi-grade classrooms versus normally stratified classrooms, the three co-enrollment articles included in their literature review all described studies of multi-grade co-enrollment programs in the United States (i.e., Bowen, 2008; Kreimeyer, Crooke, Drye, Egbert, & Klein, 2000; McCain & Antia, 2005).

Kreimeyer et al. (this volume) noted several broader benefits of multi-grade co-enrollment classrooms. Classroom teachers in the multi-grade classrooms told the investigators that having the same students from year to year gives them the opportunity to develop stronger relationships with students' families, encouraging their support and involvement in the program. Similar reports have been obtained in regular (hearing) multi-grade classrooms (e.g., Song, Spradlin, & Plucker, 2009). Indeed, family support for co-enrollment is seen as an essential ingredient for essentially all of the programs described in this volume, not only those that were parent-initiated (e.g., Abbate, this volume; Baker et al., this volume; Hennies & Hennies, this volume; Hoofard et al., this volume). Some of the students in the program described by Kereimeyer et al. also reported that having several grades in the same classroom provides greater flexibility in the pace of learning, a situation that allows them to work at different levels in different academic areas. This feature could be particularly important given the heterogeneity among deaf learners (e.g., Marschark & Leigh, 2016), although it does not appear to have been examined empirically.

Finally, it is noteworthy that multi-grade co-enrollment classrooms are not necessarily designed that way by virtue of any grand plan. For some programs, multi-grade classrooms are a convenience or a necessity due to the small number of children enrolled. Krausneker and Kramreiter (this volume), in contrast, refer to "bilingualism and mixed-age groups as the pillars of co-enrollment." They describe older or more advanced students serving as implicit academic and linguistic role models for younger or slower students, sometimes explaining content for younger ones. Knoors and Marschark (2014), however, cautioned that DHH learners who are "unskilled but unaware" can slow down or disrupt learning when peers pass along incorrect or incomplete information. Smaller multi-grade programs can avoid such potential problems through careful pairing of students.

Co-Teaching and the Presence of Deaf Adults in the Classroom

With few exceptions, co-teaching (having two teachers with expertise in supporting the two constituent groups in the classroom) serves as a hallmark of co-enrollment. Most commonly, co-teaching in co-enrollment programs involves a teacher of the deaf and a general education teacher. In some, there is a preference for the teacher of the deaf to be deaf (e.g., Hennies & Hennies, this volume; Yiu et al., this volume). Hoofard et al. (this volume), Kreimeyer et al. (this volume), and Perez et al. (this volume), however, emphasize the expense of co-teaching, a factor that eventually led two of those programs to revert to one teacher in each classroom. In both cases, that single teacher is expected to have the skills and credentials to educate both DHH and hearing children (with support from aides). Perez et al. also emphasize the difficulty of finding teachers who have the necessary sign language proficiencies for teaching higher-level academic content, particularly at the secondary level. In some programs, co-teaching is preferred, but human and financial resources as well as curricular considerations mean that they need to be flexible, sometimes having two teachers and sometimes only one.

Almost all of the co-enrollment programs described earlier adhere to standard curricula for both DHH and hearing learners, albeit with some deviation related to language programming, a point emphasized early on in the TRIPOD program (see Kirchner, this volume). The Belgian program described by Ghesquière and Meurant (this volume), for example, emphasizes co-teaching for "non-linguistic" classes, such as history, geography, mathematics, and art education and for extracurricular activities. "Linguistic" classes such as French, English, and LSFB classes are taught to DHH students separately, by bilingual teachers with appropriate skills. Such distinctions are not always philosophical in nature but may be a consequence of limited time in the school day, limited staff resources, or the diverse language needs of DHH children, who may come to school with significant language delays.

In the case of the Belgian co-enrollment program, as noted earlier, relatively few hearing staff members have sign language skills, while the bilingual co-teachers must be certified in LSFB as well as have a teaching degrees. Deaf and hearing bilingual teachers also need to pass an assessment as part of the interview process in which they are placed in a classroom and have to demonstrate pedagogical skills as well as language skills in LSFB and (written if not spoken) French. As is the case with sign language interpreters, co-enrollment programs often have needs for bilingual staff beyond the local capacity to provide them. Recognizing the relative paucity of individuals who can achieve such competencies, the programs described by Hoofard et al. (this volume) and Yiu et al. (this volume) report supporting and encouraging teacher aides to further their educations and become teachers themselves. Yiu et al. further suggest that the Junior Sign Language Interpreter training in their co-enrollment program implicitly encourages young hearing students to become sign language interpreters.

Beyond language skills, demonstrated cognitive differences between DHH and hearing learners require that their teachers recognize, understand, and are willing to accommodate differences as well as adjusting to DHH students' sometimes unique strengths and needs (Knoors &

Marschark, 2014, Chapter 6). Having teachers of the deaf and general education teachers working together allows co-enrollment programs to achieve this goal, at least assuming that the former are well informed and the latter are flexible and willing to work as a team. Many general education teachers, however, have had little experience with DHH learners, and teachers of the deaf often lack the depth of content knowledge needed for instruction to older children. At least initially, therefore, co-enrollment programming depends heavily on shared responsibility and understanding of the strengths and needs of DHH and hearing learners. This requires true teamwork and regular communication between co-teachers as well as with other staff (see de Klerk et al., Di Gregorio et al., Krausneker & Kramreiter, all this volume). Over time, that teamwork, shared experience, and professional development activities provide all teachers with the knowledge and skills necessary to better support learning by all of their students.

Given the diversity among co-enrollment programs, it may be difficult to distinguish the benefits of co-teaching from other aspects of their programming. Murawski and Swanson (2001) described co-teaching as a service delivery option particularly appropriate for serving students with special needs and conducted a meta-analysis of existing research. They noted that "although numerous authors currently espouse co-teaching as an effective alternative to service delivery for students with disabilities within the general education setting, very few provide experimental data" (p. 264). Only 3 of the 89 studies Murawski and Swanson reviewed in their meta-analysis provided sufficient information concerning students with special needs, and they cautioned against drawing any firm conclusion from their results (see also Solis, Vaughn, Swanson, & Mcculley, 2012). Nevertheless, the limited evidence available at the time, none of which pertained to DHH learners, indicated wide variability in forms of co-teaching and related outcomes but suggested that it was "moderately successful" overall. A review by Friend, Cook, Hurley-Chamberlain, and Shamberger (2008) similarly argued that diversity among forms of co-teaching in special education and the lack of fully documented research yielded only an "equivocal evidence base." Scruggs, Mastropieri, and McDuffie (2007) reviewed qualitative rather than quantitative research on co-teaching. They reported that co-teachers generally believed that the model was beneficial when implemented voluntarily. In contrast to the emphasis of chapters in this volume on equal responsibilities of co-teachers, they found a "one teacher, one assistant" model to be prevalent, a form of co-teaching they argued was not supported in the existing literature. Rather, as described by de Klerk et al. (this volume), DiGregorio et al. (this volume), and other chapters, collaboration and shared expertise are seen as touchstones for successful co-teaching.

CO-ENROLLMENT OUTCOMES

At the beginning of this volume, we noted that proponents of co-enrollment argue that such programs are more likely to result in both academic and social integration as well as improving academic achievement of DHH students. Although recent studies have suggested that DHH students in mainstream programs today are not as isolated and lonely as was suggested early on, co-enrollment programs do appear to facilitate social interactions between DHH and hearing peers (see Antia et al., this volume). It remains unclear, however, whether they do so to a significantly greater extent than in comparable mainstream classrooms. That is, thanks to societal change and technological advancement, DHH children today appear to be more readily accepted by hearing peers than in the past, a shift that hopefully will continue as current cohorts reach their teenage years and proceed into adulthood. At the same time, for a variety of reasons, even in co-enrollment programs, DHH and hearing youth frequently self-impose segregation by hearing status (de Klerk et al., this volume; Yiu & Tang, 2014; Yiu et al., this volume). To a large extent, such de facto segregation is a (perhaps understandable) consequence of ease of communication. Similar language-related segregation happens when hearing children (and sometimes adults) from different language backgrounds are put together. True, sign languages have become more accepted, and sign language increasingly is offered in schools as a "foreign language." Cochlear implants and digital hearing aids also have provided DHH children with greater opportunities than ever before to acquire spoken language (Knoors & Marschark, 2012). Assistive listening devices, however, rarely provide sufficiently "normal" hearing for most teenaged DHH learners to feel fully comfortable in social and academic settings or to develop close relationships with hearing peers.

Antia et al. (this volume) pointed out that DHH students who attend mainstream programs tend to have lesser hearing losses and better spoken language skills than those who attend separate programs specifically designed for DHH students. Such differences perhaps account, in part, for findings indicating that DHH students with access to the general education curriculum achieve better academic outcomes. In fact, recent studies involving large, diverse samples of DHH learners have indicated that by high school, attendance only at mainstream schools and use of spoken language are two of the strongest, significant predictors of academic achievement (Crowe, Marschark, Dammeyer, & Lehane, 2017; Marschark, Shaver, Nagle, & Newman, 2015; but see further discussion later in this chapter).

Most chapters in this volume indicate that their co-enrollment programs follow the general education curriculum, and that also may account for what appears to be enhanced academic achievement in programs like those described in chapters by Hennies and Hennies, Ghesquière and Meurant, and Krausneker and Kramreiter. But children in those programs also benefit academically (and perhaps social-emotionally) from the enhanced pace of instruction and higher expectations that are more typical in mainstream settings than specialized schools for the deaf. At the same time, however, those program descriptions and others also indicate that, as noted by Antia et al. (this volume), DHH students with greater hearing losses, and especially those who rely primarily on sign language, often require additional support services that consume some portion of the school day. The co-enrollment programs described in this volume largely have developed ways to accommodate those needs without jeopardizing academic progress by hearing classmates (Kreimeyer et al., 2002). Nevertheless, that does not mean that DHH and hearing students necessarily are receiving or are able to benefit fully from equivalent academic opportunities.

Academic outcomes of DHH learners in some co-enrollment programs suggest that they are performing at levels beyond those of DHH students in other settings, at least in some domains and at some points in time (Baker et al., this volume; Kreimeyer et al., 2000; Yiu et al., this volume). But, for a variety of reasons directly or indirectly associated with hearing loss, those levels frequently still are below those of hearing norms and classmates (e.g., Hermans et al., 2014; McCain & Antia, 2005; for discussion, see Marschark & Leigh, 2016; Marschark & Knoors, 2012). Other programs report academic performance of DHH children in co-enrollment programs consistently meeting or exceeding those of hearing children (Ghesquière & Meurant, this volume; Hennies & Hennies, this volume; Krausneker & Kramreiter, this volume). That performance is attributed to bilingual language abilities, motivation, and/or engagement, but longer-term research is needed to determine which factors are most important for which learners in which settings.

Given the diversity among and relative newness of many co-enrollment programs and the fact that they are situated in different parts of the world, variability in their academic outcomes perhaps should not be surprising. Perhaps for similar reasons, claims of significantly better outcomes (or at least prospects) than historically have been the case, but with limited evidence to support them, appear to parallel the situation with regard to bilingual deaf education (Marschark, Knoors, & Tang, 2014). As Antia et al. (this volume) pointed out, "While the social benefits of the dual language environment [in co-enrollment programs] seem to be consistent and positive, the academic benefits are more difficult to pin down." Günther and Hennies (2015) similarly emphasized that variability in language programming rigor, language assessment, and other factors in various descriptions of bimodal bilingual programs make it difficult to draw conclusions about their long-term value. Accordingly, they suggested that the apparent lack of evidence supporting bimodal bilingual education for DHH children (Bagga-Gupta, 2004; Marschark et al., 2014; Swanwick et al., 2014) should not be taken as an indicator of their lack of success but as a call for more rigorous evaluation.

Related to differences between some of the reports from European bimodal bilingual and co-enrollment programs and those from elsewhere as well as the aforementioned "some points in time" caveat, it is important to note that more favorable academic outcomes reported to be associated with co-enrollment and bilingual programming as well as multi-grade classrooms and co-teaching come largely from the younger grades. Marschark and Knoors (2019) noted the consistent pattern of findings indicating stronger academic performance associated with early access to sign language via deaf parents or bilingual programming and those associated with early access to spoken language via cochlear implants. However, neither early sign language nor early amplification-assisted spoken language provides DHH learners with access to the world around them comparable to that typically experienced by hearing peers. Accordingly, Marschark and Knoors also described findings from a variety of sources indicating that the early academic benefits evidenced by DHH children of deaf parents, those in bilingual programs, and those with cochlear implants are largely limited to the primary school years and are largely attenuated or absent at secondary school and university levels. They described several possible loci for such findings, including the frequent reduction or withdrawal of support services for DHH children demonstrating age-appropriate language and academic functioning during the early years and the greater complexity/difficulty of materials, tasks, and cognitive expectations in higher grades relative to lower grades. While full explication of that issue is beyond the scope of the present discussion, it is not inconsistent with the cautions raised by Hennies and Hennies (this volume) and Günther and Hennies (2015) about drawing conclusions concerning various forms of deaf education when programs vary so widely. This issue also emphasizes the importance of not drawing broad generalizations from research studies involving small samples or small age ranges when we are dealing with such a heterogeneous population.

None of the foregoing is to deny what appears to be the great potential of co-enrollment programs for DHH learners, what de Klerk et al. (this volume) and Knoors and Marschark (2014) described as offering them "the best of both worlds." Almost all of the chapters in this volume describe programs with multiple levels of flexibility and motivation, from DHH and hearing classmates to school administrations and regional authorities. Co-enrollment classrooms, by definition, aim to provide all students with access to all content at all levels at all times. A number of educators and investigators, for example, have emphasized the importance of active student engagement for learning (e.g., Hermans, de Klerk, Wauters, & Knoors, 2014; Reyes, Brackett, Rivers, White, & Salovey, 2012; Tolmie et al., 2010; Wang, Haertel, & Walberg, 1997). Active engagement in the co-enrollment programs described by several chapters of this volume are reported to be facilitated by multi-grade groupings and inclusive and thoughtful academic programming and are strongly associated with effective classroom communication for all (see also Knoors & Hermans, 2010).

Teacher expectations also are well documented to be associated with achievement among both DHH and hearing learners (see Knoors & Marschark, 2014). Chapters by Abbate (this volume), Hoofard et al. (this volume), and de Klerk et al. (this volume), among others, reflect high expectations on the part of teachers of the deaf, general education teachers, and school administrators as being a fundamental ingredient in co-enrollment. Higher expectations also appear to be appreciated by higher-performing DHH learners who might become frustrated with a slower pace, less time on task, or lower teacher expectations (Antia, Sabers, & Stinson, 2007; Knoors & Hermans, 2010; Spencer & Marschark, 2010). Co-enrollment does not necessarily eliminate differences between DHH and hearing classmates in their levels of satisfaction in the classroom, but cooperation and collaboration certainly can help to reduce them. Co-enrollment is not a panacea; it is an opportunity that is going to be influenced by the personalities of the students and adults in the classroom as well as the attitudes of the larger school community (Antia, 2015).

These factors all are clearly important for DHH learners' academic achievement, and co-enrollment programing may, indeed, promote them to a greater extent than mainstream general education classrooms. It will be difficult if not impossible, however, to distinguish the extent to which any observed academic advantages of co-enrollment programming derive from the inclusive aspect of that model or other features typical of such programs (e.g., language accessibility, social acceptance, peer and adult role models). Most likely, it is all of these things, together with teachers' greater sensitivity to DHH learners' cognitive strengths and needs, access to and expectations for handling the general curriculum, and family support, combining to enhance academic outcomes for DHH children in co-enrollment programs. These features of the co-enrollment gestalt are rarely all found together in either typical mainstream classrooms or separate classrooms for DHH learners. How they are combined in any particular co-enrollment program will depend on the individuals, resources, and support available. The specific weighting of those features likely is less important than the thoughtfulness with which they are assembled and provided by the program.

Given the heterogeneity of the DHH population, the backgrounds of DHH learners, and the diverse settings in which co-enrollment programs have been created, it should not be surprising that the limited evidence available suggests that even while co-enrollment outcomes may exceed those experienced by DHH learners in either mainstream or separate programs, results are variable. Ghesquière and Meurant (this volume) pointed out, for example, that DHH children coming into co-enrollment education programs may have relatively impoverished content knowledge and knowledge of the world due to limited personal experience and limited exposure to the informal conversations of others. Research involving DHH learners in several domains has indicated that such gaps can influence social-emotional functioning (e.g., theory of mind) as well as academic performance (e.g., mathematics). These are larger issues that co-enrollment programming may not be able to resolve fully because of their dependence on interactions among other factors such as degree of hearing loss, parent involvement, early communication access, the age at which children enter co-enrollment programming, and how long they remain there. Realistically, neither co-enrollment nor any other kind of model for deaf education can guarantee that all DHH learners will achieve long-term academic outcomes fully comparable to those of hearing peers (see Baker et al., this volume; de Klerk et al., this volume). Nevertheless, at present there do not appear to be any better alternatives than the kinds of programs described in this volume.

FINAL THOUGHTS

Kathryn Meadow-Orlans (2000) called for "informed educational placement," meaning the importance of evidence-based practice in weaving together strengths and needs of students, families, schools, and the larger community (Hennies & Hennies, this volume; see Antia, 2015). Meadow-Orlans suggested that deaf education offered too few alternative placements for too many DHH learners (see Abbate, this volume). Her point was not about the number of schools for the deaf or the number of sign language interpreters available in mainstream classrooms. Rather, it was an advocacy for recognizing diversity among deaf learners and the need for diverse, flexible programming to give them the best chances for success, the larger tricky mix described by Nelson et al. (1993; Nelson & Arkenberg, 2008). Co-enrollment programs explicitly recognize and even embrace that diversity, and thus they aim to provide flexible programming for their students and collaboration and professional development for their staff. Indeed, the co-enrollment programs described in this volume emphasize collaboration as the key to the success of the model. Most of them thus suggest that co-teaching is most beneficial when both teachers, as well as interpreters, aides, and other adults in the classroom, are responsible for all students, both deaf and hearing. Successful co-enrollment classrooms also are characterized by collaboration among their students.

Where Do We Go from Here?

Lacking a larger body of evidence concerning the long-term impact of co-enrollment on academic, personal, and employment success of DHH learners, it may be Pollyanna-ish of us to propose that it looks like the best road to deaf education in the future. Given the personnel and financial resources needed to support co-enrollment programming, as well as the changing face of deaf education brought about by digital hearing aids, cochlear implants, and increasing societal acceptance of "disability," co-enrollment is unlikely to become the universal, educational prototype for DHH (and hearing) learners. But time will tell. At a minimum, programming offers the best of mainstream and special education for DHH students in terms of its benefits to social-emotional development of DHH children (see Knoors & Marschark, 2014, Chapter 11; Wauters & Knoors, 2008; Yiu & Tang, 2014). Chapters in this volume—especially those that describe classrooms with multi-grade learners—additionally indicate that the flexibility and sense of community in co-enrollment classrooms also can lead to greater academic engagement (Knoors & Hermans, 2010), potentially supporting broader academic benefits.

Linguistic benefits also appear evident for DHH learners in co-enrollment programs, regardless of whether or the extent to which programs are explicitly bilingual. There is some evidence suggesting that the acquisition of a sign language can provide cognitive benefits for hearing children (Capirci, Cattani, Rossini, & Volterra, 1998) as well as DHH children (Ormel & Giezen, 2014), but little attention has been devoted to benefits possibly accruing to hearing children who have attended co-enrollment programs.

There remain several other areas concerning co-enrollment programming in which empirical evidence is scarce, at least partly the result of there being so few programs, and most of those relatively young. As alluded to earlier, it may be that academic benefits, as well as the social-emotional contributions of bilingual education, are inextricably intertwined in the supportive environment of the co-enrollment classroom, especially with regard to the availability of diverse models, (potentially) multi-grade/multi-talented peers, and two teachers. Such combinations may provide synergy that results in longer-term language and academic growth, but such research remains to be conducted. Research concerning multi-grade education for DHH learners also is lacking, at least in any long-term sense. Ultimately, if we want parents, schools, and school districts to accept co-enrollment as a viable option, we are going to have to provide evidence that it is worth the cost.

Co-enrollment may be expensive in the short run but, like other aspects of deaf education, it may turn out to be cost effective in the long run.

Beyond research and even the academic potential of co-enrollment programming are a number of practical issues. No one ever said that creating or running a co-enrollment program was easy. Sustaining such a program first requires long-term investment of resources and trust by multiple administrative units, schools and above. It requires cooperation, patience, and real effort from teachers and other professionals in the classroom in order to ensure that all learners are treated equally with an eye toward building on their strengths and accommodating their needs. As we noted in the introductory chapter, educating "children with disabilities" together with hearing children, co-teaching, and even just sharing one's classroom with other adults can be challenging for teachers who might have to adjust their educational beliefs, attitudes, and behaviors. This is most commonly an issue for general education teachers, but teachers of the deaf often find themselves discomforted in co-enrollment programs as well (see de Klerk et al., this volume; Hoofard et al., this volume).

Long-term buy-in for co-enrollment programming is needed by parents or, better still, whole families (Kirchner, this volume). Both Kreimeyer et al. (this volume) and Yiu et al. (this volume) note that some parents and others involved in deaf education have raised concerns that the specific needs of DHH students might be neglected in large hearing classrooms (but see Kreimeyer et al., 2000), where they may not receive as much support as they might in a self-contained classroom. Conversely, many older members of the Deaf community believe that schools for the deaf are the most appropriate/beneficial settings for educating DHH learners, even if there is little empirical evidence to support that view. In any case, support for co-enrollment programming from the local Deaf community is extremely helpful (see Baker, this volume; Di Gregorio, this volume), not only for those programs that emphasize sign language, but for all programs that seek to show both DHH and hearing learners that deaf individuals are real people with real lives.

Co-enrollment programs cannot be static. Some already have come and gone. Yiu et al. (this volume) describe the development of their program as "a continuous problem-solving process, requiring persistent reflections, reviews and modifications at all times." The Dutch program described by de Klerk et al. was built on the foundations of the earlier Twinschool project (Hermans et al., 2014), and Hoofard et al. (this volume) describe how the expansion of the Oregon program was made possible by the earlier Childswork program. Some such changes come about by virtue of practical necessity (e.g., administrative, financial) and, at least in theory, co-enrollment and other programs should evolve with the emergence of evidence concerning best practices in deaf education and inclusive education. Hettiarachchi et al. (in press) and others have suggested replacing "teacher of the deaf" training programs with "inclusive education" training programs, the potential of which is clearly exemplified in many of the program descriptions offered in this volume. Indeed, several of the programs described, even beyond the original TRIPOD program described by Kirchner (this volume), have become international models for the potential of inclusive and co-enrollment programs. Unfortunately, co-enrollment programs tend to be small, and they are not always the most visible. Hence this book.

REFERENCES

Ansari, A. (2017). Multigrade kindergarten classrooms and children's academic achievement, executive function, and socioemotional development. *Infant and Child Development, 26*(6), e2036.

Antia, S. (2015). Enhancing academic and social outcomes: Balancing individual, family, and school assets and risks for deaf and hard-of-hearing students in general education. In H. Knoors & M. Marschark (Eds.), *Educating deaf learners: Creating a global evidence base* (pp. 527–546). New York: Oxford University Press.

Antia, S. D., Sabers, D., & Stinson, M. S. (2007). Validity and reliability of the Classroom Participation Questionnaire with deaf and hard of hearing students in public schools. *Journal of Deaf Studies and Deaf Education, 12*, 158–171.

Antia, S., Stinson, M., & Gaustad, M. (2002). Developing membership in the education of deaf and hard of hearing students in inclusive settings. *Journal of Deaf Studies and Deaf Education, 7*, 214–229.

Bagga-Gupta, S. (2004). *Literacies and deaf education: A theoretical analysis of the international and Swedish literature.* Stockholm: Swedish National Agency for School Improvement.

Bowen, S. K. (2008). Coenrollment for students who are deaf or hard of hearing: Friendship patterns and social interactions. *American Annals of the Deaf, 153*, 285–293.

Capirci, O., Cattani, A., Rossini, & Volterra, V. (1998). Teaching sign language to hearing children as a possible factor in cognitive enhancement. *Journal of Deaf Studies and Deaf Education, 3*, 135–142.

Crowe, K., Marschark, M., Dammeyer, J. & Lehane, C. (2017). Achievement, language, and technology use among college-bound deaf learners. *Journal of Deaf Studies and Deaf Education, 22*, 393–401.

Friend, M., Cook, L., Hurley-Chamberlain, D., & Shamberger, C. (2008). Co-teaching: An illustration of the complexity of collaboration in special education. *Journal of Educational and Psychological Consultation, 20*, 9–27.

Frosco, A. M., Schleser, R., & Andal, J. (2004). Multiage programming effects on cognitive developmental level and reading achievement in early elementary school children. *Reading Psychology, 25*, 1–17

Günther, K.-B., & Hennies, J. (2015). Stand und Perspektiven einer bimodal-bilingualen Erziehung und Bildung für gehörlose und schwerhörige Kinder: Eine diskursive Auseinandersetzung mit dem Sammelband

Bilingualism and Bilingual Deaf Education, hrsg. von Marc Marschark, Gladys Tang & Harry Knoors. *Das Zeichen, 29*(101), 498–508.

Hermans, D., De Klerk, A., Wauters, L., & Knoors, H. (2014). The Twinschool: A co-enrollment program in the Netherlands. In M. Marschark, G. Tang, & H. Knoors (Eds.), *Bilingualism and bilingual deaf education* (pp. 396–423). New York: Oxford University Press.

Hettiarachchi, S., de Silva, M. D. K., Wijesinghe, T., Susantha, B., Amila, G., Sarani, P., & Rasak, M. (in press). "Free but not fair": A critical review of access to equal education to deaf children in Sri Lanka. In H. Knoors, M. Brons, & M. Marschark (Eds.), *Deaf education beyond the Western world*. New York: Oxford University Press.

Kirchner, C. J. (1994). Co-enrollment as an inclusion model. *American Annals of the Deaf, 139*(2), 163–164.

Knoors, H, (2016). Language use in the classroom accommodating the needs of diverse deaf and hard-of-hearing learners. In M. Marschark, V. Lampropoulou, & E. Skordilis (Eds.), *Diversity in deaf education* (pp. 219–246). New York: Oxford University Press.

Knoors, H., & Hermans, D. (2010). Effective instruction for deaf and hard-of-hearing students: Teaching strategies, school settings, and student characteristics. In M. Marschark & P. E. Spencer (Eds.), *The Oxford handbook of deaf studies, language, and education* (Vol. 2, pp. 57–71). New York: Oxford University Press.

Knoors, H., & Marschark, M. (2012). Language planning for the 21st century: Revisiting bilingual language policy for deaf children. *Journal of Deaf Studies and Deaf Education, 17*, 291–305.

Knoors, H., & Marschark, M. (2014). *Teaching deaf learners: Psychological and developmental foundations*. New York: Oxford University Press.

Kreimeyer, K. H., Crooke, P., Drye, C., Egbert, V., & Klein, B. (2000). Academic and social benefits of a coenrollment model of inclusive education for deaf and hard-of-hearing children. *Journal of Deaf Studies and Deaf Education, 5*, 174–185.

Logue, M. E. (2006). Teachers observe to learn: Differences in social behavior of toddlers and preschoolers in same-age and multiage groupings. *Young Children, 61*, (3), 70–76.

Marschark, M. (2018). *Raising and educating a deaf child* (3rd ed.). New York: Oxford University Press.

Marschark, M., & Knoors, H. (2012). Educating deaf children: Language, cognition, and learning. *Deafness and Education International, 14*, 137–161.

Marschark, M., & Knoors, H. (2019). Sleuthing the 93% solution in deaf education. In H. Knoors & M. Marschark (Eds.), *Evidence-based practice in deaf education* (pp. 1-32). New York: Oxford University Press.

Marschark, M., Knoors, H., & Tang, G. (2014). Perspectives on bilingualism and bilingual deaf education. In M. Marschark, G. Tang, & H. Knoors (Eds.), *Bilingualism and bilingual deaf education* (pp. 445–476). New York: Oxford University Press.

Marschark, M., & Leigh, G. (2016). Recognizing diversity in deaf education: Now what do we do with it?! In M. Marschark, V. Lampropoulou, & E. Skordilis (Eds.), *Diversity in deaf education* (pp. 507–535). New York: Oxford University Press.

Marschark, M., Sapere, P., Convertino, C. M., & Pelz, J. (2008). Learning via direct and mediated instruction by deaf students. *Journal of Deaf Studies and Deaf Education, 13,* 446–461.

Marschark, M., Shaver, D. M., Nagle, K., & Newman, L. (2015). Predicting the academic achievement of deaf and hard-of-hearing students from individual, household, communication, and educational factors. *Exceptional Children, 8,* 350–369.

McCain, K., & Antia, S. D. (2005). Academic and social status of hearing, deaf, and hard-of-hearing students participating in a co-enrolled classroom. *Communication Disorders Quarterly, 27,* 20–32.

Meadow-Orlans, K. P. (2000). Deafness and social change: Ruminations of a retiring researcher. In P. E. Spencer, C. Erting, & M. Marschark (Eds.), *Development in context: The deaf child in the family and at school* (pp. 293–301). Mahwah, NJ: LEA.

Murawski, W. W., & Swanson, H. L. (2001). A meta-analysis of co-teaching research. *Remedial and Special Education, 22,* 258–267.

Nelson, K. E., & Arkenberg, M. E. (2008). Language and reading development reflect dynamic mixes of learning conditions. In M. Mody & E. R. Silliman (Eds.), *Brain, behavior, and learning in language and reading disorders* (pp. 315–348). New York: Guilford Press.

Nelson, K. E., Loncke, F., & Camarata, S. (1993). Implications of research on deaf and hearing children's language learning. In M. Marschark & M. D. Clark (Eds.), *Psychological perspectives on deafness* (pp. 123–152). Hillsdale, NJ: Lawrence Erlbaum Associates.

Ormel, E., & Giezen, M. R. (2014). Bimodal bilingual cross-language interaction: Pieces of the puzzle. In M. Marschark, G. Tang, & H. Knoors (Eds.), *Bilingualism and bilingual deaf education* (pp. 74–101). New York: Oxford University Press.

Reyes, M. R., Brackett, M. A., Rivers, S. E., White, M., & Salovey, P. (2012). Classroom emotional climate, student engagement, and academic achievement. *Journal of Educational Psychology, 104*(3), 700–712.

Sapere, P., LaRock, D., Convertino, C., Gallimore, L., & Lessard, P. (2005). Interpreting and interpreter education—Adventures in Wonderland? In M. Marschark, R. Peterson, & E. Winston (Eds.), *Sign language interpreting and interpreter education: Directions for research and practice* (pp. 283–298). New York: Oxford University Press.

Scouten, E. (1984). *Turning points in the education of deaf people.* Danville, IL: Interstate Printers and Publishers, Inc.

Scruggs, T. E., Mastropieri, M. A., & McDuffie, K. A. (2007). Co-teaching in inclusive classrooms: A metasynthesis of qualitative research. *Exceptional Children, 73,* 392–416.

Solis, M., Vaughn, S., Swanson, E., & Mcculley, L. (2012). Collaborative models of instruction: The empirical foundations of inclusion and co-teaching. *Psychology in the Schools, 49,* 498–510.

Song, R., Spradlin, T. E., & Plucker, J. A. (2009). The advantages and disadvantages of multiage classrooms in the era of NCLB accountability. Center for Evaluation & Education Policy, University of Indiana. *Education Policy Brief, 7*(1), 1–3.

Spencer, P. E., & Marschark, M. (2010). *Evidence-based practice in educating deaf and hard-of-hearing students.* New York: Oxford University Press.

Swanwick, R., Hendar, O., Dammeyer, J., Kristoffersen, A., Salter, J., & Simonsen, E. (2014). Shifting contexts and practices in sign bilingual education in northern Europe: Implications for professional development and training. In M. Marschark, G. Tang, & H. Knoors (Eds.), *Bilingualism and bilingual deaf education* (pp. 292–310). New York: Oxford University Press.

Tolmie, A. K., Topping, K. J., Christie, D., Donaldson, C., Howe, C., Jessiman, E., Livingston, K., & Thruston, A. (2010). Social effects of collaborative learning in primary schools. *Learning and Instruction, 20,* 177–191.

Wang, M. C., Haertel, G. D., & Walberg, H. J. (1997). Fostering educational resilience in inner-city schools. *Children and Youth, 7,* 119–140.

Wauters, L. N., & Knoors, H. E. T. (2008). Social integration of deaf children in inclusive settings. *Journal of Deaf Studies and Deaf Education, 13,* 21–36.

Xie, Y. H., Potměšil, M., & Peters, B. (2014). Children who are deaf or hard of hearing in inclusive educational settings: A literature review on interactions with peers. *Journal of Deaf Studies and Deaf Education, 19,* 423–437.

Yiu, K. C., & Tang, G. (2014). Social integration of deaf and hard -of-hearing students in a sign bilingual and co-enrollment environment. In M. Marschark, G. Tang, & H. Knoors (Eds.), *Bilingualism and bilingual deaf education* (pp. 342–367). New York: Oxford University Press.

Index

Tables, figures, and boxes are indicated by an italic *t*, *f*, and *b* following the page/paragraph number

academic outcomes
  Austrian co-enrollment programs, 136
  of co-enrollment, 9–13, 19, 336–39
  Dutch co-enrollment program, 203–4*t*
  Madrid bilingual co-enrollment
    programs, 252
  Sainte-Marie school co-enrollment
    program, 228–29*t*
  SLCO program, Hong Kong, 101
  Southwestern U.S. co-enrollment
    program, 278–79, 292, 293*t*
  TRIPOD program, 36
  Tucker Maxon School, 315–16, 321–22
  WRSD dual-campus model, 272–73
academic support services, WRSD dual-
    campus model, 267–68
academy schools, Spain, 236. *See also*
    Gaudem academy Madrid; Ponce
    de León academy, Madrid
access for all learners, in co-enrollment
  academic outcomes and, 9–10, 11
  Dutch co-enrollment program, 191–92
  Madrid bilingual co-enrollment
    programs, 249
  need for further research, 19
  as reason for co-enrollment programs,
    3–4, 326–27, 338–39
  Sainte-Marie school, 212, 216
  Toowong State School program, 50–51
  WRSD dual-campus model, 263
achievement, academic. *See* academic
    outcomes
active participation by students, SLCO
    program, 98–99
Act of Inclusion, Israel, 107
administration
  Madrid bilingual co-enrollment
    programs, 242

SLCO program, 90*t*
successful co-enrollment programs, 189
Toowong State School program
  overview, 44
  program organization, 45
  staff, 47–48
  students and families, 45–46
  TRIPOD program, 38–39
  WRSD dual-campus model, 269–70
adult/children ratio, 111
American Sign Language (ASL)
  in Southwestern U.S. co-enrollment
    program, 280–81, 282–83, 294–95
  in TRIPOD program, 28–29, 32, 35
amplification, 285–86, 288, 292, 312
Appropriate Education Act, the
    Netherlands, 183, 184–86
assessment. *See also* monitoring progress
  Israeli preschool co-enrollment, 122–23
  WRSD dual-campus model, 263–66
attention of DHH students,
    directing, 310–11
audiological services, WRSD dual-campus
    model, 268
auditory accessibility, in preschool
    settings, 109
auditory evaluation, in Israeli system, 122
aural-oral method, 69, 109–10. *See also* oral
    deaf education
Auslan Assessment Tool, 58
Australasian Signed English, 41–42
Australian Sign Language (Auslan).
    See also Toowong bilingual
    bicultural co-enrollment program
  contact sign continuum-reading, 54–56
  contact sign continuum-writing, 56–57
  decision to use in Toowong
    program, 42–43

347

Australian Sign Language (*cont.*)
  encouraging parents to use, 62
  L1 deaf learners, 53–57
  as L1 or L2, 52–54
  L2 deaf learners, 53
  monitoring student progress, 58
  providing access for all students, 50–51
  as subject, 52
Austrian co-enrollment programs
  general discussion, 145–46
  history and experiences, 133–36
  legal and ideological context, 136–37
  model practiced in Vienna
    benefits of, 144–45
    bilingual school life, 138–39
    challenges of, 142–43
    inclusion, 140
    mixed ages, 138
    overview, 138
    progressive teaching
      approach, 140–41
Austrian Sign Language (ÖGS)
  as compulsory subject in Salzburg
    special school, 136
  legal recognition of, 137
  status in schools, 137
  as subject, 143
  teacher competence levels, 142–43
  Vienna model, 138–40

Behavior Rating Inventory of Executive
    Function (BRIEF), 199–200t
Belgium, 205. *See also* Sainte-Marie school
    co-enrollment program
Berlin School for the Deaf, 152, 153
best of both worlds approach, Dutch co-
    enrollment program, 183, 190, 201
bidirectional inclusive process, 101. *See
    also* Sign Bilingualism and Co-
    Enrollment program
bilingual co-enrollment programs. *See also*
    bimodal bilingual co-enrollment
    programs; *specific programs*
  academic participation and, 12
  bilingual-bicultural method, 110
  Dutch, 193
  general discussion, 15–16, 19–20
  history of in Italy, 165
  in Japan, 72

in Madrid, Spain
  benefits of, 251–52
  changes made to school structure and
    resources, 242
  co-enrollment, defining, 237f, 237–38
  co-teaching, 244
  emergence of programs, 238–39
  features of, 239–40
  general discussion, 252–53
  inclusive nature of, 242–43
  language education, 247f, 247–51
  language use and distribution, 245–47
  overview, 235–36
  profiles of DHH students in, 240–41t
Sainte-Marie school
  benefits of, 228–30t
  challenges to, 228, 230–31
  co-enrollment setting, 215–16
  co-teaching, 224–25
  interpreters, role of, 226–27
  overview, 211
  pedagogy, 222–23
  profiles of DHH students in, 216–21
  setting, 213–15
  start of, 211–12
Toowong bilingual bicultural program,
    Australia
  benefits of, 64
  challenges faced, 61–62
  co-teaching, 49–50
  general discussion, 65
  guiding principles for, 44t
  history of, 41–43
  key administrative
    components, 44–46
  key pedagogies used and curriculum
    directions, 51–57
  monitoring student progress, 58–60
  overview, 41
  providing access for all
    students, 50–51
bilingual deaf education, defining, 152–53
bilingual DHH students, in Sainte-Marie
    program, 220
bilingual teachers, Sainte-Marie school
  bilingual pedagogy, 222–23
  challenges for, 230–31
  co-teaching, 224–25
  and interpreters, 226–27

overview, 212
program setting, 213
bimodal bilingual co-enrollment
    programs
in Austria
    benefits of, 144–45
    bilingual school life, 138–39
    challenges of, 142–43
    general discussion, 145–46
    history and experiences, 133–36
    inclusion, 140
    legal and ideological context, 136–37
    mixed ages, 138
    model practiced in Vienna, 138–45
    progressive teaching
        approach, 140–41
in Erfurt, Germany
    characteristics of, 159–60
    establishment of, 156–57
    general discussion, 160–61
    preconditions for, 157–58
    preschool program, 158–59
in German early invention
    centers, 150–51
in German schools for DHH
    students, 151–53
interpreter use in, 331–32
ISISS Magarotto School (Italy)
    organization, 167–68
in regular schools in Germany, 155–56
SLCO program, Hong Kong
    active participation by
        students, 98–99
    deaf education in Hong Kong, 85
    deaf individual involvement in
        school practices, 92–96
    development of, 85–86
    general discussion, 101–3
    linguistic landscape of Hong
        Kong, 84
    versus other co-enrollment
        programs, 326–27
    overview, 83–84, 86–87
    preliminary evidence for, 100–1
    supporting bimodal bilingual
        development, 96–97, 98t
    whole-school approach, 87–91t
Tommaso Silvestri primary school
    (Italy)

didactic strategies, 171–72
evaluation, 177–78
learning in different disciplines,
    176f, 174–77
overview, 170–71
programs and organization of
    didactics, 172
relationships with other
    agencies, 178–79
teaching principles, 175f, 173–74
blended classrooms. See co-enrollment
    programs
Book-Creator app, 55
brainstorming, 171
BRIEF (Behavior Rating Inventory of
    Executive Function), 199–200t
Brisbane, Australia. See Toowong
    bilingual bicultural co-enrollment
    program
Burbank Unified School District (BUSD),
    TRIPOD in, 30–33

California. See TRIPOD program
Carinthia, Austria, 133–34
center-based campus, WRSD,
    258–60, 263–66
center schools (residential schools for the
    deaf), 3–4. See also special schools
    for deaf children
child-centered approach, 28, 309–10
children who are deaf and hard of
    hearing. See deaf and hard-of-
    hearing children
Childswork preschool, 307–11, 314–15
CIDS (Cultural Identity and Diversity for
    DHH Students) curriculum, 193
circle time, 171
CIs (cochlear implants), 239, 285–86,
    312, 314
civilization visual maps, 176
class membership. See inclusion;
    membership, in co-enrollment
    programs; social-emotional
    outcomes
classroom interpreters. See interpreters,
    sign language
Classroom Participation Questionnaire, 12
classroom teachers. See general education
    teachers

cochlear implants (CIs), 239, 285–86,
    312, 314
co-enrollment programs. *See also specific
    programs; specific program types;
    specific schools*
  academic outcomes, 9–13, 19, 336–39
  barriers and challenges to, 4–5,
    16–18, 298
  benefits to DHH students in, 6–15
  coining of term, 31*f*, 31
  commonalities and differences
    in, 325–27
  defined, 84
  establishment and maintenance of, 297
  foundations of
    class membership, 327–29
    communication and language, 329–31
    co-teaching and presence of deaf
      adults in classroom, 333–35
    multi-age, multi-grade
      classrooms, 332–33
  future of, 341–42
  general discussion, 20–21, 340–41
  language proficiency and, 14–15
  versus mainstreaming, 1, 101
  need for further research, 18–20, 341–42
  outcomes, 336–39
  overview, vii, 1–3
  reasons behind, 3–5
  in regular schools in Germany, 155–56
  social outcomes, 4–5, 6–8, 19, 336
  in Southwestern U.S.
    communication philosophy, 280–81
    general discussion, 297
    history of, 277–78
    interpreter perspectives on,
      281, 289–91
    versus other co-enrollment
      programs, 326–27
    overview of current program, 279–80
    parent perspectives on, 281, 295–96
    student perspectives on, 281, 291–95
    teacher perspectives on, 281–89
  TRIPOD educational principles, 32
co-learning, 141
collaboration
  in co-enrollment programs, 20
  between deaf and hearing
    educators, 87–91*t*

ISISS Magarotto School teams, 170
combined education projects, in
    Spain, 238
commitment, to co-enrollment
    program, 187
common goals, in SLCO program, 88–91*t*
communication
  access to, in Dutch co-enrollment
    program, 191–92
  challenges in co-enrollment, 17–18
  critical age hypothesis and choice of
    methods, 109–11
  evaluation of in Israeli preschool
    system, 122–23
  as foundation of co-enrollment
    programs, 329–31
  in Israeli preschool co-enrollment
    system, 121
  in preschool co-enrollment, 111
  in Southwestern U.S. program, 280–81,
    282–83, 285
  Total Communication philosophy, 28–
    29, 110–11, 222–23, 329–30
  as TRIPOD educational principle, 32
  in Tucker Maxon School
    preschool, 310–11
  in WRSD dual-campus model,
    260–61, 267–68
community membership. *See* inclusion;
    membership, in co-enrollment
    programs
comprehensive schools, in Germany, 155–
    56. *See also* Erfurt bimodal bilingual
    co-enrollment program
contact sign continuum
  moving back and forth along, 54
  reading, 54–56
  writing, 56–57
cooperative learning, 171
coordinators, Dutch co-enrollment
    program, 188–89
cost
  as barrier to co-enrollment, 18
  as challenge for Tucker Maxon
    School, 317
  Dutch co-enrollment program, 190
co-teaching
  academic integration and, 12
  challenges involved in, 17

deaf-hearing team teaching in
Austria, 134
deaf teacher involvement, in SLCO
program, 92–96
in Dutch co-enrollment program, 188,
192–93, 197
as foundation of co-enrollment
programs, 333–35
in Israeli preschool co-enrollment
system, 120
in Madrid bilingual co-enrollment
programs, 244
overview, 2–3
in Sainte-Marie co-enrollment program,
224–25, 334
in Southwestern U.S. co-enrollment
program, 282
in Toowong State School program,
43, 49–50
in TRIPOD program, 29–30, 35–36
in Tucker Maxon School, 317
in Vienna model, 142
critical age hypothesis, 109–11
critical mass of DHH students
in co-enrollment settings, 215–16, 257
foundations of co-enrollment, 327–29
in SLCO program, 96–97
Toowong State School program,
61–62, 65
in WRSD program, 261
cued articulation, 53
cued speech (CS), 213, 220–21, 249
cultural approach, in Madrid bilingual
co-enrollment, 239–40
Cultural Identity and Diversity for DHH
Students (CIDS) curriculum, 193
curricula
access, in co-enrollment, 4–5
adjusting to DHH children's needs in
preschool, 113
in Israeli preschool co-enrollment
system, 121–22
Toowong State School program
Auslan as L1 or L2, 52–54
Auslan as subject, 52
Auslan L1 deaf learners, 53–54
Auslan L2 deaf learners, 53
contact sign
continuum-reading, 54–56

contact sign
continuum-writing, 56–57
languages of instruction and
modeling bilingualism, 51–52
vertical, 168
in Vienna model, 141

databases for listening and spoken
language outcomes, 323
deaf and hard-of-hearing (DHH) children.
See also co-enrollment programs;
deaf education; diversity among
deaf learners; specific co-enrollment
courses
benefits of multi-age/multi-grade
classrooms for, 290
class membership, 327–29
critical mass of
in co-enrollment settings, 215–16, 257
foundations of co-enrollment, 327–29
in SLCO program, 96–97
Toowong State School program,
61–62, 65
in WRSD program, 261
deaf teachers as role model for, 93
full inclusion
in co-enrollment approach, 1
in Dutch co-enrollment
program, 194
in Japan, 70–71
in Southwestern U.S. co-enrollment
program, 286–89
mainstreaming
versus co-enrollment, 1
history of, 3–4
social integration and, 4–5, 6, 7–8
MH designation, 30–31
middle school co-enrollment
issues, 288–89
proportion in classes
foundations of co-enrollment, 327–29
Sainte-Marie school, 215–16
Toowong State School
program, 61–62
in regular schools in Germany, 153–55
self-contained classes for, 27
teacher expectations for, 10–11, 339
Deaf community, benefits of Madrid
programs for, 251–52

Deaf culture
   Dutch co-enrollment program and, 193
   Tommaso Silvestri primary school
      relationship with, 178
deaf education. *See also* co-enrollment
      programs; oral deaf education;
      special schools for deaf children;
      specific programs and schools
   continuum of, in WRSD dual-campus
      model, 262–63
   in Germany
      early intervention, 149–50
      inclusion in regular schools, 153–55
      overview, 149
      schools for DHH students, 151–53
   in Hong Kong, 83, 85
   in Japan, 69
   in Queensland, Australia, 42–43
   seeds of discontent related to, 33
   TRIPOD principles, 25, 26, 32
deaf educators
   deaf-hearing team teaching in
      Austria, 134
   in Dutch co-enrollment program, 193
   in Erfurt bimodal bilingual co-
      enrollment program, 157
   as foundation of co-enrollment
      programs, 333–35
   in German schools for DHH
      students, 151–52
   in ISISS Magarotto School
      organization, 170
   in Japanese deaf education, 73, 79
   in Madrid bilingual co-enrollment
      programs, 240
   professional training of in Hong
      Kong, 94
   in SLCO program
      collaboration between hearing
         educators and, 87–91*t*
      involvement in school
         practices, 92–96
      supporting bimodal bilingual
         development, 96–97
   in Southwestern U.S. co-enrollment
      program, 285
   in Toowong State School program, 43,
      47–48, 52
   in Vienna model, 138–39, 144–45, 146

Deaf Festival, SLCO program, 98*t*
deaf-specific didactics, 139
delivery of lessons, Toowong State School
      program, 50
developmental system approach, 123
DHH children. *See* co-enrollment
      programs; deaf and hard-of-
      hearing children; deaf education;
      diversity among deaf learners;
      specific co-enrollment courses
didactics
   in ISISS Magarotto School
      organization, 167–68
   Tommaso Silvestri primary
      school, 171–72
digital textbooks, 174
diplomas, high school, TRIPOD students
      receiving, 34–35
direct teaching, in Toowong
      program, 50–51
disciplinary programs, Tommaso Silvestri
      primary school, 176*f*, 172, 174–77
discipline, WRSD dual-campus
      model, 269
diversity among deaf learners
   in Dutch co-enrollment program
      case studies, 195–97
      meeting diverse needs of, 197
      overview, 194–95
   in Madrid, Spain, 240–41*t*
   overview, 325, 340–41
   preschool age, 117
   in Sainte-Marie program
      French as L1, LSFB as L2, 217
      LSFB and French bilingual, 220
      LSFB as L1, French as L2, 219–20
      no first language when entering
         school, 218–19
      overview, 216–17
      pedagogical adaptations to variety
         of, 220–21
   in Vienna model, 142
Double Discontinuity hypothesis, 54
dramatization, 172
dual-campus model of co-enrollment.
      See Willie Ross School for the Deaf
      dual-campus model
dual models of education, 235
Dutch co-enrollment program

DHH students in
case studies, 195–97
meeting diverse needs of, 197
overview, 194–95
establishment of
Appropriate Education Act, 184–86
commitment, need for, 187
educational policy of mainstream
school, 186–87
overview, 184
practical key issues, 188–90
general discussion, 206–7
key principles
access to communication and
instruction, 191–92
bilingual education, 193
co-teaching, 192–93
DHH role models and deaf
culture, 193
full members of class and school, 194
overview, 190–91
monitoring program and student
achievement
executive functioning of DHH
children, 199–201t
experiences of parents, 206
experiences of teachers, 205
language development, 203
overview, 198
research program, 199–206
school achievement, 203–4t
social outcomes, 201–2
versus other co-enrollment
programs, 326–27
overview, 183–84
parent involvement, 198
Dutch language, 193, 203
dynamic assessment, WRSD dual-campus
model, 265–66

early childhood education (ECE)
specialists, 309–10
early intervention. See also preschool co-
enrollment programs
in Germany, 149–50
Tucker Maxon School, 306–7
early intervention center of Erfurt
(ECC), 156–58
East Longmeadow Public Schools (ELPS)

deaf education continuum, 262–63
general discussion, 260–61
as model, 271
overview, 258–59
teaching and learning at
administrative and related
issues, 269–70
communication and academic
support services, 267–68
overview, 266–67
ECC (early intervention center of
Erfurt), 156–58
ECE (early childhood education)
specialists, 309–10
École et Surdité, 212, 214–15
ecological system theory, 115, 123
education, deaf. See co-enrollment
programs; deaf education; oral
deaf education; special schools for
deaf children; specific programs and
schools
Educational and Psychopedagogical Team
(EOEP), 236, 239
educational interpreters. See interpreters,
sign language
educational policies, 186–87
Education Director, WRSD, 262–63, 270
Education for All Handicapped Children
Act (Public Law 94–142), U.S., 3–4,
27–28, 33, 306
EF (executive functioning) of DHH
children, 190–91, 199–201t
elementary school co-enrollment
programs. See primary school
co-enrollment programs; specific
programs
eligibility committees, Israel, 107
ELPS. See East Longmeadow Public
Schools
El Sol state school, Madrid
language education, 248
language use and distribution
in, 246
limitations imposed from
administration, 242–43
number of DHH students in, 240–41t
transition to co-enrollment, 239
emotional outcomes. See social-emotional
outcomes

engagement, academic, 9–10, 11–12, 19,
        338–39. *See also* academic
        outcomes
English language
    Madrid bilingual co-enrollment
        programs, 250–51, 252
    Southwestern U.S. co-enrollment
        program, 280–81
    Tommaso Silvestri primary
        school, 174–75
    Toowong State School program
        access for all students, 50–51
        Auslan L1 deaf learners, 53–57
        Auslan L2 deaf learners, 52–53
        contact sign
            continuum-reading, 54–56
        contact sign
            continuum-writing, 56–57
        languages of instruction and
            modeling bilingualism, 51–52
        monitoring student progress, 58–60
enriched linguistic context, in SLCO
        program, 96–97, 98*t*
EOEP (Educational and
        Psychopedagogical Team), 236, 239
Erfurt bimodal bilingual co-enrollment
        program, Germany
    characteristics of, 159–60
    establishment of, 156–57
    general discussion, 160–61
    preconditions for, 157–58
    preschool program, 158–59
ethical principles, of interpreters, 226–27
evaluation. *See* monitoring progress
executive functioning (EF) of DHH
        children, 190–91, 199–201*t*
expectations, teacher, 10–11, 339
expense
    as barrier to co-enrollment, 18
    as challenge for Tucker Maxon
        School, 317
    Dutch co-enrollment program, 190

face-to-face language. *See* first language
families. *See also* parents
    benefits of multi-age/multi-grade
        classrooms for, 283
    Toowong State School program, 45–46
    in TRIPOD program, 29

FAPE (free and appropriate education)
        requirements, 3–4
feeder programs, Toowong State School
        program, 61–62
fidelity to source discourse,
        interpreters, 227
Fingerspelling Our Way to Reading
        Program, 56
first language (L1)
    Auslan as, 52, 53–57, 58–59
    profiles of DHH students in Sainte-
            Marie program
        French as first language, LSFB as
            second language, 217
        LSFB as first language, French as
            second language, 219–20
        no first language when entering
            school, 218–19
flipped classroom, 171
FM systems, 286, 288–89, 311, 313
free and appropriate education (FAPE)
        requirements, 3–4
French Belgian Sign Language (LSFB)
    bilingual pedagogy in Sainte-Marie
        school, 222–23
    co-enrollment setting of Sainte-Marie
        program, 216
    profiles of DHH students in Sainte-
            Marie program
        French as L1, LSFB as L2, 217
        LSFB and French bilingual, 220
        LSFB as L1, French as L2, 219–20
        no first language when entering
            school, 218–19
        pedagogical adaptations to variety
            of, 220–21
    setting of Sainte-Marie program, 213–14
French language
    bilingual pedagogy in Sainte-Marie
        school, 222–23
    co-enrollment setting of Sainte-Marie
        program, 216
    profiles of DHH students in Sainte-
            Marie program
        French as L1, LSFB as L2, 217
        LSFB and French bilingual, 220
        LSFB as L1, French as L2, 219–20
        no first language when entering
            school, 218–19

pedagogical adaptations to variety
of, 220–21
setting of Sainte-Marie program, 213
friendships. *See* social-emotional
outcomes
full inclusion
in co-enrollment programs, 1
in Dutch co-enrollment program, 194
in Japan, 70–71
in Southwestern U.S. co-enrollment
program, 286–89
full-time co-enrollment, in Israeli
preschool system, 120
Functional Diagnosis, Italy, 172–73
functional grammar approach, 56–57, 60

Gaudem academy, Madrid
language education, 248, 250, 252
language use and distribution in, 246
number of DHH students in, 241*t*
transition to co-enrollment, 239
general education classroom, WRSD
dual-campus model, 261, 264–67,
268, 269
general education teachers. *See also* co-
teaching; deaf educators; hearing
teachers
challenges to co-enrollment for, 298
in Dutch co-enrollment program, 188,
190–91, 192–93, 197, 205
expectations for DHH students,
10–11, 339
expertise in teaching DHH
students, 5–6
in ISISS Magarotto School
organization, 169–70
in Israeli preschool co-enrollment
system, 118, 119–20, 121, 122–24
in Japanese deaf education, 71,
75–77, 78
in Madrid bilingual co-enrollment
programs
co-teaching, 240, 244
language education, 247–51
language use and distribution
in, 245–47
overview, 236
preparation for participation in
co-enrollment, 187–88

in Sainte-Marie co-enrollment program,
212, 222–25, 226
in SLCO program
deaf-hearing collaboration, 87–91*t*
deaf individuals' involvement
in, 92–96
in Southwestern U.S. program,
278, 281–89
in Toowong State School program, 43,
47–48, 63
in TRIPOD program, 29–30, 35–36
in Tucker Maxon School
preschool, 309–11
in Vienna model, 138–39, 144–46
geography lessons, 176
German Method, 149
German Sign Language, 150–53, 159
Germany
bimodal bilingual co-enrollment
program in Erfurt
characteristics of, 159–60
establishment of, 156–57
preconditions for, 157–58
preschool program, 158–59
educational system for DHH
students in
early intervention, 149–50
inclusion in regular schools, 153–55
overview, 149
schools for DHH students, 151–53
general discussion, 160–61
overview, 149
goals, common, in SLCO
program, 88–91*t*
grammar, functional approach, 56–57, 60
Graz, Austria, 133, 134
group identity of SLCO classes, 97. *See
also* inclusion; membership, in co-
enrollment programs
group work, in Vienna model, 141
guided discovery, 172
guided discussions, 171
Gymnasium Karajangasse, 143

Hamburg School for the Deaf, 151–52,
153
hard-of-hearing children. *See* deaf and
hard-of-hearing children
hearing aids, 285–86

hearing students. *See also* co-enrollment
　　programs; *specific programs*
　benefits of co-enrollment for, 284–85
　benefits of multi-age/multi-grade
　　classrooms for, 290
　class membership, 327–29
　in Dutch co-enrollment program,
　　186–87, 202
　middle school co-enrollment issues,
　　288, 289
　models of preschool co-enrollment
　　full-time co-enrollment, 120
　　overview, 117–18
　　partial co-enrollment with
　　　heterogeneous age group, 119
　　side-by-side classes, 118–19
　peer relations in early education, 112
　in Sainte-Marie school co-enrollment
　　program, 212, 216, 228–29t
　in SLCO program
　　active participation in school and
　　　social activities, 98–99
　　preliminary evidence for
　　　program, 100–1
　　supporting multimodal bilingual
　　　development, 96–97
　in Southwestern U.S. co-enrollment
　　program, 291, 292–95
　Toowong State School program
　　access for all, 50–51
　　monitoring progress of, 58–60
　　overview, 45–46
　in Tucker Maxon School, 307–11,
　　314–15, 318–22
　Vienna model, 139–40, 144
hearing teachers. *See also* co-teaching;
　　general education teachers;
　　teachers of the deaf
　deaf-hearing team teaching in
　　Austria, 134
　in Erfurt bimodal bilingual co-
　　enrollment program, 157
　in Sainte-Marie school co-enrollment
　　program, 216
　in SLCO program
　　collaboration between deaf educators
　　　and, 87–91t
　　co-teaching with deaf
　　　educators, 92–96

　in Vienna model, 138–39, 144–46
heterogeneous age group, partial
　　preschool co-enrollment with, 119
high school programs. *See* secondary
　　education
history lessons, 176
HKSL. *See* Hong Kong Sign Language
Holy Family School, 305–6
Hong Kong. *See also* Sign Bilingualism
　　and Co-Enrollment program
　deaf education in, 83, 85
　linguistic landscape of, 84
Hong Kong Sign Language (HKSL)
　enriched linguistic context to support
　　bimodal bilingual development,
　　96–97, 98t
　government view on use of, 85
　Junior Sign Language Interpreter
　　training program, 99
　overview, 84
　SLCO program results, 100, 101–2
horizontal co-enrollment. *See* Willie
　　Ross School for the Deaf
　　dual-campus model
Hosford School for the Deaf, 301
House Cochlear Implant, 312
House Ear Institute, 312–13

ICPs (Individual Curriculum Plans),
　　46, 58
IDEA (Individuals with Disabilities
　　Education Act), U.S., 318–19
IEP (Individualized Education
　　Program), 123
immersion
　as insufficient to make DHH pupils
　　bilingual, 222
　two-way, 96–97
　WRSD dual-campus model, 260–61,
　　262, 263, 265
Immersion Decree, Belgium, 211–12
incidental learning. *See* overhearing/
　　incidental learning
inclusion. *See also specific inclusive programs*
　bilingualism and, 231
　in co-enrollment approach, 1
　in Dutch co-enrollment
　　program, 194
　incremental, 261, 262, 265–66, 267

in ISISS Magarotto School
    organization, 167–68
Israeli trend toward, 107–8
in Japanese deaf education, 69–71
in Madrid bilingual co-enrollment
    programs, 242–43
models of, 62–63
promotion by UNCRPD, 2
in regular schools in Germany, 153–55
in Sainte-Marie school co-enrollment
    program, 213–14
in Toowong program, 62–63
TRIPOD program, 29–30, 38–39
in Vienna program, 140
in WRSD Partnership Campus, 260–61,
    262, 263, 265–66, 267
independent learning, 190–91
Individual Curriculum Plans (ICPs),
    46, 58
individual development plans, 185–86
individual inclusion classes, 108, 111, 328
Individualized Education Program
    (IEP), 123
Individuals with Disabilities Education
    Act (IDEA), U.S., 318–19
individual weekly study plans, 140–41
informal co-enrollment, Tucker Maxon
    School, 307–11
Institute for Deaf in Rome (ISSR), 179
Institute of Cognitive Sciences and
    Technologies-Italian National
    Research Council (ISTC-CNR),
    Italy, 166, 179
instruction
    in Dutch co-enrollment program
        access to, 191–92
        pace of, 190
    language of, 51–52, 329–31
integrated approach, WRSD dual-campus
    model, 260–61
integration of schools, in Spain, 237f,
    237–38, 239. See also co-enrollment
    programs; inclusion
International Conference on the Education
    of the Deaf, vii
interpretation prominent co-enrollment
    programs, 72–73
interpreters, sign language
    academic integration and, 11–12

Dutch co-enrollment program, 192
foundations of co-enrollment, 330–31
in Japanese deaf education
    challenges of interpretation, 74–78
    general discussion, 79–80
    overview, 72, 328
    process of interventions, 73
Junior Sign Language Interpreter
    training, 99
in middle school co-enrollment, 289
in regular schools in Germany, 153–55
Sainte-Marie school co-enrollment
    program, 214, 216, 226–27, 331–32
Southwestern U.S. co-enrollment
    program, 281, 289–91
substitute, 291
teachers' aides employed as
    educational, 48
Toowong State School program,
    48, 50–51
TRIPOD program, 35–36
Vienna model, 142
WRSD dual-campus model, 268–69
INVALSI (National Institute for the
    Evaluation of the Education and
    Training Education System),
    Italy, 178
ISISS Magarotto School, Italy. See State
    Institute for Specialized Education
    for the Deaf Magarotto School
Israeli preschool co-enrollment system
    challenges to co-enrollment of
        preschool DHH children
        adjusting curriculum to needs, 113
        auditory accessibility, 109
        critical age hypothesis and choice of
            communication method, 109–11
        multidisciplinary teamwork, 114
        overview, 108–9
        parental involvement, 113–14
        peer relations, 112
        supporting communication skills, 111
    characteristics of DHH populations, 117
    class membership, 328
    communication methods, 121
    curriculum accommodations and
        mediation, 121–22
    encouraging multidisciplinary
        partnership, 123–24

Israeli preschool co-enrollment
    system (*cont.*)
  general discussion, 125
  history of, 107–8
  implementation of three models in
    full-time co-enrollment, 120
    overview, 117–18
    partial co-enrollment with
      heterogeneous age group, 119
    side-by-side classes, 118–19
  monitoring progress, 122–23
  overview, 115*f*, 116*f*, 115–16
Israeli Special Education Law, 107
ISSR (Institute for Deaf in Rome), 179
ISTC-CNR (Institute of Cognitive Sciences
    and Technologies-Italian National
    Research Council), Italy, 166, 179
Italian language, 174–75, 179–80
Italian Sign Language (LIS), 165,
    167, 179–80
Italy, deaf education in, 165. *See also*
    Tommaso Silvestri School
itinerant teachers of the deaf, 5

Japanese primary school co-enrollment
    program
  background of, 69–71
  challenges of sign language
    interpretation
    overview, 74
    related to classroom situation, 75–78
    related to DHH pupils, 74
    related to interpreters, 75
  class membership, 328
  DHH pupils in special schools and
    regular schools, 69–70*t*
  general discussion, 79–80
  process of interventions, 73
  start of, 71–72
Japanese Sign Language (JSL)
  challenges of interpretation, 74–78
  and coining of co-enrollment term,
    31*f*, 31
  general discussion, 79–80
  overview, 69
  process of interventions, 73
  start of co-enrollment program, 71–72
Junior Sign Language Interpreter (JSLI)
    training program, 99

Kentalis Academy, the Netherlands,
    184, 198
Kentalis Talent, the Netherlands, 183. *See
    also* Dutch co-enrollment program
kindergarten, 61, 309. *See also* preschool
    co-enrollment programs
Klagenfurt, Austria, 133

language. *See also* communication;
    language development; *specific
    languages*
  co-enrollment programs and
    proficiency in, 14–15
  first
    Auslan as, 52, 53–57, 58–59
    of DHH students in Sainte-Marie
      program, 217–20
    as foundation of co-enrollment
      programs, 329–31
    of instruction, Toowong State School
      program, 51–52
  second
    Auslan as, 52–53
    of DHH students in Sainte-Marie
      program, 217, 219–20
    teaching, in Madrid bilingual co-
      enrollment, 247*f*, 247–51
  third, instruction in
    in Madrid co-enrollment programs,
      250–51, 252
    in Tommaso Silvestri School, 250–51
language alternation, 222–23
language development
  auditory accessibility of DHH children
    in preschool settings, 109
  critical age hypothesis and
    choice of communication
    methods, 109–11
  Dutch co-enrollment program, 203
  Erfurt preschool program, 159
  in German early invention
    centers, 150–51
  in German schools for DHH
    students, 151–52
  Israeli preschool co-enrollment
    system, 122
  in Madrid bilingual co-enrollment
    programs, 252
  SLCO program support for, 97–98, 100

Tommaso Silvestri primary school, 176f,
174–75, 179–80
Total Communication philosophy, 28–29
Language Experience Approach
(LEA), 54–55
Language Experience Reader (LER), 55
Languages Other than English (LOTE)
curriculum, 52
lapbooks, 175f, 174
Law 104, Italy, 165
Law 517, Italy, 165
Law on School Autonomy, Italy, 167–68
LEA (Language Experience
Approach), 54–55
leadership, role in successful
co-enrollment, 189
leadership team, Toowong program, 44
lead teacher, WRSD dual-campus
model, 262–63
Leap Forward group, 193
learned helplessness, 190–91
learning
challenges of interpretation related
to, 78
co-learning, 141
cooperative, 171
by doing/thinking, 172
incidental, through overhearing,
78, 79–80
independent, 190–91
mastery, 171
self-guided, in Vienna model, 140–41
sign language early, benefits of, 101–2
in SLCO program, 90t
social construction of, 79
in Tommaso Silvestri primary school,
176f, 174–77
in WRSD dual-campus model
administrative and related
issues, 269–70
communication and academic
support services, 267–68
overview, 266–67
least restrictive educational environment
(LRE) requirements, 3–4, 107,
318–19, 323
LER (Language Experience Reader), 55
lesson delivery, Toowong State School
program, 50

LIM (multimedia interactive whiteboard),
176f, 168, 172, 174–75
linguistic context, in SLCO program,
96–97, 98t
linguistic diversity, in Vienna model, 142
linguistic landscape of Hong Kong, 84
LIS (Italian Sign Language), 165,
167, 179–80
Listening and Spoken Language Data
Repository (LSL-DR), 323
listening and spoken language programs,
315. See also Tucker Maxon School
literacy, in Toowong State School
program, 45–46, 51–57
"Little Choir of White Hands", Tommaso
Silvestri school, 176–77
logical-mathematical activities, Tommaso
Silvestri school, 175
Longmeadow Campus, WRSD,
258–60, 263–66
LOTE (Languages Other than English)
curriculum, 52
LRE (least restrictive educational
environment) requirements, 3–4,
107, 318–19, 323
LSE. See Spanish Sign Language
LSFB. See French Belgian Sign Language
LSL-DR (Listening and Spoken Language
Data Repository), 323

Madrid, Spain, bilingual co-enrollment
programs in
benefits of, 251–52
changes made to school structure and
resources, 242
co-enrollment, defining, 237f, 237–38
co-teaching, 244
emergence of programs, 238–39
features of, 239–40
general discussion, 252–53
inclusive nature of, 242–43
language education, 247f, 247–51
language use and distribution, 245–47
overview, 235–36
profiles of DHH students in, 240–41t
mainstreaming. See also co-enrollment
programs
versus co-enrollment, 1, 101
in Germany, 153–55

mainstreaming (*cont.*)
   history of, 3–4
   in the Netherlands, 183, 184–86
   seeds of discontent related to, 33
   social integration and, 4–5, 6, 7–8
   in Spain, 237*f*, 237–38, 239
   TRIPOD program, 30–31
   Tucker Maxon School, 305
mainstream schools. *See also specific co-*
     enrollment programs; specific schools
   establishment of co-enrollment
     programs with
     Appropriate Education Act, 184–86
     commitment, need for, 187
     educational policy of mainstream
      school, 186–87
     overview, 184
     practical key issues, 188–90
     Vienna model, 144
management teams, Madrid
   bilingual co-enrollment
   programs, 241–42
mastery learning, 171
maternal rubella epidemic, 258, 305
mathematical activities, 175
mediated instruction. *See also* interpreters,
   sign language
   avoidance of in Toowong
     program, 50–51
   in Japanese deaf education
     challenges of interpretation, 74–78
     general discussion, 79–80
     overview, 72
     process of interventions, 73
medical model of education, 235
membership, in co-enrollment
   programs, 2, 7–8, 194, 327–29.
   See also inclusion
mental health issues, adolescent DHH
   population, 61–62
metalinguistic understandings, 56–57
MH designation, for DHH, 30–31
microphone use, 76, 313
middle school co-enrollment. *See also*
   Willie Ross School for the Deaf
   dual-campus model
   issues with, 288–89
   in Southwestern U.S., 280, 286–89
   WRSD dual-campus model, 267, 269

mission drift, Tucker Maxon School, 317
mixed-age classrooms. *See* multi-age/
   multi-grade classrooms
modeling
   bilingualism, in Toowong State School
     program, 51–52
   Tommaso Silvestri primary
     school, 171
   as TRIPOD educational principle, 32
monitoring progress
   Dutch co-enrollment program
     executive functioning, 199–201*t*
     experiences of parents, 206
     experiences of teachers, 205
     language development, 203
     overview, 198
     research program, 199–206
     school achievement, 203–4*t*
     social outcomes, 201–2
   Israeli preschool co-enrollment
     system, 122–23
   Tommaso Silvestri primary
     school, 177–78
   Toowong State School program
     Auslan development, 58
     English development, 59–60
     overview, 58
Montessori principles, in TRIPOD
   program, 27, 28, 32
multi-age/multi-grade classrooms
   as foundation of co-enrollment
     programs, 332–33
   interpreter perspectives on, 290
   in Southwestern U.S. co-enrollment
     program, 279, 283–84, 287–88
   student perspectives on, 295
   Toowong State School philosophy
     on, 42
   Vienna bimodal bilingual mixed-age
     inclusion model
     benefits of, 144–45
     bilingual school life, 138–39
     challenges of, 142–43
     general discussion, 145–46
     inclusion, 140
     mixed ages, 138
     overview, 138
     progressive teaching
      approach, 140–41

multidisciplinary teams
    Dutch co-enrollment program,
        188, 190–91
    Israeli preschool co-enrollment system,
        116–17, 123–24
    preschool co-enrollment programs, 114
    SLCO program, 88, 89
multimedia interactive whiteboard (LIM),
        176f, 168, 172, 174–75
multiple flows of information,
        interpretation of, 75, 79
music education, 176–77

Namur, Belgium. See Sainte-Marie school
        co-enrollment program
National Center on Deafness, U.S., 25.
        See also TRIPOD program
National Institute for the Evaluation of the
        Education and Training Education
        System (INVALSI), Italy, 178
national instruction teams, Israeli
        preschool system, 116–17
Natural Sign System (NSS), 50–51, 54. See
        also contact sign continuum
Netherlands. See Dutch co-enrollment
        program
neutrality, of interpreters, 227
NMS Pfeilgasse bimodal bilingual mixed-
        age inclusion model
    benefits of, 144–45
    bilingual school life, 138–39
    challenges of, 142–43
    general discussion, 145–46
    inclusion, 140
    mixed ages, 138
    overview, 138
    progressive teaching approach, 140–41
NSS (Natural Sign System), 50–51, 54. See
        also contact sign continuum

OBS de Bolster, 183–84. See also Dutch
        co-enrollment program
observational protocol, in Israeli
        preschool system, 122–23
official languages, in Hong Kong, 84
ÖGS. See Austrian Sign Language
one person, one language rule, 222–23
OPTION schools, 315
oral deaf education

German Method, 149
    in Hong Kong, 83, 85
    in Japan, 69
    in Queensland, Australia, 42–43
    SLCO program, 97–98
    Tucker Maxon School
        benefits of co-enrollment, 318–22
        challenges to co-enrollment, 316–18
        database for listening and spoken
            language outcomes, 323
        early intervention, adding, 306–7
        general discussion, 323
        history of, 301–4
        informal co-enrollment, 307–11
        mainstreaming programs, beginning
            of, 305
        official co-enrollment, start of, 314–16
        technological advances, 312–14
overhearing/incidental learning, 78, 79–80

pace of instruction, in Dutch
        co-enrollment program, 190
Parent/Infant program, Tucker Maxon
        School, 306–7
parents
    challenges to Toowong program, 62
    in Dutch co-enrollment program,
        198, 206
    in Erfurt co-enrollment program
        establishment, 156–57, 158
    founding of Willie Ross School for the
        Deaf by, 258
    involvement in decision on educational
        setting, in Israel, 107, 113–14
    perspectives on Southwestern U.S.
        co-enrollment program, 281, 295–96
    in SLCO program, 90t
    technological advances and, 313
    in TRIPOD approach, 25–26, 32
    Tucker Maxon School preschool, views
        on, 308–9
    and WRSD placement decisions, 263–64
partially inclusive learning situations, in
        Japan, 70–71
partial preschool co-enrollment
    with heterogeneous age group, 119
    side-by-side classes, 118–19
participation in classroom activities, 11–12
participatory heuristic method, 171

partner schools, establishment of
co-enrollment programs with.
See also specific co-enrollment
programs; specific schools
Appropriate Education Act, 184–86
commitment, need for, 187
educational policy of mainstream
school, 186–87
overview, 184
practical key issues, 188–90
Partnership Campus, WRSD
academic and social outcomes, 272–73
deaf education continuum, 262–63
general discussion, 260–61, 273–74
as model, 271
overview, 258–59
placement decisions, 263–66
teaching and learning at
administrative and related
issues, 269–70
communication and academic
support services, 267–68
overview, 266–67
peer nomination task, 201–2
peer rating task, 201–2
peer relationships. *See* social-emotional
outcomes
peer teaching, 283–84
peer tutoring, 171
performance, academic. *See* academic
outcomes
phonics, 53, 249
Piruetas Nursery School, Madrid
co-teaching in, 244
language education, 247*f*, 247–48
language use and distribution
in, 246
number of DHH students in, 241*t*
placement decisions, WRSD dual-campus
model, 262–66
PM series of readers, Toowong
program, 55
Ponce de León academy, Madrid
co-teaching in, 244
language use and distribution in, 246
number of DHH students in, 241*t*
transition to co-enrollment, 239
postsecondary programs, DHH students
entering, 35

preferential schools for DHH students,
Spain, 238
preparatory classroom lectures, 171
preschool co-enrollment programs
challenges to
adjusting curriculum to DHH
children's needs, 113
auditory accessibility of DHH
children, 109
critical age hypothesis and choice of
communication method, 109–11
multidisciplinary teamwork, 114
overview, 108–9
parental involvement, 113–14
peer relations, 112
supporting communication skills, 111
Erfurt bimodal bilingual co-enrollment
program, 158–59
Israeli system
characteristics of DHH
populations, 117
class membership, 328
communication methods, 121
curriculum accommodations and
mediation, 121–22
encouraging multidisciplinary
partnership, 123–24
general discussion, 125
history of, 107–8
implementation of three models
in, 117–20
monitoring progress, 122–23
overview, 115*f*, 116*f*, 115–16
language use and distribution
in, 245–46
in Madrid, Spain, 241
Sainte-Marie school, 213, 220
in Southwestern U.S., 279–80, 282–86
TRIPOD
key components, 28–29
start of, 26–27
transfer to Burbank Unified School
District, 30–33
Tucker Maxon School, 307–11, 314–15
Willie Ross School for the Deaf, 259
primary/face-to-face language. *See* first
language
primary school co-enrollment programs.
See also Sign Bilingualism

and Co-Enrollment program;
Willie Ross School for the Deaf
dual-campus model
Dutch program
DHH students in, 194–97
establishment of, 184–90
general discussion, 206–7
key principles, 190–94
monitoring program and student
achievement, 198–206
overview, 183–84
parent involvement, 198
Japanese
challenges of sign language
interpretation, 74–78
general discussion, 79–80
process of interventions, 73
start of, 71–72
in Madrid, Spain
benefits of, 251–52
changes made to school structure and
resources, 242
co-enrollment, defining, 237f, 237–38
co-teaching, 244
emergence of programs, 238–39
features of, 239–40
general discussion, 252–53
inclusive nature of, 242–43
language education, 247f, 247–51
language use and distribution, 245–47
overview, 235–36
profiles of DHH students in, 240–41t
in Southwestern U.S.
overview of current program, 279
teacher perspectives, 282–86
Tommaso Silvestri School
didactic strategies, 171–72
evaluation, 177–78
learning in different disciplines,
176f, 174–77
overview, 170–71
programs and organization of
didactics, 172
relationships with other
agencies, 178–79
teaching principles, 175f, 173–74
Toowong bilingual bicultural program
benefits of, 64
challenges faced, 61–62

co-teaching, 49–50
general discussion, 65
guiding principles for, 44t
history of, 41–43
key administrative
components, 44–46
key pedagogies used and curriculum
directions, 51–57
monitoring student progress, 58–60
overview, 41
providing access for all
students, 50–51
TRIPOD, 29, 30–33
Tucker Maxon School, 311–12, 314–16
WRSD dual-campus model, 266–67, 269
principals, in WRSD dual-campus
model, 270
privacy, as ethical principle of
interpreters, 227
problem solving, Tommaso Silvestri
primary school, 171
professional training of deaf adults, SLCO
program, 94
program evaluations, Dutch co-
enrollment program, 199–206
program script, Dutch co-enrollment
program, 189
progressive teaching approach, 140–41
Project Impact, Tucker Maxon School, 315
project officer, Toowong State School
program, 43
proportion of DHH students in classes.
See also critical mass of DHH
students
foundations of co-enrollment, 327–29
Sainte-Marie school, 215–16
Toowong State School program, 61–62
psychological outcomes. See social-
emotional outcomes
Public Law 94-142 (Education for All
Handicapped Children Act), U.S.,
3–4, 27–28, 33, 306
public schools, deaf education in. See
also co-enrollment programs; East
Longmeadow Public Schools;
mainstreaming; specific schools
Southwestern U.S. co-enrollment
program
communication philosophy, 280–81

public schools, deaf education in (*cont.*)
    general discussion, 297
    history of, 277–78
    interpreter perspectives on,
        281, 289–91
    overview of current program, 279–80
    parent perspectives on, 281,
        295–96
    student perspectives on, 281, 291–95
    teacher perspectives on, 281–89
    TRIPOD program, 30–33
pull-out services, 5
push-in services, 5

Queensland, Australia. *See* Toowong
    bilingual bicultural co-enrollment
    program
quizzes, in Vienna model, 141

Radboud University, 198
reading. *See also* language development
    in Sainte-Marie co-enrollment
        program, 220–21
    in Toowong program, 54–56, 59
recess, self-segregation during, 321
reflection-in-action approach, 84, 91–92
regional consortia, The
    Netherlands, 185–86
regional multidisciplinary EI centers,
    Israel, 116
regular classroom situation, in Japanese
    co-enrollment, 70–71, 73–80
Rehabilitation Act of 1973, U.S., 3–4,
    306, 323
rehabilitation services, in TRIPOD
    proposal, 25
relationships, peer. *See* social-emotional
    outcomes
repetitive environment, in Toowong
    program, 50–51
research program, Dutch co-enrollment
    program, 199–206
residential schools for the deaf (center
    schools), 3–4. *See also* special
    schools for deaf children
resources, in SLCO program
    development of, 90*t*
    enriched linguistic, 97, 98*t*
    shared, 90, 91*t*

responsibility, as TRIPOD educational
    principle, 32
reverse mainstreaming, Tucker Maxon
    School, 305, 314
role models, deaf, 193
Royal Institute for the Deaf and
    Dumb. *See* State Institute for
    Specialized Education for the Deaf
    Magarotto School
rubella epidemic, 258, 305

Sainte-Marie school co-enrollment
    program, Belgium
    benefits of, 228–30*t*
    bilingual pedagogy, 222–23
    challenges to, 228, 230–31
    class membership, 327–28
    co-enrollment setting, 215–16
    co-teaching, 224–25, 334
    government decree for, 214
    interpreters, role of, 226–27, 331–32
    overview, 211
    profiles of DHH students in
        French as L1, LSFB as L2, 217
        LSFB and French bilingual, 220
        LSFB as L1, French as L2, 219–20
        no first language when entering
            school, 218–19
        overview, 216–17
        pedagogical adaptations to variety
            of, 220–21
    setting, 213–15
    start of, 211–12
Salzburg, Austria, 136
school achievement. *See* academic
    outcomes
school culture, in SLCO program, 90*t*
school integration, in Spain, 237*f*,
    237–38, 239
schools. *See* co-enrollment programs;
    mainstreaming; special schools for
    deaf children; *specific programs and
    schools*
schools specialized in deafness, Italy,
    166–68. *See also* Tommaso
    Silvestri School
science lessons, Tommaso Silvestri
    primary school, 175
script, Dutch co-enrollment program, 189

secondary education. *See also* Sign
Bilingualism and Co-Enrollment
program; Willie Ross School for the
Deaf dual-campus model
in Madrid co-enrollment
programs, 253
in Southwestern U.S. program, 289
transition from Toowong school
to, 61–62
TRIPOD, 32, 33–35*t*
WRSD dual-campus model, 267, 269
second language (L2)
Auslan as, 52–53
of DHH students in Sainte-Marie
program, 217, 219–20
self-advocacy, 289
self-contained classes, 27, 108, 328
self-guided learning, 140–41
self-segregation, 321, 336
SELPA (Special Education Local Plan
Agency), California, 32, 33
seminars, in SLCO program, 91
shared education, in Spain, 237–38.
See also Madrid, Spain, bilingual
co-enrollment programs in
shared goals and resources, SLCO
program, 88–91*t*
side-by-side classes, 118–19
Sign Bilingual Assemblies, SLCO
program, 98*t*
Sign Bilingualism and Co-Enrollment
(SLCO) program
deaf education in Hong Kong, 85
development of, 85–86
four pillars of
active participation by
students, 98–99
deaf individual involvement in
school practices, 92–96
overview, 86–87
supporting bimodal bilingual
development, 96–97, 98*t*
whole-school approach, 87–91*t*
general discussion, 101–3
linguistic landscape of Hong Kong, 84
versus other co-enrollment
programs, 326–27
overview, 83–84
preliminary evidence for, 100–1

signed bilingualism, 239–40.
See also bilingual co-enrollment
programs
signing in English, 54
sign language. *See also* bilingual co-
enrollment programs; bimodal
bilingual co-enrollment programs;
interpreters, sign language; *specific
sign languages*
benefits of learning early, 101–2
communication challenges in
co-enrollment, 17–18
contact sign continuum, 54–57
critical age hypothesis and choice of
communication methods, 109–11
proficiency in, co-enrollment programs
and, 14–15
simultaneous bilingual model, 153
successive-bilingual model, 152–53
Sign Language Day, SLCO program, 98*t*
Sign Language of the Netherlands (SLN),
192, 193, 203
Sign Language Recess, SLCO
program, 98*t*
sign supported Dutch (SSD), 192
sign supported speech, in Madrid
bilingual co-enrollment, 249
simultaneous activities, difficulty for
DHH students, 76
simultaneous bilingual model, 153
simultaneous communication, 110–11,
249, 329–30
single information flow, interpretation
of, 75
SLCO program. *See* Sign Bilingualism and
Co-Enrollment program
SLN (Sign Language of the Netherlands),
192, 193, 203
small group activities, 77
social community, as goal of
co-enrollment, 7–8
social construction of learning, 79
social-emotional outcomes
co-enrollment programs, 4–5, 6–8,
19, 336
Dutch co-enrollment program,
190, 201–2
Erfurt preschool program, 159
of having deaf role model, 93

social-emotional outcomes (*cont.*)
ISISS Magarotto School
organization, 168
Israeli preschool co-enrollment
system, 122–23
preschool co-enrollment programs, 112
Sainte-Marie school co-enrollment
program, 229–30
SLCO program, 93, 97–99, 100–1
Southwestern U.S. co-enrollment
program, 284–85, 288, 290, 291–92
Toowong State School program,
51, 61–62
Tucker Maxon School, 315, 319–21
Vienna model, 144
WRSD dual-campus model, 272–73
society, Vienna model benefits for, 145
sociometric tasks, 201–2
Southwestern U.S., co-enrollment
program in
communication philosophy, 280–81
general discussion, 297
history of, 277–78
interpreter perspectives on, 281, 289–91
versus other co-enrollment
programs, 326–27
overview of current program, 279–80
parent perspectives on, 281, 295–96
student perspectives on, 281, 291–95
teacher perspectives on, 281–89
Spanish language
language development, 252
language education, 247–51
language use and distribution, 245–47
Spanish Sign Language (LSE)
benefits of, 251–52
language education, 247–51
language use and distribution, 245–47
special classes for DHH pupils in
Japan, 70–72
special education
for DHH in Spain, 237, 238
in Israeli law, 107, 115–16
Special Education Local Plan Agency
(SELPA), California, 32, 33
special education teachers, 2–3, 17,
279–80, 281–89
special intervention programs,
Israel, 121–22

special needs children
SLCO program support for, 90*t*
in Tucker Maxon School, 316–17, 320
special schools for deaf children. *See also*
specific schools
in Austria, 136
dual models of education, 235
establishment of co-enrollment
programs by
Appropriate Education Act, 184–86
commitment, need for, 187
educational policy of mainstream
school, 186–87
overview, 184
practical key issues, 188–90
in Germany, 151–53
history of, 3–4
in Italy, 165, 166–68
in Japan, 69–70*t*
in the Netherlands, 184–86
in Spain, 238–39
Vienna model, 144
speech therapy services
Dutch co-enrollment program, 193
Tommaso Silvestri primary
school, 177
Toowong State School, 53
spoken language. *See also* language
development; *specific languages*
auditory accessibility of DHH children
in preschool settings, 109
bilingual programs, 15–16, 19–20
communication challenges in
co-enrollment, 17–18
critical age hypothesis and
choice of communication
methods, 109–11
in Dutch co-enrollment program,
193, 203
in German early invention
centers, 150–51
in German schools for DHH
students, 151–52
in Madrid bilingual co-enrollment
programs
language development, 252
language education, 247–51
language use and distribution, 245–47
third language, 250–51, 252

proficiency in, co-enrollment programs
and, 14–15
Sainte-Marie school co-enrollment
program
bilingual pedagogy, 222–23
co-enrollment setting, 216
profiles of DHH students in, 216–21
setting of, 213
simultaneous bilingual model, 153
SLCO program support for, 97–98, 100
in Southwestern U.S. co-enrollment
program, 280–81
successive-bilingual model, 152–53
in Tommaso Silvestri primary school,
174–75, 179–80
in Vienna model, 138–39
SSD (sign supported Dutch), 192
staff. *See also specific programs; specific staff
members*
Dutch co-enrollment program, 188
SLCO program, 102
Southwestern U.S. co-enrollment
program, 279–80
Toowong State School program,
47–48, 63
state-funded schools, Spain, 236. *See also*
El Sol state school, Madrid
State Institute for Specialized Education
for the Deaf (ISISS) Magarotto
School, Italy
co-enrollment aspect, 167–68
evolution to school specialized in
deafness, 166–68
general discussion, 179–80
history of, 165–66
overview, 165
school organization, 168–70*t*
team collaboration, 170
Tommaso Silvestri primary school
didactic strategies, 171–72
evaluation, 177–78
learning in different disciplines,
176*f*, 174–77
overview, 170–71
programs and organization of
didactics, 172
relationships with other
agencies, 178–79
teaching principles, 175*f*, 173–74

students. *See* co-enrollment programs;
deaf and hard-of-hearing children;
hearing students; *specific schools and
programs*
substitute interpreters, 291
successive-bilingual model, 152–53

TC (Total Communication) philosophy,
28–29, 110–11, 222–23, 329–30
Teacher Aide: Auslan Language Model
(TA:ALM), 43, 48
teachers, general education. *See* co-
teaching; deaf educators; general
education teachers; hearing
teachers
teachers' aides employed as educational
interpreters (TA:EIs), 48
teachers of the deaf (ToDs). *See also* co-
teaching; deaf educators; hearing
teachers
challenges to co-enrollment for, 298
in Dutch co-enrollment program, 188,
190–91, 192, 197, 205
in Erfurt bimodal bilingual co-
enrollment program, 157
in ISISS Magarotto School
organization, 169–70
in Israeli preschool co-enrollment
system, 118, 119–20, 121–23
itinerant teachers, 5
in Madrid bilingual co-enrollment
benefits for, 251–52
co-teaching, 240, 244
language education, 247–51
language use and distribution, 245–47
overview, 236
preparation for participation in
co-enrollment, 187–88
in Queensland, Australia, 42–43
in Sainte-Marie co-enrollment
program
bilingual pedagogy, 222–23
challenges for, 230–31
co-teaching, 224–25
and interpreters, 226–27
overview, 212
program setting, 213
training for, 216
in SLCO program, 87–91

teachers of the deaf (*cont.*)
   in Southwestern U.S. program, 281–89
   in Toowong program, 43, 63
   in TRIPOD program, 29–30
   in Tucker Maxon School preschool,
      308, 309–11
   Vienna model, 138–39
teaching assistants, 169, 170
team collaboration, ISISS Magarotto
    School, 170
team meetings, Toowong State
    School, 48
team-teaching. *See* co-teaching
technology
   ISISS Magarotto School
     organization, 168
   Tommaso Silvestri primary school, 175*f*,
     176*f*, 172, 174–75, 176
   Tucker Maxon School, 312–14
tests, 141, 177
textbook usage, 77, 174
third language education
   in Madrid co-enrollment programs,
     250–51, 252
   in Tommaso Silvestri School, 250–51
Thuringia, Germany. *See* Erfurt bimodal
    bilingual co-enrollment program
time, role in successful co-enrollment
    programs, 189
ToDs. *See* co-teaching; deaf educators;
    hearing teachers; teachers of
    the deaf
Tommaso Silvestri School
   general discussion, 179–80
   ISISS Magarotto School organization
     co-enrollment aspect, 167–68
     evolution to school specialized in
      deafness, 166–68
     history of, 165–66
     overview, 165
     school organization, 168–70*t*
     team collaboration, 170
   primary school
     didactic strategies, 171–72
     evaluation, 177–78
     learning in different disciplines, 176*f*,
      174–77
     overview, 170–71

     programs and organization of
      didactics, 172
     relationships with other
      agencies, 178–79
     teaching principles, 175*f*, 173–74
Toowong bilingual bicultural co-
    enrollment program, Australia
   benefits of, 64
   challenges faced
     feeder programs, 61–62
     models of inclusion, 62–63
     staffing program, 63
     supporting parents to sign, 62
   co-teaching, 49–50
   general discussion, 65
   guiding principles for, 44*t*
   history of, 41–43
   key administrative components
     overview, 44
     program organization, 45
     staff, 47–48
     students and families, 45–46
   key pedagogies used and curriculum
    directions
     Auslan as L1 or L2, 52–54
     Auslan as subject, 52
     Auslan L1 deaf learners, 53–54
     Auslan L2 deaf learners, 53
     contact sign
      continuum-reading, 54–56
     contact sign
      continuum-writing, 56–57
     languages of instruction and
      modeling bilingualism, 51–52
   monitoring student progress
     Auslan development, 58
     English development, 59–60
     overview, 58
   overview, 41
   providing access for all students, 50–51
Total Communication (TC) philosophy,
    28–29, 110–11, 222–23, 329–30
Toward Rehabilitation Involvement by
    Parents of the Deaf program. *See*
    TRIPOD program
training
   in Madrid co-enrollment
     programs, 242

in Sainte-Marie co-enrollment
    program, 216
in SLCO program, 91
in Toowong State School program, 48
transitional classroom, WRSD, 259
translanguaging, 222–23
TRIPOD (Toward Rehabilitation
    Involvement by Parents of the
    Deaf) program, USA
  background of, 25–26
  benefits of, 33–38t
  elementary school component, 29
  key components of, 28–29
  lessons learned from, 38–39
  mission statement, 27
  versus other co-enrollment
    programs, 326–27
  overview, 92
  role in start of co-enrollment
    programs, 277–78
  seeds of discontent, 33
  start of preschool program, 26–27
  transfer to Burbank Unified School
    District, 30–33
Tucker Maxon School, USA
  database for listening and spoken
    language outcomes, 323
  early intervention, adding, 306–7
  general discussion, 323
  history of, 301–4
  informal co-enrollment, 307–11
  mainstreaming programs, beginning
    of, 305
  official co-enrollment
    benefits of, 318–22
    challenges to, 316–18
    start of, 314–16
  technological advances, 312–14
Twinschool program, the Netherlands,
    183. See also Dutch co-enrollment
    program
two-way immersion, 96–97

UNHS (universal newborn hearing
    screening), 149–50, 314
United Nations Convention of the
    Rights of People with Disabilities
    (UNCRPD), 2, 153–55

United States. See Southwestern U.S.,
    co-enrollment program in; specific
    co-enrollment programs; specific
    schools; TRIPOD program
universal design, 2
universal newborn hearing screening
    (UNHS), 149–50, 314
University of Namur, 214
upside down model, Italy, 167–68

verification tests, Tommaso Silvestri
    primary school, 177
vertical curriculum, 168
Vienna, Austria
  bimodal bilingual mixed-age
    inclusion model
    benefits of, 144–45
    bilingual school life, 138–39
    challenges of, 142–43
    general discussion, 145–46
    inclusion, 140
    mixed ages, 138
    overview, 138
    progressive teaching
      approach, 140–41
  co-enrollment in regular school, 135–36
  pioneering bimodal bilingual co-
    enrollment program, 134–35
visual materials, challenges of
    interpretation related to, 76
visual phonics, 249
vocabulary
  in Dutch co-enrollment program, 191
  Spanish Sign Language bank of, 248
  in Toowong State School program, 57
vocational program, WRSD, 259–60
Volksschule Bilgeristraße, Vienna, 134–35

Warren unit, 312
weekly study plans, in Vienna
    model, 140–41
well-being. See social-emotional outcomes
whole class instruction, challenges of
    interpretation related to, 75–77
whole-school approach, SLCO
    program, 87–91t
whole-school commitment, role in co-
    enrollment programs, 187

Willie Ross School for the Deaf (WRSD)
    dual-campus model
  academic and social outcomes, 272–73
  administrative and related
      issues, 269–70
  class membership, 328–29
  communication and academic support
      services, 267–68
  deaf education continuum in one
      program, 262–63
  foundation of, 258
  general discussion, 273
  Longmeadow Campus, 259–60
  as model, 271
  overview, 257
  Partnership Campus, 260–61,
      266–70
  placement decisions, 263–66
work ethos, in Vienna model, 141

workshops
  language, in Madrid bilingual
      co-enrollment, 247f, 247
  in SLCO program, 91
work-study program, WRSD, 259–60
Wright School, 302
writing. See also language development
writing, in Toowong program, 56–57, 60
written language. See also language
      development; specific languages;
      spoken language
  Dutch co-enrollment program, 193
  Erfurt program, 159
  Sainte-Marie co-enrollment
      program, 222–23
WRSD. See Willie Ross School for the Deaf
      dual-campus model

ZIEN! well-being scale, 202